1994

Edmund's

VAN·PICKUP SPORT UTILITY

"THE ORIGINAL CONSUMER PRICE AUTHORITY"

Publisher: Peter Steinlauf

VAN/PICKUP/SPORT UTILITY

TABLE OF CONTENTS

JUNE 1994   VOL S2801 – 9406

Published by:
Edmund Publications Corp.
300 N Sepulveda   Suite 2050
El Segundo, CA 90245

ISBN: 0-87759-436-8
ISSN: 1043-8270

Editor:
William Badnow

*Creative
/Design Director:*
Julie Finger

Production:
Rachel Abrash
Kevin McMillan
John Ward

Advertising Manager:
Barbara Abramson

Printed in the United States

Look for Edmund's NEW Software offer on page 4
and Edmund's NEW Consumer Audio Tape offer on page 10

Dear Reader:

The "information age" is upon us!

For nearly thirty years, Edmund Publications has served consumers as an automobile price authority. With the growing complexity of automobile specification, option, and price information, Edmund's is committed to take advantage of state-of-the-art information presentation technologies to serve the emerging needs of our readers who want to get the edge and save money when purchasing or leasing a new automobile.

To meet our goals, we are using computer technology not only to maintain and update our comprehensive databases of automobile information and prices, but also to organize, highlight, and list our information on the printed page so that you can find and process the specific data you need quickly and efficiently. In the ad pages of our books, we are also promoting access to our databases and auto-buying expertise through other media products including an audio tape that tells you how to best use our pricing information, software that lets you select and price automobile alternatives on your own computer, and a 900-number information service where an expert can personally advise you on how to get the right vehicle at the right price. All of these products have already proved their value and have been well received by discerning consumers like yourselves.

To help guide our product development and information delivery efforts, we are seeking your cooperation in responding to brief questionnaires placed in our books. The responses and comments about your automobile preferences, budget categories, and information utilization strategies are very useful to us and are much appreciated.

Furthermore, we are anxious to hear your personal "success stories" about how you have been able to use the information in our price guides to save money when purchasing or leasing a new automobile. Please see our announcement in this book.

We look forward to interacting with you in the exciting times ahead so that we can continue to provide you with the automobile information you want in the best possible ways.

With warm wishes for your success in the future,

Peter Steinlauf
Publisher

Understanding the Language of Auto Buying

Buying a new vehicle is an expensive, confusing and sometimes frustrating experience. If you feel confused, you are not alone! The problem is that the language and terms used by dealers and manufacturers are often unclear. To assist you, here are some helpful definitions:

Dealer Cost The amount that dealers are initially billed for a vvehicle and/or its optional accessories. *Note:* On American models the dealer, actually ends up paying less. Here's why. On every vehicle purchased, the manufacturer withholds 2-3% of the suggested list. This "holdback allowance" is then credited to the dealer's account on a scheduled basis, usually quarterly. Consequently, the dealer can make a "small profit" selling to you at their dealer cost.

Suggested List Price The manufacturer's recommended selling price.

Destination Charge The amount charged to cover the cost of delivery from the Port of Entry or manufacturer to the dealer. This charge is passed on to the buyer without any mark-up.

Advertising Fee The amount you are charged to cover the cost of national and local advertising. This fee should be no more than 1-1½% of the suggested list price.

Dealer Charges These are highly profitable "extras" that dealers try to sell in addition to the vehicle. Items such as rustproofing, undercoating and extended warranties fall into this category. Most consumer experts do not recommend purchasing these "extras".

Manufacturer's Rebates/Dealer Incentives Programs offered by the manufacturers to increase the sales of slow-selling models or to reduce excess inventories. While manufacturer's rebates are passed directly on to the buyer, dealer incentives are passed on only to the dealer —who may or may not elect to pass the savings on to the customer.

Note: Occasionally there wll appear in the "Dealer Cost" and "Sgst'd List" columns, prices enclosed in brackets. —Example: (90). This indicates a credit or refunded amount is involved.

NOTE: All information and prices published herein are gathered from sources which, in the editor's opinion, are considered reliable, but under no circumstances is the reader to assume that this information is official or final. All prices are represented as approximations only, and are rounded to the highest whole dollar amount over 50 cents. Unless otherwise noted, all prices are effective as of 12/1/93 but are subject to change without notice. The publisher does not assume responsibility for errors of omission or interpretation. ■ The computerized consumer pricing services advertised herein are not operated by nor are they the responsibility of the publisher. ■ The publisher assumes no responsibility for claims made by advertisers regarding their products or services.

ABBREVIATIONS:

ABS	—Anti-lock Braking System	
ADJ	—Adjustable or Adjuster	
AC or AIR COND		
	—Air Conditioning	
AH	—Ampere Hours	
ALT	—Alternator	
ALUM	—Aluminum	
AMP	—Amperes	
ANT	—Antenna	
APP	—Appearance	
AT	—Automatic Transmission	
AUTO	—Automatic	
AUX	—Auxiliary	
AVAIL	—Available	
AWD	—All Wheel Drive	
B	—Betted	
BBL	—Barrel	
BLK	—Black	
BSW or BW (tires)		
	—Black Sidewall	
CAP	—Capacity	
CASS	—Cassette	
CD	—Compact Disc	
CID	—Cubic Inch Displacement	
COL	—Column	
COMP	—Compartment	
CONV	—Convertible	
CPE	—Coupe	
CTRL	—Control	
CUST	—Custom	
CU IN	—Cubic Inches	
CVT	—Convertible	
CYL	—Cylinder	
DFRS	—Dual Facing Rear Seats	
DIAM	—Diameter	
DK	—Dark	
DLX	—Deluxe	
DOHC	—Dual Overhead Camshaft	
DR	—Door	
DRW	—Dual Rear Wheels	
EFI	—Electronic Fuel Injection	
ELEC	—Electronic or Electronically	
ENG	—Engine	
EQUAL	—Equalizer	
EQUIP	—Equipment	
ETR	—Electronically Tuned Radio	
EX	—Except	
EXT	—Exterior	
EXTD	—Extended	
F (tires)	—Fiberglass	
F & R	—Front & Rear	
FB	—Fastback	
FI	—Fuel Injection	
FRT	—Front	
FS	—Flareside	
F/S	—Fleetside	
FWD	—Front Wheel Drive	
GAL	—Gallon	
GBP	—Group	
HB	—Hatchback	

HD	—Heavy Duty
HO	—High Output
HP	—Horsepower
HSC	—High Swirl Combustion
HT	—Hardtop
HUD	—Head Up Display
HVY	—Heavy
ILLUM	—Illuminated or Illumination
INCLS	—Includes
INCLD	—Included
INJ	—Injection
INT	—Interior
L (eng)	—Liter
L & R	—Left & Right
LB	—Liftback or Long Bed
LBS	—Pounds
LD	—Light Duty
LH	—Left Hand
LT	—Light
LTD	—Limited
LUX	—Luxury
LWB	—Long Wheelbase
LWR	—Lower
MAN	—Manual
MAX	—Maximum
MDLS	—Models
MED	—Medium
MH	—Must Have
MIN	—Minimum
MLDGS	—Moldings
MPI or	
MPFI	—Multi Port Fuel Injection
MPG	—Miles Per Gallon
MSR	—Minimum Size Required
MT	—Manual Transmission
NA or	
N/A	—Not Available
NB	—Notchback
NC	—No Charge
NL	—Not Listed
OD	—Overdrive
OHC	—Overhead Camshaft
OHV	—Overhead Valves
OPT	—Optional
OS	—Outside
OWL	
(tires)	—Outline White Letter
OZ	—Ounce
PASS	—Passenger
PEG	—Preferred Equipment Group
PEP	—Preferred Equipment Package
PERF	—Performance
PGM FI	—Programmed Fuel Injection
PKG	—Package
PR	—Pair
PREM	—Premium
PS	—Power Steering
PU	—Pickup
PW	—Power Windows
PWR	—Power

QTR	—Quarter
QTS	—Quarts
RBL	
(tires)	—Raised Black Letters
RDSTR	—Roadster
REQ	—Requires
REV	—Reverse
RH	—Right Hand
R or RR	—Rear
RPM	—Revolution Per Minute
RWD	—Rear Wheel Drive
RWL	
(tires)	—Raised White Letters
SB	—Short Bed
SBR (tires)	
	—Steel Belted Radial
SDN	—Sedan
SEFI or	
SFI	—Sequential Electronic Fuel Injection
SRS	—Supplemental Restraint System
SOHC	—Single Overhead Camshaft
SP or	
SPD	—Speed
SPFI	—Sequential Port Fuel Injection
SPKRS	—Speakers
SPT	—Sport
S/R	—Sunroof
SRW	—Single Rear Wheels
STD	—Standard
STRG	—Steering
SU	—Sport Utility
SW	—Station Wagon
SWB	—Short Wheelbase
SYNC	—Synchromesh or Synchronized
TACH	—Tachometer
TBI	—Throttle Body Injection
TEMP	—Temperature
TPI	—Tuned Port Injection
TRANS	—Transmission
TRU	—Truck
TW or	
T/W	—Together With
VOL	—Volume
W/	—With
WB	—Wheelbase
WGN	—Wagon
W/O	—Without
WS	—Wideside
WSW or WW	
(tires)	—White Side Wall
W/T	—Work Truck
2WD	—Two Wheel Drive
4WD	—Four Wheel Drive
4WS	—Four Wheel Steering
3A/4A	—3-Speed Automatic /4-Speed Automatic
4M/5M	—4-Speed Manual /5-Speed Manual.

How to buy your next New Automobile

Every new automobile buyer has but one thought in mind — to save money by getting a "good deal". Your goal should be to pay 2-4% over the dealer invoice, not the 8-10% the dealer wants you to pay. Use the following guide to help you plan your new vehicle purchase:

Step 1 Study the alternatives carefully, and then choose the make, model and accessories you want.

Step 2 Visit a local dealership to test drive the model you intend to buy. Pay special attention to all-around visibility, convenience of controls, seating comfort, steering response, handling, acceleration and braking.

Step 3 Once you've decided on a particular model, check with your insurance company to make sure the cost of insuring the vehicle falls within your budget.

Step 4 Contact your bank or credit union to obtain loan-rate information. Later on, you can compare their arrangement with the dealer's financing plan.

Step 5 Use the information in this book to determine the dealer's actual cost. To do this:

a) total the Dealer Invoice column costs for the model and accessories you want

b) add the destination charge and advertising fee to this amount

c) add to the dealer's cost what you think is a reasonable dealer profit. (On most vehicles, a reasonable amount is 3% over invoice – this excludes "hot selling models" which will command a higher dealer profit) *This sum represents the dealer's cost. Remember the dealer also makes an additional profit because of the "holdback allowance".*

Step 6 Bargain for the best price – visit several dealerships. The dealer who comes closest to your "target price" should get your business. Be sure that the dealer's price quote will be your final cost. Beware of dealer charges! When you buy a vehicle, you should be buying the whole vehicle – not the extras. Don't be coerced into buying items such as rustproofing, undercoating, extended warranties, etc., unless you really want them.

Step 7 Deduct any manufacturer's rebates/dealer incentives from your final cost.

Step 8 If your present vehicle will be used as a "trade-in", now is the time to negotiate the highest possible value for it. Try to accept an amount that is not less than 3% below the "trade-in" vehicle's wholesale value. (Consult Edmund's Used Car Prices book). If you trade in your old vehicle, deduct its agreed-upon value from the final cost of the new vehicle.

Step 9 Add applicable state and/or local taxes.

Step 10 Enjoy your new vehicle, knowing that you did everything to get the best possible deal.

Edmund's STEP-BY-STEP COSTING FORM

MAKE: _____   EXTERIOR COLOR: _____

MODEL: _____   INTERIOR COLOR: _____

BODY STYLE: _____   TOP COLOR (IF APPL.) _____

ITEMS	DEALER COST	LIST PRICE	BEST DEAL
Basic Model Price Only			
Optional Equipment			
1.			
2.			
3.			
4.			
5.			
6.			
7.			
8.			
9.			
10.			
11.			
12.			
13.			
14.			
15.			
16.			
17.			
18.			
19.			
20.			
Dealer Advertising Amount			
Dealer Preparation Amount			
Initial Gas & Oil			
Freight Amount (to your area)			
TOTAL COST —*Excluding Local Sales Tax, Registration & Inspection Fees*			

VANS
CONTENTS

VANS

CODE	DESCRIPTION	DEALER	LIST

CHEVROLET ASTRO CARGO VAN

ASTRO CARGO VAN 6 CYL.

CM10905 ZW9 Astro 111" WB		13886	15344
CM11005 ZW9 Extended Astro 111" WB		14314	15817
Destination Charge:		545	545

Standard Equipment

ASTRO CARGO VAN - BASE: 4-speed automatic transmission, power front disc/rear drum brakes with 4-wheel anti-lock braking system, tinted Solar Ray glass all windows, all-season steel belted radials, driver facial air bag, electronic AM radio with fixed-mast antenna, Scotchgard fabric protector, 4-spoke steering wheel with anti-theft locking feature, center high-mounted stop light, front bumper with bumper guards and rear bumpers painted lower body color, halogen headlamps, RH and LH painted black mirrors with pivoting arm and adjustable head and 15" x 6" steel painted argent wheels.

Accessories

CODE	DESCRIPTION	DEALER	LIST
AVA1	**Preferred Equip Group 1**	NC	NC
AVA2	**Preferred Equip Group 2**		
	CM10905	1016	1181
	CM11005	955	1111
C60	**Air Conditioning** — front - w/PEG AVA1	727	845
	w/PEG AVA2	NC	NC
—	**Axles, Rear**		
GU5	3.23 ratio	NC	NC
GU6	3.42 ratio	NC	NC
GT4	3.73 ratio	NC	NC
G80	locking differential	217	252
—	**Body Code**		
ZW9	standard body equip	NC	NC
E54	dutch doors	313	364
VE6	**Bumper Equip** — bumpers, F & R	45	52
V10	**Cold Climate Pkg**	40	46
DK6	**Console, Roof**	71	83

CODE	DESCRIPTION	DEALER	LIST
—	**Convenience Groups**		
ZQ2	power door locks & windows	373	434
ZQ3	speed control & tilt-wheel	NC	NC
V08	**Cooling System** — HD - w/Z82	NC	NC
	w/o Z82	170	198
C49	**Defogger, Rear Window** — electric	132	154
AU3	**Door Lock System, Power** — all doors		
	w/o ZQ2	192	223
	w/ZQ2	NC	NC
FE9	**Federal Emissions**	NC	NC
YF5	**California Emissions**	86	100
NG1	**New York Emissions**	86	100
LB4	**Engine** — 4.3 liter (262 cu. in.) EFI V6	NC	NC
—	**Glass Arrangements**		
ZW6	complete body		
	w/o AJ1	316	368
	w/AJ1	542	630
ZW2	rear panel doors		
	w/o AJ1	75	87
	w/AJ1	121	141
ZW3	sliding door & rear panel doors		
	w/o AJ1	133	155
	w/AJ1	225	262
A18	**Glass, Swing Out** — rear door & sliding side door	117	136
AJ1	**Glass, Tinted** — deep tinted	NC	NC
TL1	**Grille, Deluxe**	23	27
C36	**Heater** — rear	176	205
U52	**Instrumentation, Electronic**	168	195
TR9	**Lighting, Auxiliary** — w/o DK6	109	127
	w/DK6	81	94
D44	**Mirrors Below Eye-Line** — exterior, black		
	w/PEG AVA1	42	52
	w/PEG AVA2	NC	NC
D48	**Mirrors** — exterior, electric remote, black		
	w/PEG AVA1	129	150
	w/PEG AVA2	84	98
ZY1	**Paints, Exterior** — solid	NC	NC
—	**Radio Equipment**		
UM7	radio	83	96
	incls elect tuned AM/FM stereo radio w/seek & scan & digital clock		
UM6	radio	187	218
	incls elect tuned AM/FM stereo radio w/seek & scan, stereo cass tape & digital clock		
UL5	radio delete	(82)	(95)
—	**Seats**		
ZX1	high back bucket seat, driver only	NC	NC
ZX2	high back bucket seats w/PEG AVA1	184	214
	w/PEG AVA2	NC	NC
A78	**Seat Back Recliner & Dual Armrests**	211	245
—	**Seat Trim**		
X4	custom vinyl high back bucket	NC	NC
K4	custom cloth high back bucket	NC	NC

CODE	DESCRIPTION	DEALER	LIST
G50	**Springs, Rear** — HD w/PEG AVA1	60	70
	w/PEG AVA2	NC	NC
BA8	**Stowage Compartment**	26	30
—	**Tires** — all seasons SBR		
QCE	P205/75R15 BW	NC	NC
QCU	P215/75R15 BW	NC	NC
QCV	P215/75R15 white stripe	52	60
QCM	P215/75R15 white lettered	76	88
Z82	**Trailering Special Equip**		
	heavy duty	436	507
	w/L35 eng	266	309
MX0	**Transmission** — 4-spd auto w/overdrive	NC	NC
ZJ7	**Wheels** — rally	79	92

CHEVROLET ASTRO PASSENGER VAN

ASTRO M10 REAR WHEEL DRIVE 6 CYL

CM10906 ZW9 Astro		14732	16278
CM11006 ZW9 Extended Astro		15005	16580

ASTRO L10 ALL WHEEL DRIVE 6 CYL

CL10906 ZW9 Astro		16839	18607
CL11006 ZW9 Extended Astro		17112	18909
Destination Charge:		545	545

Standard Equipment

ASTRO PASSENGER VAN: Four-speed elec controlled auto trans w/overdrive, 100 amp alternator, pwr-assisted front disc/rear drum 4-wheel anti-lock brakes, brake/trans shift interlock, front/rear lower body color painted bumpers (includes front bumper guards), doors (driver/passenger front side, sliding RH side, RH & LH rear-load), solar-ray tinted glass, swing-out glass on sliding side door, molded plastic black grille, halogen headlamps, screw-operated scissor-type jack w/ratchet handle, extension & 2-wheel blocks; front license plate bracket, RH and LH painted mirrors with pivoting arm and adjustable heads, winch-type mounted spare tire carrier under the floor at the rear, compact spare tire/wheel mounted under floor, four all-season SBR tires, underbody corrosion protection, bright metal hub caps w/black trim, four 15" x 6" steel painted argent wheels, black painted window pillars, intermittent windshield wipers, driver's facial air bag, RH/LH armrests, front/rear pass-side assist handles, cigarette lighter with ashtray light, two LH and one RH coat hook, two dome lamps with front door actuated switches, color-keyed carpeting on wheel housing and entire load floor, gauges (coolant temperature, fuel level, odometer, oil pressure, speedometer, trip odometer and voltmeter), beverage holders on top of engine cover extension, headlamp warning, full-length color-keyed foam-backed cloth headliner, deluxe heater with side window defogger, electronically tuned AM radio with fixed-mast antenna, Scotchgard fabric protector optional cloth trims and carpeting, highback adjustable front bucket seats with vinyl trim, removable adjustable 3-passenger center bench seat (seat adjuster included on all 2nd and 3rd seats), 4-spoke black steering wheel with anti-theft locking feature, molded color-keyed storage compartment in LH rear 2nd seat area, LH/RH color-keyed cloth sunshades with RH visor mirror, color-keyed vinyl door trim panels w/front door map pockets, black plastic door sill plates, swing-out glass on sliding side door.

CL (in addition to or instead of ASTRO equipment): Air dam with fog lamps, front and rear painted lower body color bumpers with matching color-keyed end caps, black rub strips and rear combination top step surface; molded black plastic grille with argent paint on feature surfaces, black bodyside moldings with bright inserts and wheel opening moldings, 15" x 6.5" color-keyed steel rally wheels, color-keyed expanded vinyl door trim panels with carpet inserts, insulation and front door map pockets; color-keyed floor mats for all seating positions, lamps (stepwell, storage compartment, two dome with front, rear, and sliding door-actuated switches, door jamb defeat switch), molded color-keyed plastic storage compartment in LH rear quarter area, LH/RH color-keyed cloth sunshades with lighted RH visor mirror, swing-out glass on sliding side door, left front quarter panel and rear doors.

Accessories

CODE	DESCRIPTION	DEALER	LIST
ASA1	**Passenger Preferred Equipment Group 1**	NC	NC
ASA2	**Passenger Preferred Equipment Group 2 — w/YC6**	299	348
	w/o YC6...	434	505
	incls C60 front air cond, ZW6 complete body glass, UM7 AM/FM stereo radio with seek/scan and digital clock, D44 dual below eyeline mirrors		
ASA3	**Passenger Preferred Equipment Group 3 — w/o YC6**	1284	1493
	w/YC6...	884	1028
	incls ASA2 preferred equip grp 2 plus A78 seat recliners w/ dual armrests, ZQ3 convenience group, ZP8 8-passenger seating and ZL7 CS value pkg		
ASA4	**Passenger Preferred Equipment Group 4 — CM10906 - w/YC6**..............	2322	2700
	w/YC7...	2391	2780
	CM11006, CL10906 or CL11006 - w/YC6	2315	2692
	w/YC7...	2384	2772
	incls YC6 CL decor, C60 air cond,ZQ2+3 convenience grps, UM6 AM/FM stereo radio w/ cass seek/scan & digital clock, Zw6 complete body glass, ZP8 8-pass seating, A78 seat bk recliners/dual armrests, D48 elec remote blk ext. mirrors, BA8 storage compartment, QCF P205/75R15 white lettered tires (CM10906); QCM P215/75R15 white lettered tires (all ex. CM10906)		
ASA5	**Passenger Preferred Equipment Group 5 — CM10906 - w/o YC7**	3203	3724
	w/YC6...	2992	3479
	w/YC7...	2768	3219
	CM11006, CL10906 or CL11006 - w/o YC7	3195	3716
	w/YC6...	2985	3471
	w/YC7...	2761	3211
	incls ASA4 preferred equip group 4 plus, ZP8 8-passenger seating,V54 luggage carrier, DK6 roof console, PF3 alum wheels, AC3 pwr driver's seat		
—	**Radio Equipment**		
UM7	radio - w/PEG ASA1	130	151

CODE	DESCRIPTION	DEALER	LIST
	w/PEG ASA2 or ASA3	NC	NC
	incls elec tuned AM/FM stereo radio with seek and scan and digital clock		
UM6	radio - w/PEG ASA1	235	273
	w/PEG ASA2 or ASA3	105	122
	w/PEG ASA4 or ASA5	NC	NC
	incls elec tuned AM/FM stereo radio w/seek-scan, stereo cass tape & dig clock		
UX1	radio - w/PEG ASA1	364	423
	w/PEG ASA2 or ASA3	234	272
	w/PEG ASA4 or ASA5	129	150
	incls electronically tuned AM stereo/FM stereo with seek and scan, stereo cassette tape with search and repeat, graphic equalizer and digital clock		
U1C	radio - w/PEG ASA1	479	557
	w/PEG ASA2 or ASA3	349	406
	w/PEG ASA4 or ASA5	244	284
	incls elec tuned AM/FM stereo radio w/seek-scan, compact disc player and digital clock		
UL5	radio delete	(82)	(95)
—	**Air Conditioning**		
C60	front - w/PEG ASA1	727	845
	w/PEG ASA2, ASA3, ASA4 or ASA5	NC	NC
C69	front and rear - w/PEG ASA1	1176	1368
	w/PEG ASA2, ASA3, ASA4 or ASA5	450	523
—	**Axles, Rear**		
GU5	3.23 ratio	NC	NC
GU6	3.42 ratio	NC	NC
GT4	3.73 ratio	NC	NC
G80	locking differential	217	252
—	**Body**		
ZW9	standard body	NC	NC
E54	dutch doors	313	364
VE5	**Bumper Equipment** — bumpers, dlx front/rear - w/o YC6 or YC7 or ZL7	110	128
	w/YC6 or YC7 or ZL7	65	76
V54	**Carrier, Luggage** — black - w/PEG ASA1, ASA2, ASA3 or ASA4	108	126
	w/PEG ASA5	NC	NC
V10	**Cold Climate Package**	40	46
DK6	**Console, Roof** — w/o YC6 or YC7	71	83
	w/YC6 or YC7	43	50
	w/PEG ASA5	NC	NC
—	**Convenience Groups**		
ZQ2	w/PEG ASA1, ASA2 or ASA3	373	434
ZQ2	w/PEG ASA4 or ASA5	NC	NC
ZQ3	w/PEG ASA1 or ASA2	329	383
ZQ3	w/PEG ASA3, ASA4 or ASA5	NC	NC
VO8	**Cooling System** — w/Z82	NC	NC
	heavy duty	170	198
ZL7	**CS Value Package** — w/PEG ASA3	NC	NC
	w/PEG ASA1 or ASA2	400	465
—	**Decor**		
YC6	CL: custom luxury - w/PEG ASA4 or ASA5	NC	NC
	w/o ZL7	934	1086
YC7	LT: luxury touring - w/PEG ASA4 or ASA5	1551	1804
	w/o ZL7	2491	2896

CODE	DESCRIPTION	DEALER	LIST
C49	**Defogger** — electric rear window	132	154
AU3	**Door Lock System, Power** — all doors - w/o ZQ2	192	223
	w/ZQ2	NC	NC
FE9	**Federal Emission Requirements**	NC	NC
YF5	**California Emission Requirements**	86	100
NG1	**New York State Emission Requirements** — CL11006	NC	NC
	CL10906	86	100
—	**Engines**		
	gasoline		
LB4	4.3 liter (262 cu. in.) EFI V6	NC	NC
L35	4.3 liter (262 cu. in.) CPI V6 - CL10906 or CL11006	NC	NC
	CM10906 or CM11006	430	500
ZW6	**Glass Arrangement** — complete body - w/PEG ASA1	135	157
	w/PEG ASA2, ASA3, ASA4, ASA5 or YC7	NC	NC
AJ1	**Glass, Deep Tinted** — w/o YC7 or ZW6	138	161
	w/ZW6	249	290
	w/YC7	NC	NC
C36	**Heater** — rear	176	205
U52	**Instrumentation, Electronic**	168	195
TR9	**Lighting, Auxiliary** — w/o DK6 console, YC6 or YC7	109	127
	w/DK6 console	81	94
	w/YC6 or YC7	NC	NC
—	**Mirrors** — below eye line		
D44	exterior, black - w/PEG ASA1	45	52
	w/PEG ASA2 or ASA3	NC	NC
D48	exterior, electric remote, black - w/PEG ASA1	129	150
	w/PEG ASA2 or ASA3	84	98
	w/PEG ASA4 or ASA5	NC	NC
—	**Paints, Exterior**		
ZY1	solid	NC	NC
ZY2	custom two-tone - w/o YC6, YC7 or ZL7	283	329
	w/YC6, YC7 or ZL7	89	104
ZY3	special two-tone	148	172
ZY4	deluxe two-tone - w/o YC6 or ZL7	409	476
	w/YC6 or ZL7	216	251
—	**Seating Arrangements**		
ZP5	five passenger seating	NC	NC
ZP7	seven passenger seating - w/PEG ASA1 or ASA2 w/o YC6 or YC7	897	1043
	w/YC6	821	955
	w/YC7	733	852
	w/PEG ASA3 or ASA4 w/o YC6 or YC7	369	429
	w/PEG ASA3 or ASA4 and YC6	271	315
	w/PEG ASA3 or ASA4 and YC7	(22)	(25)
	w/PEG ASA5	NC	NC
ZP8	eight passenger seating - w/o YC7	340	395
	w/YC7	754	877
	w/PEG ASA3 or ASA4	NC	NC
	w/PEG ASA5 w/o YC6 or YC7	(369)	(429)
	w/PEG ASA5 and YC6	(271)	(315)
	w/PEG ASA5 and YC7	22	25
A78	**Seat Back Recliner & Dual Armrests** — w/PEG ASA1 or ASA2		
	w/o ZP7 or YC7	211	245

CODE	DESCRIPTION	DEALER	LIST
	w/PEG ASA3, ASA4 or ASA5 or w/ZP7 or YC7	NC	NC
AC3	**Seat, Power** — driver's side only, electric, 6-way control		
	w/PEG ASA1, ASA2, ASA3 or ASA4..	206	240
	w/PEG ASA5	NC	NC
—	**Seat Trim**		
X4	custom vinyl high back bucket...	NC	NC
K4	custom cloth high back bucket	NC	NC
L6	velour cloth reclining bucket	NC	NC
BA8	**Stowage Compartment** — w/PEG ASA1, ASA2 or ASA3	26	30
	w/PEG ASA4 or ASA5	NC	NC
—	**Tires** — tubeless		
QCE	P205/75R15 blackwall..	NC	NC
QCF	P205/75R15 white lettered - w/PEG ASA1, ASA2 or ASA3	83	96
	w/PEG ASA4 or ASA5	NC	NC
QCG	P205/75R15 white stripe	62	72
QCU	P215/75R15 blackwall..	NC	NC
QCV	P215/75R15 white stripe	52	60
QCM	P215/75R15 white lettered - w/PEG ASA1, ASA2 or ASA3	76	88
	w/PEG ASA4 or ASA5	NC	NC
—	P235/65R15 white outlined letter...	NA	NA
Z82	**Trailering Special Equipment** — heavy duty - w/LB4	436	507
	w/L35	266	309
MXO	**Transmission** — 4-speed automatic w/overdrive	NC	NC
—	**Wheels**		
PF3	aluminum - w/PEG ASA1, ASA2, ASA3 or ASA4 w/o YC6 or YC7	292	340
	w/YC6 or YC7 or ZL7 or FE2..	213	248
	w/PEG ASA5	NC	NC
ZJ7	rally - w/o YC6 or YC7 or ZL7 or FE2	79	92
	w/YC6 or YC7 or ZL7 or FE2..	NC	NC

CHEVROLET CHEVY VAN

4.3 LITER (262 CID) EFI 6 CYL

CODE	DESCRIPTION	DEALER	LIST
CG11005 ZW9 Chevy Van 110" WB		13745	15709
CG11305 ZW9 Chevy Van 125" WB		13906	15893
CG21005 ZW9 Chevy Van 110" WB		13718	15678
CG21305 ZW9 Chevy Van 125" WB		13898	15883
CG31305 ZW9 Chevy Van 125" WB		14009	16010
CG31606 ZW9 Extended Chevy Van 146" WB		15864	18130
Destination Charge:		580	580

Standard Equipment

G10 FULL-SIZED CHEVY VAN - BASE: Electronic 4-speed automatic transmission, 100-amp alternator, heavy-duty battery with 600 CCA, brake/transmission shift interlock, heady-duty power front disc/rear drum brakes with 4-wheel anti-lock system, front and rear silver painted bumpers, side window defoggers, Solar-Ray tinted glass, single rectangular halogen headlamps, black bodyside molding, heavy-duty front and rear shocks 32mm, power steering, driver's facial air bag, electronic AM radio with digital clock and fixed-mast antenna, Scotchgard seats, center high-mounted stop lamp, side door guard beams, stowage box with latched door, deluxe outside air heater and defogger, full gauges, five P215/75R15 blackwall steel belted radial tires and five 15" x 6" argent painted steel wheels.

G20 FULL-SIZED CHEVY VAN - BASE: Electronic 4-spd auto trans, 100-amp alternator, heavy-duty battery w/600 CCA, brake/trans shift interlock, heady-duty pwr front disc/rear drum brakes w/4-whl anti-lock sys, front/rear silver painted bumpers, side window defoggers, Solar-Ray tinted glass, single rectangular halogen headlamps, blk bodyside molding, heavy-duty front/ear shocks 32mm, pwr steering, driver's facial air bag, elec AM radio w/digital clock/fixed-mast antenna, Scotchgard seats, center high-mtd stop lamp, side door guard beams, stowage box w/atched door, dlx outside air heater/defogger, full gauges, four P225/75R15 blackwall steel belted radial tires & five 15" x 6" argent painted steel wheels.

G30 FULL-SIZED CHEVY VAN - BASE: Electronic 4-speed auto trans, 100-amp alternator, heavy-duty battery with 600 CCA, brake/trans shift interlock, heady-duty power front disc/rear drum brakes with 4-wheel anti-lock system, front and rear silver painted bumpers, side window defoggers, Solar-Ray tinted glass, single rectangular halogen headlamps, black bodyside molding, heavy-duty front and rear shocks 35mm, power steering, driver's facial air bag, electronic AM radio w/ digital clock and fixed-mast antenna, Scotchgard seats, center high-mounted stop lamp, side door guard beams, stowage box w/latched door, deluxe outside air heater and defogger, full gauges, four LT 225/75R16 blackwall steel belted radial tires, five 16" x 6.5" argent painted steel wheels and 33-gallon fuel tank.

CODE	DESCRIPTION	DEALER	LIST

Accessories

CODE	DESCRIPTION	DEALER	LIST
GVA1	**Preferred Equipment Group 1**	NC	NC
GVA2	**Preferred Equipment Group 2**	961	1118
—	**Air Conditioning**		
C60	front	839	975
	w/PEG GVA2	NC	NC
C69	front & rear	1354	1574
	w/PEG GVA2	515	599
V22	**Appearance, Deluxe Front**	122	142
—	**Axles, Rear**		
GU5	3.23 ratio	NC	NC
GU6	3.42 ratio	NC	NC
GT4	3.73 ratio	NC	NC
GT5	4.10 ratio (CG31*05)	NC	NC
HC4	4.56 ratio (CG31305)	NC	NC
G80	locking differential	217	252
ZW9	**Body Code, Standard**	NC	NC
V37	**Bumper Equip** — bumpers, F & R, chromed	65	76
V10	**Cold Climate Pkg**	41	48
—	**Convenience Groups**		
ZQ2	power door locks & power windows	373	434
ZQ3	includes speed control & tilt wheel	329	383
V08	**Cooling Systems** — w/Z82 or C5Y	NC	NC
	w/o Z82 or C5Y	170	198
C49	**Defogger, Rear Window** — w/A12 or ZW3 glass	132	154
	w/ZX6 glass	82	95
YA2	**Door** — side, sliding	NC	NC
AU3	**Door Lock System, Power** — w/o ZQ2 convenience pkg	192	223
	w/ZQ2 convenience pkg	NC	NC
YF5	**California Emissions**	86	100
NA6	**High Altitude Emissions**	NC	NC
FE9	**Federal Emissions**	NC	NC
NG1	**New York Emissions** — w/o C5J 6000 GVW	NC	NC
	w/C5J 6000 GVW	86	100
—	**Engines**		
	gasoline		
LB4	4.3 liter (262 cu. in) EFI V6 w/o C6P	NC	NC
	w/C6P	(727)	(845)
L03	5.0 liter (350 cu. in.) EFI V8	495	575
L05	5.7 liter (350 cu. in.) EFI V8 w/CG21305	727	845
	w/CG31***	NC	NC
L19	7.4 liter (454 cu. in.) EFI V8 (w/CG31*05)	520	605
	diesel		
L49	6.5 liter (395 cu. in.) naturally aspirated diesel V8	2468	2870
L57	6.5 liter (395 cu. in.) HD naturally aspirated diesel V8	1423	1655
KL5	alternative fuel	108	125
B30	**Floor Covering** — carpeting, wheelhousing & floor	135	157
—	**Glass**		
ZX6	swing out glass pkg	194	226
A07	full body, 6 windows (w/ZX6)	124	144
A08	RH rear body side window - w/o A07 glass	45	52

CODE	DESCRIPTION	DEALER	LIST
	w/A07 glass	NC	NC
A12	rear door, fixed - w/o A07 or ZW3 glass or ZX6	43	50
	w/A07 or ZW3 glass or ZX6	NC	NC
A18	rear door, swing out - w/o A07 or ZX6 glass	94	109
	w/A07 glass	51	59
	w/ZX6 glass	NC	NC
ZW3	fixed glass pkg	77	90
—	**GVWR**		
C5J	6000#	NC	NC
C5S	6600#	NC	NC
C6Q	6875# - w/L49	NC	NC
	w/o L49	274	319
C5Y	7100#	NC	NC
C6C	7400# - w/L05	720	837
C6P	8600# - w/CG31605	NC	NC
	w/CG31305	870	1012
C6W	9200# - w/CG31605	206	240
	w/CG31305	1077	1252
C36	**Heater** — rear	176	205
TR9	**Lighting, Auxiliary**	134	156
AX3	**Lock, Remote Keyless Entry** — w/ZQ2 & TR9	151	175
DG9	**Mirrors, Exterior - Below Eye-Line**		
	stainless steel, electric	84	98
B98	**Molding Delete**	NC	NC
ZY1	**Paint, Exterior** — solid	NC	NC
—	**Radio Equip**		
UM7	radio	83	96
	w/PEG GVA2	NC	NC
	incls elect tuned AM/FM stereo radio w/seek & scan & digital clock		
UM6	radio	187	218
	w/PEG GVA2	105	122
	incls elect tuned AM/FM stereo radio w/stereo cass tape, seek & scan & digital clock		
UX1	radio	316	368
	w/PEG GVA2	234	272
	incls elect tuned AM stereo/FM stereo w/stereo cass tape w/ search & repeat, seek & scan, graphic equalizer, & digital clock		
U1C	radio	445	517
	w/PEG GVA2	362	421
	incls elect tuned AM/FM stereo w/compact disc player, seek & scan & digital clock		
U75	radio antenna, power	73	85
UL5	radio delete	(82)	(95)
A57	**Seat** — front auxiliary	161	187
	w/PEG GVA2	NC	NC
YG4	auxiliary seat not desired	NC	NC
—	**Seat Trim**		
X4	custom vinyl high back bucket seats	NC	NC
NP5	**Steering Wheel** — leather wrapped	52	60
NL7	**Tank, Fuel** — approx 33-gal capacity	83	96
—	**Tires**		
	tubeless all-season SBR		

CHEVROLET

CODE	DESCRIPTION	DEALER	LIST
	P215/75R15 BW		
XCU	front	NC	NC
YCU	rear	NC	NC
ZCU	spare	NC	NC
	P215/75R15 WW		
XCV	front	26	30
YCV	rear	26	30
ZCV	spare	13	15
	P225/75R15 BW		
XET	front	NC	NC
YET	rear	NC	NC
ZET	spare	118	137
	P225/75R15 WW		
XEU	front	31	36
YEU	rear	31	36
ZEU	spare	133	155
	P225/75R15 white lettered		
XEV	front	43	50
YEV	rear	43	50
ZEV	spare	139	162
	LT225/75R16E BW		
XHF	front		
	CG31305		
	w/o C6P or C6W	29	34
	w/C6P or C6W	NC	NC
YHF	rear		
	CG31305		
	w/o C6P or C6W	29	34
	w/C6P or C6W	NC	NC
ZHF	spare	193	224
	LT225/75R16D BW		
XHP	front	NC	NC
YHP	rear	NC	NC
ZHP	spare	178	207
	P235/75R15 BW		
XFL	front	NC	NC
YFL	rear	NC	NC
ZFL	spare	130	151
	P235/75R15 white stripe		
XFM	front	31	36
YFM	rear	31	36
ZFM	spare	145	169
R6Z	spare tire not desired	NC	NC
—	**Trailering Special Equipment**		
Z82	heavy duty		
	w/L49, L19 or L57 or C5Y	267	310
	w/o L49, L19 or L57 or C5Y	437	508
Z72	light duty	114	132
MX0	**Transmission** — 4-spd automatic w/overdrive	NC	NC
—	**Wheels**		
P01	bright metal, full cover	36	42
N67	rally	104	121

22		EDMUND'S VAN/PICKUP/SPORT UTILITY BUYER'S GUIDE

CHEVROLET LUMINA CARGO MINIVAN

LUMINA VARGO MINIVAN 6 CYL

	DEALER	LIST
1UM05 Lumina Minivan 109.8" WB	14014	15485
Destination Charge:	530	530

Standard Equipment

LUMINA CARGO MINIVAN - BASE: 3-speed automatic transmission, integrated roof antenna, power front disc/rear drum brakes with 4-wheel anti-lock braking system, accent-color front and rear bumpers and rocker moldings, sliding side door with fixed glass, Solar-Ray tinted glass all windows, composite halogen headlamps, power rack and pinion steering, independent front MacPherson strut suspension, P205/70R15 blackwall tires, rear window washer/wiper, driver's air bag, front carpeting, console with lockable storage center, electronic AM/FM stereo with seek feature, digital clock and coaxial front speakers; Scotchgard fabric protection and vinyl highback bucket seats.

Accessories

CODE	DESCRIPTION	DEALER	LIST
—	**Lumina Cargo Minivan Base Equip Group** incl'd w/model	NC	NC
—	**Interior Trim**		
V2	vinyl high back bucket seats, standard	NC	NC
C2	cloth high back bucket seats	157	182
—	**Exterior Color** — paint solid	NC	NC
LG6	**Engine** — 3.1 liter EFI V6	NC	NC
C67	**Air Conditioning**	714	830
VK3	**Bracket, Front License Plate**	NC	NC
C49	**Defogger, Rear Window** - electric	146	170
YF5	**California Emissions**	NC	NC
FE9	**Federal Emissions**	NC	NC
NG1	**New York Emissions**	NC	NC
AJ1	**Glass, Deep Tinted**	92	107
K05	**Heater, Engine Block**	17	20
AB5	**Locks, Power** — door & tailgate	258	300
MX1	**Transmission** — automatic	NC	NC

CHEVROLET

CHEVROLET LUMINA PASSENGER MINIVAN

LUMINA PASSENGER MINIVAN 6 CYL

		DEALER	LIST
1UM06	Minivan..	15218	16815
	Destination Charge:..	530	530

Standard Equipment

LUMINA PASSENGER MINIVAN: 3.1 liter EFI V6 eng, 3-speed auto trans, integrated roof antenna, pwr front disc/rear drum brakes, 4-wheel anti-lock brake system, accent color front/rear/rocker moldings (body color - LS trim), sliding side door, stainless steel exhaust sys, tinted glass, solar-ray windshield, liftgate handle, composite halogen headlamps, one-piece rear liftgate, LH remote/RH manual black painted fold-away mirrors, basecoat/clearcoat paint, body color pillars, roof and windshield; compact spare tire w/underbody spare tire carrier, power rack/pinion steering, independent front suspension w/MacPherson struts, P205/70R15 BW tires, bolt-on wheel covers, rear wiper/washer, intermittent windshield wipers, driver side air bag sys, forward instrument panel carpeting, full floor carpeting, lockable center storage console w/permanently mtd cup holders, front/rear color-keyed carpeted floor mats, lamps (glove box, ashtray, front/rear reading, footwell, sliding door, tailgate), auxiliary lighting, rear auxiliary power outlet, elect tuned AM/FM stereo radio w/seek feature, digital clock, coaxial front/extended range rear speakers; Scotchgard fabric protector (seats, door trim, floor covering), cloth highback reclining bucket seats with adjustable head restraints and driver's side 4-way manual seat adjuster.

Accessories

CODE	DESCRIPTION	DEALER	LIST
—	**Lumina Minivan Base Equipment Group**..	NC	NC
UM6	w/UM6 radio, add	120	140
U1C	w/U1C radio, add	341	396
	incld w/model		
—	**Lumina Minivan Preferred Equipment Group 1**	669	778
UM6	w/UM6 radio, add	120	140
U1C	w/U1C radio, add	341	396
	incls air conditioning, electric twin remote fold-away mirrors, power door/tailgate locks with side door delay, electronic speed control with resume speed, adjustable steering column tilt wheel		
—	**Lumina Minivan Preferred Equipment Group 2**	1998	2323
U1C	w/U1C radio, add	220	256
	incls air cond, elec tuned AM/FM stereo w/seek feature, digital clock, stereo		

CODE	DESCRIPTION	DEALER	LIST
	cass tape, coaxial front/extended range rear spkrs; luggage area cargo convenience net, pwr windows w/driver's express down, pwr door/ tailgate locks w/side door delay, elec speed control w/resume speed, adjustable steering column tilt wheel, elec fold-away twin remote mirrors, elec rear window defogger, deep tinted glass, remote keyless entry, 7-pass seating		
—	**Lumina Minivan Preferred Equipment Group 3**	2445	2843
U1C	w/U1C radio, add	220	256
	incls elec tuned AM/FM stereo w/seek feature, digital clock, stereo cass tape, coaxial front/extended range rear spkrs, power windows w/ driver's express down, power door/tailgate locks w/side door delay, luggage area cargo convenience net, elec speed control w/resume speed, elec fold-away twin remote mirrors, air cond, adjustable steering column tilt wheel, elec rear window defogger, deep tinted glass, remote keyless entry, 7-pass seating, LS trim package, driver side power seat with 6-way adjuster		
—	**Radio Equipment** — see pkgs		
UM6	radio	NA	NA
	incls electronically tuned AM/FM stereo radio with seek feature, digital clock, stereo cassette tape, coaxial front and extended range rear speakers		
U1C	radio	220	256
	incls electronically tuned AM/FM stereo radio with seek-scan, digital clock, compact disc player, Delco-Loc II, coaxial front and ext range rear spkrs		
—	**Interior Trim**		
C2	cloth bucket seat - std	NC	NC
F2	custom cloth bucket seats	NC	NC
—	**Exterior Color** — paint, solid	NC	NC
D84	custom two-tone	127	148
—	**Engines**		
LG6	3.1 liter EFI V6	NC	NC
L27	3.8 liter SFI V6	532	619
C67	**Air Conditioning**	714	830
C34	**Air Conditioning** — front & rear, - w/PEG WPA2 or WPA3	387	450
VK3	**Bracket, Front License Plate**	NC	NC
V54	**Carrier, Roof**	125	145
C49	**Defogger** — rear window, electric	146	170
E58	**Door, Power Sliding**	254	295
YF5	**California Emission Requirements**	NC	NC
FE9	**Federal Emission Requirements**	NC	NC
NG1	**New York State Emission Requirements**	NC	NC
AUO	**Entry, Keyless, Remote**	108	125
AJ1	**Glass, Deep Tinted**	211	245
KO5	**Heater, Engine Block**	17	20
AB5	**Locks, Power** — door & tailgate	258	300
AP9	**Luggage Area, Cargo Convenience Net**	26	30
DD9	**Mirrors, Twin Remote Fold-Away, Electric**	67	78
AG9	**Seat, Power** — driver's side only, electric 6-way control	232	270
AD9	**Seats, Child** — integral	194	225
—	**Seating Arrangements**		
ZP5	five-passenger seating	NC	NC
	incls two front bucket seats, three pasgr bench seat - also incls seat belts		
ZP7	seven-passenger seating	568	660
	incls two front bucket seats, five modular rear seats - also incls seat belts		
K34	**Speed Control, Electronic w/Resume Speed**	194	225

CODE	DESCRIPTION	DEALER	LIST
C54	**Sunroof, Manual, Non-Removable**	258	300
G67	**Suspension, Load Leveling**	146	170
N33	**Tilt-Wheel, Adjustable Steering Column**	125	145
—	**Tires**		
XIN	P205/70R15 touring radial BW	30	35
P42	self-sealing option (req's XIN tires)	129	150
NW9	**Traction Control**	301	350
V92	**Trailering Package**	275	320
—	**Transmissions**		
MX1	3-speed automatic	NC	NC
MX0	4-speed automatic	172	200
PH3	**Wheels** — aluminum cast, w/locks 15"	237	275
A31	**Windows, Power w/Driver's Express Down**	237	275

CHEVROLET SPORTVAN

4.3 LITER (262 CID) EFI 6 CYL

CG21306 ZW9 Sportvan - 8 pass 125" WB	16317	18648

5.7 LITER (350 CID) EFI 8 CYL

CG31306 ZW9 Sportvan - 12 pass 125" WB	17500	20000
CG31606 ZW9 Extended Sportvan - 12 pass 146" WB	18512	21156
Destination Charge:	580	580

Standard Equipment

G20 FULL-SIZED SPORTVAN - BASE: Electronic four-speed automatic transmission, 100-amp alternator, heavy-duty battery with 600 CCA, brake/transmission shift interlock, heavy-duty power front disc/rear drum brakes with 4-wheel anti-lock braking system, front and rear chromed bumpers, side window defoggers, tinted Solar Ray glass, swing-out rear door glass, RH and LH stainless steel below eye-line mirrors with adjustable heads, black bodyside moldings, 32mm heavy-duty front and rear shocks and heavy duty springs, power steering, four P225/75R15 blackwall steel radials, driver's facial air bag, side door guard beams, full gauges, deluxe outside air heater and defogger, electronic AM radio with digital clock and fixed-mast antenna, Scotchgard seat protector and adjustable highback bucket seats and two removable three-passenger bench seats with custom vinyl trim.

BEAUVILLE (in addition to or instead of BASE equipment): Deluxe front appearance group, chrome grille, dual halogen high-beam headlamps, black bodyside moldings and rear moldings with bright inserts, full-length cloth headliner with garnish moldings, front and rear dome lamps with door activated switches, color-keyed cloth on door and carpeting on lower areas, and locking storage compartment.

G30 FULL-SIZED SPORTVAN - BASE: Electronic four-speed auto trans, 100-amp alternator, heavy-duty battery w/600 CCA, brake/trans shift interlock, heavy-duty power front disc/rear drum brakes w/4-wheel anti-lock braking system, front/rear chromed bumpers, side window defoggers, tinted Solar Ray glass, swing-out rear door glass, RH and LH stainless steel below- eyeline mirrors with adjustable heads, black bodyside moldings, 35mm heavy-duty front and rear shocks and heavy duty springs, power steering, four LT225/75R16-D blackwall steel belted radials, five 16.0" x 6.5" argent painteJ steel wheels, driver's facial air bag, side door guard beams, full gauges, deluxe outside air heater and defogger, electronic AM radio with digital clock and fixed-mast antenna, Scotchgard seat protector and adjustable highback bucket seats and two removable three-passenger bench seats with custom vinyl trim.

BEAUVILLE (in addition to or instead of BASE equipment): Deluxe front appearance group, chrome grille, dual halogen high-beam headlamps, black bodyside moldings and rear moldings with bright inserts, full-length cloth headliner with garnish moldings, front and rear dome lamps with door activated switches, color-keyed cloth on door and carpeting on lower areas, and locking storage compartment.

Accessories

CODE	DESCRIPTION	DEALER	LIST
SVA1	**Preferred Equip Group 1**	NC	NC
SVA2	**Preferred Equip Group 2**	831	966
SVA3	**Beauville Preferred Equip Group 3**	1528	1777
SVA4	**Beauville Preferred Equip Group 4**		
	CG21306	2774	3225
	CG31**6	2706	3146
—	**Air Conditioning**		
C60	front	839	975
	w/SVA2 or SVA3	NC	NC
C69	front & rear	1354	1574
	w/SVA2 or SVA3	515	599
	w/SVA4	NC	NC
—	**Axles, Rear**		
GU5	3.23 ratio	NC	NC
GU6	3.42 ratio	NC	NC
GT4	3.73 ratio	NC	NC
GT5	4.10 ratio	NC	NC
G80	locking differential	217	252
ZW9	**Body Code - Standard**	NC	NC
V10	**Cold Climate Pkg**	41	48
—	**Convenience Group**		
ZQ2	incls AU3 power door locks & power windows	373	434
	w/SVA3 or SVA4	NC	NC
ZQ3	incls speed control & tilt wheel	329	383
	w/SVA3 or SVA4	NC	NC
V08	**Cooling System**		
	w/Z82 trailering	NC	NC

CODE	DESCRIPTION	DEALER	LIST
	w/o Z82 trailering	170	198
C49	**Defogger, Rear Window**	82	95
YA2	**Door** — sliding side	NC	NC
AU3	**Door Lock System, Power** — all doors		
	w/o ZQ2 convenience group	192	223
	w/ZQ2 convenience group	NC	NC
YF5	**California Emissions**	86	100
NA6	**High Altitude Emissions**	NC	NC
FE9	**Federal Emissions**	NC	NC
NG1	**New York Emissions**	NC	NC
—	**Engines**		
	gasoline		
LB4	4.3 liter (262 cu. in.) EFI V6	NC	NC
L03	5.0 liter (305 cu. in.) EFI V8	495	575
L05	5.7 liter (350 cu. in.) EFI V8		
	CG21306	727	845
	CG31**6	NC	NC
L19	7.4 liter (454 cu. in.) EFI V8	520	605
	diesel		
L49	6.5 liter (395 cu. in.) diesel naturally aspirated	2468	2870
L57	6.5 liter (394 cu. in.) HD diesel naturally aspirated	1423	1655
KL5	alternative fuel	108	125
AJ1	**Glass** — deep tinted	327	380
	w/SVA3	NC	NC
—	**GVWR**		
C5S	6600#	NC	NC
C6Q	6875# - w/L05	274	319
	w/L49	NC	NC
C6C	7400#	NC	NC
C6P	8600#		
	CG31606	NC	NC
	CG31306	216	251
C6W	9200#		
	CG31606	206	240
	CG31306	319	371
C36	**Heater** — rear seat	176	205
TR9	**Lighting, Auxiliary**	134	156
	w/SVA3 or SVA4	NC	NC
AX3	**Lock Remote** — keyless entry	151	175
DG9	**Mirror, Exterior** — LH & RH, below eye-line type, stainless steel, electric	84	98
	w/SVA4	NC	NC
DH6	**Mirror, Interior** — lighted visor/vanity	65	75
—	**Paints, Exterior**		
ZY1	solid	NC	NC
ZY2	custom two-tone - w/o E94 Beauville decor	231	269
	w/E94 Beauville decor	118	137
—	**Radio Equip**		
UM7	radio	121	141
	w/SVA2 or SVA3	NC	NC
	incls elect tuned AM/FM stereo radio w/seek & scan & digital clock		
UM6	radio	226	263
	w/SVA2 or SVA3	105	122

CODE	DESCRIPTION	DEALER	LIST
	w/SVA4	NC	NC
	incls elect tuned AM/FM stereo radio w/stereo cass tape, seek & scan & digital clock		
UX1	radio	355	413
	w/SVA2 or SVA3	234	272
	w/SVA4	129	150
	incls elect tuned AM stereo/FM stereo w/stereo cass tape w/search & repeat, seek & scan, graphic equalizer & digital clock		
U1C	radio	462	537
	w/SVA2 or SVA3	341	396
	w/SVA4	236	274
	incls elect tuned AM/FM stereo w/compact disc player, seek & scan & digital clock		
U75	radio antenna, power	73	85
UL5	radio delete	(82)	(95)
—	**Seat, Rear**		
ZP3	one additional rear seat for 15-pass seating	319	371
YG4	seat not desired	(319)	(371)
—	**Seat Trim**		
X4	custom vinyl high back bucket seats	NC	NC
K4	custom cloth high back bucket seats	NC	NC
K6	custom cloth reclining bucket seats		
	w/o SVA4	346	402
	w/SVA4	NC	NC
NP5	**Steering Wheel** — leather wrapped	52	60
—	**Tires** — all-season SBR		
	P225/75R15 BW		
XET	front	NC	NC
YET	rear	NC	NC
ZET	spare	118	137
	P225/75R15 WW		
XEU	front	31	36
YEU	rear	31	36
ZEU	spare	133	155
	P225/75R15 white lettered		
XEV	front	43	50
YEV	rear	43	50
ZEV	spare	139	162
	LT225/75R16/E BW		
XHF	front		
	CG31306		
	w/C6C w/o C6P or C6W	29	34
	w/C6P or C6W	NC	NC
	CG31606	NC	NC
YFH	rear		
	CG31306		
	w/C6C w/o C6P or C6W	29	34
	w/C6P or C6W	NC	NC
	CG31606	NC	NC
ZHF	spare	193	224
	LT225/75R16/D BW		
XHP	front	NC	NC

CODE	DESCRIPTION	DEALER	LIST
YHP	rear	NC	NC
ZHP	spare - CG31306	178	207
	P235/75R15 BW		
XFL	front - w/L05 & C6Q or L49...	NC	NC
YFL	rear w/L05 & C6Q or L49..	NC	NC
ZFL	spare - CG21306	130	151
R6Z	**Spare Tire Not Desired**..	NC	NC
—	**Trailering Special Equip**		
Z82	heavy duty - w/diesel, L19 or C5Y.....................................	267	310
	w/o diesel, L19 or C5Y	437	508
Z72	light duty	114	132
MX0	**Transmission** — 4-spd automatic w/overdrive.......................	NC	NC
—	**Wheel Trim**		
P01	wheel covers - w/SVA4	NC	NC
	w/o SVA4...	36	42
N67	rally w/SVA4	NC	NC
	w/o SVA4...	104	121

CHRYSLER TOWN & COUNTRY

TOWN & COUNTRY 6 CYL

YP53	FWD Wagon..	24700	27284
CP53	AWD Wagon..	26544	29380
Destination Charge:		560	560

Standard Equipment

TOWN & COUNTRY: Front and rear air conditioning, lower bodyside and sill body color applique with bright nerf, headlamps on/seat belt/key in ignition chimes, forward storage console with coin holder, overhead console with compass, outside temperature, 4-function trip computer, front and rear reading

CHRYSLER

lamps; cup holders, rear window electric defroster, power door locks, front and rear body color fascias with bright nerf, floor mats, fog lights, sunscreen glass (side, quarter, rear window), tinted glass (front doors, windshield), locking glove box, rear heater, inside hood release, dual horns, illuminated entry system, padded instrument panel with wood tone bezels, deluxe body sound insulation, remote keyless entry, power liftgate release, automatic time delay headlights, lamps (front door courtesy and rear dome with time out feature, ignition switch with time delay, headlight switch, ash receiver, liftgate, underhood, glove box), roof-mounted luggage rack, heated dual power remote control body color outside mirrors, right and left illuminated visor mirrors, AM/FM stereo ETR radio with cassette, graphic equalizer, seek and scan, clock and four Infinity amplified speakers; front reclining bucket seats with adjustable head rests, leather and cloth trim seats, power 6-way driver seat, Quad command reclining buckets (2) with tilting right seat and 3-passenger quick release rear bench, electronic speed control, tilt steering column, leather-wrapped steering wheel, storage compartments, conventional spare tire (underslung with cable winch), four cast aluminum "Spiralcast" wheels, front door and rear quarter vent power windows, side and sliding door vented windows, windshield and rear window wiper/washer with intermittent wipe, woodgrain bodyside and liftgate moldings, 3.8 liter SMPI V6 engine, 4-speed automatic transmission, power assisted rack and pinion steering, power front disc/rear drum brakes.

Accessories

CODE	DESCRIPTION	DEALER	LIST
Y	**Woodgrain Delete Pkg Y**	NC	NC
	incls gold stripe & gold painted aluminum wheels		
NAE	**California Emissions**	87	102
NBY	**New York Emissions**	87	102
GAC	**Tinted Glass**	NC	NC
NHK	**Engine Block Heater** — avail in Alaska only - FWD Wagon	29	34
CYK	**Seating Group** — 7-pass w/integrated child seat	NC	NC
RBC	**Radio**	145	170
	incls AM/FM stereo w/CD player, graphic equalizer, clock & 6 Infinity spkrs		
TPC	**Tires** — P205/70R15 WSW SBR	59	69
AHT	**HD Trailer Tow Group**	230	270
	incls 120 amp alternator, 685 amp battery, HD brakes, flasher, radiator, susp'n trailer tow wiring harness		
WJ6	**Wheels** — cast aluminum, gold - w/o pkg Y	NC	NC
WJ7	**Wheels** — cast aluminum, white - w/pkg Y	NC	NC
—	**Seats** — cloth/leather low back buckets (NA w/CYK)	STD	STD
—	**Seats** — leather low back buckets	NC	NC
—	**Paint** — special color or metallic	82	97

CHRYSLER

DODGE CARAVAN C/V

CARAVAN C/V 4 CYL
KE12   Caravan C/V 112" WB 13108   14412

EXTENDED CARAVAN C/V 6 CYL
KE13   Extended Caravan C/V 119" WB.. 15267   16866

Destination Charge: 560   560

Standard Equipment

CARAVAN C/V COMPACT CARGO VAN - BASE: 5-speed manual transmission, coil spring front suspension with gas shocks, power front disc/rear drum brakes, power rack and pinion steering, driver's air bag, front and side door guard beams, 90-amp alternator, maintenance-free 600-amp battery, rear liftgate with fixed glass and gas-assisted props, front and rear full wraparound fascias with black nerf, tinted glass all windows, inside hood release, front headliner, analog instrument cluster, outside dual mirrors, AM/FM electronic stereo with digital clock and two speakers.

Accessories

—	**Quick Order Pkgs** — Caravan C/V 112" WB		
A	**Base Pkg** — Caravan C/V 112" WB	STD	STD
	incls vehicle w/std equip		
B	**Commercial Pkg B** — Caravan C/V 112" WB	236	278
	incls 685 amp battery, full gauge cluster (tach, oil pressure, volt, deck gauge lights, door ajar/low washer fluid), LT195/75R14 BSW tires (5), 2000 lb. maximum GVW		
Z	**Commercial Pkg Z** — Caravan C/V 112" WB..	1000	1177
	incls commercial pkg B plus air conditioning, deluxe convenience group (cruise/tilt), light group, lockable storage drawer under front passenger seat, AM/FM radio w/cassette (non-seek & scan), 4 speakers		
C	**Conversion Pkg C** — Caravan C/V 112" WB...	1077	1267
	incls commercial pkg Z plus vented glass sliding cargo door, temporary plastic driver seat, vanity mirrors on sunvisors (non-illuminating), bodyside & rear quarter vented windows		
D	**Conversion Pkg D** — Caravan C/V 112" WB..	1770	2082
	incls conversion pkg C plus power convenience (locks, windows, mirrors, keyless entry), sunscreen glass, dual electric horns, deluxe sound insulation, power liftgate release		
—	**Quick Order Pkgs** — Extended Caravan C/V 119" WB		
A	**Base Pkg** — Extended Caravan C/V 119" WB	STD	STD
	incls vehicle w/std equip		
B	**Commercial Pkg B** — Extended Caravan C/V 119" WB	56	66
	incls 685 amp battery plus full gauge cluster (tach, oil pressure, volt, check gauge lights, door ajar/washer fluid lights)		
Z	**Commercial Pkg Z** — Extended Caravan C/V 119" WB	820	965
	incls commercial pkg B plus air conditioning, deluxe convenience group (cruise/tilt), light group, lockable storage drawer under front passenger seat, AM/FM radio w/cassette (non-seek & scan), 4 speakers		
C	**Conversion Pkg C** — Extended Caravan C/V 119" WB................................	812	955
	incls commercial pkg Z plus temporary plastic driver seat, vented glass sliding cargo door, vanity mirrors on sunvisors (non-illuminating), bodyside & rear quarter vented windows		
D	**Conversion Pkg D** — Extended Caravan C/V 119" WB	1675	1970

CODE	DESCRIPTION	DEALER	LIST
	incls conversion pkg C plus power convenience group (locks, windows, mirrors, keyless entry), sunscreen glass, dual electric horns, deluxe sound insulation, power liftgate release		
DGA	**Transmission** — 3-spd automatic - Caravan C/V 112" WB	511	601
EFA	**Engine** — 3.0L V6 - Caravan C/V 112" WB	590	694
HAA	**Air Conditioning** — models w/base pkg or commercial pkg B	728	857
BRL	**Anti Lock Brakes** — Extended Caravan C/V 119" WB	509	599
AJK	**Deluxe Convenience Group** — models w/base pkg or commercial pkg B ..	317	372
	incls cruise/tilt		
AJP	**Power Convenience Group** — models w/conversion pkg C	621	730
	incls locks, windows, mirrors, keyless entry		
GFA	**Rear Window Electric Defroster**	143	168
NAE	**California Emissions**	87	102
NAF	**High Altitude Emissions**	NC	NC
NBY	**New York Emissions**	87	102
NHK	**Engine Block Heater** — available in Alaska only	29	34
Z1C	**GVW Pkg 5060** — Caravan C/V 112" WB w/base pkg	265	312
	incls LT195/75R14 BSW tires		
GKC	**Sliding Cargo Door w/Vented Glass**		
	models w/base pkg or commercial pkg	100	118
JPB	**Power Door Locks** — front & side door	225	265
	incl in conversion pkg D		
RA8	**Radio Delete** — deletes standard radio	(118)	(139)
RAS	**Radio** — models w/base pkg or commercial pkg B	187	220
	incls AM/FM radio w/cassette & 4 speakers		
SUA	**Tilt Steering Column** — models w/base pkg or commercial pkg B	126	148
TBB	**Spare Tire** — Caravan Cargo C/V 112" WB w/base pkg	93	109
GAE	**Sunscreen Glass** — models w/base pkg or commercial pkg	218	256
	models w/commercial pkg C	352	414
	reqs GKC		
AHT	**Trailer Towing Group** — Extended Caravan C/V 119" WB w/base pkg	224	264
	Extended Caravan C/V 119" WB w/commercial pkg or conversion pkg	176	207
	incls 120 amp alternator, 685 amp battery, HD flasher/variable load turn signal, HD radiator, HD transaxle oil cooler, trailer tow wiring harness		
—	**Paint** — special color or metallic	82	97
—	**Seats**		
	vinyl highback buckets - models w/base pkg or commercial pkg	STD	STD
	models w/conversion pkg	60	70
—	deluxe cloth highback buckets - models w/base pkg or commercial pkg	41	48
	models w/conversion pkg	41	48
—	temporary plastic driver's seat - see quick order pkgs		

DODGE CARAVAN FWD

CARAVAN FWD 4 CYL

KL52	Base	13629	14919

CARAVAN FWD 6 CYL

KH52	SE	16462	18139
KP52	LE	19827	21963
KP52	ES	20275	22472
Destination Charge:		560	560

Standard Equipment

CARAVAN FWD - BASE: Chimes (headlights on, seat belt, key in ignition), cupholders, child protection side door locks, stainless steel exhaust system, front and rear body color fascias with accent nerf, tinted glass, inside hood release, single horn, body sound insulation, front/rear dome lamps, fold away exterior aero manual mirrors, non-illuminated visor mirrors, AM/FM stereo ETR radio with digital clock, seek and four speakers; five-passenger seating, quick release intermediate and rear seats, driver and passenger highback reclining bucket seats, molded deluxe cloth seat trim, underbody spare tire carrier with cable winch, electronic speed control, storage compartments, compact spare tire, four "Virgo" wheel covers, vented side/quarter/sliding door windows, liftgate window wipers/washers with fixed intermittent wipe, 2-speed windshield wipers with variable intermittent wipe.

SE (in addition to or instead of Base equipment): Dual horn, power liftgate release, power fold away exterior aero black mirrors, bodyside accent color (2 colors) moldings, AM/FM stereo ETR radio with cass, seek, Dolby/four speakers, seven-passenger seating, tilt steering col, four "Triad" wheel covers.

LE (in addition to or instead of SE equipment): Front air conditioning, front storage console with coin holder, overhead console (compass, outside temperature, 4-function trip computer, front and rear reading lights), electric rear window defroster, power front and side door locks, front and rear body color fascias, floor mats, automatic time delay headlights, deluxe body sound insulation, remote keyless entry, front dome lamp deleted, map and liftgate lamps, light group (ash receiver, front map/reading [header mounted], glove box, ignition switch [time delayed], rear cargo dome, underhood, illuminated entry system, liftgate-mounted dual floodlights), roof luggage rack, heated power foldaway exterior aero black mirrors, illuminated visor mirrors, driver and passenger reclining bucket seats, luxury cloth molded seat trim, power quarter vent windows, lower bodyside and sill accent color cladding.

CODE	DESCRIPTION	DEALER	LIST

Accessories

CODE	DESCRIPTION	DEALER	LIST
T	**Base Family Value Pkg T**	181	213
	incls air conditioning, dual horns, accent color bodyside molding, under front passenger seat storage drawer, power liftgate release, map and cargo lighting enhancements		
B	**SE Family Value Pkg B**	181	213
	incls air conditioning, map and cargo lighting enhancements, rear window defroster		
D	**SE Family Value Pkg D**	985	1159
	incls air conditioning, map and cargo lighting enhancements, rear window defroster, forward and overhead consoles, power door locks, floor mats, gauges (oil pressure, voltage and tachometer), deluxe insulation, light group, power rear quarter vent windows		
K	**Two Tone Pkg K** — LE	260	306
	incls power driver seat, power windows, radio (AM/FM with cassette, equalizer and six Infinity speakers), sunscreen glass		
M	**"ES" Pkg M** — ES	366	431
	incls power driver's seat, power windows, radio (AM/FM with cassette, equalizer and six Infinity speakers), sunscreen glass, sport handling group, "ES" decor group		
HAA	**Climate Group I** — Base	728	857
	incls air conditioning		
AAA	**Climate Group II** — w/family value pkg	352	414
	incls air conditioning and sunscreen glass [NA w/ASK]		
AJK	**Convenience Group I** — Base w/Pkg T	316	372
	incls speed control and tilt		
AAC	**Convenience Group II** — Base w/Pkg T	590	694
	SE w/Pkg B	225	265
	incls speed control and tilt, power mirrors and power door locks		
AAD	**Convenience Group III** — SE w/Pkg B	572	673
	SE w/Pkg D	347	408
	incls speed control and tilt, power mirrors, power door locks, power windows and keyless remote entry		
CYE	**Seating Group I** — 7-passenger seating - Base	294	346
CYK	**Seating Group II** — 7-passenger seating w/integrated child seat - Base	485	570
	SE, LE, ES	191	225
CYS	**Seating Group III** — 7-passenger quad command - SE, LE, ES	507	597
CYT	**Seating Group IV** — 7-passenger convert-a-bed - SE, LE, ES	470	553
TBB	**Loading & Towing Group I**	93	109
	incls conventional spare		
AAE	**Loading & Towing Group II** — Base w/Pkg T	151	178
	SE, LE	151	178
	w/AAG (SE w/Pkg B or D, LE w/Pkg K, ES)	124	146
	incls conventional spare tire and firm ride heavy load suspension		
AAF	**Loading & Towing Group III** — SE w/Pkg B or D	473	556
	w/ASH (SE w/Pkg B or D)	376	442
	LE w/Pkg K	376	442
	w/AAG or ASK (SE w/Pkg B or D, LE w/Pkg K, ES)	349	410
	incls conventional spare tire, firm ride heavy load suspension and trailer tow group		
WJV	**Wheels I** — 15" aluminum wheels - LE w/Pkg K	309	363
AAG	**Sport Handling Group** — SE w/Pkg B or D (NA w/ASK)	203	239

DODGE

CODE	DESCRIPTION	DEALER	LIST
	LE w/Pkg K (incls WJV)	415	488
—	**Radio Equipment**		
RAS	radio - Base...	145	170
	incls AM/FM stereo with cassette, clock & four speakers		
RCE	Infinity speaker system - SE..	172	202
RBC	radio - SE w/Pkg D	426	501
	incls AM/FM stereo with CD player, equalizer, clock and six Infinity speakers		
BRL	**Brakes** — anti-lock - SE w/Pkg B or D..	584	687
	w/AAF, AAG, ASH, ASK or WJV (SE w/Pkg B or D)....................	509	599
	LE, ES...	509	599
ASH	**Gold Special Edition Decor Group** — SE w/Pkg B or D.............	213	250
	incls gold badging, 15" front disc/rear drum brakes, gold day light opening accent stripe, bodyside body color molding, P205/70R15 BSW SBR tires, 15" cast aluminum "Lace" wheels with gold accents		
ASK	**Sport Wagon Decor Group** — SE w/Pkg B or D.........................	638	750
	incls accent color fascias with black rub strips, fog lights, leather-wrapped steering wheel, sunscreen glass, sport handling group, 15" cast aluminum 5-spoke wheels		
—	**Paint** — special color or metallic	82	97
—	**Seats** — leather lowback buckets - LE......................................	735	865
	ES...	735	865
GFA	**Rear Window Defroster** — SE	143	168
JPB	**Power Door Locks** — Base w/Pkg T	225	265
NAE	**California Emissions**	87	102
NBY	**New York Emissions**	87	102
NHK	**Engine Block Heater** — available in Alaska only	29	34
MWG	**Luggage Rack**	122	143
TLB	**Tires** — Base w/Pkg T, SE w/Pkg B or D	122	143
	incls P205/70R14 WSW SBR tires (NA w/AAF, AAG, BRL, ASH or ASK)		
TPC	**Tires** — SE w/Pkg B or D, LE w/Pkg K.....................................	59	69
	incls P205/70R15 WSW SBR tires (req's BRL or AAF on SE models; NA w/AAG, ASH or ASK)		
EDM	**Engine** — 2.5L EFI 4 cylinder - Base..	STD	STD
EFA	**Engine** — 3.0L MPI V6 - SE, LE, ES	STD	STD
	Base	652	767
EGA	**Engine** — 3.3L MPI V6 - SE, LE, ES	87	102
DDM	**Transmission** — 5-speed manual - Base	STD	STD
DGA	**Transmission** — 3-speed automatic - Base	511	601
	SE, LE...	STD	STD
DGB	**Transmission** — 4-speed automatic - Base	679	799
	SE, LE...	168	198
	ES...	STD	STD

CODE	DESCRIPTION	DEALER	LIST

DODGE GRAND CARAVAN AWD

GRAND CARAVAN AWD 6 CYL

Code	Description	Dealer	List
DH53	SE	19869	21982
DP53	LE	23018	25560
DP53	ES	23466	26069
	Destination Charge:	560	560

Standard Equipment

GRAND CARAVAN AWD - SE: Chimes (headlights on, seat belt, key in ignition), cupholders, child protection side door locks, stainless steel exhaust system, front and rear body color fascias with accent nerf, tinted glass, dual horn, body sound insulation, power liftgate release, front/rear dome lamps, power fold away exterior aero black mirrors, non-illuminated visor mirrors, accent color (2 colors) bodyside moldings, AM/FM ETR stereo radio with cassette, seek, Dolby and four speakers; seven-passenger seating, quick release intermediate and rear seats, driver and passenger highback reclining bucket seats, deluxe cloth molded seat trim, underbody spare tire carrier with cable winch, electronic speed control, tilt steering column, storage compartments, compact spare tire, four "Triad" wheel covers, vented side/quarter/sliding door windows, liftgate window wipers and washers with fixed intermittent wipe, 2-speed wipers with variable intermittent wipe.

LE (in addition to or instead of SE equipment): Front air cond, lower bodyside & sill accent color cladding, front storage console w/coin holder, overhead console (compass, outside temperature, 4-function trip computer, front/rear reading lights), electric rear window defroster, power front and side door locks, front and rear body color fascias, floor mats, automatic time delay headlights, deluxe body sound insulation, remote keyless entry, front dome lamps deleted, map and liftgate lamps, light group (ash receiver, front map/reading [header mounted], glove box, ignition switch [time delayed], rear cargo dome, underhood, illuminated entry system, liftgate-mounted dual floodlights), roof luggage rack, heated power fold away exterior aero black mirrors, illuminated visor mirrors, accent color bodyside moldings deleted, driver and passenger reclining bucket seats, molded luxury cloth seat trim, power quarter vent windows.

Accessories

B	**SE Family Value Pkg B**	985	1159
	incls air cond, map, cargo lighting enhancements, rear window defroster		
D	**SE Family Value Pkg D**	985	1159

DODGE

CODE	DESCRIPTION	DEALER	LIST
	incls air conditioning, map and cargo lighting enhancements, rear window defroster, forward and overhead consoles, deluxe insulation, floor mats, gauges (oil pressure, voltage and tachometer), illuminated visor vanity mirrors, light group, power door locks, power rear quarter vent windows		
K	**Two-Tone Pkg K** — LE	260	306
	incls power driver's seat, power windows, radio (AM/FM stereo w/cassette, equalizer, clock and 6 speakers), sunscreen glass		
L	**Woodgrain Pkg L** — LE	818	962
	incls power windows, power driver's seat, radio (AM/FM stereo w/cassette, equalizer, clock and 6 speakers), sunscreen glass, woodgrain group		
M	**"ES" Pkg M** — ES	60	306
	incls power driver's seat, power windows, radio (AM/FM stereo w/cassette, equalizer, clock and 6 speakers), "ES" decor group		
AAC	**Convenience Group I** — SE w/Pkg B	225	265
	incls power mirrors and power locks		
AAD	**Convenience Group II** — SE w/Pkg B	572	673
	SE w/Pkg D	347	408
	incls power mirrors, power locks, power windows and keyless remote entry		
AAA	**Climate Group I** — SE w/Pkg B or D	352	414
	incls sunscreen glass		
AAB	**Climate Group II** — SE w/Pkg B	840	988
	SE w/Pkg D	748	880
	w/ASK (SE w/Pkg B)	488	574
	w/ASK (SE w/Pkg D)	396	466
	w/AAF (SE w/Pkg B)	786	925
	w/AAF (SE w/Pkg D)	695	818
	w/ASK & AAF (SE w/Pkg B)	434	511
	incls sunscreen glass and rear heater/air conditioning		
CYK	**Seating Group II** — 7-passenger seating w/integrated child seat	191	225
CYS	**Seating Group III** — 7-passenger quad command	507	597
CYT	**Seating Group IV** — 7-passenger convert-a-bed	470	553
TBB	**Loading & Towing Group I**	93	109
	incls conventional spare tire		
AAF	**Loading & Towing Group II** — SE w/Pkg B or D	317	373
	LE w/Pkg K or L, ES	317	373
	incls conventional spare tire and heavy duty trailer tow group		
—	**Radio Equipment**		
RCE	Infinity speaker system - SE w/Pkg B or D	172	202
RBC	radio - SE w/Pkg D	426	501
	LE w/Pkg K or L, ES	145	170
	incls AM/FM stereo w/CD player, graphic equalizer, clock, 6 Infinity spkrs		
ASH	**Gold Special Edition Decor Group** — SE w/Pkg B or D	213	250
	incls gold badging, gold day light opening accent stripe, bodyside body color moldings, 15" cast alum "Lace" wheels w/gold accents [NA w/ASK]		
ASK	**Sport Wagon Decor Group** — SE w/Pkg B or D	638	750
	incls accent color fascias with black rub strip, fog lights, leather-wrapped steering wheel, sunscreen glass, P205/70R15 all-season touring LBL SBR tires, 15" cast aluminum 5-spoke wheels		
GFA	**Rear Window Defroster** — SE	143	168
NAE	**California Emissions**	87	102
NBY	**New York Emissions**	87	102

CODE	DESCRIPTION	DEALER	LIST
NHK	**Engine Block Heater** — available in Alaska only	29	34
MWG	**Luggage Rack**	122	143
TPC	**Tires** — SE w/Pkg B or D	59	69
	LE w/Pkg K or L	59	69
	incls P205/70R15 WSW SBR (NA w/ASH or ASK)		
WJV	**Wheels** — 15" cast aluminum - LE w/Pkg K	309	363
EGA	**Engine** — 3.3L MPI V6..	STD	STD
EGH	**Engine** — 3.8L MPI V6 - LE w/Pkg K or L, ES...	257	302
—	**Seats** — cloth highback buckets - SE	STD	STD
—	**Seats** — cloth lowback buckets - LE, ES...	STD	STD
—	**Seats** — leather lowback buckets - LE, ES	735	865
	NA w/CYK		
—	**Paint** — special color or metallic	82	97

DODGE GRAND CARAVAN FWD

GRAND CARAVAN FWD 6 CYL

CODE	DESCRIPTION	DEALER	LIST
KL53	Base..	16522	18178
KH53	SE..	17513	19304
KP53	LE...	20662	22883
KP53	ES...	21110	23392
	Destination Charge:..	560	560

Standard Equipment

GRAND CARAVAN FWD - BASE: Chimes (headlights on, seat belt, key in ignition), cupholders, child protection side door locks, stainless steel exhaust system, front and rear body color fascias with accent nerf, tinted glass, single horn, body sound insulation, front/rear dome lamps, fold away exterior aero manual mirrors, non-illuminated visor mirrors, AM/FM ETR stereo radio with digital clock, seek and four speakers; seven-passenger seating, quick release intermediate and rear seats, driver and passenger highback reclining bucket seats, deluxe cloth molded seat trim, underbody spare tire carrier with cable

DODGE

CODE	DESCRIPTION	DEALER	LIST

winch, electronic speed control, compact spare tire, four "Triad" wheel covers, vented side/quarter/sliding door windows, liftgate window wipers/washers with fixed intermittent wipe, 2-speed wipers with variable intermittent wipe.

SE (in addition to or instead of BASE equipment): Dual horn, power liftgate release, power fold away exterior aero black mirrors, bodyside accent color (2 colors) moldings, AM/FM ETR stereo radio with cassette, seek, Dolby, four speakers; tilt steering column, storage compartments.

LE (in addition to or instead of SE equipment): Front air cond, lower bodyside and sill accent color cladding, front storage console w/coin holder, overhead console (compass, outside temperature, 4-function trip computer, front/rear reading lights), electric rear window defroster, power front and side door locks, front/rear body color fascias, floor mats, automatic time delay headlights, deluxe body sound insulation, remote keyless entry, front dome lamps deleted, map and liftgate lamps, light group (ash receiver, front map/reading [header mounted], glove box, ignition switch [time delayed], rear cargo dome, underhood, illuminated entry system, liftgate-mounted dual floodlights), roof luggage rack, heated power fold away exterior aero black mirrors, illuminated visor mirrors, bodyside accent color moldings deleted, driver and passenger reclining bucket seats, molded luxury cloth seat trim, pwr quarter vent windows.

Accessories

Code	Description	Dealer	List
T	**Base Family Value Pkg T** .... *incls air conditioning, dual horns, bodyside accent color molding, under front passenger seat storage drawer, power liftgate release, map and cargo lighting enhancements*	181	213
B	**SE Family Value Pkg B** .... *incls air conditioning, map and cargo lighting enhancements, rear window defroster*	181	213
D	**SE Family Value Pkg D** .... *incls air conditioning, map and cargo lighting enhancements, rear window defroster, forward and overhead consoles, power door locks, floor mats, gauges (oil pressure, voltage, tachometer), deluxe insulation, light group, illuminated visor vanity mirror, power rear quarter vent windows*	985	1159
K	**Two-Tone Pkg K —** .... LE *incls power driver seat, power windows, radio (AM/FM w/cassette, equalizer and six Infinity speakers), sunscreen glass*	260	306
L	**Woodgrain Pkg L — LE** .... *incls power driver seat, power windows, radio (AM/FM w/cassette, equalizer and six Infinity speakers), sunscreen glass, woodgrain group*	818	962
M	**"ES" Pkg M — ES** .... *incls power driver seat, power windows, radio (AM/FM w/cassette, equalizer and six Infinity speakers), sunscreen glass, sport handling group, "ES" decor group*	366	431
HAA	**Climate Group I** — Base .... *incls air conditioning*	728	857
AAA	**Climate Group II** — w/family value pkg .... *incls air conditioning and sunscreen glass [NA w/ASK]*	352	414
AAB	**Climate Group III** — Base w/Pkg T	840	988
	SE w/Pkg B	840	988
	SE w/Pkg D	748	880
	w/ASK (SE w/Pkg B)	488	574
	w/ASK (SE w/Pkg D)	396	466
	w/AAF (SE w/Pkg B)	786	925
	w/AAF (SE w/Pkg D)	695	818
	w/ASK & AAF (SE w/Pkg B)	434	511

CODE	DESCRIPTION	DEALER	LIST
	w/ASK & AAF (SE w/Pkg D)	343	404
	LE w/Pkg K or L, ES	396	466
	w/AAF (LE w/Pkg K or L, ES)	343	404
	incls air conditioning, sunscreen glass, rear heat/air conditioning		
AJK	**Convenience Group I** — Base w/Pkg T	316	372
	incls speed control and tilt		
AAC	**Convenience Group II** — Base w/Pkg T	590	694
	SE w/Pkg B	225	265
	incls speed control and tilt, power mirrors and power door locks		
AAD	**Convenience Group III** — SE w/Pkg B	572	673
	SE w/Pkg D	347	408
	incls speed control and tilt, power mirrors, power locks, power windows and keyless entry		
CYK	**Seating Group I** — 7-passenger seating w/integrated child seat - Base	191	225
CYS	**Seating Group II** — 7-passenger quad command - SE, LE, ES	507	597
CYT	**Seating Group IV** — 7-passenger convert-a-bed - SE, LE, ES	470	553
TBB	**Loading & Towing Group I**	93	109
	incls conventional spare		
AAE	**Loading & Towing Group II** — Base w/Pkg T	151	178
	SE, LE	151	178
	w/AAG (SE w/Pkg B or D, LE w/Pkg K or L, ES)	124	146
	incls conventional spare tire and firm ride heavy load suspension		
AAF	**Load & Towing Group III** — SE w/Pkg B or D	376	442
	LE w/Pkg K or L	376	442
	w/AAG or ASK (SE w/Pkg B or D, LE w/Pkg K or L, ES)	349	410
	incls conventional spare tire, firm ride heavy load suspension and trailer tow group		
WJV	**Wheels I** — 15" aluminum wheels - LE w/Pkg K	309	363
AAG	**Sport Handling Group** — SE w/Pkg B or D (NA w/ASK)	106	125
	LE w/Pkg L (NA w/ASK)	106	125
	LE w/Pkg K (incls WJV)	415	488
—	**Radio Equipment**		
RAS	radio - Base	145	170
RCE	Infinity speaker system - SE w/Pkg B or D	172	202
RBC	radio - SE w/Pkg D	426	501
	LE w/Pkg K or L, ES	145	170
	incls AM/FM stereo w/CD player, equalizer, clock and 6 Infinity speakers		
BRL	**Brakes** — anti-lock - SE w/Pkg B or D	509	599
	LE, ES	509	599
ASH	**Gold Special Edition Decor Group** — SE w/Pkg B or D	213	250
	incls gold badging, gold day light opening accent stripe, bodyside body color molding, 15" cast aluminum "Lace" wheel with gold accents		
ASK	**Sport Wagon Decor Group** — SE w/Pkg B or D	638	750
	incls accent color fascias w/blk rub strips, fog lights, leather-wrapped steering whl, sunscreen glass, sport handling group, 15" cast alum/ 5-spoke whls		
GFA	**Rear Window Defroster** — Base, SE	143	168
JPB	**Power Door Locks** — Base w/Pkg T	225	265
NAE	**California Emissions**	87	102
NBY	**New York Emissions**	87	102
NHK	**Engine Block Heater** — available in Alaska only	29	34
MWG	**Luggage Rack**	122	143
TPC	**Tires** — Base w/Pkg T	59	69

DODGE

DODGE

CODE	DESCRIPTION	DEALER	LIST
	SE w/Pkg B or D	59	69
	LE w/Pkg K or L	59	69
	incls P205/70R15 WSW SBR tires (NA w/AAG, ASH or ASK)		
—	**Paint** — special color or metallic	82	97
—	**Seats** — cloth highback buckets - Base, SE....................	STD	STD
—	**Seats** — cloth lowback buckets - LE, ES....................	STD	STD
—	**Seats** — leather lowback buckets (NA w/CYK) - LE, ES	735	865
EFA	**Engine** — 3.0L MPI V6 - Base....................................	STD	STD
EGA	**Engine** — 3.3L MPI V6 - SE, LE, ES..............................	STD	STD
EGH	**Engine** — 3.8L MPI V6 - LE, ES.................................	257	302
DGA	**Transmission** — 3-speed automatic - Base	STD	STD
DGB	**Transmission** — 4-speed automatic - Base	168	198
	SE, LE, ES..	STD	STD

DODGE RAM VAN

B150 6 CYL

AB1L11	Van 109" WB	11847	12951
AB1L12	Van 127" WB	13936	15866

B250 6 CYL

ABL11	Van 109" WB	13974	15911
AB2L12	Van 127" WB	14287	16279
AB2L13	Maxivan 127" WB	15126	17266

B350 8 CYL

AB3L12	Van 127" WB	15375	17559
AB3L13	Maxivan 127" WB	16195	18524

Destination Charge:	595	595

Standard Equipment

B150 RAM CARGO VAN - BASE: 3-speed automatic lock-up transmission, power steering, power front disc/rear drum brakes with rear anti-lock braking system, front and rear painted bumpers, stainless steel exhaust system, tinted glass windows, halogen headlamps, dual black exterior foldaway mirrors, ETR AM/FM stereo with seek, clock and two speakers; non-reclining highback bucket seats.

TRADESMAN (in addition to or instead of BASE equipment): Color-keyed "Eurograin" vinyl door trim panels, 6" x 9" black dual exterior mirrors, fixed rear, dual-door windows, heavy-duty suspension, intermittent windshield wipers with low warning washer fluid.

B250 RAM CARGO VAN - BASE: 3-speed automatic lockup transmission, power steering, power front disc/rear drum brakes with rear anti-lock braking system, front and rear painted bumpers, stainless steel exhaust system, tinted glass windows, halogen headlamps, dual black exterior foldaway mirrors, ETR AM/FM stereo with seek, clock and two speakers; non-reclining highback bucket seats.

TRADESMAN (in addition to or instead of BASE equipment): Color-keyed "Eurograin" vinyl door trim panels, 6" x 9" black dual exterior mirrors, fixed rear, dual-door windows, heavy-duty suspension, intermittent windshield wipers with low warning washer fluid.

CONVERSION (in addition to or instead of TRADESMAN equip): Air cond, bright front/rear bumpers, Deluxe Convenience Group (tilt steering, speed control, 4-spoke sport steering wheel), bright grille, dual tone horn, conventional-size spare tire, styled steel wheels w/bright hub covers, fixed side/ear windows.

B350 RAM CARGO VAN - BASE: 4-speed automatic lockup transmission, power steering, power front disc/rear drum brakes with rear anti-lock braking system, front and rear painted bumpers, stainless steel exhaust system, tinted glass windows, halogen headlamps, dual black exterior foldaway mirrors, ETR AM/FM stereo with seek, clock and two speakers; non-reclining highback bucket seats.

MAXI SPECIAL (in addition to or instead of BASE equip): Air cond, bright front/rear bumpers, maximum eng cooling, auxiliary auto trans oil, Deluxe Convenience Grp (tilt steering column, speed control, 4-spoke sport steering wheel), dual tone horn, color-keyed door assist straps, dual power exterior mirrors, Power Convenience Group (power locks, pwr windows, keyless & illum entry system), heavy-duty suspension.

Accessories

CODE	DESCRIPTION	DEALER	LIST
HAA	**Air Conditioning**	825	970
	models w/3.9 liter V6 engine include 90 amp alternator		
MBF	**Bumper, Bright Rear Step**		
	w/o AEA	184	216
	w/AEA		
	B150 w/commercial pkg	50	59
	B250 w/commercial pkg or conversion pkg	50	59
	B350 w/commercial or shuttle pkg	50	59
NAE	**California Emissions**	87	102
NBY	**New York Emissions — B150**	87	87
NAF	**High Altitude Emissions**	NC	NC
JHA	**Intermittent Windshield Wipers**	51	60
—	**Tires**		
TRE	P225/75R15 SBR all-season BW (5) - B150	109	128
TRF	P225/75R15 SBR all-season WW (5)		
	B250 109" WB, w/22E, 24E or 26E	77	91
TSF	P235/75R15XL SBR all-season OWL (5)		
	B150 w/commercial pkg	312	367
	B250 109" WB		
	w/22C, 24C, 26C, 22E, 24E or 26E	204	240
	w/22F, 24F, 26F	127	149

DODGE

CODE	DESCRIPTION	DEALER	LIST
	B250 127" WB		
	w/conversion pkg	26	31
	non-maxi w/commercial pkg	204	240
	maxivan w/commercial pkg	105	123
TSC	P235/75R15XL SBR all-season BW (4)		
	B250 ex. maxivan		
	w/o quick order pkg	80	94
	non-maxi 127" WB w/commercial pkg	99	117
TWR	LT225/75R16E SBR all-season BW (4)		
	B350 non-maxi		
	w/o commercial pkg	128	151
	w/commercial pkg	143	168
TBB	spare tire		
	w/TRE tires - B250 ex. maxivan	122	144
	w/TSC tires - B250	142	167
	w/TWP tires - B350 non-maxi	201	236
	w/TWR tires - B350	215	253
	w/TYB tires - B350 maxivan	240	282
CSR	**Pull Handle Strap** — B250 109" WB conversion	31	37
WJA	**Styled Steel Wheels (4)** — B150 & B250 w/commercial pkg	209	246
DSA	**Anti-Spin Differential**	218	257
DM	**Optional Rear Axle Ratio**	33	39
—	**Engines**		
ELF	5.2 liter V8 EFI - B150, B250	499	587
EML	5.9 liter V8 EFI - B250 127" WB	728	857
	B350	230	270
NHK	**Engine Block Heater**	29	34
SUA	**Tilt Steering Column**	114	134
GXE	**Lock Group**	7	8
—	**Seats**		
K5	cloth & vinyl highback front bucket	129	152
N6	vinyl highback front bucket	57	67
CYA	driver seat delete	(156)	(184)
DGA	**Transmission** — 4 speed automatic	213	250
	std on B350, reqs 5.2 liter V8 engine		
CUB	**Console** — w/commercial, conversion or shuttle pkg	130	153
BGK	**Anti-Lock Brakes** — 4 wheel	425	500
NFF	**Fuel Tank** — 35 gallon	96	113
BAN	**Alternator** — 120 amp	131	154
BCQ	**Battery** — 750 amp	48	57
—	**Mirrors**		
GPU	dual black manual	80	94
GPS	dual black power - w/commercial pkg	54	64
	B250 w/22E, 24E or 26E	54	64
—	**Doors**		
GMF	rear single	NC	NC
GKF	right side sliding	NC	NC
CLP	**Scuff Pads**	34	40
—	**Glass**		
GAE	sunscreen		
	B150 w/commercial pkg		
	w/GHB	102	120

CODE	DESCRIPTION	DEALER	LIST
	w/GHD	205	241
	w/GHG or GHJ	348	409
	B250		
	w/GHG or GHJ (commercial)	348	409
	w/GHD (conversion)	205	241
	w/GHB (commercial)	102	120
	B350 w/commercial or shuttle pkg		
	w/GHB (commercial)	102	120
	w/GHD (commercial or shuttle conversion)	205	241
	w/GHG or GHJ (commercial or shuttle conversion)	348	409
GAH	vented		
	w/GHB	51	60
	w/GHD or GHJ	118	139
	w/GHG	184	217
ADC	**Convenience Group** — B250, B350 (see pkgs)		
	incls intermittent wipers, lights for ashtray, glove box & underhood; ignition key light & headlight switch		
AJK	**Deluxe Convenience Group**		
	w/commercial pkg	340	400
	incls tilt steering col, cruise control premium soft vinyl steering wheel [B250 127" WB reqs intermittent wipers]		
ADP	**Heavy Duty Suspension Group** — std on B250 maxivan	31	37
	incls HD front & rear gas shock absorbers		
AEA	**Exterior Appearance Group** — w/commercial pkg	317	373
	incls bright bumpers & grille, bumper step pads & rectangular halogen headlamps		
—	**Springs**		
SKS	heavy duty front	13	15
SNG	heavy duty rear (1980#)	60	71
SNE	heavy duty rear, 1810 lb - B150 w/commercial pkg	60	71
SNG	heavy duty rear, 1980 lb. - B250 (std on maxivan)	60	71
SNL	heavy duty rear, 2770 lb. - B350 (reqs Z3B)	60	71
—	**Radio Equipment**		
RA8	AM/FM delete	(104)	(122)
RAS	AM/FM ETR stereo radio w/cassette & 4 speakers		
	w/commercial or conversion pkg	178	210
	B250 109" WB	178	210
RAY	premium AM/FM ETR radio w/cassette & graphic equalizer B250 109" WB		
	conversion w/22E, 24E or 26E	454	534
	conversion w/22F, 24F or 26F	130	153
RCE	radio speaker system (Infinity sound) (reqs RAS)		
	B250 109" WB conversion w/22E, 24E or 26E	145	171
—	**Cooling**		
NHB	auxiliary auto trans oil (reqs NMC)	54	64
NMC	maximum engine	56	66
AJP	**Power Convenience Group** — B250 109" WB	534	628
	w/22E, 24E or 26E	534	628
	incls pwr windows, pwr door locks, door lock delay, keyless entry system w/remote transmitters		
—	**GVWR Pkgs**		
Z1B	5,300 lb. - B150	74	87

DODGE

CODE	DESCRIPTION	DEALER	LIST
Z2B	6,400 lb. - B250 127" WB (std maxivan)		
	w/o quick order pkg	184	217
	w/commercial pkg	173	203
	incls P235/75R15XL all-season BW tires (4); vans w/commercial pkg incl matching spare		
Z3B	8,510 lb. B350 non-maxi		
	w/o commercial pkg	233	274
	w/commercial pkg	216	254
	B350 maxivan w/o quick order pkg	105	123
	B350 w/shuttle pkg	105	123
	incls LT225/75R16E all-season BW tires; vans w/commercial pkg incl matching spare		
Z3D	9,000 lb. - B350 maxivan		
	w/o quick order pkg	441	519
	w/28C	361	425
	w/28H	337	396
	incls LT245/75R16E SBR all-season BW tires & thermal insulation group [reqs 5.9 liter V8 engine]		
ZZ	**Temporary Plastic Seat Group** — w/o AHC	72	85
	B250 w/AHC or conversion pkg	(59)	(69)
	B350 w/AHC or shuttle pkg	(59)	(69)
AEB	**Van Conversion Appearance Group** — B250, B350 (see pkgs)		
	incls exterior appearance group, van window group, 120 amp alternator, dual horns, sport steering wheel, accessory wiring harness, woodtone instrument panel applique rubber scuff pads		
—	**Van Window Groups**		
GHB	**Group GHB**	51	60
	incls fixed window glass on rear dual doors		
GHD	**Group GHD** — vans w/o quick order pkg	88	103
	vans w/commercial pkg	37	43
	incls fixed window glass on rear dual doors & right side dual doors		
GHJ	**Group GHJ (Vision Van Curb Side)** — vans w/o quick order pkg	114	134
	vans w/commercial pkg	63	74
	incls fixed window glass on rear dual doors, right-side rear quarter window		
GHG	**Group GHG (Vision Van Curb Side)** — vans w/o quick order pkg	178	209
	van w/commercial pkg	127	149
	B350 w/shuttle pkg	156	184
	incls window glass on right & left sides and on dual rear doors; B350 w/shuttle pkg also incls vented glass		
GHA	**Group GHA (Window Delete)** — vans w/commercial pkg	(51)	(60)
AHC	**Trailer Tow Prep Group**		
	B250 109" WB		
	w/commercial pkg	319	375
	w/conversion pkg	171	201
	B250 127" WB		
	w/commercial pkg	319	375
	w/conversion pkg	139	164
	B350 w/o quick order pkg		
	w/o Z3B or Z3D	350	412
	w/Z3B	319	375
	B350 w/commercial pkg	208	245
	B350 non-maxi w/26H or 28H		

CODE	DESCRIPTION	DEALER	LIST
	w/o Z3B	171	201
	w/Z3B	139	164
	B350 maxivan w/26H or 28H	139	164
	incls maximum engine cooling, HD suspension group, auto trans oil auxiliary cooling, 120 amp alternator, HD flashers, trailer wiring harness, [NA w/3.9 liter engine on B250 109" WB; NA w/3.9 liter engine & auto trans on B250 127" WB]		
—	**Quick Order Pkgs - B150 Vans**		
22C	**Commercial** — B150 109" WB	158	186
24C	w/ELF engine, add	499	587
26C	w/ELF engine and DGB trans, add	711	837
	incls rear door windows, 35 gal fuel tank, GVW upgrade, intermittent wipers, dual black 6"x9" mirrors, scuff pads		
22C	**Commercial** — B150 127" WB	(256)	(301)
24C	w/ELF engine, add	499	587
26C	w/ELF engine and DGB trans, add	711	837
	incls rear door windows, 35 gal fuel tank, GVW upgrade, intermittent wipers, dual black 6"x9" mirrors, scuff pads		
—	**Quick Order Pkgs - B250 Vans**		
22C	**Commercial** — B250 109" WB	122	143
24C	w/ELF engine, add	499	587
26C	w/ELF engine and DGB trans, add	711	837
	incls P225/75R15 SBR all-season BW tires w/matching spare, intermittent wipers, rear dual door glass, HD suspension group, dual black 6"x9" mirrors, scuff pads, 35 gal fuel tank		
22E	**Conversion** — B250 109" WB	800	941
24E	w/ELF engine, add	499	587
26E	w/ELF engine and DGB trans, add	711	837
	incls van conversion appearance group, P225/75R15 SBR all-season BW tires w/matching spare, air conditioning, HD alternator, dual black 6"x9" mirrors, 35 gal fuel tank, HD battery, exterior appearance group, scuff pads, intermittent wipers, convenience group, deluxe convenience group, spare tire, glass on rear dual doors & right side doors, vented glass on dual rear doors & dual right cargo doors		
22F	**Conversion** — B250 109" WB	1522	1791
24F	w/ELF engine, add	499	587
26F	w/ELF engine and DGB trans, add	711	837
	incls convenience group, deluxe convenience group, dual black power mirrors, P225/75R15 SBR all-season WW tires w/matching spare, 35 gal fuel tank, pwr convenience group, air conditioning, exterior appearance group, cast aluminum wheels, AM/FM ETR stereo radio w/cassette, graphic equalizer & 4 spkrs; van conversion appearance group, intermittent wipers, HD alternator, scuff pads, HD battery, glass on rear dual doors & right side doors, vented glass on dual rear doors & dual right cargo doors		
22C	**Commercial** — B250 non-maxi	(176)	(207)
24C	w/ELF engine, add	499	587
26C	w/ELF engine and DGB trans, add	711	837
	incls HD suspension group, intermittent wipers, rear dual door glass, P225/75R15 SBR all-season BW tires w/matching spare, scuff pads, 35 gal fuel tank, dual black manual 6"x9" mirrors		
24C	**Commercial** — B250 maxivan	(188)	(221)
26C	w/ELF engine and DGB trans, add	711	837

CODE	DESCRIPTION	DEALER	LIST
	incls rear dual door glass, intermittent wipers, P235/75R15XL SBR all-season BW tires w/matching spare, dual black 6"x9" mirrors, 35 gal fuel tank, scuff pads [reqs 5.2 liter engine]		
24F	**Conversion** — B250 non-maxi van	1393	1639
	B250 maxivan	1209	1422
26F	w/ELF engine and DGB trans, add	711	837
28F	w/EML engine and DGB trans, add	941	1107
	incls P235/75R15XL SBR all-season WW tires w/matching spare, 35 gal fuel tank, air conditioning, convenience group, deluxe convenience group, van conversion appearance group, HD battery, scuff pads, pwr convenience group, intermittent wipers, dual black pwr mirrors, cast aluminum wheels, exterior appearance group, GVW upgrade (std on maxivan), AM/FM ETR stereo radio w/cassette, graphic equalizer & 4 spkrs; HD suspension group (std on maxivan), glass on rear dual doors & right side doors, vented glass on dual rear doors & dual right cargo doors [reqs 5.2 liter V8 engine]		
—	**Quick Order Pkgs - B350 Vans**		
26C	**Commercial** — B350 non-maxi	13	15
28C	w/EML engine, add	230	270
	incls HD suspension group, intermittent wipers, dual black manual 6"x9" mirrors, 35 gal fuel tank, scuff pads, LT225/75R16D SBR all-season BW tires w/matching spare, fixed glass on rear dual doors, auto trans oil cooler, maximum engine cooling		
26H	**Shuttle Conversion** — B350 non-maxi	1025	1206
28H	w/EML engine, add	230	270
	incls air conditioning, pwr convenience group, convenience group, deluxe convenience group, exterior appearance group, wheel trim rings, vented glass on rear dual doors & right side doors, HD battery, dual black pwr mirrors, van conversion appearance group, 35 gal fuel tank, scuff pads, AM/FM ETR stereo radio w/cassette, graphic equalizer & 4 spkrs, intermittent wipers		
26C	**Commercial** — B350 Maxivan	(410)	(482)
28C	w/EML engine, add	230	270
	incls HD suspension group, maximum engine cooling, intermittent wipers, GVW upgrade, LT235/75R16E SBR all-season BW tires w/matching spare, 35 gal fuel tank, glass on rear dual doors, scuff pads, auxiliary trans oil cooling, dual black manual 6"x9" mirrors		
26H	**Shuttle Conversion** — B350 Maxivan	1037	1220
28H	w/EML engine, add	230	270
	incls convenience group, deluxe convenience group, air conditioning, pwr convenience group, 35 gal fuel tank, HD suspension group, dual black pwr mirrors, HD battery, scuff pads, 120 amp alternator, wheel trim rings, van conversion appearance group, glass on dual rear doors & right side doors, vented glass for rear dual doors & right side doors, exterior appearance group, AM/FM ETR stereo radio w/cassette, graphic equalizer & 4 spkrs		

DODGE RAM WAGON

B150 6 CYL
AB1L51 Wagon 109" WB 13252   14491

B250 6 CYL
AB2L52 Non-Maxiwagon 127" WB 16021   18260
AB2L53 Maxiwagon 127" WB (8 cyl) 17114   19546

B350 8 CYL
AB3L52 Non-Maxiwagon 127" WB 17116   19548
AB3L53 Maxiwagon 127" WB 17980   20565

Destination Charge: 595   595

Standard Equipment

B150 RAM PASSENGER WAGON - BASE: 3-speed automatic transmission with lockup torque converter, side door guard beams, power front disc/rear drum brakes, power steering, painted front and rear bumpers, dual side rear door compartments, stainless steel exhaust, tinted glass windows, 5" x 6" black foldaway exterior mirrors, ETR AM/FM stereo with seek, clock and four speakers; five-passenger seating package, non-reclining highback bucket front seats, conventional spare tire.

FAMILY VALUE (in addition to or instead of BASE equipment): Air cond, front and rear bright bumpers, dual side compartments, color-keyed front and rear carpeting, eight-passenger seating package, 6" x 9" black manually-operated dual exterior mirrors, conventional spare mounted inside, bright wheel covers.

LE (in addition to or instead of FAMILY VALUE equipment): Engine carpeted engine cover, sunscreen rear glass, tinted windshield and front doors, sound insulation, full-length color-keyed carpeting with pad and silencer, dual power exterior mirrors, ETR AM/FM stereo with seek Dolby sound, clock, cassette and four speakers; Power Convenience Package (power locks and windows, keyless and illuminated entry system), reclining highback bucket front seats, cloth and vinyl seat trim, styled steel wheels.

B250 RAM PASSENGER WAGON - BASE: 3-speed automatic transmission non-lockup, side door guard beams, power front disc/rear drum brakes, power steering, painted front and rear bumpers, dual side rear door compartments, stainless steel exhaust, tinted glass windows, 5" x 6" black foldaway exterior mirrors, ETR AM/FM stereo with seek, clock and four speakers; eight-passenger seating package, non-reclining highback bucket front seats, conventional spare tire.

DODGE

CHURCH VALUE (in addition to or instead of BASE equipment): Air cond, front and rear bright bumpers, dual side compartments, color-keyed front and rear carpeting, 12-passenger seating package, 6" x 9" black manually-operated dual exterior mirrors, conventional spare mounted inside, bright wheel covers.

LE (in addition to or instead of CHURCH VALUE equipment): Engine carpeted engine cover, sunscreen rear glass, tinted windshield and front doors, sound insulation, full-length color-keyed carpeting with pad and silencer, dual power exterior mirrors, ETR AM/FM stereo with seek Dolby sound, clock, cassette and four speakers; Power Convenience Package (power locks and windows, keyless and illuminated entry system), reclining highback bucket front seats, cloth and vinyl seat trim, styled steel wheels.

B350 RAM PASSENGER WAGON - BASE: 3-speed automatic transmission, side door guard beams, power front disc/rear drum brakes, power steering, painted front and rear bumpers, dual side rear door compartments, stainless steel exhaust, tinted glass windows, 5" x 6" black foldaway exterior mirrors, ETR AM/FM stereo with seek, clock and four speakers; eight-passenger seating package, non-reclining highback bucket front seats, conventional spare tire.

CHURCH VALUE (in addition to or instead of BASE equipment): Air conditioning, front and rear bright bumpers, dual side compartments, color-keyed front and rear carpeting, 12-passenger seating package (15-passenger on Maxi), 6" x 9" black manually-operated dual exterior mirrors, conventional spare mounted inside, bright wheel covers.

LE (in addition to or instead of CHURCH VALUE equipment): Engine carpeted engine cover, sunscreen rear glass, tinted windshield and front doors, sound insulation, full-length color-keyed carpeting with pad and silencer, dual power exterior mirrors, ETR AM/FM stereo with seek Dolby sound, clock, cassette and four speakers; Power Convenience Package (power locks and windows, keyless and illuminated entry system), reclining highback bucket front seats, cloth and vinyl seat trim, styled steel wheels.

Accessories

CODE	DESCRIPTION	DEALER	LIST
HAA	**Air Conditioning** — front	825	970
	incls 90 amp alternator		
HBA	**Air Conditioning** — auxiliary rear w/o heater		
	w/o AHC		
	B250 Maxiwagon w/o LE pkg	519	611
	B250 w/LE or value pkg	388	457
	B350 w/value pkg	388	457
	w/AHC		
	B250 non-maxiwagon w/LE or value pkg	340	400
	B250 maxiwagon	340	400
	B350 w/o LE pkg	340	400
	B350 w/LE pkg	(179)	(211)
	reqs front air conditioning		
HBB	**Air Conditioning** — auxiliary rear w/heater		
	w/o AHC		
	B250 maxiwagon w/o LE pkg	699	822
	B350 w/o LE or value pkg	699	822
	B250 w/LE or value pkg	568	668
	B350 w/value pkg	568	668
	w/AHC		
	B250 non-maxiwagon w/LE or value pkg	519	611
	B250 maxiwagon	519	611
	B350	519	611
	incls 810 amp battery & 120 amp alternator [reqs front air conditioning; NA on B250 vans w/3.9 liter V6 engine]		
ADC	**Convenience Group**	94	110

DODGE

CODE	DESCRIPTION	DEALER	LIST
	incls intermittent wipers & lights for ashtray, glove box & underhood, headlight & ignition		
SUA	**Tilt Steering Column**	114	134
JHA	**Windshield Wipers** — intermittent	51	60
NFF	**Fuel Tank** — 35 gallon	96	113
ADP	**Heavy Duty Suspension Group** — std on B250 maxiwagon	31	37
	incls HD gas front & rear shock absorbers		
—	**Engines**		
ELF	5.2 liter EFI V8 - B150, B250 non-maxiwagon	499	587
EML	5.9 liter EFI V8 - B250 non-maxiwagon	728	857
	B350 non-maxiwagon	230	270
DGB	**Transmission** — 4-spd automatic - B150, B250	213	250
	reqs 5.2 liter V6 engine		
6P	**Paint** — two-tone center band - w/o LE pkg	303	357
	w/LE pkg	207	243
6L	**Paint** — two-tone lower break - w/o LE pkg	258	304
	w/LE pkg	162	190
BAN	**Alternator** — 120 amp	131	154
BCM	**Battery** — 810 amp	48	57
CUB	**Console** — w/value pkg	130	153
GFA	**Rear Window Defroster**	94	110
	reqs single rear door w/vented glass		
RAS	**Radio** — AM/FM ETR - w/value pkg	179	210
	incls cassette & 4 spkrs		
RAY	**Radio** — AM/FM ETR - B250 w/LE	130	153
	B350 w/LE	130	153
	incls cass w/graphic equalizer, 4 spkrs		
GAE	**Glass** — sunscreen	348	409
	incls sunscreen glass on all windows except windshield & front door glass		
BGK	**Anti-Lock Brakes** — 4 wheel	425	500
NAE	**California Emissions**	87	102
NBY	**New York Emissions** — B150	87	102
NAF	**High Altitude Emissions**	NC	NC
HDA	**Auxiliary Rear Heater**		
	B150		
	w/LE or value pkg	179	211
	w/o LE or value pkg	310	365
	B250		
	w/o AHC w/o LE or value pkg	310	365
	w/o AHC w/LE or value pkg	179	211
	w/AHC w/o LE or value pkg	179	211
	B350		
	w/o AHC w/o LE or value pkg	310	365
	w/AHC w/value pkg	179	211
	non-maxiwagon w/AHC w/o LE or value pkg	179	211
AJK	**Deluxe Convenience Group**	282	332
	incls sp t steering wheel w/tilt col, cruise control [reqs intermittent wipers]		
—	**Doors**		
GMC	single rear w/vented glass	59	69
GKC	sliding side w/vented glass	NC	NC
GLC	dual rear w/vented glass - w/LE or value pkg	NC	NC
	w/o LE or value pkg	59	69

CODE	DESCRIPTION	DEALER	LIST
NHK	**Engine Block Heater**	29	34
DSA	**Axle** — rear anti-spin differential	218	257
DM	**Axle** — rear optional ratio	33	39
—	**Cooling**		
NHB	auxiliary transmission oil	54	64
	reqs maximum engine cooling; NA on B150 w/3.9 liter V6 eng & man trans		
NMC	maximum engine	56	66
GPU	**Mirrors** — dual black manual	80	94
—	**Tires** — steel belted radial		
TSC	P235/75R15 BW - B150	208	245
	B250 non-maxiwagon	80	94
TSD	P235/75RXL WW - B150 w/LE pkg	78	92
TSF	P235/75R15XL OWL - B150 w/LE pkg	105	123
	B250 w/LE pkg	26	31
TBB	conventional spare		
	w/P225/75R15 tires - B250 non-maxiwagon	122	144
	w/P235/75R15 tires - B250	142	167
	w/LT225/75R16D tires - B350 non-maxiwagon	201	236
	w/LT225/75R16E tires - B350	215	253
W5A	**Wheel Covers (4)** — bright (NA on B350)	56	66
WMC	**Wheel Trim Rings (4)** — bright - B350	107	126
WJC	**Wheels (4)** — cast aluminum - B150 & B250 w/LE pkg	111	130
WJA	**Wheels (4)** — styled steel - B150 & B250 w/value pkg	153	180
MBF	**Bumper** — bright, rear step - w/LE pkg	50	59
	w/o LE pkg	184	216
—	**GVW Pkgs**		
Z1D	6010 lb. - B150	282	332
	incls P235/75R15XL SBR all-season BW tires		
Z2B	6400 lb. - B250 non-maxiwagon	184	217
	incls P235/75R15XL SBR all-season tires		
Z3B	8510 lb. - B350 non-maxiwagon w/LE or value pkg	217	255
	B350 non-maxiwagon w/o quick order pkg	202	238
	B350 maxiwagon	105	123
	incls LT225/75R16E SBR all-season BW tires		
CKZ	**Carpeting Delete** — B150 w/value pkg	NC	NC
	B250 non-maxiwagon w/value pkg	NC	NC
	carpet replaced by rubber floor mat		
CKE	**Carpeting** — driver compartment - B350 w/value pkg	49	58
	reqs rear carpeting		
CKN	**Carpeting** — rear compartment - B350 w/value pkg	84	99
	reqs driver compartment carpeting		
K5	**Seats** — cloth & vinyl	72	85
AJP	**Power Convenience Group** — (see pkgs)		
	incls pwr windows, pwr door locks & keyless entry system w/remote transmitters		
—	**Springs**		
SKS	heavy duty front	13	15
SNE	heavy duty rear, 1810 lb. - B150 w/o Z1D	60	71
SNG	heavy duty rear, 1980 lb. - B150, B250 non-maxiwagon	60	71
SNL	heavy duty rear, 2770 lb. - B350	60	71
AHC	**Trailer Towing Prep Group**		
	B250 maxiwagon w/6400 lb. GVW w/o LE pkg	319	375

CODE	DESCRIPTION	DEALER	LIST
	B250 maxiwagon w/LE pkg	188	221
	B250 non-maxiwagon w/LE or value pkg	188	221
	B350 w/o 8510 lb. GVW		
	w/o LE or value pkg	350	412
	non-maxiwagon w/LE pkg	171	201
	non-maxiwagon w/value pkg	219	258
	B350 w/8510 lb. GVW		
	w/o LE or value pkg	319	375
	w/LE pkg	139	164
	w/value pkg	188	221
	incls HD suspension group, maximum engine cooling, auxiliary auto trans oil cooling, 810 amp battery, 120 amp alternator, trailer wiring harness, HD flashers [B250 reqs 5.2 liter V8 engine & 4-spd auto trans]		
—	**Seating**		
CYF	8-passenger	291	342
	B150 reqs 6010 lb. GVW		
CYP	8-passenger, travel seat - B250 w/LE pkg	776	913
	B350 non-maxiwagon w/LE pkg	468	551
	B350 maxiwagon w/LE pkg	226	266
CYH	12-passenger - B350 w/o LE or value pkg	598	704
	B350 w/LE or value pkg	(242)	(285)
	reqs dual rear doors w/vented glass or single rear door w/vented glass		
CYJ	15-passenger - B350 maxiwagon	841	989
	reqs dual rear doors w/vented glass or single rear door w/vented glass, 8510 lb. GVW pkg		
ASP	**LE Decor Group** — (see pkgs)		
	incls halogen headlamps, driver & pass highback reclining front bucket seats, rear bench seat, color-keyed carpeting, spare tire cover, dual horns, door pull straps, bright grille, color-keyed cloth headliner, sport steering wheel, map/reading light, front rubber floor mats, bright front & rear bumpers, woodgrain instrument panel trim, console (models w/auto trans), stepwell courtesy lights, illuminated pass visor vanity mirror, moldings for lower bodyside & rear, headliner insulation [B250 & B350 req conventional spare tire]		
—	**Quick Order Pkgs - B150**		
22C	**Value** — B150	425	500
24C	w/ELF engine, add	499	587
26C	w/ELF engine & DGB trans, add	711	837
	incls convenience group, 35 gal fuel tank, dual black manual mirrors, 8-pas seating, bright grille, air conditioning, spare tire cover, P235/75R15XL SBR all-season BW tires, 120 amp alternator, full carpeting, bright wheel covers (4), bright front & rear bumpers, 2 additional radio spkrs, vented glass on single rear door		
22E	**LE** — B150	2728	3209
24E	w/ELF engine, add	499	587
26E	w/ELF engine & DGB trans, add	711	837
	incls LE decor group, pwr convenience group, 22C value pkg, sunscreen glass, deluxe convenience group, dual black pwr mirrors, styled steel wheels (4), AM/FM ETR stereo radio w/cass, graphic equalizer & 4 spkrs		
—	**Quick Order Pkgs - B250**		
22C	**Value** — B250 non-maxiwagon	934	1099
24C	w/ELF engine, add	499	587

DODGE

CODE	DESCRIPTION	DEALER	LIST
26C	w/ELF engine & DGB trans, add	711	837
28C	w/EML engine & DGB trans, add	941	1107
	incls convenience group, air conditioning, 35 gal fuel tank, 8-pass seating, P235/75R15XL SBR all-season BW tires, spare tire & cover, HD suspension group, vented glass on single rear door, full carpeting, 2 additional radio spkrs, bright grill, bright wheel covers (4), dual black manual mirrors, 120 amp alternator, bright front & rear bumpers		
24E	**LE** - B250 non-maxiwagon	2831	3330
26E	w/ELF engine & DGB trans, add	711	837
28E	w/EML engine & DGB trans, add	941	1107
	incls LE decor group, P235/75R15XL SBR all-season WW tires (5), sunscreen glass, pwr convenience group, dual black pwr mirrors, 22C value pkg, auto trans, deluxe convenience group, AM/FM ETR stereo radio w/cassette, graphic equalizer & 4 spkrs, styled steel wheels, spare tire		
26E	**LE** — B250 maxiwagon..	2831	3330
	w/DGB trans, add...	213	250
	incls LE decor group, P235/75R15XL SBR all-season WW tires (5), sunscreen glass, pwr convenience group, dual black pwr mirrors, 22C value pkg, auto trans, deluxe convenience group, AM/FM ETR stereo radio w/cassette, graphic equalizer & 4 spkrs, styled steel wheels, spare tire		
—	**Quick Order Pkgs — B350**		
26B	**Value** — B350 non-maxiwagon	991	1166
28B	w/EML engine, add	230	270
	incls bright grille, dual black manual mirrors, front air conditioning, 12-pass seating, 35 gal fuel tank, vented glass on single rear door, 120 amp alternator, convenience group, bright wheel trim rings, bright front & rear bumpers, LT225/75R16D SBR all-season BW tires, spare tire & cover		
26B	**Value** — B350 maxiwagon	1480	1741
	incls frt air conditioning, 120 amp alternator, F & R bumpers w/bright step caps, convenience group (light & 2-spd wipers), single rear door w/vented glass, 35 gal fuel tank, bright grille, spare tire cover, spare tire & wheel, wheel trim rings		
28E	w/EML engine, add	230	270
26E	**LE** — B350 non-maxiwagon...	3420	4023
28E	w/EML engine, add	230	270
	incls convenience group, dual black manual mirrors, 15-pass seating, vented glass on single rear door, front air conditioning, HD suspension group, 35 gal fuel tank, bright front & rear bumpers, LT225/75R16E SBR all-season BW tires, spare tire & cover, 120 amp alternator, bright wheel trim rings, bright grille, 2 additional radio spkrs		
26E	**LE** — B350 maxiwagon..	3781	4448
28E	w/EML engine, add	230	270
	incls LE decor group, rear air conditioning w/auxiliary heater, deluxe convenience group, dual black pwr mirrors, pwr convenience group, 26B value pkg, sunscreen glass, AM/FM ETR stereo radio w/cassette, graphic equalizer & 4 spkrs		

FORD AEROSTAR VAN

AEROSTAR VAN 6 CYL

Code	Description	Dealer	List
A14	Cargo Regular Length 2WD	13395	15040
A34	Cargo Extended Length 2WD	13879	15590
A24	Cargo Regular Length 4WD	15591	17535
A44	Cargo Extended Length 4WD	16119	18135
A15	Window Regular Length 2WD	13655	15335
A35	Window Extended Length 2WD	14139	15885
A25	Window Regular Length 4WD	15851	17830
A45	Window Extended Length 4WD	16378	18430
A15	RV-Prep Regular Length 2WD	13620	15295
A35	RV-Prep Extended Length 2WD	14082	15820
A25	RV-Prep Regular Length 4WD	15067	16940
A45	RV-Prep Extended Length 4WD	15599	17545
	Destination Charge:	535	535

Standard Equipment

AEROSTAR COMPACT CARGO VAN - BASE: 5-speed manual transmission, 95-amp alternator, independent front suspension and gas shocks, power rack and pinion steering, power front disc/rear drum brakes, P215/70R14SL all-season radials, tinted glass, center high-mounted stop light, driver's air bag, electronic AM/FM radio with digital clock, dual front highback bucket seats, color-keyed vinyl seat trim, front carpeting only and premium wheel covers.

Accessories

Code	Description	Dealer	List
—	**Preferred Equipment Pkgs** — prices include pkg discounts		
420A	**Standard Cargo Pkg 420A**	NC	NC
423A	**Standard Cargo Pkg 423A**	1030	1212
430A	**Standard Window Pkg 430A**	NC	NC
431A	**Standard Window Pkg 431A**	1157	1362
463A	**RV-Prep Van Pkg 463A**	NC	NC
99U	**Engine** — 3.0L EFI V6 - 2WD	STD	STD
99X	**Engine** — 4.0L EFI V6 - 2WD	268	316
	4WD	STD	STD
44M	**Transmission** — 5-speed manual overdrive - 2WD	STD	STD
44T	**Transmission** — automatic overdrive (std on E4WD)	638	750
—	**Limited Slip Axle** — use w/o Trailer Towing Pkg	215	252
	use w/Trailer Towing Pkg	NC	NC
422	**California Emissions System**	85	100
428	**High Altitude Emissions System**	NC	NC
—	**Tires**		
T85	P215/70R14SL steel radial BSW all-season	STD	STD
T86	P215/75R14SL steel radial BSW all-season	NC	NC
—	**Seats**		
211	dual bucket, vinyl	STD	STD
212	dual captain's chairs, cloth	398	468
21Y	dual captain's chairs, w/o trim (w/power lumbar; req's Y Trim Type)	83	98
572	**Air Conditioning** — use w/Pkg 420 or 430	738	868
184	**Bright Package**	88	104
414	**Console, Floor**	148	174
57Q	**Defroster, Electric Rear Window** — req's rear liftgate	143	168

CODE	DESCRIPTION	DEALER	LIST
60L	Door, Rear Liftgate w/Glass	NC	NC
151	Electronics Group — use w/RV-Prep Van	729	857
924	Glass, Privacy	351	413
41H	Heater, Engine Block	28	33
153	License Plate Bracket	NC	NC
542	Mirrors, Swing Lock "A" Pillar	45	52
20P	1950# Payload Package	88	104
20M	1870# Payload Package	88	104
903	Power Convenience Group	457	538
512	Spare Tire, Underbody Space Saver	19	22
514	Spare Tire, Underbody Space Saver Delete		
—	spare tire mounted inside vehicle	(19)	(22)
52N	Speed Control/Tilt Steering Wheel	315	371
534	Trailer Towing Package	239	282
434	Underseat Stowage Bin — front passenger side	31	37
17C	Washer/Wiper, Rear	118	139
646	Wheels, Forged Aluminum	309	363
175	Window, Side Door Fixed	58	68
—	Radio Systems		
587	electronic AM/FM stereo w/clock	188	221
589	electronic AM/FM stereo w/cassette & clock - use w/Pkg 423 or 431	104	122
	use w/all other packages	291	343
58Y	radio credit option - use w/RV-Prep Van	(155)	(183)
	use w/all other packages	(52)	(61)

FORD AEROSTAR WAGON

AEROSTAR WAGON 6 CYL

CODE	DESCRIPTION	DEALER	LIST
A11	XL Regular Length 2WD	13342	14980
A31	XL Extended Length 2WD	14614	16425
A21	XL Regular Length 4WD	16397	18450
A41	XL Extended Length 4WD	17183	19345

CODE	DESCRIPTION	DEALER	LIST
A11	XL Plus Regular Length 2WD	14693	16515
A31	XL Plus Extended Length 2WD	15609	17555
A21	XL Plus Regular Length 4WD	17342	19525
A41	XL Plus Extended Length 4WD	18068	20350
A11	XLT Regular Length 2WD	18130	20420
A31	XLT Extended Length 2WD	18552	20900
A21	XLT Regular Length 4WD	19498	21975
A41	XLT Extended Length 4WD	20259	22840
A11	Eddie Bauer Regular Length 2WD	20664	23300
A31	Eddie Bauer Extended Length 2WD	21368	24100
A21	Eddie Bauer Regular Length 4WD	22345	25210
A41	Eddie Bauer Extended Length 4WD	23146	26120
	Destination Charge:	535	535

Standard Equipment

AEROSTAR - XL: Color-coordinated front and rear bumpers with bright moldings, tinted glass, aero headlights, black aero fold-away LH and RH mirrors, bodyside moldings, underbody spare tire carrier (except Regular Length 4WD), black aero front spoiler, full face wheel cover, rear washer/wiper, RH/LH bodyside sliding and liftgate windows, front interval windshield wipers, driver air bag, color-keyed carpeting, front cigarette lighter, coat hooks, convenience group (includes courtesy lamp switches and cargo lamp, carpet-covered engine cover, inside fuel filler release, headlamps-on warning, four-gauge mechanical instrument cluster, front dome lights, rearview 10" day/night mirror, electronic AM/FM stereo radio with digital clock, color-coordinated scuff plates, color-keyed dual front high-back bucket seats, one three-passenger rear bench seat with folding seat back, bodyside storage bins with fishnet covers, RH and LH color-keyed sunvisors with sunglass strap and vanity mirror.

XLT (in addition to or instead of XL equipment): Dual-note horn, lower two-tone paint, premium wheel covers, front air conditioning, carpet-covered lower door trim with map pocket and vinyl accent stripe, liftgate convenience net, light group, carpet-covered lower quarter trim panels and vinyl accent color stripe, dual captain's chairs with recliners, inboard fold-down armrests and power lumbar support, one two-passenger and one three-passenger bench seat with folding seat back, color-keyed deluxe leather-wrapped tilt steering wheel, speed control.

EDDIE BAUER (in addition to or instead of XLT equipment): Luggage rack, Eddie Bauer two-tone paint with tape stripe, forged aluminum wheels, rear air conditioning with auxiliary heater, electric rear window defroster, electronics group (includes autolamp, electrochromic day/night mirror, electronic instrument cluster and super sound system), mini floor consolette, carpeted front and rear floor mats, electronic cluster including trip computer, power equipment group (includes power windows, power door locks, electric remote mirrors), unique Eddie Bauer cloth seat trim.

Accessories

—	**Preferred Equipment Pkgs** — prices include pkg discounts		
400A	**XL Base Pkg**	31	37
401A	**XL Plus Pkg**	624	734
401A	**XL Plus Regular Length 2WD Pkg** — double bonus discount	(808)	(950)
403A	**XLT Pkg**	267	315
403A	**XLT Extended Length 4WD Pkg**		
—	bonus discount	(680)	(800)
405A	**Eddie Bauer Pkg**	287	338
99U	**Engine** — 3.0L EFI V6 - 2WD models	STD	STD
99X	**Engine** — 4.0L EFI V6 - 2WD models	255	300

FORD

VANS

CODE	DESCRIPTION	DEALER	LIST
	4WD models	STD	STD
44M	**Transmission** — 5-speed manual overdrive - 2WD models	STD	STD
44T	**Transmission** — automatic overdrive (std on 4WD models)	638	750
—	**Limited Slip Axle** — use w/o trailer towing pkg	215	252
	use w/trailer towing pkg	NC	NC
—	**Optional Axle Ratio**	32	38
422	**California Emissions System**	85	100
428	**High Altitude Emissions System**	NC	NC
—	**Tires**		
T85	P215/70R14SL steel radial BSW all-season	STD	STD
T8E	P215/70R14SL steel radial WSW all-season	72	84
T86	P215/75R14SL steel radial BSW all-season	NC	NC
—	**Optional Seating**		
214	5-passenger w/dual captain's chairs	547	644
21D7	passenger w/dual captain's chairs and 2 & 3 passenger seat/bed		
	use w/Pkg 401 or 403	470	552
21B7	passenger w/dual captain's chairs -use w/XL Base	886	1043
21E7	passenger w/quad captain's chairs - use w/XLT	508	598
21F7	passenger w/quad captain's chairs and 3-passenger seat/bed - use w/XLT	529	622
	use w/Eddie Bauer	NC	NC
21F	7-passenger w/quad captain's chairs and 3-pass seat/bed (leather trim)	720	848
87C	**Child Safety Seat**	191	224
572	**Air Conditioning**	729	857
574	**Air Conditioning, High Capacity & Auxiliary Heater**	489	576
414	**Console, Floor**	148	174
—	**Console, Floor Delete**	(52)	(61)
57Q	**Defroster, Electric Rear Window**	143	168
151	**Electronics Group** — use w/Pkg 403	691	813
558	**Exterior Appearance Group**		
—	use w/Pkg 400	489	576
	use w/Pkg 401	148	174
	use w/Pkg 403	80	94
	use w/XLT trim w/o Privacy Glass & Power Convenience Group	436	513
94A	**XL Plus Convenience Group** — use w/Pkg 401 only	703	827
94B	**XLT Convenience Group** — use w/Pkg 403 only		
	use w/Exterior Appearance Group	721	849
	use w/o Exterior Appearance Group	766	901
924	**Glass, Privacy**	351	413
41H	**Heater, Engine Block**	28	33
153	**License Plate Bracket**	NC	NC
593	**Light Group**	135	159
615	**Luggage Rack**	121	143
542	**Mirrors, Swing Lock "A" Pillar** — use w/o 558 or 903	45	52
	use w/558 or 903	NC	NC
963	**Molding, Bodyside Protection**	54	63
853	**Paint Stripe, Deluxe**	36	43
—	**Paint Stripe, Deluxe Credit** — use w/XL Plus	(25)	(29)
903	**Power Convenience Group** — use w/Exterior Appearance Group	413	485
	use w/o Exterior Appearance Group	457	538
52N	**Speed Control/Tilt Steering Wheel**	315	371
552	**Sport Appearance Package**	623	733
534	**Trailer Towing Package**	239	282

FORD

CODE	DESCRIPTION	DEALER	LIST
434	**Underseat Stowage Bin** — front passenger side - use w/captain's chairs .	NC	NC
	use w/o captain's chairs	31	37
646	**Wheels, Forged Aluminum**	309	363
589	**Radio** — electronic AM/FM stereo w/cassette & clock (incls headphones)...	166	195

FORD CLUB WAGON

CLUB WAGON 6 CYL

E11	XL Regular Club Wagon..	15544	18099
E31	XL HD Regular Club Wagon	16404	19111
S31	XL Super Club Wagon	18210	21234
E11	XLT Regular Club Wagon..	18265	21300
E31	XLT HD Regular Club Wagon	19059	22234
S31	XLT Super Club Wagon	19637	22914
E11	Chateau Regular Club Wagon.......................................	20855	24348
E31	Chateau HD Regular Club Wagon	21265	24829
	Destination Charge:	575	575

Standard Equipment

CLUB WAGON FULL-SIZED VAN - BASE XL: 4-speed automatic transmission, Twin I-Beam front suspension, single-stage multi-leaf rear suspension, 3600-lb. front/3800 rear axle capacity, power front disc/rear drum brakes with 4-wheel anti-lock braking system, power steering, 15.0" x 6.0" steel disc wheels, tinted glass all windows, high-mounted rear stop light, hub caps, driver's air bag, electronic AM radio with digital clock and two speakers, front dome light.

XLT (in addition to or instead of BASE XL equipment): Chrome front and rear bumpers, wheel covers, air conditioning, auxiliary heater, full-length color-keyed carpeting, deluxe insulation package, illuminated entry reading light, electronic AM/FM stereo with digital clock and six speakers, dual cloth-covered captain's chairs.

CHATEAU (in addition to or instead of XLT equipment): Privacy glass, power sail-mounted outside mirrors, two-tone paint on lower rocker panel, cast alum wheels, color-keyed engine cover with map pocket and color-keyed console, speed control and tilt steering wheel, leather-wrapped steering wheel.

CODE	DESCRIPTION	DEALER	LIST

Accessories

CODE	DESCRIPTION	DEALER	LIST
—	**Preferred Equip Pkgs** — prices include pkg discounts		
700A	**Pkg 700A** — XL Regular Club Wagon	NC	NC
710A	**Pkg 710A** — XL HD Regular Club Wagon	NC	NC
721B	**Pkg 721B** — XL Super Club Wagon	684	805
705A	**Pkg 705A** — XLT Regular Club Wagon w/4.9L or 5.0L engine	626	737
	XLT Regular Club Wagon w/5.8L engine	796	937
713A	**Pkg 713A** — XLT HD Regular Club Wagon	753	887
722A	**Pkg 722A** — XLT Super Club Wagon	797	938
723A	**Pkg 723A** — XLT Super Club Wagon	1852	2179
706A	**Pkg 706A** — Chateau Regular Club Wagon	NC	NC
714A	**Pkg 714A** — Chateau HD Regular Club Wagon	NC	NC
—	**Tires - Steel Radial**		
T77	P235/75Rx15XL BSW all-season - Regular Club Wagon	STD	STD
T78	P235/75Rx15XL WSW all-season - Regular Club Wagon	87	102
T37	LT225/75Rx16E BSW all-season - HD Regular Club Wagon	STD	STD
T38	LT245/75Rx16E BSW all-season - HD Regular Club Wagon	119	139
T38	LT245/75Rx16E BSW all-season - Super Club Wagon	STD	STD
—	**Engines**		
99Y	4.9L EFI I-6	STD	STD
99N	5.0L EFI V-8 (Regular only)	608	716
99H	5.8L EFI V-8	796	937
99G	7.5L EFI V-8 (HD Regular/Super only)	1208	1421
99M	7.3 Diesel V-8 (HD Regular/Super only)	3173	3733
—	**Transmissions**		
44E	electronic 4-spd automatic - use w/Regular only	STD	STD
	use w/HD Regular/Super only	254	299
44G	automatic (HD Regular/Super only)	STD	STD
44U	electronic automatic overdrive (Regular w/5.0L engine)	NC	NC
—	**Limited Slip Axle**	215	252
—	**Optional Axle Ratio Upgrade**	37	44
422	**California Emissions** — use w/Regular	85	100
	use w/HD Regular/Super	NC	NC
428	**High Altitude Emissions**	NC	NC
—	**Optional Seating**		
21G	7-passenger capacity w/quad captian's chairs & seat/bed w/XLT Regular Club Wagon	848	998
21G	7-passenger capacity w/quad captian's chairs & seat/bed w/XLT HD Regular Club Wagon	575	677
218	12-passenger capacity w/bucket seats w/Custom - Super Club Wagon	(119)	(140)
572	**Air Conditioning** — front only	827	973
574	**Air Conditioning, High Capacity** — front & rear w/Custom Wagons	1603	1885
	use w/XLT Wagon	472	555
	use w/PEP 721	599	705
633	**Alternator, Heavy Duty**	56	66
904	**Anti-Theft System**	236	278
634	**Battery, Heavy Duty/Auxiliary**	114	134
769	**Bumpers, Rear Step, Argent** — XL	104	122
768	**Bumpers, Rear Step, Chrome** — XLT, Chateau	104	122
951	**Chateau Two-Tone Delete**	NC	NC
415	**Console, Engine Cover**	130	152

CODE	DESCRIPTION	DEALER	LIST
94D	**Deluxe Interior Upgrade Pkg** — Custom only	277	326
60S	**Door, Sliding Side Cargo**	NC	NC
924	**Glass, Privacy**	330	388
57H	**Heater, Auxiliary (Rear)**	176	207
41H	**Heater, Engine Block** — use w/4.9L, 5.0L or 5.8L eng (single element)	28	33
	use w/7.5L eng (dual element)	56	66
551	**Insulation Pkg, Deluxe**	31	37
153	**License Plate Bracket**	NC	NC
593	**Light & Convenience Group**	128	150
548	**Mirrors, Bright Swing-Out Recreational**	50	59
543	**Mirrors, Power Sail Mount**	136	160
181	**Optional Equip Group 1**	459	540
432	**Optional Equip Group 2**	592	696
183	**Optional Equip Group 3**	1078	1268
434	**Optional Equip Group 4**	1055	1241
—	**Paint, Clearcoat**	145	171
953	**Paint, Deluxe Two-Tone**	178	210
903	**Power Door Locks/Windows**	555	652
90P	**Power Driver's Seat**	330	388
52N	**Speed Control/Tilt Steering Wheel**	325	383
535	**Trailer Towing Pkg (Class II, III, IV)**	126	149
64B	Wheel Covers (Regular Only)	84	99
644	**Wheel Covers, Sport**	84	99
647	**Wheels, Aluminum**	240	283
—	**Radio Systems**		
587	electronic AM/FM stereo w/clock - XL	121	143
589	electronic AM/FM stereo w/cassette/clock - XL	252	296
	w/XLT Wagons	131	154
588	electronic AM/FM premium w/cassette/clock - XLT	252	296
582	electronic AM/FM premium w/CD/clock - XLT	503	591
582	electronic AM/FM premium w/CD/clock - Chateau	251	295
965	**Molding, Bodyside (Black)**	114	134
76X	**Bumpers, Painted, Black**	NC	NC
76W	**Bumpers, Painted, White**	NC	NC

CODE	DESCRIPTION	DEALER	LIST

FORD ECONOLINE VAN

E150 ECONOLINE VAN 6 CYL

E14	Regular Cargo	13857	16115

E250 ECONOLINE VAN 6 CYL

E24	Regular Cargo	14193	16510
S24	Super Cargo	14795	17217
E24	H.D. Regular Cargo	14463	16827
S24	H.D. Super Cargo	15142	17626

E350 ECONOLINE VAN 6 CYL

E34	Regular Cargo	15127	17608
S34	Super Cargo	15951	18577
	Destination Charge:	575	575

Standard Equipment

E150 ECONOLINE FULL-SIZED VAN - BASE: 3-speed automatic transmission, twin I-Beam front suspension, power steering, power front disc/rear drum brakes, steel disc 15.0" x 6.0" wheels, tinted glass, halogen headlamps, electronic AM radio with digital clock and two speakers, dual bucket vinyl trimmed front seats, medium titanium front and rear bumpers and grille, black sail-mounted tubular mirrors, color-keyed hardboard headliner.

XL (in addition to or instead of BASE equipment): Chrome front/rear bumpers and grille, halogen aero headlights, wheel covers, full-length color-keyed carpeting, color-keyed door trim/acoustical headliner, reading light, illuminated entry, underhood light, power door locks/power windows, elec AM/FM stereo w/digital clock, four speakers, cloth captain's chairs, color-keyed sun visors and plastic stepwell pads.

RV (in addition to or instead of XL equipment): Four-wheel anti-lock braking system, tinted glass on the fixed side and rear cargo door, RH convex mirrors, air conditioning, color-keyed engine cover, electronic AM/FM stereo with digital clock, cassette player and six speakers; underseat stowage bin, modified vehicle wiring kit (for add-ons such as towing).

E250 ECONOLINE FULL-SIZED VAN - BASE: 3-speed automatic transmission, twin I-Beam front suspension, heavy 4600-lb. front axle/5400-lb. rear axle capacity, two-stage multi-leaf spring suspension, power steering, power front disc/rear drum brakes, steel disc 15.0" x 6.0" wheels, tinted glass, halogen headlamps, electronic AM radio with digital clock and two speakers, dual bucket vinyl trimmed front seats, medium titanium front and rear bumpers and grille, black sail-mounted tubular mirrors, color-keyed hardboard headliner.

XL (in addition to or instead of BASE equipment): Chrome front and rear bumpers and grille, halogen aero headlights, wheel covers, full-length color-keyed carpeting, color-keyed door trim and acoustical headliner, reading light, illuminated entry, underhood light, power door locks and power windows, electronic AM/FM stereo with digital clock and four speakers, cloth captain's chairs, color-keyed sun visors and plastic stepwell pads.

RV (in addition to or instead of XL equipment): Four-wheel anti-lock braking system, tinted glass on the fixed side and rear cargo door, RH convex mirrors, air conditioning, color-keyed engine cover, electronic AM/FM stereo with digital clock; cassette player and six speakers; underseat stowage bin, modified vehicle wiring kit (for add-ons such as towing).

E350 ECONOLINE FULL-SIZED VAN - BASE: 3-speed automatic transmission, twin I-Beam front suspension, heavy 4600-lb. front axle/5400-lb. rear axle capacity, two-stage multi-leaf spring suspension, power steering, power front disc/rear drum brakes, steel 16.0" x 7.0" wheels, tinted glass, halogen headlamps, electronic AM radio with digital clock and two speakers, dual bucket vinyl trimmed front seats, medium titanium front and rear bumpers and grille, black sail-mounted tubular mirrors, color-keyed hardboard headliner.

XL (in addition to or instead of BASE equipment): Chrome front and rear bumpers and grille, halogen aero headlights, wheel covers, full-length color-keyed carpeting, color-keyed door trim and acoustical headliner, reading light, illuminated entry, underhood light, power door locks and power windows, electronic AM/FM stereo with digital clock and four speakers, cloth captain's chairs, color-keyed sun visors and plastic stepwell pads.

RV (in addition to or instead of XL equipment): Four-wheel anti-lock braking system, tinted glass on the fixed side and rear cargo door, RH convex mirrors, air conditioning, color-keyed engine cover, electronic AM/FM stereo with digital clock, cassette player and six speakers; underseat stowage bin, modified vehicle wiring kit (for add-ons such as towing).

Accessories

CODE	DESCRIPTION	DEALER	LIST
—	**Preferred Equipment Pkgs** — prices include pkg discounts		
740A	**Standard Pkg 740A** — E150	NC	NC
741A	**XL Pkg 741A** — E150	1175	1383
743A	**RV Pkg 743A** — E150	2045	2406
750A	**Standard Pkg 750A** — E250	NC	NC
751A	**XL Pkg 751A** — E250	1175	1383
753A	**RV Pkg 753A** — E250	2189	2574
755A	**Standard Pkg 755A** — E250 H.D.	NC	NC
	w/H.D. E24 model, 4.9L engine & 44E trans	NC	NC
756A	**XL Pkg 756A** — E250 H.D.	1175	1383
758A	**RV Pkg 758A** — E250 H.D.	2189	2574
760A	**Standard Pkg 760A** — E350	NC	NC
762A	**XL Pkg 762A** — E350	1175	1383
763A	**RV Pkg 763A** — E350	1936	2278
—	**Payload Pkgs** — E150		
201	**Pkg 201** — E150 Regular Cargo	STD	STD
202	**Pkg 202** — E150 Regular Cargo	87	102
203	**Pkg 203** — E150 Regular Cargo (incl w/PEP 743A)	NC	NC
—	**Payload Pkgs** — E250		
201	**Pkg 201** — E250 Regular Cargo	STD	STD
	E250 Super Cargo	STD	STD
203	**Pkg 203** — E250 H.D. Regular Cargo	STD	STD

FORD

CODE	DESCRIPTION	DEALER	LIST
	E250 H.D. Super Cargo	STD	STD
—	**Payload Pkgs** — E350		
201	**Pkg 201** — E350 Regular Cargo	STD	STD
202	**Pkg 202** — E350 Regular Cargo	NC	NC
205	**Pkg 205** — E350 Super Cargo	STD	STD
—	**Tires** — steel radial		
T76	P225/75R15SL BSW all-season - E150 Regular Cargo	STD	STD
T77	P235/75R15XL BSW all-season - E150 Regular Cargo w/o RV pkg	72	84
	E150 Regular Cargo w/RV pkg	NC	NC
T78	P235/75R15XL WSW all-season - E150 Regular Cargo w/o RV pkg	158	185
	E150 Regular Cargo w/RV pkg	87	101
T7Q	P235/75R15XL OWL all-season - E150 Regular Cargo w/o RV pkg	177	209
	E150 Regular Cargo w/RV pkg	106	124
T32	LT225/75R16D BSW all-season - E250 Regular/Super Cargo	STD	STD
T37	LT225/75R16E BSW all-season - E250 Regular/Super Cargo	73	85
	E250 H.D. Regular/H.D. Super Cargo	STD	STD
T38	LT245/75R16E BSW all-season - E350 Regular/Super Cargo	STD	STD
516	**Spare Tire & Wheel Delete** — all models		
	P225/75R15SL steel radial BSW all-season	(116)	(137)
	P235/75R15XL steel radial BSW all-season	(129)	(151)
	P235/75R15XL steel radial WSW all-season	(146)	(172)
	P235/75R15XL steel radial OWL all-season	(149)	(176)
	LT225/75R16D steel radial BSW all-season	(215)	(252)
	LT225/75R16E steel radial BSW all-season	(229)	(270)
	LT245/75R16E steel radial BSW all-season	(253)	(297)
—	**Seats**		
	cloth on standard vans	17	20
	dual captain's chairs w/premium cloth on XL vans	204	240
21W	**Seat Delete** — captain's chairs deleted	(288)	(339)
—	**Engines**		
99Y	4.9L EFI I6	STD	STD
99N	5.0L EFI V8 (E150 only)	608	716
99H	5.8L EFI V8	796	937
99G	7.5L EFI V8 (E350 only)	1208	1421
99M	7.3L diesel V8 (E350 only)	2975	3500
—	**Transmissions**		
44G	automatic	STD	STD
44U	electronic automatic overdrive - E150 w/5.0L	254	299
44E	electronic 4-speed automatic	254	299
—	**Limited Slip Axle**	215	252
—	**Optional Axle Ratio Upgrade**	37	44
422	**California Emissions System** — use w/E150, E250	85	100
	use w/E250 H.D., E350	NC	NC
428	**High Altitude Emissions System**	NC	NC
572	**Air Conditioning**	827	973
574	**Air Conditioning w/Auxiliary Heater** — high capacity	1582	1861
	use w/XL pkgs w/o front air conditioning	1475	1735
	use w/pkgs which incl front air conditioning	648	762
904	**Anti-Theft System**	216	254
67B	**Brakes, Anti-Lock, 4-Wheel**	518	610
634	**Battery, Heavy-Duty/Auxiliary**	114	134
764	**Bumper, Chrome**	114	134

CODE	DESCRIPTION	DEALER	LIST
769	**Bumper, Rear Step, Argent**..	104	122
768	**Bumper, Rear Step, Chrome, Std**.......................................	251	295
768	**Bumper, Rear Step, Chrome** — XL, RV.............................	137	161
415	**Console, Engine Cover**...	130	152
60S	**Door, Sliding Side Cargo**..	NC	NC
173	**Glass, Fixed Rear Cargo Door**..	50	59
178	**Glass, Fixed Side/Rear Cargo Door**.................................	85	100
924	**Glass, Privacy** — use w/side/rear cargo door glass.............	229	270
	use w/window all around	330	388
179	**Glass, Swing-Out Side/Rear Cargo Door**	207	244
	use w/RV pkg..	122	144
684	**Handling Pkg** — use w/E150 & E250..................................	67	79
	use w/trailer tow pkg..	NC	NC
	use w/H.D. service pkg..	NC	NC
57H	**Heater, Auxiliary** — rear...	176	207
41H	**Heater, Engine Block** — use w/4.9L, 5.0L or 5.8L engine (single element)	28	33
	use w/7.5L engine (dual element)...	56	66
551	**Insulation Pkg, Deluxe**...	140	165
153	**License Plate Bracket**...	NC	NC
593	**Light & Convenience Group**..	128	150
548	**Mirrors, Bright Swing-Out Recreational**	50	59
543	**Mirrors, Power Sail Mount**	136	150
	use w/pkgs which incl bright swing-out recreational mirrors......	86	101
—	**Paint, Clearcoat**..	145	171
953	**Paint, Deluxe Two-Tone**..	178	210
903	**Power Door Locks/Windows**..	555	652
90P	**Power Driver's Seat**...	330	388
53C	**Service Pkg, Heavy-Duty** — use w/E150, E250 w/o air conditioning	226	266
	use w/E150, E250 w/air conditioning....................................	140	165
	use w/RV pkg..	NC	NC
	use on E350 w/4.9L or 5.8L...	159	187
	use on E350 w/7.5L or 7.3L or air conditioning	73	85
52N	**Speed Control/Tilt Steering Wheel**	325	383
683	**Suspension, Heavy-Duty** — use w/E150	75	88
	use w/E150 w/RV pkg..	NC	NC
	use w/E250...	275	323
534	**Trailer Tow Pkg (Class I)**	174	205
	credit w/AC (except 7.3L or 7.5L eng or RV pkg).................	(86)	(101)
535	**Trailer Tow Pkg (Class II/III/IV)** — use w/E150, E250.....	314	370
	use w/E350 (std or XL trim)...	140	165
	use w/E150, E250 w/RV pkgs..	140	165
	credit w/AC (std or XL trim only)...	(86)	(101)
64B	**Wheel Covers** — E150..	84	99
644	**Wheel Covers, Sport**	84	99
645	**Wheels, Bright Cast Aluminum**	265	312
647	**Wheels, Forged Aluminum**	240	283
64X	**Wheel Trim Delete**..	(35)	(41)
—	**Radio Systems**		
587	electronic AM/FM stereo w/clock...	121	143
589	electronic AM/FM stereo w/cassette & clock............................	252	296
	use w/XL trim..	131	154
588	radio, AM/FM premium w/cassette & clock - w/XL..................	213	250

CODE	DESCRIPTION	DEALER	LIST
	w/RV	63	74
582	radio, AM/FM premium w/CD & clock - w/XL	463	545
	w/RV	314	370
58R	radio prep pkg	(119)	(140)
58Y	radio credit option	(52)	(61)
633	**Alternator, Heavy-Duty** — 130 ampere	56	66
57J	**Auxiliary Heater Connector Pkg**	21	24
57L	**Auxiliary Heater** — AC connector pkg	52	61
57X	**Auxiliary Heater** — AC connector pkg w/rear AC controls	62	73
	use w/prep pkg	10	12
76X	**Bumper, Painted Black**	NC	NC
76W	**Bumper, Painted White**	NC	NC
17M	**Display Van, Swing-Out Side/Rear Cargo Windows**	252	296
166	**Floor Mat, Full Length** — credit w/XL	(50)	(59)
965	**Moldings, Bodyside** — black	114	134
17W	**Windows, All-Around**	300	352
	use w/RV pkgs	215	252
671	**Front GAWR** — one up	12	15

CODE	DESCRIPTION	DEALER	LIST

GMC

GMC RALLY WAGON

2500 RALLY WAGON 6 CYL
TG21306 Rally 125" WB 16502   18859

3500 RALLY WAGON 8 CYL
TG31306 Rally 125" WB 17625   20143
TG31606 Extended Rally 146" WB 18637   21299

Destination Charge: 580   580

Standard Equipment

G2500 FULL-SIZED RALLY WAGON - BASE: Electronic four-speed automatic transmission, 100-amp alternator, heavy-duty battery with 600 CCA, brake/transmission shift interlock, heavy-duty power front disc/rear drum brakes with 4-wheel anti-lock braking system, front and rear chromed bumpers, side window defoggers, tinted Solar Ray glass, swing-out rear door glass, RH and LH stainless steel below-eyeline mirrors with adjustable heads, black bodyside moldings, 32mm heavy-duty front and rear shocks and heavy duty springs, power steering, four P225/75R15 blackwall steel radials, driver's facial air bag, side door guard beams, full gauges, deluxe outside air heater and defogger, electronic AM radio with digital clock and fixed-mast antenna, Scotchgard seat protector and adjustable highback bucket seats and two removable three-passenger bench seats with custom vinyl trim.

STX (in addition to or instead of BASE equipment): Deluxe front appearance group, chrome grille, dual halogen high-beam headlamps, black bodyside moldings and rear moldings with bright inserts, full-length cloth headliner with garnish moldings, front and rear dome lamps with door activated switches, color-keyed cloth on door and carpeting on lower areas, and locking storage compartment.

G3500 FULL-SIZED RALLY - BASE: Electronic four-speed automatic transmission, 100-amp alternator, heavy-duty battery with 600 CCA, brake/transmission shift interlock, heavy-duty power front disc/rear drum brakes with 4-wheel anti-lock braking system, front and rear chromed bumpers, side window defoggers, tinted Solar Ray glass, swing-out rear door glass, RH and LH stainless steel below- eyeline mirrors with adjustable heads, black bodyside moldings, 35 mm heavy-duty front and rear shocks and heavy duty springs, power steering, four LT225/75R16-D blackwall steel belted radials, five 16.0" x 6.5" argent painted steel wheels, driver's facial air bag, side door guard beams, full gauges, deluxe outside air heater and defogger, electronic AM radio with digital clock and fixed-mast antenna, Scotchgard seat protector and adjustable highback bucket seats and two removable three-passenger bench seats with custom vinyl trim.

GMC

VANS

CODE	DESCRIPTION	DEALER	LIST

STX (in addition to or instead of BASE equipment): Deluxe front appearance group, chrome grille, dual halogen high-beam headlamps, black bodyside moldings and rear moldings with bright inserts, full-length cloth headliner with garnish moldings, front and rear dome lamps with door activated switches, color-keyed cloth on door and carpeting on lower areas, and locking storage compartment.

Accessories

CODE	DESCRIPTION	DEALER	LIST
—	**Option Pkgs** — decor price incl'd in pkgs		
1SA	**Pkg 1SA** — w/R9S std decor	NC	NC
	w/E94 STX decor	721	838
	incls vehicle w/std equip		
1SB	**Pkg 1SB** — w/R9S std decor	931	1083
	w/E94 STX decor	1652	1921
	incls pkg 1SA plus frt air conditioning, tilt wheel & speed control		
1SC	**Pkg 1SC** — w/E94 STX decor	1465	1704
	incls pkg 1SB plus UM6 radio, deep tinted solar glass & auxiliary lamps		
1SD	**Pkg 1SD** — w/E94 STX decor	2147	2496
	incls pkg 1SC plus pwr radio antenna, remote keyless entry system, dual elec control exterior mirrors, pwr door locks & windows		
—	**Decor**		
R9S	**Standard Decor**	NC	NC
	incls std equip		
E94	**STX Decor**	721	838
	incls black body side moldings w/bright strip, chrome wheel opening moldings, deluxe frt appearance, full floor carpeting w/Scotchgard protection, F & R floor mats, frt seat storage compartments, spare tire cover, interior trim molding & visor mirror [w/L57 eng & AQ4 seating deletes wheel opening moldings]		
—	**Body**		
ZW9	standard body - incl'd in 1SA, 1SB, 1SC, 1SD	NC	NC
—	**GVW Pkgs**		
C5S	6600 lb	NC	NC
C6Q	6875 lb - w/L49 eng	NC	NC
	w/L05 eng	274	319
C6C	7400 lb	NC	NC
C6P	8600 lb - TG31606 model	NC	NC
	w/TG31306	216	251
C6W	9200 lb - w/TG31306 model	319	371
	w/TG31606	206	240
Z72	**Light Duty Trailering Equip**	114	132
	incls trailer hitch & 5-wire harness		
Z82	**Heavy Duty Trailering Equip** — w/eng L19, L49 or L57	267	310
	w/eng LB4, L03 or L05	437	508
	incls trailer hitch & 7-wire harness [incls V08 HD cooling w/LB4, L03 or L05 eng] [NA w/ZP3 seat arrangement; NA w/GVW C6C]		
—	**Emissions**		
FE9	Federal	NC	NC
NA6	high altitude	NC	NC
YF5	California	NA	NA
NG1	New York	NC	NC
—	**Engines**		
LB4	4.3L (262 CID) V6 EFI gas	NC	NC
L03	5.0L (305 CID) V8 EFI gas	NC	NC

GMC

8888888888888

CODE	DESCRIPTION	DEALER	LIST
L05	5.7L (350 CID) V8 EFI gas - w/TG21306 model	727	845
	w/TG31306 or TG31606 models	NC	NC
L19	7.4L (454 CID) V8 EFI gas	520	605
L49	6.5L (395 CID) V8 EFI diesel	2468	2870
	incls dual batteries, pwr brakes, eng oil cooler, HD radiator, extra sound		
	insulation, eng block heater, glow plugs, integral two stage fuel filter, fuel &		
	water separator w/instrument panel warning light & fuel filter change signal		
L57	6.5L (395 CID) V8 diesel	1423	1655
	incls dual batteries, pwr brks, eng oil cooler, HD radiator, extra sound insu-		
	lation, eng block htr, glow plugs, integral two stage fuel filter, fuel & water		
	separator w/instrument panel warning light & fuel filter change signal		
—	**Transmissions**		
M30	4-spd automatic w/overdrive (4L60E)	NC	NC
MT1	4-spd automatic w/overdrive (4L80E)	NC	NC
—	**Rear Axles**		
GU5	3.23 ratio	NC	NC
GU6	3.42 ratio	NC	NC
GT4	3.73 ratio	NC	NC
GT5	4.10 ratio	NC	NC
G80	**Locking Rear Differential**	217	252
V08	**Heavy Duty Cooling**	170	198
	incls eng oil cooler, trans oil cooler & HD radiator [incl'd w/Z82 trailering]		
	[NA w/eng L19, L49 or L57]		
V10	**Cold Climate Pkg** — incls eng block heater	41	48
	reqs eng LB4, L03, L05 or L19		
—	**Wheels**		
P01	bright metal, full wheel covers - TG31306 or TG31606	36	42
N67	rally wheels (spare is steel) - TG21306	104	121
N90	aluminum cast wheels - TG21306	266	310
—	**Front Tires - G2500**		
XET	P225/75R15 all season BW SBR	NC	NC
XEU	P225/75R15 all season WW SBR	31	36
XEV	P225/75R15 all season WL SBR	43	50
XFL	P235/75R15 all season BW SBR	NC	NC
—	**Rear Tires - G2500**		
YET	P225/75R15 all season BWSBR	NC	NC
YEU	P225/75R15 all season WW SBR	31	36
YEV	P225/75R15 all season WL SBR	43	50
YFL	P235/75R15 all season BW SBR	NC	NC
—	**Spare Tires - G2500**		
ZET	P225/75R15 all season BW SBR	118	137
ZEU	P225/75R15 all season WW SBR	133	155
ZEV	P225/75R15 all season WL SBR	139	162
ZFL	P235/75R15 all season BW SBR	130	151
—	**Front Tires - G3500**		
XHP	LT225/75R16/D all season BW SBR	NC	NC
XHF	LT225/75R16/E all season BW SBR - w/GVW C6P or C6W	NC	NC
	w/GVW C6C	29	34
—	**Rear Tires - G3500**		
YHP	LT225/75R16/D all season BW SBR	NC	NC
YHF	LT225/75R16/E all season BW SBR - w/GVW C6P or C6W	NC	NC
	w/GVW C6C	29	34

GMC

CODE	DESCRIPTION	DEALER	LIST
—	**Spare Tires - G3500**		
ZHP	LT225/75R16/D all season BW SBR	178	207
ZHF	LT225/75R16/E all season BW SBR	193	224
R6G	**Air Conditioning Delete** - reqs 1SA	NC	NC
C60	**Air Conditioning** — front (incl in 1SB, 1SC, 1SD)..................	839	975
C69	**Air Conditioning** — F & R (NA w/ZP3)	1354	1574
—	**Convenience Pkgs**		
AU3	power door locks (incl w/ZQ2)	192	223
ZQ2	power door locks & windows (incl in 1SD)...................................	373	434
ZQ3	tilt wheel & speed control (incl in 1SB, 1SC, 1SD)...................	329	383
C36	**Rear Heater**	176	205
TR9	**Auxiliary Lamps** —incl in 1SC, 1SD	134	156
DH6	**Mirrors** — illuminated RH/LH visor vanity	65	75
—	**Radio Equip**		
UM7	radio .... *incls AM/FM stereo w/seek-scan w/2 frt coaxial spkrs & 2 ext range rear spkrs [reqs 1SA or 1SB]*	NC	NC
UT5	radio .... *incls AM radio [reqs 1SA]*	(121)	(141)
UM6	radio .... *incls AM/FM stereo w/seek-scan, cass, clock w/2 frt coaxial spkrs & 2 ext range rear spkrs [incl in 1SC, 1SD]*	105	122
UX1	radio .... *incls AM/FM w/seek-scan, cass, equalizer, clock w/2 frt coaxial spkrs & 2 ext range rear spkrs*	234	272
U1C	radio .... *incls AM/FM w/seek-scan, CD player, clock w/2 frt coaxial spkrs & 2 ext range rear spkrs*	341	396
UL5	radio delete - reqs 1SA	(203)	(236)
U75	power radio antenna - incl in 1SD..	73	85
—	**Seats**		
AV5	front high back buckets	NC	NC
A95	front reclining high back buckets .... *incls dual armrests [reqs E94]*	346	402
—	**Seat Arrangements**		
AQ3	8 passenger - TG21306	NC	NC
AQ4	12 passenger - TG31306, TG31606..	NC	NC
ZP3	15 passenger - TG31606 (NA w/Z82 or C69).............................	(319)	(371)
YG4	rear seat delete - TG21306, TG31306	(319)	(371)
NP5	**Leather-Wrapped Steering Wheel**	52	60
C49	**Rear Window Electric Defogger** — incls fixed rear glass	82	95
YA2	**Sliding Side Door** — NA on TG31606......................................	NC	NC
AX3	**Remote Keyless Entry System**.. *incl'd in 1SD; reqs ZQ2 & TR9*	151	175
DG9	**Mirrors** — dual elec control, stainless steel .... *incl'd in 1SD; reqs ZQ2 conv pkg*	84	98
AJ1	**Deep Tinted Solar Ray Glass** — incl'd in 1SC, 1SD	327	380
—	**Paint**		
ZY1	solid	NC	NC
ZY2	conventional two-tone - w/Y94 decor..	118	137
	w/R9S decor *incls body side moldings*....................................	231	269

CODE	DESCRIPTION	DEALER	LIST

GMC SAFARI CARGO VAN

SAFARI RWD 6 CYL

TM10905	Panel Doors	13950	15414
TM11005	XT Panel Doors	14378	15887

SAFARI AWD 6 CYL

TL10905	Panel Doors	16059	17733
TL11005	XT Panel Doors	16476	18206
	Destination Charge:	545	545

Standard Equipment

SAFARI COMPACT CARGO VAN - BASE: 4-speed automatic transmission, power front disc/rear drum brakes with 4-wheel anti-lock braking system, tinted Solar Ray glass all windows, all-season steel belted radials, driver facial air bag, electronic AM radio with fixed-mast antenna, Scotchgard fabric protector, 4-spoke steering wheel with anti-theft locking feature, center high-mounted stop light, front bumper with bumper guards and rear bumpers painted lower body color, halogen headlamps, RH and LH painted black mirrors with pivoting arm and adjustable head and 15" x 6" steel painted argent wheels.

Accessories

CODE	DESCRIPTION	DEALER	LIST
R9S	**SL Decor**	NC	NC
YF7	**RV Conversion Group** - w/TL10905 or TM10905	1514	1760
	w/TL11005 or TM11005	1453	1690
	incls air cond, ext mirrors, UM7 radio, stepwell lamps w/override switch, glove box lamp, tilt whl & spd cntrl pkg (incls G50 springs w/TM10905 or TL10905)		
—	**Body**		
ZW9	panel doors - incl'd in 1SA, 1SB, 1SC 1SD, 1SE, 1SF	NC	NC
E54	dutch doors	313	364
	incls elec remote release, rear washer/wiper		
—	**Option Pkgs** — *incls decor group pricing*		
1SA	**Pkg 1SA** — w/SL decor R9S	NC	NC
	incls panel doors [TL models req YF0 upfitter]		
1SB	**Pkg 1SB** — w/SL decor R9S	802	932
	incls pkg 1SA plus frt air cond, rear panel door windows [TL models req YF0 upfitter]		
1SC	**Pkg 1SC** — w/SL decor R9S	929	1080
	incls pkg 1SB plus UM7 AM/FM radio w/seek-scan & clock & below eye-line mirrors [TL models req YF0 upfitter]		
1SD	**Pkg 1SD** — w/RV conversion group YF7 (TM10905, TL10905 models).......	590	686
w/RV	conversion group YF7 (TM11005, TL11005 models).................................	530	616
	incls RV conversion group, panel doors, pwr locks & windows, rally wheels		
1SE	**Pkg 1SE** — w/RV conversion group YF7 (TM10905, TL10905 models).......	1052	1223
w/RV	conversion group YF7 (TM11005, TL11005 models).................................	992	1153
	incls pkg 1SD plus deluxe F & R chrome bumpers, sliding door & rear panel door windows, deep tinted solar-ray windows, deluxe black grille w/argent highlights, UM6 radio, dual elec control mirrors		
1SF	**Pkg 1SF** — w/RV conversion group YF7 (TM10905, TL10905 models).......	1489	1731
w/RV	conversion group YF7 (TM11005, TL11005 models).................................	1428	1661
	incls pkg 1SE plus aluminum wheels, air deflector w/fog lamps, elect instrumentation, UX1 radio		
—	**GVW Pkgs**		
C5C	5000 lb	NC	NC

GMC

CODE	DESCRIPTION	DEALER	LIST
C5E	5400 lb	NC	NC
C5G	5600 lb	NC	NC
DA3	5700 lb	NC	NC
C5R	5800 lb	NC	NC
C7X	5850 lb	NC	NC
C6M	5950 lb	NC	NC
C5M	6100 lb	NC	NC
Z82	**HD Trailering Equip** — w/L35 eng	266	309
	w/LB4 eng	436	507
	incls platform hitch & 7-wire harness (incls V08 HD cooling w/LB4 eng) [NA w/LB4 & GU5] [NA w/TL11005 & GU6]		
G50	**HD Rear Springs**	60	70
	reqs models TM10905 or TL10905 & NA w/GVW C5C or C5R		
—	**Emissions**		
FE9	federal	NC	NC
YF5	California	NA	NA
NG1	New York - w/C5M	NC	NC
	w/o C5M	86	100
—	**Engines**		
LB4	4.3L (262 CID) EFI V6 gas	NC	NC
	NA w/TL models		
L35	4.3L (262 CID) CPI V6 gas - w/TL models	NC	NC
	w/TM models	430	500
M30	**Transmission** — 4-spd auto w/overdrive	NC	NC
—	**Rear Axles**		
GU5	3.23 ratio	NC	NC
GU6	3.42 ratio	NC	NC
GT4	3.73 ratio	NC	NC
G80	**Locking Rear Differential**	217	252
V08	**HD Cooling**	170	198
	incls eng oil cooler & trans oil cooler (incl w/Z82 trailering equip w/LB4) [reqs LB4 engine]		
V10	**Cold Climate Pkg**	40	46
	incls eng block heater & extra coolant protection		
ZJ7	**Rally Wheels - (4)**	79	92
	incl'd in 1SD, 1SE; NA w/1SF		
PF3	**Aluminum Wheels - (4)** — w/YF7 decor	292	340
—	**Tires** — incls spare tire		
QCE	P205/75R15 BW SBR	NC	NC
QCF	P205/75R15 WL SBR	83	96
QCG	P205/75R15 WW SBR	62	72
QCU	P215/75R15 BW SBR	NC	NC
QCV	P215/75R15 WW SBR	52	60
QCM	P215/75R15 WOL SBR	76	88
R6G	**Air Conditioning Delete** - reqs 1SA	NC	NC
C60	**Air Conditioning** — front	727	845
	incl'd w/YF7 decor, 1SB, 1SC		
ZQ2	**Convenience Pkg**	373	434
	incls pwr locks & windows (incl'd in 1SD, 1SE, 1SF)		
AU3	**Convenience Pkg**	192	223
	incls pwr door locks (incl in ZQ2)		
ZQ3	**Convenience Pkg**	329	383

CODE	DESCRIPTION	DEALER	LIST
	incls tilt wheel & speed control (incl'd w/YF7)		
C36	**Rear Heater**	176	205
U52	**Electronic Instrumentation**	168	195
	incls voltmeter, oil pressure & water temp gauges, trip odometer & speedometer		
TR9	**Auxiliary Lamps** — w/DK6 roof console	81	94
	w/o DK6 roof console	109	127
	NA w/YF7 decor		
—	**Radio Equip**		
UT5	radio - w/1SA or 1SB & R9S decor	NC	NC
	w/1SD & YF7 decor	(130)	(151)
	incls AM radio w/2 std frt spkrs		
UM7	radio	83	96
	incls AM/FM stereo w/seek-scan & clock, 2 ext range frt spkrs [NA w/1SE or 1SF]		
UM6	radio - w/YF7 decor	105	122
	w/R9S decor	187	218
	incls AM/FM stereo w/seek-scan, cass, clock, 2 coaxial frt spkrs [NA w/1SF]		
UX1	radio	234	272
	incls AM/FM stereo w/seek-scan, cass, equalizer, clock, 2 coaxial frt spkrs [reqs YF7 decor]		
U1C	radio	349	406
	incls AM/FM stereo w/seek-scan, CD player, clock, 2 coaxial frt spkrs [reqs YF7 decor]		
UL5	radio delete - w/1SA & R9S decor	(82)	(95)
	w/1SD & YF7 decor	(212)	(246)
DK6	**Roof Console**	71	83
	reqs TR9 or YF7 decor		
—	**Seats**		
VK5	temporary driver seat - reqs YF7 decor	NC	NC
AV4	front high back bucket seats less trim	318	370
	reqs YF7 decor		
AV5	front high back bucket seats - reqs R9S decor	NC	NC
—	**Seating Arrangements**		
ZX1	driver only (NA YF7 decor or AV4 seats)	NC	NC
ZX2	driver & passenger - w/AV5 seats	184	214
	w/AV4 seats	NC	NC
A78	**Seat Back Recliner**	211	245
	incls dual armrests; reqs ZX2 seats		
AC3	**Power Seat** — 6-way driver (reqs YF7 decor)	206	240
BA8	**Stowage Compartment** — under front pass seat	26	30
	reqs ZX2 seats)		
NP5	**Leather-Wrapped Steering Wheel**	46	54
ANL	**Air Deflector/Fog Lamps** — w/YF7 decor	99	115
VE6	**Bumpers** — color-keyed F & R w/rub strip	45	52
	NA w/1SE or 1SF		
VE5	**Deluxe Bumpers** — w/YF7 decor	110	128
C49	**Rear Window Electric Defogger** — reqs E54	132	154
TL1	**Grille** — deluxe black w/argent highlights	23	27
	incl'd in 1SE, 1SF		
V54	**Roof Mounted Luggage Carrier** — w/YF7 decor	108	126

GMC

CODE	DESCRIPTION	DEALER	LIST
—	**Mirrors**		
D44	below eye-line, black (NA w/1SE or 1SF)..	45	52
D48	dual electric control, black below eye-line type		
	w/YF7 decor	84	98
	w/R9S decor	129	150
—	**Window Arrangements**		
R6A	standard window arrangement	NC	NC
	reqs 1SA or 1SD		
ZW2	rear panel door windows - w/o AJ1 tinted glass..	75	87
	w/AJ1 tinted glass	121	141
	reqs ZW9 body; incl'd in 1SB, 1SC		
ZW3	sliding door & rear panel door windows		
	w/o AJ1 tinted glass	133	155
	w/AJ1 tinted glass	225	262
ZW6	complete body window arrangement - w/o AJ1 tinted glass........................	316	368
	w/AJ1 tinted glass	541	630
—	**Window Options**		
A19	rear swing out door glass..	66	77
	reqs E54 body & window arrangements ZW3 or ZW6		
A18	rear & side cargo swing out door glass	117	136
	reqs ZW9 body & window arrangements ZW3 or ZW6		
AJ1	**Deep Tinted Solar Ray Glass**	NC	NC
	reqs window arrangements ZW2, ZW3 or ZW6		
ZY1	**Paint** — solid...	NC	NC
YF0	**Upfitter Pkg** — TL models & R9S decor..	NC	NC

GMC SAFARI PASSENGER VAN

SAFARI RWD 6 CYL
TM10906	Panel Doors	14932	16499
TM11006	XT Panel Doors	15205	16801

SAFARI AWD 6 CYL
TL10906	Panel Doors	17039	18828
TL11006	XT Panel Doors	17313	19130
	Destination Charge:	545	545

Standard Equipment

SAFARI COMPACT PASSENGER VAN - BASE SLX: 4-speed electronic automatic transmission, power front disc/rear drum brakes with 4-wheel anti-lock braking, Solar-Ray tinted glass all windows, center high-mounted rear stop light, four all-season steel belted radial tires, 15" x 6" steel painted argent wheels, side impact guard beams in driver, passenger and sliding door; front high-back bucket seats with all vinyl trim, full instrumentation and gauges, full-length color-keyed cloth headliner, deluxe heater with window defogger, electronic AM radio with fixed antenna.

SLE (in addition to or instead of SLX equipment): Air dam with fog lights, front and rear painted lower body color with matching color-keyed inserts, molded black plastic grille, 15" x 6.5" steel color-keyed wheels, color-keyed expanded vinyl trim door panels and carpet inserts, full interior laps, storage compartment, swing-out glass on sliding side door.

SLT (in addition to or instead of SLE equipment): Deep-tinted Solar Ray side glass windows, special nameplates on front side door, striping, color-keyed door sill plates and scuff plates, special front bucket seats with reclining backs, folding integral armrests and adjustable headrests, split back center seat (includes fold-down center console with convenience tray and cup pockets; RH seat back folds forward for easy access to rear); special velour fabric seat trim on all seats, storage compartment (includes storage pouch with zipper on LH trim panel).

Accessories

—	**Decor**		
R9S	**SLX Decor**	NC	NC
YC6	**SLE Decor**	934	1086

CODE	DESCRIPTION	DEALER	LIST
	incls aux lamps, color-keyed floor mats, illuminated visor vanity mirror, deluxe w/argent highlights grille, F & R color-keyed bumpers, rally wheels, air deflector w/fog lamps, wide body side moldings & map pockets on back of driver & pass seats (w/ZW9 panel doors incls swing out rear door glass) [Note: decor pricing incl'd in option pkgs]		
YC7	**SLT Decor**...	2490	2896
	incls air deflector w/fog lamps, aux lamps, color-keyed decal striping, color-keyed floor mats, deep tinted solar ray glass, deluxe blk w/argent highlights grille, rally wheels, F & R color-keyed bumpers, illuminated visor vanity mirror, special reclining wide frt & split rear bench seat backs, wide bodyside molding, adjustable head restraints		
—	**Option Pkgs** — incls decor group pricing		
1SA	**Pkg 1SA** — w/SLX decor R9S	NC	NC
	w/SLE decor YC6	934	1086
	incls panel doors & 5 person seating		
1SB	**Pkg 1SB** — w/SLX decor R9S...	587	682
	w/SLE decor YC6	1520	1768
	incls pkg 1SA plus frt air cond, tilt whl/spd control, below eye-line mirrors, seat back recliners w/dual armrests, complete body window arrangement		
1SC	**Pkg 1SC** — w/SLX decor R9S	1048	1219
	w/SLE decor YC6	1873	2178
	w/SLT decor YC7	3084	3586
	incls pkg 1SB plus roof mounted luggage carrier, roof console, aux lamps, pwr locks & windows		
1SD	**Pkg 1SD** — w/SLE decor YC6	2493	2899
	w/SLT decor YC7	3704	4307
	incls pkg 1SC plus aluminum wheels, F & R air cond, dual elec control exterior mirrors, AM/FM w/seek-scan cass, clock (may be upgraded to UX1 or U1C radio), map pockets on back of driver & pass seats (incls ZW6 complete body glass & leather-wrapped steering wheel) (w/ZW9 panel doors incls swing out rear door glass) [Note: decor pricing incl'd in option pkgs]		
—	**Body**		
ZW9	panel doors - incl'd in 1SA, 1SB, 1SC, 1SD..............................	NC	NC
E54	dutch doors	313	364
	incls elec remote release, rear washer/wiper		
-	**GVW Pkgs**		
DA3	5700 lb...	NC	NC
C6M	5950 lb...	NC	NC
C5M	6100 lb...	NC	NC
Z82	**HD Trailering Equip** — w/L35 eng..	266	309
	w/LB4 eng	436	507
	incls platform hitch & 7-wire harness (incls V08 HD cooling w/LB4 eng) [NA w/LB4 & GU5] [NA w/TL10906 or TL11006 & GU6]		
—	**Emissions**		
FE9	federal..	NC	NC
YF5	California	NA	NA
NG1	New York - w/C5M...	NC	NC
	w/o C5M	86	100
—	**Engines**		
LB4	4.3L (262 CID) EFI V6 gas	NC	NC
	NA w/TL models		
L35	4.3L (262 CID) CPI V6 gas - w/TL models...................................	NC	NC

CODE	DESCRIPTION	DEALER	LIST
	w/TM models......	430	500
	incls eng oil cooler, radiator & trans oil cooler		
M30	**Transmission** — 4-spd auto w/overdrive......	NC	NC
—	**Rear Axles**		
GU5	3.23 ratio......	NC	NC
GU6	3.42 ratio......	NC	NC
GT4	3.73 ratio......	NC	NC
G80	**Locking Rear Differential**......	217	252
V08	**HD Cooling**......	170	198
	incls eng oil cooler & trans oil cooler (incl'd w/Z82 trailering equip w/LB4) [reqs LB4 eng]		
V10	**Cold Climate Pkg**......	40	46
	incls eng block heater & extra coolant protection		
ZJ7	**Rally Wheels - (4)**......	79	92
	incl'd w/YC6 & YC7 decor & ZL7 appearance pkg		
PF3	**Aluminum Wheels (4)** — w/YC6, YC7 or ZL7......	213	248
	w/R9S decor......	292	340
—	**Tires** — incls spare tire		
QCE	P205/75R15 BW SBR......	NC	NC
QCF	P205/75R15 WL SBR......	83	96
QCG	P205/75R15 WW SBR......	62	72
QCU	P215/75R15 BW SBR......	NC	NC
QCV	P215/75R15 WW SBR......	52	60
QCM	P215/75R15 WOL SBR......	76	88
R6G	**Air Conditioning Delete** — reqs 1SA......	NC	NC
C60	**Air Conditioning** — front (NA w/1SD)......	727	845
C69	**Air Conditioning** — front & rear......	1176	1368
	incls 105 amp alternator		
ZQ2	**Convenience Pkg**......	373	434
	incls pwr locks & windows (incl'd in 1SC & 1SD)		
AU3	**Convenience Pkg**......	192	223
	incls pwr door locks (incl'd in ZQ2)		
ZQ3	**Convenience Pkg**......	329	383
	incls tilt wheel & speed control (incl'd in 1SB, 1SC, 1SD)		
C36	**Rear Heater**......	176	205
U52	**Electronic Instrumentation**......	168	195
	incls voltmeter, oil pressure, water temp gauges, trip odometer & speedometer		
TR9	**Auxiliary Lamps** — w/DK6 roof console......	81	94
	w/o DK6 roof console......	109	127
	incl'd w/YC6 & YC7 decor		
—	**Radio Equip**		
UM7	radio......	NC	NC
	incls AM/FM stereo w/seek-scan & clock, 2 ext range frt spkrs & 2 std, 2 ext range rear spkrs		
UT5	radio......	(130)	(151)
	incls AM radio w/2 std frt spkrs		
UM6	radio......	105	122
	incls AM/FM stereo w/seek-scan, cass, clock, 2 coaxial frt spkrs & 4 ext range rear spkrs		
UX1	radio......	234	272
	incls AM/FM stereo w/seek-scan, cass, equalizer, clock, 2 coaxial frt spkrs & 4 ext range rear spkrs		

CODE	DESCRIPTION	DEALER	LIST
U1C	radio	349	406
	incls AM/FM stereo w/seek-scan, CD player & clock, 2 coaxial frt spkrs & 4 ext rear spkrs		
UL5	radio delete - reqs 1SA	(212)	(246)
DK6	**Roof Console** — w/YC6 or YC7 decor	43	50
	w/R9S	71	83
	incl'd in 1SC, 1SD [reqs TR9]		
AV5	**Seats** — front high back buckets	NC	NC
—	**Seating Arrangements**		
ZP5	5 person seating	NC	NC
ZP8	8 person seating - w/YC7 decor	754	877
	w/YC6 or R9S	340	395
ZP7	7 person seating - w/YC7	733	852
	w/YC6	821	955
	w/R9S	897	1043
	incls 4 high back buckets		
A78	**Seat Back Recliner**	211	245
	incls driver & pass dual armrests		
AC3	**Power Seat** — 6-way driver (reqs A78)	206	240
BA8	**Stowage Compartment** — under frt pass seat	26	30
NP5	**Leather-Wrapped Steering Wheel** — incl'd w/YC7	46	54
ZL7	**SLX Enhanced Appearance Pkg**	172	200
	incls ZJ7 rally wheels, deluxe F & R color-keyed bumpers, deluxe wide body side molding, deluxe black w/argent highlights grille, F & R color-keyed rubber floor mats [reqs R9S decor & 1SA or 1SB]		
VE5	**Deluxe Bumpers** — w/YC6 or YC7 or ZL7	65	76
	w/R9S decor	110	128
	incls deluxe F & R chrome bumpers w/rub strip		
C49	**Rear Window Electric Defogger** - reqs E54	132	154
V54	**Roof Mounted Luggage Carrier**	108	126
	incl'd in 1SC, 1SD		
—	**Mirrors**		
D44	below eye-line, black (NA w/1SD)	45	52
D48	dual elec control, black below eye-line type	129	150
—	**Window Arrangements**		
R6A	standard window arrangement	NC	NC
	reqs 1SA & NA w/YC7		
ZW6	complete body window arrangement	135	157
	incl'd w/YC7 decor, 1SB, 1SC, 1SD		
AJ1	**Deep Tinted Solar Ray Glass** — w/YC7	NC	NC
	w/ZW6 window arrangement	249	290
	w/R6A window arrangement	138	161
—	**Paint**		
ZY1	solid	NC	NC
ZY2	two-tone conventional - w/YC6 or YC7 or ZL7	89	104
	w/R9S decor	283	329
	incls decal striping w/YC7 [reqs VE5 bumper w/o ZL7 appearance pkg or YC6 decor or YC7]		
ZY4	deluxe two-tone - w/YC6 or ZL7	216	251
	w/R9S decor	409	476
	reqs VE5 bumper w/o ZL7 appearance pkg or YC6 decor; NA w/YC7 decor		

GMC VANDURA SERIES

VANDURA G1500 SERIES
TG11005 Vandura 110" WB 13807   15779
TG11305 Vandura 125" WB 13968   15963

VANDURA G2500 SERIES
TG21005 Vandura 110" WB 13780   15748
TG21305 Vandura 125" WB 13959   15953

VANDURA G3500 SERIES
TG31305 Vandura 125" WB 14011   16012
TG31605 Vandura 146" WB 15866   18132

Destination Charge: 580   580

Standard Equipment

VANDURA: Driver's side air bag (models with GVWR under 8600 lbs.), LH padded armrest, beverage holder, cigarette lighter, LH coat hook, two dome lamps with door-operated switches, driver's side black rubber floor mat, gauges (includes speedometer, odometer, trip odometer, fuel level, voltmeter, engine temperature, oil pressure and telltale lights), light-on warning buzzer, color-keyed headliner, deluxe outside air-tight heater with side window defoggers, parcel tray, electronically-tuned AM radio with digital clock and fixed-mast antenna, adjustable high-back driver's seat with custom trim, full sized spare tire and wheel (spare wheel only on G2500 and G3500 models), RH rear spare tire carrier, safety step pads on front and rear side step panels, instrument panel stowage box, RH and LH color-keyed sun shades with padded cloth trim, mechanical jack and wheel wrench, intermittent windshield wiper system, painted silver front and rear bumpers, front bumper guards, rear load doors, 60/40 hinged swing-out side loading door, single rectangular headlamps, single note electric horn, bright metal hubcaps with black trim, stainless steel below-eyeline mirrors with adjustable head, black bodyside rub strips, undercoating (on body rocker panels, step panels and wheel housings), light tinted solar ray windshield and front side doors, 4.3 liter (262 CID) V6 EFI engine (G1500 and G2500, G3500 125" WB), 5.7 liter (350 CID) V8 EFI engine (G3500 146" WB), 4-speed automatic transmission with overdrive, power front disc/rear drum brakes with 4-wheel anti-lock, power steering, 100 amp alternator, P215/70R15 BW tires (G1500), P225/75R15 BW tires (G2500), LT225/75R16/D SBR tires (G3500 125" WB), LT225/75R15/E SBR tires (G3500 146" WB).

GMC

CODE	DESCRIPTION	DEALER	LIST

Accessories

CODE	DESCRIPTION	DEALER	LIST
—	**Decor**		
R9S	STD Decor	NC	NC
YF7	**RV Conversion Group**		
	w/model TG21005 or TG31605	2215	2576
	w/model TG21305 and engine L49	2215	2576
	w/model TG11305 or TG21305 or TG31305	2298	2672

incls C60 air cond, VK5 temp driver seat, V22 deluxe frt appearance, V37 F & R chromed bumpers, ZQ2 pwr locks/windows pkg, ZQ3 tilt whl/spd control pkg, UM6 AM/FM stereo, cass, NL7 fuel tank (w/o TG21005), A12 glass, stepwell lamps, underhood lamps, override switch, electrical junction box w/gas engines, driver/pass frt seat riser, track/belts (deletes the following std equip: seat, headliner dome lamp, interior paint & rubber frt floor mats) (spare tire reqd) (incl'd in 1SD, 1SE, 1SF, 1SG, 1SH, 1SJ, 1SK, 1SL, 1SM)

—	**Option Pkgs - w/o RV Conversion Group YF7**		
1SA	Pkg 1SA	NC	NC

incls vehicle w/std equip

1SB	Pkg 1SB	999	1162

incls pkg 1SA plus C60 frt air cond (may be upgraded to C69 air cond), A57 pass seat

1SC	Pkg 1SC	1125	1308

incls pkg 1SB plus A12 fixed rear door glass (may be upgraded to A18, ZW3,m ZX6, A08, R7L, A07 or R7T glass pkg), UM7 AM/FM w/seek-scan & clock (may be upgraded to UM6 or UX1 radios)

—	**Option Pkgs - w/RV Conversion Group YF7**		
1SD	Pkg 1SD — G1500 Series	1257	1462

incls ZW9 std body, ZW9 fixed glass pkg (may be upgraded to ZX6, R7L, A07 or R7T glass pkgs), rub strip delete, RV conversion group

1SE	Pkg 1SE — G1500 Series	1828	2125

incls pkg 1SD plus ZX6 swing out glass pkg 1 (may be upgraded to A08, R7L, A07 or R7T glass pkgs), V06 HD cooling, DH6 interior RH/LH visor vanity mirrors, DG9 dual elec control exterior mirrors, N67 rally wheels (may be upgraded to N90 alum cast wheels), leather-wrapped steering wheel, XCV frt P215/75R15 all-season WW tires (may be upgraded XCM, YCM or ZCM tires), YCV rear P215/75R15 all-season WW tires, ZCV spare P215/75R15 all-season WW tires

1SF	Pkg 1SF — G1500 Series	1935	2250

incls pkg 1SE plus U75 pwr radio antenna, UX1 AM/FM w/seek-scan, cass, equalizer (may be upgraded to U1C radio), AJ1 deep tinted solar ray glass

1SG	Pkg 1SG — G2500 Series		
	TG21005 w/gas engine	1175	1366
	TG21305 w/gas engine	1257	1462
	TG21305 w/diesel engine	1175	1366

incls ZW9 std body, ZW3 fixed glass pkg (may be upgraded to ZX6, A08, R7L, A07 or R7T glass pkgs), rub strip delete, RV conversion group

1SH	Pkg 1SH — G2500 Series		
	TG21005 w/gas engine	1876	2181
	TG21305 w/gas engine	1958	2277
	TG21305 w/diesel engine	1640	1907

incls pkg 1SG plus ZX6 swing out glass pkg (may be upgraded to A08, R7L, A07 or R7T glass pkgs), V08 HD cooling (when upgrading to L49 diesel eng V08 is not included), DH6 interior RH/LH visor vanity mirrors, DG9 dual

80   EDMUND'S VAN/PICKUP/SPORT UTILITY BUYER'S GUIDE

CODE	DESCRIPTION	DEALER	LIST

electric control exterior mirrors, N67 rally wheels (may be upgraded to N90 alum cast wheels), leather wrapped steering wheel XEU frt P225/75R15 all-season WW tires (may be upgraded to XEV, YEV, ZEV tires w/gas eng; reqs XFL, YFL, ZFL tires w/L49 diesel engine), YEU rear P225/75R15 all-season WW tires, ZEU spare P225/75R15 all-season WW tires

CODE	DESCRIPTION	DEALER	LIST
1SJ	**Pkg 1SJ** —G2500 Series		
	TG21305 w/gas engine	2352	2735

incls pkg 1SH plus U75 pwr radio antenna, UX1 AM/FM w/seek-scan, cass, equalizer (may be upgraded to U1C radio), AJ1 deep tinted solar ray glass, C6Q 6875 lbs. GVWR, XFM frt P235/75R15 all-season white tires, YFM rear P235/75R15 all-season white tires, ZFM spare P235/75R15 all-season white tires

CODE	DESCRIPTION	DEALER	LIST
1SK	**Pkg 1SK** — G3500 Series		
	TG31305 w/LB4 gas engine & C5Y GVWR	1257	1462
	TG31305 w/diesel engine	1257	1462
	TG31605 w/gas engine	1175	1366
	TG31605 w/diesel engine	1175	1366

incls ZW9 std body, ZW3 fixed glass pkg (may be upgraded to ZX6, A08, R7L, A07 or R7T glass pkgs), rub strip delete, RV conversion group

CODE	DESCRIPTION	DEALER	LIST
1SL	**Pkg 1SL** — G3500 Series		
	TG31305 w/LB4 gas engine & C5Y GVWR	1740	2023
	TG31305 w/diesel engine	1681	1955
	TG31605 w/gas engine	1769	2057
	TG31605 w/diesel engine	1599	1859

incls pkg 1SK plus ZX6 swing out glass pkg (may be upgraded to A08, R7L, A07 or R7T glass pkgs), V08 HD cooling (when upgrading to L19 or L57 engines, V08 is not included; V08 incl'd w/LB4 engine & C5Y GVWR), DH6 interior RH/LH visor vanity mirrors, DG9 dual elec control exterior mirrors, NP5 leather-wrapped steering wheel, XHF frt LT225/75R16E all-season tires (XHP, YHP, ZHP tires may be selected in place of XHF), YHF rear LT225/75R16E all-season tires, spare LT225/75R16E all-season tires

CODE	DESCRIPTION	DEALER	LIST
1SM	**Pkg 1SM** — G3500 Series		
	TG31305 w/LB4 gas engine & C5Y GVWR	1847	2148
	TG31305 w/diesel engine	1789	2080
	TG31605 w/gas engine	1877	2182
	TG31605 w/diesel engine	1706	1984

incls pkg 1SL plus U75 pwr radio antenna, UX1 AM/FM w/seek-scan, cass, equalizer (may be upgraded to U1C radio), AJ1 deep tinted solar ray glass

CODE	DESCRIPTION	DEALER	LIST
—	**Body**		
ZW9	standard body	NC	NC
	incl'd in 1SA, 1SB, 1SC, 1SD, 1SE, 1SF, 1SG, 1SH, 1SJ, 1SL, 1SM		
—	**GVW Pkgs**		
C5J	6000 lb.	NC	NC
C5S	6600 lb.	NC	NC
C6Q	6875 lb. - w/model TG21305 & engine L49	NC	NC
	w/model TG21305 & engine L05	274	319
C5Y	7100 lb.	NC	NC
C6C	7400 lb.	720	837
C6P	8600 lb. - w/model TG31605	NC	NC
	w/model TG31305	870	1012
C6W	9200 lb. - w/model TG31305	1077	1252
	w/model TG31605	206	240

GMC

CODE	DESCRIPTION	DEALER	LIST
Z72	**Light Duty Trailering Equip**..	114	132
	incls trailer hitch & 5-wire harness		
Z82	**Heavy Duty Trailering Equip**		
	w/GVW C5Y or engines L19 or L49 or L57....................................	267	310
	w/o GVW C5Y or engines L19 or L49 or L57.................................	437	508
	incls trailer hitch & 7-wire harness (incls V08 HD cooling w/LB4, L03 or L05 engines)		
NL7	**Fuel Tank** — 33 gal...	83	96
	incl'd w/YF7 decor; reqs model TG11305 or TG21305 or TG31305		
—	**Emissions**		
FE9	federal	NC	NC
NA6	high altitude..	NC	NC
YF5	California	NA	NA
NG1	New York w/o GVW C5J	NC	NC
	w/GVW C5J..	86	100
—	**Engines**		
LB4	4.3L (262 CID) V6 EFI		
	w/model TG11005 or TG11305 or TG21105 or TG21305	NC	NC
	w/model TG31305 & GVWR C5Y	NC	NC
	w/model TG31305 & GVWR C6P	(727)	(845)
L03	5.0L (305 CID) V8 EFI gas...	495	575
L05	5.7L (350 CID) V8 EFI gas - w/model TG21305	727	845
	w/model TG31305 or TG31605	NC	NC
L19	7.4L (454 CID) V8 EFI gas...	520	605
L49	6.5L (395 CID) 155 HP V8 diesel	2468	2870
	incls dual batteries, pwr brakes, eng oil cooler, HD radiator, extra sound insulation, eng block heater, glow plugs, integral two-stage fuel filter, fuel & water separator w/instrument panel warning light & fuel filter change signal		
L57	6.5L (395 CID) 160 HP V8 diesel	1423	1655
	incls dual batteries, pwr brakes, eng oil cooler, HD radiator, extra sound insulation, eng block heater, glow plugs, integral two-stage fuel filter, fuel & water separator w/instrument panel warning light & fuel filter change signal		
—	**Transmissions**		
M30	4-spd automatic w/overdrive (4L60E)...	NC	NC
MT1	4-spd automatic w/overdrive (4L80E)...	NC	NC
—	**Rear Axles**		
GU5	3.23 ratio..	NC	NC
GU6	3.42 ratio..	NC	NC
GT4	3.73 ratio..	NC	NC
GT5	4.10 ratio..	NC	NC
HC4	4.56 ratio..	NC	NC
G80	**Locking Rear Differential**	217	252
V08	**Heavy Duty Cooling**..	170	198
	incls eng oil cooler, trans oil cooler & HD radiator (incl'd w/Z82 trailering, GVWR C5Y, 1SE, 1SF, 1SH, 1SJ, 1SL & 1SM) (NA w/engines L19, L49 or L57)		
V10	**Cold Climate Pkg** — incls engine block heater..............................	41	48
	reqs engines LB4, L03, L05 or L19		
—	**Wheels**		
P01	bright metal, full wheelcovers - TG31305 or TG31605	36	42
N67	rally wheels (spare is steel)..	104	121
	reqs model TG11005, TG11305, TG21005 or TG21305		

GMC

CODE	DESCRIPTION	DEALER	LIST
N90	aluminum cast wheels	266	310
	reqs TG11305, TG21005 or TG21305 and decor YF7		
—	**Front Tires** — G1500		
XCU	P215/75R15 all season BW SBR	NC	NC
XCV	P215/75R15 all season WW SBR	26	30
XCM	P215/75R15 all season white outline letter SBR	38	44
—	**Rear Tires** — G1500		
YCU	P215/75R15 all season BW SBR	NC	NC
YCV	P215/75R15 all season WW SBR	26	30
	incl'd in pkg 1SE, 1SF		
YCM	P215/75R15 all season white outline letter SBR........	38	44
—	**Spare Tires** — G1500		
ZCU	P215/75R15 all season BW SBR	NC	NC
ZCV	P215/75R15 all season WW SBR	13	15
	incl'd in pkg 1SF		
ZCM	P215/75R15 all season white outline letter SBR	19	22
—	**Front Tires** — G2500		
XET	P225/75R15 all season BW SBR	NC	NC
XEU	P225/75R15 all season WW SBR	31	36
	incl'd in pkg 1SH		
XEV	P225/75R15 all season white lettered SBR	43	50
XFL	P235/75R15 all season SBR	NC	NC
XFM	P235/75R15 all season WW SBR	31	36
	incl'd in pkg 1SJ		
—	**Rear Tires** — G2500		
YET	P225/75R15 all season BW SBR	NC	NC
YEU	P225/75R15 all season WW SBR	31	36
	incl'd in pkg 1SH		
YEV	P225/75R15 all season white lettered SBR	43	50
YFL	P235/75R15 all season BW SBR	NC	NC
YFM	P235/75R15 all season WW SBR	31	36
	incl'd in pkg 1SJ		
—	**Spare Tire** — G2500		
ZET	P225/75R15 all season BW SBR	118	137
ZEU	P225/75R15 all season WW SBR	133	155
	incl'd in pkg 1SH		
ZEV	P225/75R15 all season white lettered SBR	139	162
ZFL	P235/75R15 all season BW SBR	130	151
ZFM	P235/75R15 all season WW SBR	145	169
	incl'd in pkg 1SJ		
—	**Front Tires** — G3500		
XHP	LT225/75R16D all season BW SBR	NC	NC
XHF	LT225/75R16E all season BW SBR		
	w/GVWR C6P or C6W	NC	NC
	w/GVWR C5Y or C6C........................	29	34
	incl'd in pkg 1SL, 1SM		
—	**Rear Tires** — G3500		
YHP	LT225/75R16D all season BW SBR	NC	NC
YHF	LT225/75R16E all season BW SBR		
	w/GVWR C6P or C6W	NC	NC
	w/GVWR C5Y or C6C........................	29	34
	incl'd in pkg 1SL, 1SM		

GMC

CODE	DESCRIPTION	DEALER	LIST
—	**Spare Tires** — G3500		
ZHP	LT225/75R16D all season BW SBR	178	207
ZHF	LT225/75R16E all season BW SBR	193	224
	incl'd in pkg 1SL, 1SM		
R6G	**Air Conditioning Delete** — reqs 1SA	NC	NC
C60	**Air Conditioning** — front (incl'd in 1SB, 1SC)	839	975
C69	**Air Conditioning** — front & rear - w/decor YF7	515	599
	w/decor R9S	1354	1574
—	**Convenience Pkgs**		
AU3	power door locks (incl'd w/ZQ2 conv pkg)	192	223
ZQ2	power door locks & windows (incl'd w/YF7 decor)	373	434
ZQ3	tilt wheel & speed control (incl'd w/YF7 decor)	329	383
B30	**Floor Covering**	135	157
	incls floor & wheelhouse carpeting (reqs pass seat A57 & decor R9S)		
C36	**Rear Heater**	176	205
TR9	**Auxiliary Lamps** — NA w/decor YF7	134	156
DH6	**Mirrors** — interior RH/LH visor vanity	65	75
	incl'd in pkgs 1SE, 1SF, 1SH, 1SJ, 1SL, 1SM (reqs decor YF7)		
—	**Radio Equip**		
UT5	radio	NC	NC
	incls AM radio (reqs 1SA or 1SB)		
UM7	radio	83	96
	incls AM/FM stereo w/seek-scan & clock, 2 frt coaxial spkrs w/wiring for rear spkrs (incl'd in pkg 1SC; NA w/decor YF7)		
UM6	radio	187	218
	incls AM/FM stereo w/seek-scan, cass, clock, 2 frt coaxial spkrs w/wiring for rear spkrs (incl'd w/YF7 decor) (NA w/1SF, 1SJ or 1SM)		
UX1	radio - w/decor YF7	129	150
	w/decor R9S	316	368
	incls AM/FM stereo w/seek-scan, cass, equalizer, clock & 2 frt coaxial spkrs w/wiring for rear spkrs (incl'd in pkg 1SF, 1SJ, 1SM)		
U1C	radio	257	299
	incls AM/FM stereo w/seek-scan, CD player, clock, 2 frt coaxial spkrs w/wiring for rear spkrs (reqs decor YF7)		
UL5	radio delete - reqs pkg 1SA or 1SB	(82)	(95)
U75	power radio antenna - incl'd in pkg 1SF, 1SJ, 1SM	73	85
—	**Seats**		
AV5	high back bucket driver's seat (reqs decor R9S)	NC	NC
VK5	temporary driver seat (incl'd in YF7 decor)	(80)	(93)
AV4	front high back bucket seats less seat fabric	237	276
	reqs decor YF7		
A57	passenger seat	161	187
	incl'd in pkg 1SB, 1SC (NA w/YF7)		
NP5	**Leather-Wrapped Steering Wheel**	52	60
	incl'd in 1SE, 1SF, 1SH, 1SJ, 1SL, 1SM		
V22	**Deluxe Front Appearance Pkg** — incl'd w/YF7 decor	122	142
V37	**Bumpers** — chromed front & rear (incl'd w/YF7 decor)	65	76
C49	**Rear Window Electric Defogger**	132	154
	reqs A12 or ZW3 or A08 or A07		
YA2	**Sliding Side Door** — NA on model TG31605	NC	NC
AX3	**Remote Keyless Entry System**		
	reqs decor YF7 or lighting TR9 & convenience pkg ZQ2		

GMC

CODE	DESCRIPTION	DEALER	LIST
DG9	**Mirrors** — dual electric control, stainless steel	84	98
	incl'd in 1SE, 1SF, 1SH, 1SJ, 1SL, 1SM (reqs convenience pkg ZQ2 & NA w/window R6A)		
B98	**Rub Strip Delete** — reqs decor YF7..	NC	NC
—	**Window Arrangements**		
R6A	standard window arrangement	NC	NC
	incls windshield, frt driver & frt pass windows w/adjustable vent windows (NA w/DG9 mirrors & C49 defogger; reqs pkg 1SA or 1SB)		
A12	fixed rear door glass..	43	50
	incls windshield, frt driver & frt pass windows w/adjustable vent windows, fixed LH & RH rear cargo door glass (reqs pkg 1SA, 1SB or 1SC)		
A18	swing out rear door glass..	94	109
	incls windshield, front driver & frt pass windows w/adjustable vent windows, swing out LH & RH cargo door glass (NA w/C49 defogger or decor YF7)		
ZW3	fixed glass pkg I - w/decor YF7	34	40
	w/decor R9S	77	90
	incls windshield, frt driver & frt pass windows w/adjustable vent windows, fixed LH & RH rear cargo door glass & fixed sliding side cargo door glass (reqs decor R9S or pkg 1SD or 1SG or 1SK)		
ZX6	swing out glass pkg I - w/decor YF7	151	176
	w/decor R9S	194	226
	incls windshield, frt driver/frt pass windows w/adjustable vent windows, swing out LH & RH rear cargo door glass/swing out sliding side cargo door glass (incl'd in pkg 1SE, 1SF, 1SH, 1SJ, 1SL, 1SM) (NA w/C49 defogger)		
A08	fixed glass pkg II - w/decor YF7	79	92
	w/decor R9S	122	142
	incls windshield, frt driver & frt pass windows w/adjustable vent windows, fixed LH & RH rear cargo door glass, fixed sliding side cargo door glass & fixed RH rear body glass		
R7L	swing out glass pkg II - w/decor YF7..	196	228
	w/decor R9S	239	278
	incls windshield, frt driver & frt pass windows w/adjustable vent windows, swing out LH & RH rear cargo door glass, swing out sliding side cargo door glass & fixed RH rear body glass (NA w/C49 defogger)		
A07	fixed full body glass pkg - w/decor YF7	158	184
	w/decor R9S	201	234
	incls windshield, frt driver & frt pass windows w/adjustable vent windows, fixed LH & RH rear cargo door glass, fixed sliding side cargo door, fixed RH rear body glass & fixed LH center & LH rear body glass		
R7T	swing out full body glass pkg - w/decor YF7	275	320
	w/decor R9S	318	370
	incls windshield, frt driver & frt pass windows w/adjustable vent windows, swing out LH & RH rear cargo door glass, swing out sliding side cargo door glass, fixed RH rear body glass & fixed LH center & LH rear body glass (NA w/C49 defogger)		
AJ1	**Tinted Glass** — w/windows A07 or R7T	327	380
	w/windows A08 or R7L...	194	225
	w/windows ZW3 or ZX6..	120	140
	incls deep tinted solar ray glass (incl'd in pkg 1SF, 1SJ, 1SM; reqs decor YF7)		
ZY1	**Paint** — solid..	NC	NC

GMC

MAZDA MPV

4 CYLINDER

Code	Description	Dealer	List
LV521	MPV 2-Row Wagon/Van (auto)	16212	18195
LV521	MPV 3-Row Wagon (auto)	17460	19595

6 CYLINDER

Code	Description	Dealer	List
LV522	MPV 3-Row Wagon (auto)	18172	20395
LV523	MPV 4WD 3-Row Wagon (auto)	20845	23395
	Destination Charge: Alaska	645	645
	Other States	445	445

Standard Equipment

MPV 5-PASSENGER WAGON/VAN 4 CYLINDER: 2.6L SOHC 12-valve 4 cylinder engine, 4-speed automatic transmission w/overdrive, rack-and-pinion steering w/variable assist, power assisted front and rear disc brakes, rear wheel anti-lock braking system (ABS), 15-inch wheels w/full wheel covers, P195/75R15 tires, protective bodyside moldings, dual manual mirrors, variable intermittent wipers w/rear wiper washer, tinted glass w/dark-tinted windshield sunshade band, high-mount stop light, 5-passenger seating w/3-passenger 2nd row seat, reclining front bucket seats w/adjustable head restraints, driver side airbag supplemental restraint system, child safety lock on rear side door, remote hood and fuel door releases, tachometer, tilt steering column, rear window defogger w/auto shut-off, AM/FM cassette stereo w/4 speakers.

MPV 7-PASSENGER WAGON 4 CYLINDER (in addition to or instead of MPV 5-PASSENGER WAGON/VAN 4 CYLINDER equipment): Dual power mirrors, 7-passenger seating w/2-passenger 2nd row seat & 3-passenger 3rd row, removable 2nd row seat w/recline, easy-fold and flip-forward 3rd row seats, fold-flat function for 2nd and 3rd row seats, AM/FM cassette stereo w/6 speakers.

MPV 7-PASSENGER WAGON V6 (in addition to or instead of MPV 7-PASSENGER WAGON 4 CYLINDER equipment): 3.0L SOHC 18-valve V6 engine, 4-speed electronically controlled automatic transmission w/overdrive.

MPV 7-PASSENGER 4WD WAGON V6 (in addition to or instead of MPV 7-PASSENGER WAGON V6 equipment): Multi-mode four-wheel-drive system w/lockable center diff, 15-inch aluminum alloy wheels, P215/65R15 tires.

CODE	DESCRIPTION	DEALER	LIST

Accessories

CODE	DESCRIPTION	DEALER	LIST
ACB	**Dual Air Conditioning** — LV522, LV523	1230	1500
ACA	**Single Air Conditioning** — NA on models w/Pkg D	705	860
MR1	**Power Moon Roof** — LV522, LV523	820	1000
	models w/Pkg A & B require dual air conditioning, towing pkg and alloy wheel pkg		
1TP	**Towing Pkg** — LV522	430	500
	LV523	344	400
	models w/Pkg A & B require alloy wheels		
1CO	**Cold Pkg**	258	300
	incls 65 amp battery, 5.1 liter washer tank, rear heater		
CD1	**CD Player** — models w/Pkg D	560	700
1TR	**Touring Pkg** — LV522	490	570
	incls 8-passenger seating, 2nd row w/3 seats, fold-down armrests, beverage holders and outboard armrests [models w/Pkg A & B require FLE floor mats]		
JCP	**Two-Tone Paint**	246	300
	std on LV522 w/Pkg D; NA on LV523 w/Pkg D		
FLM	**Floor Mats** — 2-Row	47	65
	3-Row	65	90
FLE	**Floor Mats** — 3-Row	69	95
1PA	**Pkg A** — LV521 3-Row	872	1050
	incls power windows, power door locks, cruise control, rear privacy glass, bronze tinted windows		
1PB	**Pkg B** — LV522 3-Row	1121	1350
	incls Pkg A items plus body-color grille and license plate illumination bar, keyless entry system		
1PC	**Pkg C** — LV523 3-Row	1121	1350
	incls Pkg A items plus body-color grille and license plate illumination bar and keyless entry		
2LX	**Pkg D** — LV522 3-Row	3316	3995
	incls Pkg B & C items plus lace alloys wheels, leather seating surfaces, wheel special two-tone paint, color-keyed bodyside moldings [dual air conditioning mandatory, towing pkg mandatory, moonroof mandatory]		

MERCURY

1993 MERCURY VILLAGER

NOTE: Information for the 1994 Villager was unavailable at time of publication.

1993 VILLAGER 6 CYL

		Dealer	List
V11	GS 3-Dr Wagon	15138	17015
V11	LS 3-Dr Wagon	19605	22090
	Destination Charge:	540	540

Standard Equipment

VILLAGER GS: "Light bar" grille, halogen aero headlamps, front cornering lamps, black sail-mounted breakaway mirrors, clearcoat metallic paint (except black and white body colors), lower bodyside urethane protection, interval windshield wipers w/washer, rear window wiper/washer, color-keyed aero wheel covers, color-keyed cut-pile carpets w/full coverage floor mats, front/rear dome lamps w/courtesy switches at all doors (w/time delay on front lamp), color-keyed door trim panels w/ower carpeting/cloth inserts/map pockets/courtesy lamps; three entry assist handles w/integral coat hooks, front/ear full coverage floor mats, remote fuel filler door release, warning lamps for low fuel/low washer fluid/low oil/door ajar/temperature gauge/reminder chime for headlamp on, fasten seat belt, & key-in-ignition; backlighted mechanical instrument cluster w/achometer and trip odometer, side window defoggers, locking glove box w/amp, two stowage bins w/removable rubber mat, slide out coinholder tray, interior hood release, day/night rearview mirror, elec AM/FM radio w/four speakers and clock, cupholders at each seating position (except at sliding door), flat load floor, cloth reclining bucket front seats with adjustable headrests/inboard armrests/two cupholders mounted (unique cloth trim on LS), cloth 3-pass rear bench seat, 110 amp alternator, 60 amp/hr. maintenance-free battery, power front disc/rear drum brakes with four-wheel anti-lock, child safety seat provision, 3.0 liter V6 OHC engine with multi-port electronic fuel injection, electric fan drive, front wheel drive, fuel cap tether, 20 gallon fuel tank, interior hood release, dual-note horn, childproof side sliding door, nitrogen gas-filled shocks/struts, temporary spare tire mounted underbody, front stabilizer bar, power rack and pinion steering, MacPherson strut front suspension, Hotchkiss rear suspension, P205/75R15 BSW all-season radial tires, 4-speed electronic automatic overdrive transaxle with electronic power/economy switch, flip-out 2nd and 3rd row bodyside windows, color-keyed front and rear 5-mph impact bumpers with black bumper rub strips, tinted glass, black bodyside molding, 4-spoke steering wheel, cloth visors with dual covered mirrors.

LS (in addition to or instead of GS equipment): Color-keyed bumper rub strips, privacy glass, luggage rack, color-keyed bodyside moldings, color-keyed bodyside accent tape stripe, front air conditioning, rear window defroster, light group includes overhead map lights/front door step lamps/under I/P lamps with time delay; electronic AM/FM stereo cassette radio, cargo net, rear seat adjustable recliner which folds forward flat with tray surface, additional quick release 2-passenger bench seat with fold flat back (with tray surface and seat back recliner), map pockets on front seat backs, lockable storage under passenger seat, leather-wrapped steering wheel with tilt column, cloth visors with dual illuminated mirrors, power locks with side sliding door "memory," automatic fingertip speed control, power front door windows, remote power flip-out 3rd row bodyside windows.

Accessories

CODE	DESCRIPTION	DEALER	LIST
—	**Preferred Equipment Pkgs**		
691A	**Villager GS Pkg 691A**..	1281	1507
	incls front air conditioning, electric rear window defroster, dual power mirrors, tilt wheel/speed control, power windows, power locks		
692A	**Villager LS Pkg 692A**..	2166	2549
	incls equipment in Preferred Equipment Pkg 691A plus luggage rack, electronic AM/FM stereo cassette radio, underseat storage, 8-way power driver's seat, aluminum wheels with locking lug nuts		
695A	**Villager LS Pkg 695A**..	293	345
	incls 8-way power driver's seat, aluminum wheels with locking lug nuts, flip open liftgate window, high level AM/FM cassette radio, two-tone paint		
696A	**Villager LS Pkg 696A**..	1485	1748
	incls equipment in Preferred Equipment Pkg 695A plus rear air cond/ auxiliary heater, electronic instrument cluster, keyless entry and autolamp on/off delay system, 4-way power passenger seat, quad bucket seats		
99W	**Engine** — 3.0L EFI 6 cyl	STD	STD
44P	**Automatic Overdrive Transaxle**...	STD	STD
422	**California Emissions System**...	87	102
428	**High Altitude Emissions System**	NC	NC
T70	**Tires** — P205/75R15 BSW	STD	STD
64V	**Wheels** — aluminum w/locking lug nuts...................................	322	379
—	**Optional Seating**		
21A	7-passenger seating - std on LS...	282	332
21H	quad bucket seats - LS	508	598
R	leather trim - LS	735	865
90F	seat, 4-way power pass - LS	165	194
90P	seat, 8-way power driver	335	394
572	**Air Conditioning** — std on LS..	729	857
574	**Rear Air Conditioning & Auxiliary Heater** — GS	1125	1323
	w/PEP's 692A, 695A..	396	466
57Q	**Electric Rear Window Defroster** — std on LS	143	168
17F	**Flip Open Liftgate Window**	77	90
153	**Front License Plate Bracket**	NC	NC
924	**Glass, Privacy** — std on LS...	351	413
15A	**Instrument Cluster, Electronic** — LS	207	244
60A	**Keyless Entry & Autolamp On/Off Delay System** — LS..............	256	301
593	**Light Group & Power Rear Vent Windows** — std on LS..............	132	155
615	**Luggage Rack** — std on LS	121	143
543	**Mirrors, Dual Power** — std on LS..	83	98
951	**Paint, Monotone** — LS...	NC	NC
943	**Power Windows/Locks** — std on LS	451	530
434	**Storage, Underseat** — std on LS..	31	37
85C	**Stripes, Bodyside Tape** — std on LS	36	43

CODE	DESCRIPTION	DEALER	LIST
439	**Sunroof, Power — LS**	659	776
684	**Suspension, Handling — LS**..	74	87
52N	**Tilt Wheel/Speed Control — GS**	316	372
534	**Trailer Tow Package**...	211	249
—	**Radio Systems**		
58T	electronic AM/FM stereo cassette - std on LS	203	239
588	high level AM/FM cassette - LS..	282	332
91Q	supersound AM/FM cassette & CD player - LS	764	899
58Y	standard radio credit - GS	(78)	(91)

MITSUBISHI EXPO

EX35-L	LRV Base 3-Dr Liftback (5-spd).................................	11716	13019
EX35-L	LRV Base 3-Dr Liftback (auto)	12474	13859
EX35-N	LRV Sport 3-Dr Liftback (5-spd)...............................	14619	16799
EX35-N	LRV Sport 3-Dr Liftback (auto).................................	15219	17489
EX45-N	4-Dr Liftback (5-spd)	13648	15689
EX45-N	4-Dr Liftback (auto)	14248	16379
EX45-W	4-Dr AWD Liftback (5-spd)	14900	17129
EX45-W	4-Dr AWD Liftback (auto)	15500	17819
	Destination Charge:	445	445

Standard Equipment

EXPO LRV: Removable/tumbling rear bench w/0/50 split folding/reclining seatbacks, rear seat head-rests, full-face cloth upholstery, heating/ventilation system w/4-speed fan, dial-type controls and dual bi-level output; rear window defogger w/heavy-duty timer, tilt steering column, sliding rear passenger door w/inner rail sliding mechanism, dome and cargo area lights, remote fuel filler door w/tethered cap, low fuel warning light, analog instrumentation: 140 mph speedometer/fuel-level gauge/tripmeter/coolant temperature gauge; warning lights: engine check/brake system/low oil pressure/charging system/door-hatch ajar; driver side airbag, child protection rear door locks, variable intermittent wipers, 5 mph bumpers, protective bodyside molding, two-tone paint, dual manual remote sideview mirrors, 185/75R14 all-season tires, 14 x 5.5 full wheel covers, 1.8L SOHC 16V 4 cylinder engine, electronic multi-point fuel injection, stainless steel exhaust system, 5-speed manual overdrive transmission, power assist front disc/rear drum brakes, power assist rack and pinion steering, strut-type independent front suspension, semi-trailing arm independent rear suspension, front stabilizer bar, on-board diagnostic system.

EXPO LRV SPORT (in addition to or instead of EXPO LRV equipment): Rear-seat heater ducts (2nd seat), CFC-free refrigerant air cond, Power Package includes power windows w/driver side auto down/remote keyless entry system/dual power remote side view mirrors/cruise control; rear window wiper/washer with intermittent, power tailgate release, digital quartz clock, Convenience Package includes: center armrest/upgraded door trim w/cloth inserts and map pockets/rear cargo cover/power door and tailgate lock; tachometer, rear cargo cover, ETR AM/FM cassette w/4 speakers, tailgate deflector with LED stop lamp, dual power remote sideview mirrors, 205/70R14 all season tires, 14 x 5.5 alloy wheels, 2.4L SOHC 16V 4 cylinder engine, dual engine stabilizers, automatic valve lash adjusters, rear stabilizer bar.

EXPO/EXPO AWD (in addition to or instead of EXPO LRV SPORT equipment): 2nd and 3rd row seats w/50/50 folding/reclining; rear seat heater ducts (2nd and 3rd seat), air conditioning deleted, Power Package deleted, underseat front passenger tray, remote keyless entry system deleted, sliding rear passenger door w/inner rail sliding mechanism deleted, cruise control deleted, Convenience Package deleted, ETR AM/FM cassette w/4 speakers deleted, tailgate deflector w/LED stop lamp deleted, 14 x 5.5 full wheel covers, 14 x 5.5 alloy wheels deleted, rear stabilizer bar deleted.

Accessories

CODE	DESCRIPTION	DEALER	LIST
FM	**Floor Mats** — LRV	47	73
	4-Door	55	85
AW	**Alloy Wheels** — AWD models	233	291
AC	**Air Conditioning** — std LRV Sport	680	829
RR	**Luggage Rack**	178	274
KC	**Cargo Kit Pkg** — LRV	70	99
	incls cargo area net, cargo tray		
PP	**Power Pkg** — LRV Base	575	719
	incls dual power mirrors, cruise control, remote keyless entry system, power windows (req's 4-speed automatic transmission)		
PP	**Power Pkg** — 4-Door	715	894
	incls cruise control, remote keyless entry sys, power door locks, pwr windows		
CP	**Convenience Pkg** — LRV Base	477	596
	incls digital clock, power door locks, power tailgate locks, rear tonneau cover, rear window wiper/washer, front seat center armrest, door trim panels w/cloth inserts		
ER	**AM/FM ETR Stereo Radio** — LRV Base	217	334
	incls four speakers		
EQ	**AM/FM ETR Stereo Radio w/Cassette** — std LRV Sport	312	466
	incls four speakers		
ED	**Compact Disc Player**	407	626
PI	**Power Tilt/Slide Sunroof** — LRV Sport, 4-Door FWD	548	685
	incls inner sunshade		
AB	**Four-Wheel Anti-Lock Power Brakes** — all except LRV Base	800	976
TL	**Wheel Locks** — 4-Door FWD	24	37
MG	**Front & Rear Mud Guards**	54	84

MITSUBISHI

NISSAN QUEST

Code	Description	Dealer	List
00314	XE 7-Passenger (auto)	16065	18529
00414	GXE (auto)	19975	23039
	Destination Charge:	375	375

Standard Equipment

QUEST - XE: 3.0L SOHC V6 engine, sequential multi-point fuel injection, front wheel drive, electronically controlled 4-speed automatic overdrive transmission, power-assisted rack-and-pinion steering, power-assisted front vented disc/rear drum brakes, independent front suspension w/stabilizer bar, beam rear axle with leaf springs, full wheel covers, aerodynamic halogen headlamps, flush-mounted cornering lamps, tinted glass with upper windshield band, body-color body side moldings, sliding passenger side door, rear window wiper/washer, 7-passenger seating (2nd and 3rd row bench), 4-way reclining front bucket seats, Quest Trac flexible seating system, moquette seat trim, full carpeting, carpeted floor mats, air conditioning (non-CFC refrigerant), power-boosted ventilation system, tilt steering column, 2-speed variable intermittent windshield wipers/twin-stream washers, rear wiper with intermittent setting, electric rear window defroster, remote fuel-filler door and hood releases, center console w/cassette and CD storage, lockable glove box, entry/exit fade-out system, tabletop surfaces w/cupholders, cargo area net, tachometer, trip odometer, speedometer/coolant temperature/fuel level gauges, electronically-tuned AM/FM cassette stereo audio system/Dolby noise reduction/4 speakers, diversity antenna system, passive motorized front shoulder belt system/active lap belt, driver side airbag (SRS), 3-point manual rear seatbelts (outboard, 2nd and 3rd row/center lap belt), 5 mph energy-absorbing front/rear bumpers, steel side-door guard beams and pillar/roof reinforcement, child-safety lock on sliding side door.

GXE (in addition to or instead of XE equip): Anti-lock braking system (ABS) incls rear disc brakes, alum alloy wheels, side & rear privacy glass, dual liftgate w/opening glass hatch, dual power remote-controlled outside mirrors w/passenger-side convex, roof luggage rack, 8-way power driver's seat, 4-way reclining front bucket seats deleted, velour seat trim, leather-wrapped steering wheel, rear air cond, rear heater controls, power front windows, power rear quarter windows, power door locks, cruise control, pass under-seat storage bin, dual illuminated visor vanity mirrors, deluxe elec-tuned AM/FM cassette stereo audio system/Dolby noise reduction/4 speakers/rear seat audio controls, power antenna, Power Package includes power front windows/dual power mirrors/power door locks, Convenience Package includes privacy glass/deluxe AM/FM cassette stereo audio system/cruise control/luggage rack/lockable under-seat storage/leather-wrapped steering wheel/illuminated passenger visor vanity mirror.

NISSAN

NISSAN

CODE	DESCRIPTION	DEALER	LIST

Accessories

CODE	DESCRIPTION	DEALER	LIST
S02	**Power Pkg** — XE.. *incls power windows w/driver's side down feature, power door locks w/central locking, power mirrors [std on GXE]*	699	825
F05	**Convenience Pkg** — XE .... *incls cruise control, privacy glass, lockable underseat storage, illuminated passenger side visor vanity mirror, luggage rack, leather-wrapped steering wheel, AM/FM stereo radio w/cassette [reqs power pkg]*	677	800
T02	**XE Extra Performance Pkg** — XE .... *incls 215/70R15 97H tires, full-size spare tire, rear stabilizer bar, heavy-duty battery and radiator, tuned shocks and springs, 3500 lb. towing pkg*	805	950
T02	**GXE Extra Performance Pkg** — GXE... *incls 215/70R15 97H tires, full-size spare tire, rear stabilizer bar, heavy-duty battery and radiator, tuned shocks and springs, alloy wheels, 3500 lb. towing pkg*	445	525
V01	**Luxury Pkg** — GXE... *incls 2nd row captain's chairs, digital illuminated entry system, power passenger seat, automatic headlamp feature*	677	800
X03	**Leather Trim Pkg** — GXE .... *reqs luxury pkg; GXE extra performance pkg required when power sunroof and leather pkg are combined*	847	1000
J01	**Power Sunroof** — GXE .... *GXE extra performance pkg required when power sunroof and leather pkg are combined*	699	825
A04	**Rear Air Conditioning** — XE (std on GXE)... *reqs power pkg*	529	625
B07	**4-Wheel Anti-Lock Braking System** — XE (std on GXE)	593	700
E10	**Two-Tone Paint** — GXE	254	300
H07	**Premium Audio Pkg** — GXE... *incls CD player (reqs luxury pkg)*	859	1015
C01	**California Emissions**...	127	150

OLDSMOBILE SILHOUETTE

SILHOUETTE 6 CYL

		DEALER	LIST
M06UR	3-Dr Minivan	18186	20095
Destination Charge:		530	530

Standard Equipment

SILHOUETTE: Front touch-control air conditioner, front and rear air distribution system, ashtrays include: front/center row/third row; Freedom battery, pwr front disc/rear drum anti-lock brakes, front/rear body color bumper fascias, front/third-row cigar lighters, lower center console w/ocking storage/HVAC and radio controls/dual cupholders; defoggers include: side window/front/rear; 3.1 liter V6 engine w/throttle-body fuel injection (transverse-mounted w/front-wheel drive), deluxe cut-pile wall-to-wall floor carpeting with carpeted lower door panels, carpeted front and rear floor mats, foglamps, composite halogen headlamps, headlamp-on reminder, interior operated hood release, carpeted instrument panel cover, instrument panel Rallye Cluster includes: electrically driven needle speedometer/tachometer/trip and total odometer/voltmeter/temperature gauge/oil pressure gauge; driver and passenger side outside fold-away electrically operated mirrors, bodyside body color moldings, rear cargo area 12-volt concealed auxiliary power outlet, Delco ETR AM/FM stereo radio with seek-scan/digital display clock/dual front/rear spkrs/integrated roof radio antenna; seven-psgr seating includes: front buckets w/folding armrests/3 center seats/2 rear modular seats; driver-side 4-way man seat adjuster; front, center/rear row full-foam seat cushions, power rack-and-pinion steering, MacPherson front strut suspension sys, rear variable-rate coil spring suspension, P205/70R15 steel-belted radial-ply blackwall all-season tires, automatic trans w/column shifter, flo-thru ventilation, 15" x 6" aluminum-styled wheels, pulse wiper system, rear window wiper, deluxe tilt steering wheel, tinted glass, solar treated windshield, driver's side air bag, instrument panel lamp, glove box courtesy lamp, driver and passenger side covered visor vanity mirrors.

Accessories

			DEALER	LIST
1SA	**Option Pkg 1SA**		NC	NC
	incls vehicle plus standard equipment			
1SB	**Option Pkg 1SB**		1428	1660
	incls convenience pkg (incls pwr side windows w/auto-down feature, programmable auto pwr door locks w/sliding door delay feature, cruise			

		DEALER	LIST
	control w/resume & acceleration features, convenience net, deep tint glass (all glass behind frt doors), overhead console, rooftop luggage carrier, remote lock control pkg (incls door lock release, illuminated entry feature, & key-chain transmitter), Delco ETR AM/FM stereo radio (incls seek-scan, auto reverse cass & digital display clock)		
1SC	**Option Pkg 1SC** — w/o C54	2812	3270
	w/C54	2662	3095
	incls pkg 1SB equip plus pwr sliding door, 3800 V6 eng, seat adjuster (6-way pwr bucket seat - driver side), leather-wrapped steering wheel w/steering wheel touch controls		
AD9	**Integrated Child Seats, Dual**	194	225
AG9	**Seat Adjuster, 6-Way Power, Driver** — incl'd w/pkg 1SC	232	270
AJ1	**Deep Tint Glass** — incl'd w/pkgs 1SB, 1SC	211	245
AP9	**Convenience Net, Cargo Area** — incl'd w/pkgs 1SB, 1SC	26	30
B4A	**Black Roof Delete**	NC	NC
C34	**Air Conditioner, Auxiliary Rear**	387	450
C54	**Sunroof, Pop-Up** — NA w/pkg 1SA/1SB	301	350
E58	**Power Sliding Door** — incl'd w/pkg 1SC	254	295
FE3	**Touring Suspension System** — incl'd w/V92	176	205
K05	**Heater, Engine Block**	15	18
L27	**Engine, 3800 V6 w/4-Spd Auto Trans**	688	800
	incl'd w/pkg 1SC		
NW9	**Traction Control System**	301	350
R9T	**Convenience Pkg** — incl'd w/pkgs 1SB, 1SC	688	800
UM6	**Radio, AM/FM Stereo w/Cassette**	120	140
	avail w/pkg 1SA, incl w/pkg 1SB		
UN6	**Radio, AM/FM Stereo w/Cassette**	26	30
	available w/pkg 1SB, incl'd w/pkg 1SC		
U1C	**Radio, AM/FM Stereo w/Compact Disc** — w/pkg 1SB	220	256
	w/pkg 1SC	194	226
	NA w/pkg 1SA		
V54	**Luggage Carrier, Rooftop** — incl'd w/pkgs 1SB, 1SC	125	145
V92	**Towing Pkg, 3,000 Lb Capacity**	305	355
WJ7	**Custom Leather Trim** — w/o pkg 1SC	748	870
	w/pkg 1SC	671	780
	NA w/pkg 1SA		
NG1	**New York Emissions**	NC	NC
YF5	**California Emissions**	NC	NC

PLYMOUTH COLT VISTA

PM52	Base Wagon (5-spd)	12036	12979
PH52	SE Wagon (5-spd)	13130	14194
MM52	AWD Wagon (5-spd)	13751	14884
	Destination Charge:	430	430

Standard Equipment

COLT VISTA - BASE: Body color fascias, black side window opening moldings, gray bodyside moldings, upper black tailgate applique, 5-mph bumpers, cigarette lighter, cupholders, side sliding door, child protection sliding door locks, stainless steel exhaust system, remote release fuel filler door, halogen aero headlights, rear heat ducts, remote hood release, single horn, three assist grips, floor console, full vinyl front door trim, molded cloth covered headliner, driver's sun visor with ticket holder, inner tailgate assist handle, dome and cargo area lamps, passenger-side covered visor mirror, outside dual manual mirrors, lowback reclining front bucket seats with adjustable head rests, removable fold and tumble rear bench seat, full-face fabric seat trim, tilt steering column, door map pockets, flat cargo floor storage, four argent styled steel wheels with bright center caps, side and rear quarter vented windows, 2-speed variable intermittent wipers/washers, 1.8 liter SMPI 16-valve 4-cylinder engine, 5-speed manual transmission, power assisted rack and pinion steering, power front disc/rear drum brakes.

SE (in addition to or instead of BASE equip): Upper red/black tailgate applique, two-tone paint w/accent color fascias, bodyside moldings & lower tailgate applique; power door locks, tinted glass, dual horn, front door trim w/cloth insert, driver foot rest, driver side covered visor mirror, outside dual power mirrors, front ctr armrest, reclining split back bench seat, Premium full-fabric seat trim (vinyl on back of front seats), pass seat back pocket storage, left rear side shelf storage, power lock/unlock tailgate, four 7-spoke full-wheel covers, fixed rear intermittent wipers/washers, 2.4 liter SMPI 16-valve 4-cyli eng.

AWD (in addition to or instead of SE equipment): Body color fascias, lower gray tailgate applique, single horn, front full vinyl door trim, front and rear mudguards, rear bench seat, full-face fabric seat trim, two-tone paint with accent color fascias deleted, power door locks deleted, tinted glass deleted, driver foot rest deleted, front seat center armrest deleted, passenger seat back pocket storage deleted, left rear side shelf deleted, power lock/unlock tailgate deleted.

CODE	DESCRIPTION	DEALER	LIST

Accessories

		DEALER	LIST
C	**Pkg C** — Base Wagon..	994	1156
	incls rear window defroster, air conditioning, tinted glass, pwr remote dual o/s mirrors, radio (AM/FM w/clock & 4 speakers), pwr remote tailgate lock, rear stabilizer bar, 9-spoke full wheel covers, rear window wiper/washer		
D	**Pkg D** — Base Wagon..	1545	1796
	incls Pkg C contents plus pwr door locks, floor mats, radio (AM/FM w/cassette, clock & 4 speakers), speed control		
K	**Pkg K** — SE Wagon	1384	1609
	incls air conditioning, cargo security cover, rear window defroster, floor mats, radio (AM/FM w/cassette, clock & 6 speakers)		
S	**Pkg S** — AWD Wagon	579	673
	incls cargo security cover, custom group, rear window defroster, floor mats, tinted glass, keyless entry, radio (AM/FM w/clock & 4 speakers)		
W	**Pkg W** — AWD Wagon	1839	2138
	incls Pkg S contents plus air conditioning, radio (AM/FM w/cassette, clock & 6 speakers), speed control, tach, pwr windows		
HAA	**Air Conditioning** — AWD Wagon...	679	790
BGF	**Brakes** — rear disc w/anti-lock - Base Wagon..	601	699
	SE Wagon..	601	699
BGF	**Brakes** — 4-wheel disc anti-lock - AWD Wagon.....................................	601	699
	SE Wagon..	57	66
	AWD Wagon..	57	66
NAE	**California Emissions**	NC	NC
NBY	**New York Emissions**	NC	NC
MWA	**Roof Rack**	130	151
CLA	**Floor Mats** — Base Wagon w/Pkg C	47	55
RAT	**Radio** — Base Wagon	248	288
	incls AM/FM w/clock & 4 speakers		
RAW	**Radio** — Base Wagon w/Pkg C	156	181
	AWD Wagon..	156	181
—	**Paint** — two-tone	166	193
EJA	**Engine** — 1.8L MPI 16-valve 4-cyl - Base Wagon.....................................	STD	STD
EY7	**Engine** — 2.4L MPI 16-valve 4-cyl - SE Wagon	STD	STD
	AWD Wagon..	STD	STD
	Base Wagon..	156	181
DDR	**Transmission** — 5-spd manual..	STD	STD
DGB	**Transmission** — 4-spd auto	622	723

PLYMOUTH VOYAGER FWD

VOYAGER FWD 4 CYL

HL52	Base	13629	14919

VOYAGER FWD 6 CYL

HH52	SE	16462	18139
HP52	LE	19827	21963
HP52	LX	20275	22472
	Destination Charge:	560	560

Standard Equipment

VOYAGER FWD - BASE: Chimes (headlights on, seat belt, key in ignition), cupholders, child protection side door locks, stainless steel exhaust system, front and rear body color fascias with accent nerf, tinted glass, inside hood release, single horn, body sound insulation, front/rear dome lamps, fold away exterior aero manual mirrors, non-illuminated visor mirrors, AM/FM stereo ETR radio with digital clock, seek and four speakers; five-passenger seating (three-passenger fixed rear bench seat), quick release intermediate and rear seats, driver and passenger highback reclining bucket seats, molded deluxe cloth seat trim, underbody spare tire carrier with cable winch, storage compartments, compact spare tire, four "Commodore" wheel covers, vented side/quarter/sliding door windows, liftgate window wipers/washers with fixed intermittent wipe, 2-speed windshield wipers with variable intermittent wipe.

SE (in addition to or instead of BASE equipment): Dual horn, pwr liftgate release, power fold away exterior aero black mirrors, non-illuminated visor mirrors, bodyside accent color (2 colors) moldings, AM/FM stereo ETR radio w/cass, digital clock, seek, Dolby, four spkrs, seven-pass seating (two-pass fixed bench, three-passenger), elec speed control, tilt steering column, four "Conclave" wheel covers.

LE (in addition to or instead of SE equipment): Front air cond, lower bodyside and sill accent appliques, front storage console with coin holder, overhead console (compass, outside temperature, 4-function trip computer, front and rear reading lights), electric rear window defroster, front and rear body color fascias with bright nerf, floor mats, automatic time delay headlights, deluxe body sound insulation, remote keyless entry, map and liftgate lamps, light package (ash receiver, front), roof luggage rack, heated power foldaway exterior aero black mirrors, illuminated visor mirrors, accent color bodyside molding deleted, power front and side door locks, front dome lamp deleted, driver and passenger reclining bucket seats with adjustable headrests, molded luxury cloth seat trim, power quarter vent windows.

CODE	DESCRIPTION	DEALER	LIST

Accessories

CODE	DESCRIPTION	DEALER	LIST
T	**Base Family Value Pkg T**	181	213
	incls air conditioning, dual horns, accent color bodyside molding, under front passenger seat storage drawer, power liftgate release, map and cargo lighting enhancements		
B	**SE Family Value Pkg B**	181	213
	incls air cond, map and cargo lighting enhancements, rr window defroster		
D	**SE Family Value Pkg D**	985	1159
	incls air conditioning, map and cargo lighting enhancements, rear window defroster, forward and overhead consoles, power door locks, floor mats, gauges (oil pressure, voltage and tachometer), deluxe insulation, light group, power rear quarter vent windows		
K	**Two Tone Pkg K** — LE	260	306
	incls power driver seat, power windows, radio (AM/FM with cassette, equalizer and six Infinity speakers), sunscreen glass		
M	**"LX" Pkg M** — LX	366	431
	incls power driver's seat, power windows, radio (AM/FM with cassette, equalizer and six Infinity speakers), sunscreen glass, sport handling group, "LX" decor group		
HAA	**Climate Group I** — Base	728	857
	incls air conditioning		
AAA	**Climate Group II** — w/family value pkg	352	414
	incls air conditioning and sunscreen glass [NA w/ASK]		
AJK	**Convenience Group I** — Base w/Pkg T	316	372
	incls speed control and tilt		
AAC	**Convenience Group II** — Base w/Pkg T	590	694
	SE w/Pkg B	225	265
	incls speed control and tilt, power mirrors and power door locks		
AAD	**Convenience Group III** — SE w/Pkg B	572	673
	SE w/Pkg D	347	408
	incls speed control and tilt, power mirrors, power door locks, power windows and keyless remote entry		
CYE	**Seating Group I** — 7-passenger seating - Base	294	346
CYK	**Seating Group II** — 7-passenger seating w/integrated child seat - Base	485	570
	SE, LE, LX	191	225
CYS	**Seating Group III** — 7-passenger quad command - SE, LE, LX	507	597
CYT	**Seating Group IV** — 7-passenger convert-a-bed - SE, LE, LX	470	553
TBB	**Loading & Towing Group I**	93	109
	incls conventional spare		
AAE	**Loading & Towing Group II** — Base w/Pkg T	151	178
	SE, LE	151	178
	w/AAG (SE w/Pkg B or D, LE w/Pkg K, LX)	124	146
	incls conventional spare tire and firm ride heavy load suspension		
AAF	**Loading & Towing Group III** — SE w/Pkg B or D	473	556
	w/ASH (SE w/Pkg B or D)	376	442
	LE w/Pkg K	376	442
	w/AAG or ASK (SE w/Pkg B or D, LE w/Pkg K, LX)	349	410
	incls conventional spare tire, firm ride heavy load suspension and trailer tow group		
WJF	**Wheels I** — 15" aluminum wheels - LE w/Pkg K	309	363
AAG	**Sport Handling Group** — SE w/Pkg B or D (NA w/ASK)	203	239
	LE w/Pkg K (incls WJF)	415	488

PLYMOUTH

CODE	DESCRIPTION	DEALER	LIST
—	**Radio Equipment**		
RAS	radio - Base	145	170
	incls AM/FM stereo with cassette, clock & four speakers		
RCE	Infinity speaker system - SE	172	202
RBC	radio - SE w/Pkg D	426	501
	LE w/Pkg K or L	145	170
	incls AM/FM stereo with CD player, equalizer, clock and six Infinity		
	speakers		
BRL	**Brakes** — anti-lock - SE w/Pkg B or D	584	687
	w/AAF, AAG, ASH, ASK or WJF (SE w/Pkg B or D)	509	599
	LE, LX	509	599
ASH	**Gold Special Edition Decor Group** — SE w/Pkg B or D	213	250
	incls gold badging, 15" front disc/rear drum brakes, gold day light opening		
	accent stripe, bodyside body color molding, P205/70R15 BSW SBR tires,		
	15" cast aluminum "Lace" wheels with gold accents		
ASK	**Sport Wagon Decor Group** — SE w/Pkg B or D	638	750
	incls accent color fascias with black rub strips, fog lights, leather-wrapped		
	steering wheel, sunscreen glass, sport handling group, 15" cast aluminum		
	5-spoke wheels		
GFA	**Rear Window Defroster** — SE	143	168
JPB	**Power Door Locks** — Base w/Pkg T	225	265
NAE	**California Emissions**	87	102
NBY	**New York Emissions**	87	102
NHK	**Engine Block Heater** — available in Alaska only	29	34
MWG	**Luggage Rack**	122	143
TLB	**Tires** — Base w/Pkg T, SE w/Pkg B or D	122	143
	incls P205/70R14 WSW SBR tires (NA w/AAF, AAG, BRL, ASH or ASK)		
TPC	**Tires** — SE w/Pkg B or D, LE w/Pkg K	59	69
	incls P205/70R15 WSW SBR tires (req's BRL or AAF on SE models; NA		
	w/AAG, ASH or ASK)		
EDM	**Engine** — 2.5L EFI 4 cylinder - Base	STD	STD
EFA	**Engine** — 3.0L MPI V6 - SE, LE, LX	STD	STD
EGA	**Engine** — 3.3L MPI V6 - SE, LE, LX	87	102
DDM	**Transmission** — 5-speed manual - Base	STD	STD
DGA	**Transmission** — 3-speed automatic - Base	511	601
	SE, LE	STD	STD
DGB	**Transmission** — 4-speed automatic - Base	679	799
	SE, LE	168	198
	LX	STD	STD
—	**Seats** — cloth highback buckets - Base, SE	STD	STD
—	**Seats** — cloth lowback buckets - LE, LX	STD	STD
—	**Seats** — leather lowback buckets - LE, LX	735	865
—	**Paint** — special color or metallic	82	97

CODE	DESCRIPTION	DEALER	LIST

PLYMOUTH GRAND VOYAGER AWD

GRAND VOYAGER AWD 6 CYL

PH53	SE	19869	21982
PP53	LE	23018	25560
Destination Charge:		560	560

Standard Equipment

GRAND VOYAGER AWD - SE: Chimes (headlights on, seat belt, key in ignition), cupholders, child protection side door locks, stainless steel exhaust system, front and rear body color fascias with accent nerf, tinted glass, dual horn, body sound insulation, power liftgate release, front/rear dome lamps, power fold away exterior aero black mirrors, non-illuminated visor mirrors, accent color (2 colors) bodyside moldings, AM/FM ETR stereo radio with cassette, digital clock, seek, Dolby and four speakers; seven-passenger seating, quick release intermediate and rear seats, driver and passenger highback reclining bucket seats, deluxe cloth molded seat trim, underbody spare tire carrier with cable winch, electronic speed control, tilt steering column, storage compartments, compact spare tire, four "Conclave" wheel covers, vented side/quarter/sliding door windows, liftgate window wipers and washers with fixed intermittent wipe, 2-speed windshield wipers with variable intermittent wipe.

LE (in addition to or instead of SE equipment): Front air conditioning, lower bodyside and sill accent appliques, front storage console with coin holder, overhead console (compass, outside temperature, 4-function trip computer, front and rear reading lights), electric rear window defroster, power front and side door locks, front and rear body color fascias with bright nerf, floor mats, automatic time delay headlights, deluxe body sound insulation, remote keyless entry, front dome lamp deleted, map and liftgate lamps, light package (ash receiver, front) roof luggage rack, heated power fold away exterior aero black mirrors, illuminated visor mirrors, accent color bodyside moldings deleted, driver and passenger reclining bucket seats, molded luxury cloth seat trim, power quarter vent windows.

Accessories

B	**SE Family Value Pkg B**	181	213
	incls air conditioning, map and cargo lighting enhancements, rear window defroster		
D	**SE Family Value Pkg D**	985	1159
	incls air conditioning, map and cargo lighting enhancements, rear window		

CODE	DESCRIPTION	DEALER	LIST
	defroster, forward and overhead consoles, deluxe insulation, floor mats, gauges (oil pressure, voltage and tachometer), illuminated visor vanity mirrors, light group, power door locks, power rear quarter vent windows		
K	**Two-Tone Pkg K** — LE..	260	306
	incls power driver's seat, power windows, radio (AM/FM stereo w/cassette, equalizer, clock and 6 speakers), sunscreen glass		
L	**Woodgrain Pkg L** — LE...	818	962
	incls power windows, power driver's seat, radio (AM/FM stereo w/cassette, equalizer, clock and 6 speakers), sunscreen glass, woodgrain group		
AAC	**Convenience Group I** — SE w/Pkg B...................................	225	265
	incls power mirrors and power locks		
AAD	**Convenience Group II** — SE w/Pkg B..................................	572	673
	SE w/Pkg D..	347	408
	incls power mirrors, power locks, power windows and keyless remote entry		
AAA	**Climate Group I** — SE w/Pkg B or D...................................	352	414
	incls sunscreen glass		
AAB	**Climate Group II** — SE w/Pkg B	840	988
	SE w/Pkg D..	748	880
	w/ASK (SE w/Pkg B)...	488	574
	w/ASK (SE w/Pkg D)...	396	466
	w/AAF (SE w/Pkg B)...	786	925
	w/AAF (SE w/Pkg D)...	695	818
	w/ASK & AAF (SE w/Pkg B)..	434	511
	incls sunscreen glass and rear heater/air conditioning		
CYK	**Seating Group II** — 7-passenger seating w/integrated child seat	191	225
CYS	**Seating Group III** — 7-passenger quad command	507	597
CYT	**Seating Group IV** — 7-passenger convert-a-bed........................	470	553
TBB	**Loading & Towing Group I**..	93	109
	incls conventional spare tire		
AAF	**Loading & Towing Group II** — SE w/Pkg B or D..................	317	373
	LE w/Pkg K or L...	317	373
	incls conventional spare tire and heavy duty trailer tow group		
—	**Radio Equipment**		
RCE	Infinity speaker system - SE w/Pkg B or D	172	202
RBC	radio - SE w/Pkg D	426	501
	LE w/Pkg K or L...	145	170
	incls AM/FM stereo w/CD player, graphic equalizer, clock and 6 Infinity speakers		
ASH	**Gold Special Edition Decor Group** — SE w/Pkg B or D.............	213	250
	incls gold badging, gold day light opening accent stripe, bodyside body color moldings, 15" cast aluminum "Lace" wheels with gold accents [NA w/ASK]		
ASK	**Sport Wagon Decor Group** — SE w/Pkg B or D.......................	638	750
	incls accent color fascias with black rub strip, fog lights, leather-wrapped steering wheel, sunscreen glass, P205/70R15 all-season touring LBL SBR tires, 15" cast aluminum 5-spoke wheels		
GFA	**Rear Window Defroster** — SE	143	168
NAE	**California Emissions**..	87	102
NBY	**New York Emissions**...	87	102
NHK	**Engine Block Heater** — available in Alaska only	29	34
MWG	**Luggage Rack**..	122	143

CODE	DESCRIPTION	DEALER	LIST
TPC	**Tires** — SE w/Pkg B or D	59	69
	LE w/Pkg K or L	59	69
	incls P205/70R15 WSW SBR (NA w/ASH or ASK)		
WJV	**Wheels** — 15" cast aluminum - LE w/Pkg K	309	363
EGA	**Engine** — 3.3L MPI V6	STD	STD
EGH	**Engine** — 3.8L MPI V6 - LE w/Pkg K or L	257	302
—	**Seats** — cloth highback buckets - SE	STD	STD
—	**Seats** — cloth lowback buckets - LE..	STD	STD
—	**Seats** — leather lowback buckets - LE.....................................	735	865
	NA w/CYK		
—	**Paint** — special color or metallic	82	97

PLYMOUTH GRAND VOYAGER FWD

GRAND VOYAGER FWD 6 CYL

HL53	Base	16522	18178
HH53	SE..	17513	19304
HP53	LE..	20662	22883
	Destination Charge:	560	560

Standard Equipment

GRAND VOYAGER FWD - BASE: Chimes (headlights on, seat belt, key in ignition), cupholders, child protection side door locks, stainless steel exhaust system, front and rear body color fascias with accent nerf, tinted glass, single horn, body sound insulation, front/rear dome lamps, fold away exterior aero manual mirrors, non-illuminated visor mirrors, AM/FM ETR stereo radio with digital clock, seek and four speakers; seven-passenger seating (two-passenger fixed bench and three-passenger), quick release intermediate and rear seats, driver and passenger highback reclining bucket seats, deluxe cloth molded seat trim, underbody spare tire carrier with cable winch, storage compartments, compact spare tire, four "Conclave" wheel covers, vented side/quarter/sliding door windows, liftgate window wipers/washers with fixed intermittent wipe, 2-speed windshield wipers with variable intermittent wipe.

SE (in addition to or instead of BASE equip): Dual horn, power liftgate release, power fold away exterior aero black mirrors, accent color (2 colors) bodyside moldings, AM/FM ETR stereo radio w/cass, digital clock, seek, Dolby and four speakers; elec speed control, tilt steering column, storage compartments.

CODE	DESCRIPTION	DEALER	LIST

LE (in addition to or instead of SE equipment): Front air cond, lower bodyside and sill accent appliques, front storage console with coin holder, overhead console (compass, outside temperature, 4-function trip computer, front and rear reading lights), electric rear window defroster, power front and side door locks, front and rear body color fascias with bright nerf, floor mats, automatic time delay headlights, deluxe body sound insulation, remote keyless entry, map and liftgate lamps, light package (ash receiver, front), roof luggage rack, heated power fold away exterior aero black mirrors, illuminated visor mirrors, driver and passenger reclining bucket seats, molded luxury cloth seat trim, power quarter vent windows.

Accessories

CODE	DESCRIPTION	DEALER	LIST
T	**Base Family Value Pkg T**	181	213
	incls air cond, dual horns, bodyside accent clr mldg, under front pass seat storage drawer, pwr liftgate release, map, cargo lighting enhancements		
B	**SE Family Value Pkg B**	181	213
	incls air cond, map, cargo lighting enhancements, rear window defroster		
D	**SE Family Value Pkg D**	985	1159
	incls air conditioning, map and cargo lighting enhancements, rear window defroster, forward and overhead consoles, power door locks, floor mats, gauges (oil pressure, voltage, tachometer), deluxe insulation, light group, illuminated visor vanity mirror, power rear quarter vent windows		
K	**Two-Tone Pkg K — LE**	260	306
	incls power driver seat, power windows, radio (AM/FM w/cassette, equalizer and six Infinity speakers), sunscreen glass		
L	**Woodgrain Pkg L — LE**	818	962
	incls power driver seat, power windows, radio (AM/FM w/cassette, equalizer and six Infinity speakers), sunscreen glass, woodgrain group		
HAA	**Climate Group I — Base**	728	857
	incls air conditioning		
AAA	**Climate Group II — w/family value pkg**	352	414
	incls air conditioning and sunscreen glass [NA w/ASK]		
AAB	**Climate Group III — Base w/Pkg T**	840	988
	SE w/Pkg B	840	988
	SE w/Pkg D	748	880
	w/ASK (SE w/Pkg B)	488	574
	w/ASK (SE w/Pkg D)	396	466
	w/AAF (SE w/Pkg B)	786	925
	w/AAF (SE w/Pkg D)	695	818
	w/ASK & AAF (SE w/Pkg B)	434	511
	w/ASK & AAF (SE w/Pkg D)	343	404
	LE w/Pkg K or L	396	466
	w/AAF (LE w/Pkg K or L)	343	404
	incls air conditioning, sunscreen glass, rear heat/air conditioning		
AJK	**Convenience Group I — Base w/Pkg T**	316	372
	incls speed control and tilt		
AAC	**Convenience Group II — Base w/Pkg T**	590	694
	SE w/Pkg B	225	265
	incls speed control and tilt, power mirrors and power door locks		
AAD	**Convenience Group III — SE w/Pkg B**	572	673
	SE w/Pkg D	347	408
	incls speed control and tilt, power mirrors, power locks, power windows and keyless entry		
CYK	**Seating Group I — 7-passenger seating w/integrated child seat - Base**	191	225
CYS	**Seating Group II — 7-passenger quad command - SE, LE**	507	597

PLYMOUTH

CODE	DESCRIPTION	DEALER	LIST
CYT	**Seating Group IV** — 7-passenger convert-a-bed - SE, LE	470	553
TBB	**Loading & Towing Group I**	93	109
	incls conventional spare		
AAE	**Loading & Towing Group II** — Base w/Pkg T	151	178
	SE, LE	151	178
	w/AAG (SE w/Pkg B or D, LE w/Pkg K or L)	124	146
	incls conventional spare tire and firm ride heavy load suspension		
AAF	**Load & Towing Group III** — SE w/Pkg B or D	376	442
	LE w/Pkg K or L	376	442
	w/AAG or ASK (SE w/Pkg B or D, LE w/Pkg K or L)	349	410
	incls conventional spare tire, firm ride heavy load suspension and trailer tow group		
WJF	**Wheels I** — 15" aluminum wheels - LE w/Pkg K	309	363
AAG	**Sport Handling Group** — SE w/Pkg B or D (NA w/ASK)	106	125
	LE w/Pkg L (NA w/ASK)	106	125
	LE w/Pkg K (incls WJF)	415	488
—	**Radio Equipment**		
RAS	radio - Base	145	170
	incls AM/FM stereo w/cassette, clock & 4 speakers		
RCE	Infinity speaker system - SE w/Pkg B or D	172	202
RBC	radio - SE w/Pkg D	426	501
	LE w/Pkg K or L	145	170
	incls AM/FM stereo w/CD player, equalizer, clock and 6 Infinity speakers		
BRL	**Brakes** — anti-lock - SE w/Pkg B or D	509	599
	LE	509	599
ASH	**Gold Special Edition Decor Group** — SE w/Pkg B or D	213	250
	incls gold badging, gold day light opening accent stripe, bodyside body color molding, 15" cast aluminum "Lace" wheel with gold accents		
ASK	**Sport Wagon Decor Group** — SE w/Pkg B or D	638	750
	incls accent color fascias with black rub strips, fog lights, leather-wrapped steering wheel, sunscreen glass, sport handling group, 15" cast aluminum 5-spoke wheels		
GFA	**Rear Window Defroster** — Base, SE	143	168
JPB	**Power Door Locks** — Base w/Pkg T	225	265
NAE	**California Emissions**	87	102
NBY	**New York Emissions**	87	102
NHK	**Engine Block Heater** — available in Alaska only	29	34
MWG	**Luggage Rack**	122	143
TPC	**Tires** — Base w/Pkg T	59	69
	SE w/Pkg B or D	59	69
	LE w/Pkg K or L	59	69
	incls P205/70R15 WSW SBR tires (NA w/AAG, ASH or ASK)		
—	**Paint** — special color or metallic	82	97
—	**Seats** — cloth highback buckets - Base, SE	STD	STD
—	**Seats** — cloth lowback buckets - LE	STD	STD
—	**Seats** — leather lowback buckets (NA w/CYK) - LE	735	865
EFA	**Engine** — 3.0L MPI V6 - Base	STD	STD
EGA	**Engine** — 3.3L MPI V6 - SE, LE	STD	STD
EGH	**Engine** — 3.8L MPI V6 - LE	257	302
DGA	**Transmission** — 3-speed automatic - Base	STD	STD
DGB	**Transmission** — 4-speed automatic - Base	168	198
	SE, LE	STD	STD

PLYMOUTH

CODE	DESCRIPTION	DEALER	LIST

PONTIAC TRANS SPORT SE

TRANS SPORT SE 6 CYL

M06R	Minivan	15719	17369
	Destination Charge:	530	530

Standard Equipment

TRANS SPORT SE: Integrated roof antenna, polymer composite bumpers w/integral rub strips, composite body panels that resist dents & rust, fog lamps, heat-repelling solar-coated glass windshield, rear flip-out side glass windows, tinted glass, composite halogen headlamps, one-piece liftgate, LH remote & RH manual w/old-and-stow feature sport mirrors, black roof treatment moldings, lower aero molding, monotone paint theme, rear liftgate two-speed wiper/washer, P205/70R15 BW all-season tires, compact spare w/hoist cable, 15" styled bolt-on wheel covers, controlled-cycle "wet-arm" windshield wipers, "quiet pkg" acoustical insulation, driver-side air bag, front side windows defoggers, child safety door locks, fabric seats, instrumentation (mechanical analog speedometer, odometer, tachometer, coolant temperature, oil presure indicator, voltmeter/trip odometer), lamp group (overhead map lights, rear dome reading lamps, cargo area lamps, underhood light), front/rear floor mats, day/night rearview mirror, RH & LH covered visor vanity mirrors, rear auxiliary power socket, ETR AM/FM stereo radio w/clock, reclining front bucket seats with headrests, four-way manual driver-side seat adjuster, four-spoke sport steering wheel, front and side door map pockets, cup and mug holder tray with center instrument panel lower console, lockable under-dash storage, glove box, mesh net front seatback pockets, rear quarter storage compartments, Freedom II battery, power disc/drum brakes, 4-wheel anti-lock braking system, engine coolant recovery system, stainless steel exhaust system, front wheel drive, 3.1 liter V6 engine, 3-speed auto transmission, power rack and pinion steering, fully independent MacPherson strut suspension.

Accessories

Code	Description	DEALER	LIST
1SA	**SE Pkg 1SA**	NC	NC
	incls vehicle w/std equip		
1SB	**SE Pkg 1SB**	1073	1248
	incls front air conditioning, tilt steering wheel, cruise control, pwr sport mirrors, ETR AM/FM stereo radio w/auto reverse cass		
1SC	**SE Pkg 1SC**	2070	2383
	incls SE pkg 1SB equip plus single key pwr door locks, pwr windows w/drivers side express down, elec rear window defogger, deep tinted glass, 7-pass seating, convenience net		
1SD	**SE Pkg 1SD**	2543	2933
	incls SE pkg 1SC equip plus drivers 6-way pwr seat, remote keyless entry, luggage rack		
1SE	**SE Pkg 1SE**	3382	3908
	incls SE pkg 1SD equip plus auto level control, 15" self sealing touring tires, 15" alum sport wheels, ETR AM stereo FM stereo w/auto reverse cass & 5-band equalizer, clock, seek up/down, search & replay, leather wrapped steering wheel w/radio controls		
—	**Engines**		
LG6	3.1 liter FI V6	STD	STD
	incls 3-spd auto trans		
L27	3800 V6	704	819
	incls 4-spd auto trans		
FE9	**Federal Emissions**	NC	NC
YF5	**California Emissions**	NC	NC
NG1	**New York Emissions**	NC	NC

CODE	DESCRIPTION	DEALER	LIST
—	**Tires**		
XGY	P205/70R15 BSW STL	STD	STD
XIN	P205/70R15 BSW STL touring w/o P42 & 1SE	30	35
	w/P42 or 1SE	NC	NC
—	**Interiors**		
—	5-passenger seating w/Milliweave cloth	STD	STD
ZP7	7-passenger seating w/Milliweave cloth w/o 1SC, 1SD & 1SE	606	705
	w/1SC, 1SD or 1SE	NC	NC
ZP7	7-passenger seating w/Prado leather w/1SD or 1SE	748	870
C67	**Air Conditioning, Electronic Front** — w/1SB, 1SC, 1SD, 1SE	NC	NC
	w/o 1SB, 1SC, 1SD, 1SE	714	830
C34	**Air Conditioning & Heater Rear (Incls Front)**		
	w/o 1SB, 1SC, 1SD & 1SE	1101	1280
	w/1SB, 1SC, 1SD or 1SE	387	450
C40	**Air Conditioning Delete**	NC	NC
G67	**Automatic Level Control**	172	200
B2Q	**Black Roof Delete**	NC	NC
C49	**Defogger, Electric Rear Window**	146	170
K05	**Engine Block Heater**	15	18
VK3	**Front License Plate Bracket**	NC	NC
AJ1	**Glass, Deep Tint**	211	245
AD8	**Integral Child Seat** — one	108	125
AD9	**Integral Child Seat** — two	194	225
V54	**Luggage Rack**	151	175
DD9	**Mirrors, Sport LH Power, RH Power Breakaway**	41	48
AB5	**Power Door Locks, Single Key**	258	300
AG9	**Power Seat, Driver 6-Way**	232	270
E58	**Power Sliding Door**	254	295
A31	**Power Windows, Drivers Side Express Down**	237	275
—	**Radios**		
UM6	ETR AM/FM stereo w/auto reverse cass - w/o 1SB, 1SC, 1SD	120	140
	w/1SB, 1SC, 1SD	NC	NC
UX1	ETR AM/FM cass & 5-band equalizer - w/1SD	271	315
	w/1SE	NC	NC
U1A	ETR AM/FM compact disc & 5-band equalizer - w/1SD	465	541
	w/1SE	177	206
AU0	**Remote Keyless Entry**	116	135
C54	**Sunroof, Pop-Up**	258	300
NW9	**Traction Control**	301	350
V92	**Trailer Provisions**	129	150
P42	**15" Touring Tires** — self sealing	159	185
PH3	**15" Aluminum Wheels**	237	275
15P	**15" Aluminum Wheels, Bright Faced**	237	275

PONTIAC

CODE	DESCRIPTION	DEALER	LIST

TOYOTA PREVIA

		DEALER	LIST
5122	DX (auto)	18937	22148
5142	DX All-Trac (auto)	21580	25388
5132	LE (auto)	21928	25798
5152	LE All-Trac (auto)	24521	28848
	Destination Charge: approximate	400	400

Standard Equipment

PREVIA DX: Full wheel covers, front and rear assist grips, rear heater ducts, trip odometer, digital clock, diagnostic warning lights, front stabilizer bar, tilt steering column, sliding side door, engine oil auto-feeder, power front disc/rear drum brakes, power steering, cloth upholstery, driver and front passenger airbags, swing-out side windows, full carpeting (includes cargo area), door trim panels w/cloth inserts, P215/65R15 SBR all-season BW tires, full-size spare tire, electric rear window defroster, reclining front bucket seats, 2-passenger removable second row bench seat, 3-passenger split fold-down third-row bench seat, headlights with automatic off, dual manual remote mirrors, right visor vanity mirror, remote fuel-filler door release, glove box/ashtray lights, key-in-ignition warning chime, variable intermittent front wipers, fixed intermittent rear window wiper/washer, 2.4L 4 cylinder EFI 16-valve engine, protective lower bodyside cladding, 4-speed ECT automatic transmission, child-safety sliding side door locks, deluxe AM/FM ETR stereo radio w/6 speakers.

LE (in addition to or instead of DX equipment): Cruise control, power windows, dual air conditioning, power 4-wheel disc brakes, front seatback map pockets, deluxe AM/FM ETR stereo radio w/cassette and 6 speakers, adjustable front armrests, power door locks w/anti lockout feature, dual power mirrors, illuminated right visor vanity mirror.

Accessories

			DEALER	LIST
AC	**Air Conditioning** — DX		1348	1685
PO	**Power Pkg** — DX		596	745
	incls power windows w/driver side express down, power door locks, dual power mirrors			

CODE	DESCRIPTION	DEALER	LIST
CC	**Seats** — captain's chairs - LE..	632	790
CL	**Cruise Control** — DX...	220	275
EX	**Deluxe AM/FM ETR Radio** — w/cassette - DX	127	170
	incls 6 speakers		
CE	**Premium AM/FM ETR Radio** — w/cassette - LE....................................	326	435
	incls programmable equalization, 7 speakers (reqs privacy glass		
DC	**Premium 3-In-1 Combo Radio** —	956	1275
	incls 9 speakers, programmable equalization, AM/FM ETR stereo radio		
	w/cass & compact disc, antenna w/diversity reception (reqs privacy glass)		
PN	**Security Pkg** — DX	756	945
	incls Power Pkg, anti-theft device		
PN	**Security Pkg** — LE...	160	200
	incls anti-theft device		
CA	**California Emissions**..	130	153
SR	**Dual Moonroofs** — LE 2WD	1240	1550
	incls rear pwr sliding moonroof, front pop-up moonrf, rr spoiler, sunshade		
AB	**Anti-Lock Power Brakes** — 4-wheel disc - DX	889	1100
	LE..	779	950
	incls rear disc brakes (std on LE), anti-lock brakes (reqs cruise control)		
PG	**Privacy Glass** — LE	308	385
AW	**Aluminum Wheels** — LE...	336	420
	incls P215/65R15 all-season tires, aluminum wheels		

PICKUPS
CONTENTS

CODE	DESCRIPTION	DEALER	LIST

CHEVROLET C-K CREW CAB PICKUP

5.7 LITER (350 CID) EFI 8 CYL

C3500 SERIES 2WD

		DEALER	LIST
CC30943 E63 Crew Cab 168.5" WB		16934	19357

K3500 SERIES 4WD

		DEALER	LIST
CK30943 E63 Crew Cab 168.5" WB		19614	22420
Destination Charge:		600	600

Standard Equipment

C/K 3500 CREW CAB PICKUP - BASE: 5.7-liter V-8, 5-speed heavy-duty manual transmission w/deep low gear and overdrive, power front disc/rear drum w/rear-wheel anti-lock system, power steering, chrome bumpers, RH and LH below-eyeline 9.0" x 6.5" mirrors, four steel belted radials (single rear wheel models), argent painted steel wheels, side impact guard beams, full instrumentation and gauges, tinted Solar Ray glass all window, heavy-duty heater/defogger, electronic AM/FM stereo with seek-scan and digital clock, Scotchgarded carpeting cloth and door panels, full-width front bench seat in vinyl trim and matching rear seat, center high-mounted stop light.

SILVERADO (in addition to or instead of BASE equipment): Chrome front and black bumper guards, chrome grille and front lamp bezels, dual RH and LH composite dual halogen headlamps, color-keyed door trim panels with map pockets, carpet trim and padded armrests, full color-keyed carpeting, auxiliary lighting all door-operated, full-width three-passenger front cloth bench and cloth rear seats (optional buckets include console).

Accessories

		DEALER	LIST
CCK1	**Cheyenne Preferred Equip Group**	NC	NC
CCK2	**Cheyenne Preferred Equip Group**	692	805
CCK3	**Silverado Preferred Equip Group**	1490	1732
CCK4	**Silverado Preferred Equip Group**	2390	2779
V22	**Appearance Pkg**	164	191
—	**Axles, Rear**		
GT4	3.73 ratio	NC	NC
GT5	4.10 ratio	NC	NC
HC4	4.56 ratio	NC	NC
G80	locking differential	217	252
TP2	**Battery, Auxiliary** — w/Z81	NC	NC
	w/o Z81	115	134
BZY	**Bedliner**	194	225
—	**Bumper Equip**		
VB3	chromed, rear step	197	229
V43	painted, rear	112	130
Z81	**Camper Special Chassis Equip** — basic camper group	200	233
P13	**Carriers, Spare Wheel & Tire** — side mounted	NC	NC
V10	**Cold-Climate Pkg**	28	33
—	**Convenience Group**		
ZQ2	power locks & windows - w/PEG CCK4	NC	NC
	w/PEGS CCK1, CCK2 or CCK3	466	542
ZQ3	tilt wheel & speed control - w/PEG CCK4	NC	NC
	w/PEGS CCK1, CCK2 or CCK3	329	383
C49	**Defogger, Rear Window**	132	154

CODE	DESCRIPTION	DEALER	LIST
NG1	**New York Emissions**	NC	NC
YF5	**California Emissions**	NC	NC
—	**Engines**		
	gasoline		
L05	5.7 liter (350 cu. in.) EFI V8	NC	NC
L19	7.4 liter (454 cu. in.) EFI V8	404	470
L65	6.5 liter (400 cu. in.) turbo diesel V8	2430	2825
AJ1	**Glass** — deep tinted	155	180
U01	**Lamps** — roof marker (5)		
	w/o R04	45	52
	w/R05	NC	NC
VK3	**License Plate Bracket**	NC	NC
TR9	**Lighting, Auxiliary** — w/PEGS CCK3 or CCK4	NC	NC
	w/PEGS CCK1 or CCK2	52	61
—	**Mirrors, Exterior** — LH & RH		
D48	below-eye-line type, remote control	84	98
DF2	camper type, stainless steel - w/Z81	NC	NC
	w/o Z81	46	53
—	**Paints, Exterior**		
ZY1	solid	NC	NC
ZY2	conventional two-tone	114	132
ZY4	deluxe two-tone	209	243
—	**Radio Equip**		
UM6	radio - w/PEG CCK4	NC	NC
	w/PEGS CCK1, CCK2, CCK3	105	122
	incls elect tuned AM/FM stereo radio w/seek & scan, stereo cass tape & digital clock		
UX1	radio - w/PEG CCK4	129	150
	w/PEGS CCK1, CCK2, or CCK3	234	272
	incls elect tuned AM stereo/FM stereo radio w/seek & scan, stereo cass tape w/search & repeat, digital clock & graphic equalizer, extended range sound system		
UL5	radio delete	(247)	(287)
AG9	**Seating, Power Driver's Seat**	206	240
—	**Seat Trim**		
V1	vinyl bench	NC	NC
L1	custom cloth bench	NC	NC
L3	custom cloth reclining split bench	150	174
L6	custom cloth reclining high back bucket	464	540
NZZ	**Skid Plate Pkg**	82	95
F60	**Springs - Front, HD**	54	63
U16	**Tachometer**	51	59
—	**Tires** — all seasons SBR		
	LT225/75R16D BW		
XHP	front	(58)	(70)
YHP	rear	370	428
ZHP	spare	258	300
	LT245/75R16E BW		
XHH	front	NC	NC
YHH	rear	NC	NC
ZHH	spare	287	335
	LT225/75R16D BW		

CODE	DESCRIPTION	DEALER	LIST
XHR	front	(40)	(48)
YHR	rear	408	472
ZHR	spare	267	311
	LT245/75R16E BW		
XGK	front	19	22
YGK	rear	19	22
ZGK	spare	297	346
V76	**Tow Hooks**	33	38
Z82	**Trailering Pkg**	181	210
—	**Transmissions**		
MT8	5-spd HD manual	NC	NC
MX0	4-spd automatic w/overdrive	765	890
—	**Wheel Trim**		
P01	wheel covers - w/CCK2	36	42
P06	wheels, rally trim - w/PEGS CCK3 or CCK4	NC	NC
	w/PEGS CCK1 or CCK2	52	60
—	**Wheels, Rear**		
R05	dual	737	857
R04	single	NC	NC
A28	**Window** — sliding rear	97	113

CHEVROLET C-K 1500 PICKUP

4.3 LITER (262 CID) EFI 6 CYL

C1500 SERIES 2WD

CC10703 E62 Sportside (6 ft.) 117.5" WB		12854	14690
CC10703 E63 Fleetside (6 ft.) 117.5" WB		12274	14027
CC10903 E63 Fleetside (8 ft.) 131.5" WB		12519	14307
CC10703 E63 & X81 Fleetside - w/T pkg (6 ft.) 117.5" WB		11180	12354
CC10903 E63 & X81 Fleetside - w/T pkg (8 ft.) 131.5" WB		11180	12354
CC10753 E62 Sportside Ext (6 ft.) 141.5" WB		14233	16266
CC10753 E63 Fleetside Ext (6 ft.) 141.5" WB		13872	15854

PICKUPS **CHEVROLET**

CODE	DESCRIPTION	DEALER	LIST

K1500 SERIES 4WD

		DEALER	LIST
CK10703 E62 Sportside (6 ft.) 117.5" WB		14902	17031
CK10703 E63 Fleetside (6 ft.) 117.5" WB		14410	16469
CK10903 E63 Fleetside (8 ft.) 131.5" WB		14672	16768
CK10703 E63 & X81 Fleetside - w/T pkg (6 ft.) 117.5" WB		13979	15446
CK10903 E63 & X81 Fleetside - w/T pkg (8 ft.) 131.5" WB		13979	15446
CK10753 E62 Sportside Ext (6 ft.) 141.5" WB		16264	18591
CK10753 E63 Fleetside Ext (6 ft.) 141.5" WB		15903	18179

5.0 LITER (305 CID) EFI 8 CYL

		DEALER	LIST
CC10953 E63 Fleetside Ext (8 ft.) 155.5" WB		14610	16697
WB		16580	18953
Destination Charge:		600	600

Standard Equipment

C/K 1500 REGULAR CAB PICKUP - BASE CHEYENNE: 5-speed manual transmission, power front disc/rear drum brakes with rear-wheel anti-lock system, power steering, chrome bumpers and painted argent grille, black RH and LH below-eyeline mirrors, side impact door guard beams, full gauges and instrumentation, tinted Solar Ray glass all windows, color-keyed headliner, deluxe heater with windshield and side window defoggers, heavy-duty radiator, electronic AM radio with fixed-mast antenna, Scotchgarded carpeting and cloth trim, three-passenger all-vinyl front bench seat with folding backrest.

SILVERADO (in addition to or instead of BASE equip): Bumpers w/blk rub strip, bright trim, dlx front appearance grille, dual composite halogen headlamps, blk bodyside moldings w/bright trim, Rally whl trim, rr quarter swing-out windows, color-keyed carpeting, elec AM/FM stereo w/seek-scan, dig clock, three-pass front seat w/choice of vinyl or custom cloth front bench w/headrest, fldg backrest, spt steering whl.

C/K 1500 EXTENDED CAB PICKUP - BASE CHEYENNE: 5-speed manual transmission, power front disc/rear drum brakes with rear-wheel anti-lock system, chrome bumper and painted argent grille, black RH and LH below-eyeline mirrors, side impact door guard beams, full gauges and instrumentation, tinted Solar Ray glass all windows, color-keyed headliner, deluxe heater with windshield and side window defoggers, heavy-duty radiator, electronic AM radio with fixed-mast antenna, Scotchgarded carpeting and cloth trim, 60/40 vinyl split bench seat includes folding rear seat, power steering.

SILVERADO (in addition to or instead of BASE equipment): Chrome front bumpers with black rub strip and bright trim, deluxe front appearance grille, dual composite halogen headlamps, black bodyside moldings with bright trim, Rally wheel trim, rear quarter swing-out windows, color-keyed carpeting, electronic AM/FM stereo with seek-scan and digital clock, 60/40 split bench seat, sport steering wheel.

Accessories

		DEALER	LIST
—	**W/T1500 Preferred Equip Groups**		
PWT1		NC	NC
PWT2	C1500	139	162
PWT2	K1500	192	223
PSP1	**C/K 1500 Sport Truck Preferred Equip Group**		
	C10703		
	w/ZQ8	1761	2048
	w/o ZQ8	2088	2428
	K10703	2239	2608
—	**Cheyenne Preferred Equip Group**		
P1A1	C1500 w/LB4 & MX0 & E63	(765)	(890)
P1A2	C1500 w/LB4 & MX0 & E63	851	990
P1A3	**Silverado Preferred Equip Group**	1085	1262
	w/MX0 & LB4 or L03	655	762

CHEVROLET

CODE	DESCRIPTION	DEALER	LIST
P1A4	**Silverado Preferred Equip Group**...........................	1620	1884
	w/MX0 & LB4 or L03.............................	1190	1384
C60	**Air Conditioning**		
	w/PEGS PSP1, P1A2, P1A3 or P1A4....................	NC	NC
	w/PEGS PWT1, PWT2 or P1A1........................	692	805
V22	**Appearance Pkg** — w/PEG P1A3 or P1A4...........	NC	NC
	w/PEG P1A1 or P1A2.............................	164	191
—	**Axles, Rear**		
GU4	3.08 ratio....................................	NC	NC
GU6	3.42 ratio....................................	NC	NC
GT4	3.73 ratio....................................	NC	NC
GT5	4.10 ratio....................................	NC	NC
G80	locking differential.............................	217	252
TP2	**Battery** — auxiliary............................	115	134
BZY	**Bedliner**....................................	194	225
—	**Body Code**		
E62	Sportside body................................	NC	NC
E63	Fleetside body	NC	NC
—	**Bumper Equipment**		
V43	painted, rear step w/PEG PWT2....................	NC	NC
	w/PEGS PWT1, P1A1, P1A2, P1A3 or P1A4........	112	130
VG3	chromed, deluxe front w/rub strip		
	w/PEGS P1A3 or P1A4.........................	NC	NC
	w/PEGS P1A1 or P1A2.........................	22	26
VB3	chromed, rear step w/rub strip....................	197	229
V27	guards, front bumper, black		
	Silverado or E62 w/o diesel......................	28	32
	Silverado w/diesel.............................	NC	NC
P13	**Carrier, Spare Wheel & Tire** — side mounted.......	NC	NC
—	**Chassis Equipment**		
F44	heavy duty		
	w/diesel eng.................................	NC	NC
	w/o diesel eng...............................	198	230
Z71	off-road pkg.................................	232	270
ZQ8	sport handling pkg w/PEGS P1A4 or P1A3..........	838	974
	w/PEGS P1A1, P1A2 or PSP1....................	916	1065
V10	**Cold Climate Pkg**	28	33
—	**Convenience Group**		
ZQ2	power door locks & power windows		
	w/PEGS P1A4 or PSP1	NC	NC
	w/PEGS P1A1, P1A2 P1A3	316	367
ZQ3	tilt wheel & cruise control		
	w/PEGS PSP1 or P1A4.........................	NC	NC
	w/PEGS P1A1, P1A2 or P1A3....................	329	383
—	**Cooling Systems**		
KC4	engine oil w/Z82..............................	NC	NC
	w/o Z82....................................	116	135
V08	engine & transmission oil w/Z82..................	NC	NC
	w/o Z82....................................	170	198
C49	**Defogger, Rear Window - Electric**...............	132	154
FE9	**Federal Emissions**...........................	NC	NC
NA6	**High Altitude Emissions**	NC	NC

CODE	DESCRIPTION	DEALER	LIST
YF5	**California Emissions**	86	100
NG1	**New York Emissions** — w/o C5G GVW	NC	NC
	w/C5G GVW	86	100
—	**Engines**		
	gasoline		
LB4	4.3 liter (262 cu. in.) EFI V6	NC	NC
L03	5.0 liter (305 cu. in.) EFI V8 w/C-K 10953	NC	NC
	w/o C-K 10953	495	575
L05	5.7 liter (350 cu. in.) EFI V8 w/C-K 10953	232	270
	w/o C-K 10953	727	845
	diesel		
L49	6.5 liter V8 naturally aspirated diesel (395 cu. in.)		
	w/C-K 10953	1974	2295
	w/o C-K 10953	2468	2870
L56	6.5 liter V8 turbo diesel (395 cu. in.)		
	w/C-K 10953	2662	3095
	w/o C-K 10953	3156	3670
KL5	alternative fuel	108	125
BG9	**Floor Covering, Full** — rubber w/C-K 10*03	(17)	(20)
	w/o C-K 10*03	(31)	(36)
AJ1	**Glass, Deep Tinted**		
	w/P1A3 or P1A4 & A28 or C49	62	72
	w/P1A3 or P1A4 w/o A28 or C49	92	107
	w/P1A1 or P1A2 w/A28 or C49	99	115
	w/P1A1 or P1A2 w/o A28 or C49	129	150
—	**Lamps**		
C95	dome & reading w/TR9	NC	NC
	w/o TR9	28	33
U01	roof marker	45	52
VK3	**License Plate Bracket, Front**	NC	NC
TR9	**Lighting, Auxiliary**		
	w/PEGS PSP1, P1A3 or P1A4	NC	NC
	w/o R9A or w/PEGS P1A1 or P1A2	81	94
—	**Mirrors, Exterior** — LH & RH		
D45	stainless steel		
	w/PEGS P1A3 or P1A4	NC	NC
	w/PEGS P1A1 or P1A2	39	45
DF2	camper type, stainless steel		
	w/PEGS P1A3 or P1A4	7	8
	w/PEGS P1A1 or P1A2	46	53
B85	**Moldings** — body side bright		
	w/PEGS P1A3 or P1A4	NC	NC
	w/PEGS P1A1 or P1A2 w/E63 w/o ZQ8	92	107
	w/PEGS P1A1 or P1A2	65	76
—	**Paints, Exterior**		
ZY1	solid	NC	NC
ZY2	conventional two-tone	114	132
ZY4	deluxe two-tone	209	243
—	**Radio Equipment**		
UP4	radio - w/PEG PWT2	NC	NC
	w/PEG PWT1 *incls elect tuned AM radio*	139	162
UM7	radio - w/PEGS P1A2 or P1A3	NC	NC

CHEVROLET

CODE	DESCRIPTION	DEALER	LIST
	w/PEGS PWT2 or P1A1	146	170
	w/PEG PWT1	286	332
	incls elect tuned AM/FM stereo radio w/seek & scan & digital clock		
UM6	radio - w/PEGS P1A4 or PSP1	NC	NC
	w/PEGS P1A2 or P1A3	105	122
	w/PEGS P1A1 or PWT2	251	292
	w/PEG PWT1	390	454
	incls elect tuned AM/FM stereo radio w/seek & scan, stereo cass tape & digital clock		
UX1	radio - w/PEGS P1A4 or PSP1	129	150
	w/PEGS P1A2 or P1A3	234	272
	w/PEG P1A1	380	442
	incls elect tuned AM stereo/FM stereo radio w/seek & scan, stereo cass tape w/search & repeat, graphic equalizer & digital clock		
UL5	radio delete..	(101)	(117)
AG9	**Seat, Power Driver's Seat**	206	240
YG4	**Seat Delete, Rear**	(340)	(395)
—	**Seat Trim**		
V1	vinyl bench	NC	NC
V3	vinyl split bench w/C-K 10*53	NC	NC
	w/C-K 10*03	150	174
C1	cloth bench	NC	NC
C3	cloth reclining split bench w/C-K 10*53	NC	NC
	w/C-K 10*03	150	174
L1	custom cloth bench	NC	NC
L3	custom cloth reclining split bench w/C-K 10*53	NC	NC
	w/C-K 10*03	150	174
L6	custom cloth reclining high back bucket w/C-K 10*53	250	291
	w/C-K 10*03	421	490
F51	**Shock Absorbers** — HD F & R w/Z82 or VYU	NC	NC
	w/o Z82 or VYU	34	40
NZZ	**Skid Plate** — off-road w/Z71	NC	NC
	w/o Z71	82	95
VYU	**Snow Plow Prep Pkg** — w/Z71	47	55
	w/o Z71	136	158
F60	**Springs, Front** — HD w/VYU	NC	NC
	w/o VYU	54	63
U16	**Tachometer**	51	59
—	**Tires**		
	All Seasons SBR		
	P225/75R15 BW		
XET	front	NC	NC
YET	rear	NC	NC
ZET	spare - w/PEG PWT1	138	160
	w/PEG PWT2	NC	NC
	w/o PEGS PWT1 or PWT2	NC	NC
	P225/75R15 white lettered		
XEV	front	43	50
YEV	rear	43	50
ZEV	spare	22	25
	P235/75R15 BW		
XFL	front - w/PEG PSP1	NC	NC

CODE	DESCRIPTION	DEALER	LIST
	w/diesel eng or C-K 1**53	NC	NC
	w/o diesel eng or C-K 1**53	24	28
YFL	rear - w/PEG PSP1	NC	NC
	w/diesel eng or C-K 1**53	NC	NC
	w/o diesel eng or C-K 1**53	24	28
ZFL	spare - w/PEG PSP1	NC	NC
	w/PEG PWT1	150	174
	w/diesel eng or C-K 1**53	NC	NC
	w/o diesel eng, PEG PWT1 or C-K 1**53	12	14
	P235/75R15 white stripe		
XFM	front - w/o diesel eng or C-K 1**53	55	64
	w/diesel eng or C-K 1**53	31	36
YFM	rear - w/o diesel eng or C-K 1**53	55	64
	w/diesel eng or C-K 1**53	31	36
ZFM	spare - w/o diesel eng or C-K 1**53	28	32
	w/diesel eng or C-K 1**53	15	18
	P235/75R15 white lettered		
XFN	front - w/o diesel eng or C-K 1**53	67	78
	w/diesel eng or C-K 1**53	43	50
YFN	rear - w/o diesel eng or C-K 1**53	67	78
	w/diesel eng or C-K 1**53	43	50
ZFN	spare - w/o diesel eng or C-K 1**53	34	39
	w/diesel eng or C-K 1**53	22	25
	LT245/75R16C BW		
XBK	front	NC	NC
YBK	rear	NC	NC
ZBK	spare	NC	NC
	LT225/75R16C BW		
XHE	front	NC	NC
YHE	rear	NC	NC
ZHE	spare - w/PEG PWT1	190	221
	w/PEG PWT2	NC	NC
	w/o PEGS PWT1 or PWT2	NC	NC
	P275/60R15 BW		
XCN	front	NC	NC
YCN	rear	NC	NC
ZCN	spare	NC	NC
	On-Off Road SBR		
	LT225/75R16C BW		
XHJ	front	19	22
YHJ	rear	19	22
ZHJ	spare - w/o PEG PWT1	9	11
	w/PWT1	200	232
	LT225/75R16C white outlined lettered		
XHN	front	62	72
YHN	rear	62	72
ZHN	spare	31	36
	LT245/75R16C BW		
XBN	front	19	23
YBN	rear	19	23
ZBN	spare	9	11
	LT245/75R16 white outlined lettered		

CHEVROLET

CODE	DESCRIPTION	DEALER	LIST
XBX	front	62	73
YBX	rear	62	73
ZBX	spare	31	36
	LT265/75R16C BW		
XGL	front - w/PEG PSP1	NC	NC
	w/K 1**03	114	134
	w/K 1**53	65	76
YGL	rear - w/PEG PSP1	NC	NC
	w/K 1**03	114	134
	w/K 1**53	65	76
ZGL	spare - w/PEG PSP1	NC	NC
	w/K 1**03	57	67
	w/K 1**53	33	38
	LT265/75R16C white outlined lettered		
XGM	front - w/C-K 1**03	157	184
	w/C-K 1**53	108	126
YGM	rear - w/C-K 1**03	157	184
	w/C-K 1**53	108	126
ZGM	spare - w/C-K 1**03	78	92
	w/C-K 1**53	54	63
V76	**Tow Hooks**	33	38
Z82	**Trailering Special** — HD		
	w/diesel eng		
	w/Z71	181	210
	w/o Z71	215	250
	w/o diesel eng		
	w/MX0 & ZQ8 or Z71 or VYU	351	408
	w/MX0 w/o ZQ8 or Z71 or VYU	385	448
	w/MT8		
	w/o ZQ8 or Z71 or VYU	331	385
	w/ZQ8 or Z71 or VYU	297	345
—	**Transmissions**		
MM5	5-spd manual w/overdrive	NC	NC
MT8	5-spd manual w/deep low & overdrive, HD	84	98
MX0	4-spd automatic w/overdrive	765	890
—	**Wheel Trim**		
P01	wheel covers, bright metal	36	42
P06	rally wheel trim w/PEGS P1A3, P1A4 or PWT2	NC	NC
	w/PEGS P1A1, P1A2 or PWT1	52	60
—	**Wheels, Optional**		
N90	aluminum, cast - 4 wheels only - w/PEGS P1A3 or P1A4	215	250
	w/PEGS P1A1 or P1A2	267	310
PF4	aluminum, cast - 4 wheels only - w/PEGS P1A3 or P1A4	215	250
	w/PEGS P1A1 or P1A2	267	310
N83	chrome - w/ZQ8 sport chassis	NC	NC
	w/PEGS P1A3 or P1A4	206	239
	w/PEGS P1A1 or P1A2 or w/o ZQ8	257	300
—	**Window**		
A20	swing-out, rear quarter w/PEGS P1A3, P1A4 or AJ1	NC	NC
	w/PEGS P1A1, P1A2 w/o AJ1	37	43
A28	sliding rear	97	113

CHEVROLET C-K 2500 PICKUP

4.3 LITER (262 CID) EFI 6 CYL
C2500 SERIES 2WD
CC20903 E63 Fleetside (8 ft.) 131.5" WB...... 13225 15114

K2500 SERIES 4WD
CK20903 E63 Fleetside (8 ft.) 131.5" WB...... 15000 17143

5.0 LITER (305 CID) EFI 8 CYL
C2500 SERIES 2WD
CC20753 E63 Fleetside (6 1/2 ft.) 141.5" WB...... 15437 17642

K2500 SERIES 4WD
CK20753 E63 Fleetside (6 1/2 ft.) 141.5" WB...... 17024 19459

5.7 LITER (350 CID) EFI 8 CYL
C2500 SERIES 2WD
CC20903 E63 & C6P Fleetside (8 ft.) 131.5" WB...... 14682 16783
CC20953 E63 & C6P Fleetside (8 ft.) 155.5" WB...... 16210 18530

K2500 SERIES 4WD
CK20903 E63 & C6P Fleetside (8 ft.) 131.5" WB...... 16827 19235
CK20953 E63 & C6P Fleetside (8 ft.) 155.5" WB...... 18373 21002

Destination Charge: 600 600

Standard Equipment

C/K 2500 REGULAR CAB PICKUP - BASE CHEYENNE: 5-speed manual transmission, black air dam (7200 GVW only), 600-amp battery, power front disc/rear drum brakes with rear-wheel anti-lock system, power steering, chrome front bumper and painted argent grille, heavy duty radiator, LT225/75R16D all-season radials with 7,200-lb. GVW, LT245/75R16E all-season radials with 8,600-lb. GVW, side door guard beams, full gauges, tinted Solar Ray glass all windows, deluxe heater with windshield and side window defoggers, electronic AM radio with fixed-mast antenna, Scotchgarded carpeting, cloth trim and door panels, three-passenger all-vinyl trim front bench seat with head restraints and folding backrest.

SILVERADO (in addition to or instead of BASE CHEYENNE equipment): Bumpers with black rub strip and bright trim, deluxe front appearance grille, dual composite halogen headlamps, black bodyside moldings with bright trim and bright wheel openings, Rally wheel trim, color-keyed carpeting, electronic AM/FM stereo with seek-scan and digital clock, three-passenger front seat with choice of custom vinyl or custom cloth front bench with folding backrest (optional bucket seats include console).

C/K 2500 EXTENDED CAB PICKUP - BASE CHEYENNE: 5-speed manual transmission, black air dam (7200 GVW only), 600-amp battery, power front disc/rear drum brakes with rear-wheel anti-lock system, power steering, chrome front bumper and painted argent grille, heavy duty radiator, LT225/75R16D all-season radials w/7,200-lb. GVW, LT245/75R16E all-season radials with 8,600-lb. GVW, side door guard beams, full gauges, tinted Solar Ray glass all windows, deluxe heater with windshield and side window defoggers, electronic AM radio with fixed-mast antenna, Scotchgarded carpeting, cloth trim and door panels, 60/40 vinyl reclining split bench seats with driver and passenger easy entry feature.

SILVERADO (in addition to or instead of BASE CHEYENNE equipment): Bumpers with black rub strip and bright trim, deluxe front appearance grille, dual composite halogen headlamps, black bodyside moldings with bright trim and bright wheel openings, Rally wheel trim, color-keyed carpeting, electronic AM/FM stereo w/seek-scan and digital clock, custom vinyl reclining 60/40 split bench seat w/easy entry feature.

Accessories

Code	Description	Dealer	List
—	**Cheyenne Preferred Equip Group**		
P2A1		NC	NC
P2A2		495	575
—	**Silverado Preferred Equip Group**		
P2A3	Regular cab	1214	1412
P2A3	Extended cab	1128	1312
P2A4	Regular cab	1792	2084
P2A4	Extended cab	1620	1884
C60	**Air Conditioning**		
	w/PEGS P2A2, P2A3 or P2A4	NC	NC
	w/PEG P2A1	692	805
V22	**Appearance Pkg**		
	w/PEGS P2A3 or P2A4	NC	NC
	w/PEGS P2A1 or P2A2	164	191
—	**Axles, Rear**		
GU6	3.42 ratio	NC	NC
GT4	3.73 ratio	NC	NC
GT5	4.10 ratio	NC	NC
HC4	4.56 ratio	NC	NC
G80	locking differential	217	252
TP2	**Battery** — auxiliary w/Z81	NC	NC
	w/o Z81	115	134
BZY	**Bedliner**	194	225
E63	**Body: Fleetside**	NC	NC
—	**Bumper Equipment**		
VB3	chromed, rear step w/rub strip	197	229
V43	painted rear step	112	130
V27	guards, front bumper - black		
	w/o diesel w/PEGS P2A3 or P2A4	28	32
	w/diesel & PEGS P2A3 or P2A4	NC	NC
Z81	**Camper Special Chassis Equip**		
	w/PEGS P2A3 or P2A4 & diesel	46	54
	w/PEGS P2A3 or P2A4 w/o diesel	162	188
	w/PEGS P2A1 or P2A2 & diesel	85	99
	w/PEGS P2A1 or P2A2 w/o diesel	200	233

CODE	DESCRIPTION	DEALER	LIST
P13	**Carrier, Spare Wheel & Tire** — side mounted	NC	NC
V10	**Cold-Climate Pkg**	28	33
—	**Convenience Group**		
ZQ2	power door locks & power windows - w/PEG P2A4	NC	NC
	w/o PEG P2A4	316	367
ZQ3	tilt-wheel & speed control - w/PEG P2A4	NC	NC
	w/o PEG P2A4	329	383
—	**Cooling Systems**		
KC4	engine oil	116	135
V08	radiator & transmission oil	170	198
C49	**Defogger, Electric - Rear Window**	132	154
FE9	**Federal Emissions**	NC	NC
NA6	**High Altitude Emissions**	NC	NC
YF5	**California Emissions** — w/o C6P	86	100
	w/C6P	86	100
NG1	**New York Emissions**	NC	NC
—	**Engines**		
	gasoline		
LB4	4.3 liter (262 cu. in.) EFI V6	NC	NC
L03	5.0 liter (305 cu. in.) EFI V8 - w/C-K20753	NC	NC
	w/C-K20903 w/o C6P	495	575
L05	5.7 liter (350 cu. in.) EFI V8 - w/C6P	NC	NC
	w/C-K20753 w/o C6P	232	270
	w/C-K20903 w/o C6P	727	845
L19	7.4 liter (454 cu. in.) EFI V8	520	605
	diesel		
L49	6.5 liter (395 cu. in) V8 diesel - w/C-K20753 w/o C6P	1974	2295
	w/C-K20903 w/o C6P	2468	2870
L56	6.5 liter (395 cu. in.) turbo V8 diesel		
	w/C-K20753 w/o C6P	2662	3095
	w/C-K20903 w/o C6P	3156	3670
L65	6.5 liter (395 cu. in.) turbo diesel	2430	2835
KL5	alternative fuel	108	125
BG9	**Floor Covering, Full-Rubber** — w/C-K20*03	(17)	(20)
	w/C-K20*53	(31)	(36)
AJ1	**Glass, Deep Tinted**		
	w/PEGS P2A3 or P2A4 & A28 or C49	62	72
	w/PEGS P2A3 or P2A4 w/o A28 or C49	92	107
	w/PEGS P2A1 or P2A2 & A28 or C49	99	115
	w/PEGS P2A1 or P2A2 w/o A28 or C49	129	150
C6P	**GVWR** — 8600#	NC	NC
—	**Lamps**		
C95	dome & reading - w/o TR9	28	33
	w/TR9	NC	NC
U01	roof marker	45	52
VK3	**License Plate Bracket, Front**	NC	NC
TR9	**Lighting, Auxiliary** — w/PEGS P2A3 or P2A4	NC	NC
	w/PEGS P2A1 or P2A2	81	94
—	**Mirrors, Exterior** — LH & RH		
D45	stainless steel w/PEGS P2A3 or P2A4	NC	NC
	w/PEGS P2A1 or P2A2	39	45
DF2	camper type, stainless steel - w/Z81	NC	NC

CODE	DESCRIPTION	DEALER	LIST
	w/PEGS P2A3 or P2A4	7	8
	w/PEGS P2A1 or P2A2	46	53
B85	**Molding Exterior, Bright** — w/PEGS P2A3 or P2A4	NC	NC
	K2500 w/C6P	65	76
	K2500 w/o C6P or C2500	92	107
—	**Paints, Exterior**		
ZY1	solid	NC	NC
ZY2	conventional two-tone	114	132
ZY4	deluxe two-tone	209	243
—	**Radio Equipment**		
UM7	radio - w/PEGS P2A2 or P2A3	NC	NC
	w/PEG P2A1	146	170
	incls elect tuned AM/FM stereo radio w/seek & scan & digital clock		
UM6	radio - w/PEG P2A4	NC	NC
	w/PEGS P2A2 or P2A3	105	122
	w/PEG P2A1	251	292
	incls elect tuned AM/FM stereo radio w/seek & scan, stereo cass tape & digital clock		
UX1	radio - w/PEG P2A4	129	150
	w/PEGS P2A2 or P2A3	234	272
	w/PEG P2A1	380	442
	incls elect tuned AM stereo/FM stereo radio w/seek & scan, stereo cass tape w/search & repeat, graphic equalizer & digital clock		
UL5	radio delete	(101)	(117)
AG9	**Seat, Power Driver's Seat**	206	240
YG4	**Seat Delete, Rear**	(340)	(395)
—	**Seat Trim**		
V1	vinyl bench	NC	NC
C1	cloth bench	NC	NC
V3	vinyl reclining split bench - w/C-K20953	NC	NC
	w/C-K20903	150	174
C3	cloth reclining split bench - w/C-K20953	NC	NC
	w/C-K20903	150	174
L1	custom cloth bench	NC	NC
L3	custom cloth reclining split bench - w/C-K20953	NC	NC
	w/C-K20903	150	174
L6	custom cloth reclining high back bucket		
	w/C-K20953	250	291
	w/C-K20903	421	490
NZZ	**Skid Plate** — off road	82	95
VYU	**Snow Plow Prep Pkg**	101	118
F60	**Springs, Front** — HD - w/o VYU	54	63
	w/VYU	NC	NC
U16	**Tachometer**	51	59
—	**Tires**		
	All Seasons SBR		
	LT225/75R16D BW		
XHP	front	NC	NC
YHP	rear	NC	NC
ZHP	spare	249	289
	LT245/75R16C BW		
XBK	front	NC	NC

CODE	DESCRIPTION	DEALER	LIST
YBK	rear	NC	NC
ZBK	spare	258	301
	LT245/75R16E BW		
XHH	front - w/o C6P	77	92
	w/C6P	NC	NC
YHH	rear - w/o C6P	77	92
	w/C6P	NC	NC
ZHH	spare	287	335
	On-Off Road SBR		
	LT225/75R16D BW		
XHR	front	19	22
YHR	rear	19	22
ZHR	spare	258	300
	LT245/75R16C BW		
XBN	front	19	23
YBN	rear	19	23
ZBN	spare	267	312
	L245/75R16C white outlined letter		
XBX	front	62	73
YBX	rear	62	73
ZBX	spare	289	337
	LT245/75R16E BW		
XGK	front - w/o C6P	96	114
	w/C6P	19	22
YGK	rear - w/o C6P	96	114
	w/C6P	19	22
ZGK	spare	297	346
V76	**Tow Hooks**	33	38
Z82	**Trailering Special** — HD		
	w/diesel or L19 or GT5 or HC4	181	210
	w/MX0	351	408
	w/MT8	297	345
—	**Transmissions**		
MM5	5-spd manual w/overdrive	NC	NC
MT8	5-spd manual w/deep low & overdrive, HD - w/C6P	NC	NC
	w/o C6P	84	98
MX0	4-spd automatic w/overdrive	765	890
—	**Wheel Trim**		
P01	wheel covers	36	42
P06	rally wheel trim - w/PEGS P2A3 or P2A4	NC	NC
	w/PEGS P2A1 or P2A2	52	60
—	**Windows**		
A20	swing-out rear quarter - w/PEGS P2A3 or P2A4 or AJ1	NC	NC
	w/PEGS P2A1, P2A2 w/o AJ1	37	43
A28	sliding rear	97	113

CHEVROLET

CODE	DESCRIPTION	DEALER	LIST

CHEVROLET C-K 3500 PICKUP

5.7 LITER (350 CID) EFI 8 CYL

C3500 SERIES 2WD

CC30903 E63 Fleetside (8 ft.) 131.5" WB		14739	16848
CC30953 E63 Fleetside - Ext (8 ft.) 155.5" WB		17581	20092

K3500 SERIES 4WD

CK30903 E63 Fleetside (8 ft.) 131.5" WB		17023	19459
CK30953 E63 Fleetside - Ext (8 ft.) 155.5" WB		19504	22290
Destination Charge:		600	600

Standard Equipment

C/K 3500 REGULAR CAB PICKUP - BASE CHEYENNE: 5.7 liter V-8, 5-speed manual transmission with deep low gear and overdrive, 600-amp battery, power front disc/rear drum brakes with rear-wheel anti-lock system, chrome front bumper and argent painted grille, single rectangular halogen headlamps, RH and LH below-eyeline black painted mirrors, heavy-duty radiator, LT245/75R16-E all-season radial tires, silver painted steel wheels, side door guard beams, full gauges and instrumentation, tinted Solar Ray glass all windows, deluxe heater with windshield and side window defoggers, electronic AM radio with fixed-mast antenna, Scotchgarded carpeting, cloth trim and door panels, three-passenger all-vinyl trim front bench seat with head restraints and folding backrest.

SILVERADO (in addition to or instead of BASE CHEYENNE equipment): Bumpers with black rub strip and bright trim, deluxe front appearance grille, dual composite halogen headlamps, black bodyside moldings with bright trim, Rally wheel trim, swing-out rear quarter windows, color-keyed carpeting, electronic AM/FM radio with seek-scan and digital clock, three-passenger seats with choice of custom vinyl or custom cloth front bench with head restraint and folding backrest.

C/K 3500 EXTENDED CAB PICKUP - BASE CHEYENNE: 5.7 liter V-8, 5-speed manual transmission with deep low gear and overdrive, 600-amp battery, power front disc/rear drum brakes with rear-wheel anti-lock system, chrome front bumper and argent painted grille, single rectangular halogen headlamps, RH and LH below-eyeline black painted mirrors, heavy-duty radiator, LT245/75R16-E all-season radial tires, silver painted steel wheels, side door guard beams, full gauges and instrumentation, tinted Solar Ray glass all windows, deluxe heater with windshield and side window defoggers, electronic AM radio with fixed-mast antenna, Scotchgarded carpeting, cloth trim and door panels, three-passenger all-vinyl trim front 60/40 reclining split bench seat with driver and passenger easy entry.

SILVERADO (in addition to or instead of BASE CHEYENNE equipment): Bumpers with black rub strip and bright trim, deluxe front appearance grille, dual composite halogen headlamps, black bodyside moldings with bright trim, Rally wheel trim, swing-out rear quarter windows, color-keyed carpeting, electronic AM/FM radio with seek-scan and digital clock, three-passenger seats with choice of custom vinyl or custom cloth front bench with head restraint and folding backrest.

Accessories

—	**Cheyenne Preferred Equip Group**		
P3A1		NC	NC
P3A2		495	575
P3A3	**Silverado Preferred Equip Group**		
	Regular cab	1300	1512
	Extended cab	1128	1312
P3A4	**Silverado Preferred Equip Group**		
	Regular cab	1835	2134
	Extended cab	1620	1884
C60	**Air Conditioning** — w/PEGS P3A2, P3A3 or P3A4	NC	NC

CHEVROLET

CODE	DESCRIPTION	DEALER	LIST
	w/PEG P3A1	692	805
V22	**Appearance Package** — w/PEGS P3A3 or P3A4	NC	NC
	w/PEGS P3A1 or P3A2	164	191
—	**Axles, Rear**		
GT4	3.73 ratio	NC	NC
GT5	4.10 ratio	NC	NC
HC4	4.56 ratio	NC	NC
G80	locking differential	217	252
TP2	**Battery** — auxiliary - w/Z81	NC	NC
	w/o Z81	115	134
BZY	**Bedliner**	194	225
E63	**Body Code - Fleetside**	NC	NC
—	**Bumper Equip**		
VB3	chromed, rear step w/rub strip	197	229
V43	painted, rear step	112	130
V27	guards, front bumper, black		
	w/diesel & PEGS P3A3 or P3A4	NC	NC
	w/o diesel w/PEGS P3A3 or P3A4	28	32
Z81	**Camper Special Chassis Equip**		
	w/PEGS P3A3 or P3A4 & diesel	46	54
	w/PEGS P3A3 or P3A4 w/o diesel	162	188
	w/PEGS P3A1 or P3A2 & diesel	85	99
	w/PEGS P3A1 or P3A2 w/o diesel	200	233
P13	**Carrier, Spare Wheel & Tire** — side mounted	NC	NC
V10	**Cold-Climate Pkg**	28	33
—	**Convenience Group**		
ZQ2	power door locks & power windows - w/PEG P3A4	NC	NC
	w/PEGS P3A1, P3A2 or P3A3	316	367
ZQ3	tilt-wheel & speed control — w/PEG P3A4	NC	NC
	w/PEGS P3A1, P3A2 or P3A3	329	383
C49	**Defogger - Rear Window**	132	154
FE9	**Federal Emissions**	NC	NC
NG1	**New York Emissions**	NC	NC
YF5	**California Emissions**	86	100
—	**Engines**		
	gasoline		
L05	5.7 liter (350 cu. in.) EFI V8	NC	NC
L19	7.4 liter (454 cu. in.) EFI V8	404	470
	diesel		
L65	6.5 liter (400 cu. in.) turbo diesel	2430	2825
KL5	alternative fuel	108	125
BG9	**Floor Covering, Full-Rubber** — C-K3**03	(17)	(20)
	C-K3**53	(31)	(36)
AJ1	**Glass, Deep Tinted Solar-Ray**		
	w/PEGS P3A3 or P3A4 & A28 or C49	62	72
	w/PEGS P3A3 or P3A4 w/o A28 or C49	92	107
	w/PEGS P3A1 or P3A2 & A28 or C49	99	115
	w/PEGS P3A1 or P3A2 w/o A28 or C49	129	150
—	**Lamps**		
C95	dome & reading - w/TR9	NC	NC
	w/o TR9	28	33
U01	roof marker - w/R04	45	52

CHEVROLET

CODE	DESCRIPTION	DEALER	LIST
	w/R05	NC	NC
VK3	**License Plate Bracket, Front**	NC	NC
TR9	**Lighting, Auxiliary** — w/PEGS P3A3 or P3A4	NC	NC
	w/PEGS P3A1 or P3A2	81	94
—	**Mirrors, Exterior**		
D45	below eyeline, stainless steel		
	w/PEGS P3A3 or P3A4	NC	NC
	w/PEGS P3A1 or P3A2	39	45
DF2	camper type, stainless steel - w/Z81	NC	NC
	w/PEGS P3A3 or P3A4	7	8
	w/PEGS P3A1 or P3A2	46	53
B85	**Moldings** — exterior, bright		
	w/PEGS P3A3 or P3A4	NC	NC
	w/K30903	65	76
	w/C309*3	92	107
—	**Paints, Exterior**		
ZY1	solid	NC	NC
ZY2	conventional two-tone	114	132
ZY4	deluxe two-tone	209	243
—	**Radio Equip**		
UM7	radio - w/PEGS P3A2 or P3A3	NC	NC
	w/PEG P3A1	146	170
	incls elect tuned AM/FM stereo radio w/seek & scan & digital clock		
UM6	radio - w/PEG P3A4	NC	NC
	w/PEGS P3A2 or P3A3	105	122
	w/PEG P3A1	251	292
	incls elect tuned AM/FM stereo radio w/seek & scan, stereo cass tape & digital clock		
UX1	radio - w/PEG P3A4	129	150
	w/PEGS P3A2 or P3A3	234	272
	w/PEG P3A1	380	442
	incls elect tuned AM stereo/FM stereo radio w/seek & scan, stereo cass tape w/search & repeat, graphic equalizer & digital clock		
UL5	radio delete	(101)	(117)
AG9	**Seat, Power Driver's Seat**	206	240
YG4	**Seat Delete, Rear**	(340)	(395)
—	**Seat Trim**		
V1	vinyl bench	NC	NC
C1	cloth bench	NC	NC
V3	vinyl reclining split bench w/C-K30953	NC	NC
	w/C-K30903	150	174
C3	cloth reclining split bench w/C-K30953	NC	NC
	w/C-K30903	150	174
L1	custom cloth bench	NC	NC
L3	custom cloth reclining split bench w/C-K30953	NC	NC
	w/C-K30903	150	174
L6	custom cloth reclining high back bucket		
	w/C-K30953	250	291
	w/C-K30903	421	490
NZZ	**Skid Plate** — off road	82	95
VYU	**Snow Plow Prep Pkg**	101	118
F60	**Springs, Front** — HD w/VYU	NC	NC

CODE	DESCRIPTION	DEALER	LIST
	w/o VYU	54	63
U16	**Tachometer**	51	59
—	**Tires**		
—	**All Seasons SBR**		
	LT225/75R16C BW		
XHE	front - w/C30903	(88)	(104)
	w/C30953	NC	NC
	LT225/75R16D BW		
XHP	front - w/C-K30903	(58)	(70)
	w/C-K30953	NC	NC
YHP	rear - w/C-K30903	370	428
	w/C-K30953	NC	NC
ZHP	spare	258	300
	LT245/75R16E BW		
XHH	front	NC	NC
YHH	rear	NC	NC
ZHH	spare	287	335
—	**On-Off Road SBR**		
	LT225/75R16D BW		
XHR	front - w/K30903	(40)	(48)
	w/K30953	18	22
YHR	rear - w/C-K30903	408	472
	w/C-K30953	38	44
ZHR	spare	267	311
	LT245/75R16E BW		
XGK	front - w/K30903	19	22
YGK	rear - w/C-K30903	19	22
ZGK	spare - w/C-K30903	297	346
V76	**Tow Hooks**	33	38
Z82	**Trailering Special** — HD	181	210
—	**Transmissions**		
MT8	5-spd manual w/deep low & overdrive, HD	NC	NC
MX0	4-spd automatic w/overdrive	765	890
—	**Wheel Trim**		
P01	wheel covers	36	42
P06	rally wheel trim - w/PEGS P3A3 or P3A4	NC	NC
	w/PEGS P3A1 or P3A2	52	60
—	**Wheels, Rear**		
R04	single	NC	NC
R05	dual	821	955
—	**Windows**		
A28	sliding rear	97	113
A20	swing-out quarter - w/PEGS P3A3 or P3A4 or AJ1	NC	NC
	w/PEGS P3A1 or P3A2 w/o AJ1	37	43

CODE	DESCRIPTION	DEALER	LIST

CHEVROLET S/T 10 PICKUP

2.2 LITER MFI 4 CYL
S10 SERIES 2WD
BASE MODEL

	Dealer	List
CS10603 E63 Fleetside (6 ft.) 108.3" WB	9124	9655
CS10803 E63 Fleetside (7 1/3 ft.) 117.9" WB	9407	9955

LS MODEL

	Dealer	List
CS10603 E63 Fleetside (6 ft.) 108.3" WB	9765	10790
CS10803 E63 Fleetside (7 1/3 ft.) 117.9" WB	10286	11366
CS10653 E63 Fleetside (6 ft.) 122.9" WB	10670	11790

4.3 LITER EFI 6 CYL
T10 SERIES 4WD
BASE MODEL

	Dealer	List
CT10603 E63 Fleetside (6 ft.) 108.3" WB	13376	14155
CT10803 E63 Fleetside (7 1/3 ft.) 117.9" WB	13660	14455

LS MODEL

	Dealer	List
CT10603 E63 Fleetside (6 ft.) 108.3" WB	13837	15290
CT10803 E63 Fleetside (7 1/3 ft.) 117.9" WB	14359	15866
CT10653 E63 Fleetside (6 ft.) 122.9" WB	14761	16310
Destination Charge:	470	470

Standard Equipment

S10 REGULAR CAB PICKUP - BASE: 5-speed manual transmission, 100-amp alternator, air dam, 525-amp battery, power front disc/rear drum brakes with rear-wheel anti-lock braking on 4-cylinder engine and 4-wheel anti-lock braking system on V-6, power steering, front and rear step bumpers, tinted Solar Ray glass windows, halogen headlamps, full-sized spare (mounted under bed), center high-mounted stop light, coil spring front suspension 2WD and torsion bar on 4WD models, semi-floating rear axle and 2-stage multi-leaf springs, P205/75R15 all-season radials, 15" x 7" steel argent painted wheels, deluxe heater with windshield and side window defoggers, full instrumentation and gauges, ETR AM radio with digital clock and two speakers, Scotchgarded for cloth trim, color-keyed seat and shoulder belts, deluxe steering wheel, door-operated interior lamps, dark gray vinyl floor covering.

LS (in addition to or instead of BASE equipment): Chrome grille with halogen headlamps, door trim panels with LH and RH molded pockets, molded plastic with soft cloth upper insert, full-floor color-keyed carpeting, day/night mirror with dual reading lamps, ETR AM/FM stereo with digital clock, Scotchgarded cloth trim, door panels and carpeting, deluxe 2-spoke black steering wheel, color-keyed padded sunshades with slider extensions.

S10 EXTENDED CAB PICKUP - BASE (standard equipment same as uplevel LS series on Regular Cab S10): 5-speed manual trans/, 100-amp alternator, air dam, 525-amp battery, power front disc/rear drum brakes with rear-wheel anti-lock braking on 4-cylinder engine and 4-wheel anti-lock braking system on V-6, power steering, front/rear step bumpers, tinted Solar Ray glass windows, full-sized spare, center high-mounted stop light, coil spring front suspension 2WD and torsion bar on 4WD models, P205/75R15 all-season radials, 15" x 7" steel argent painted wheels, deluxe heater with windshield and side window defoggers, full instrumentation and gauges, chrome grille with halogen headlamps, door trim panels with LH and RH molded pockets, and cloth upper insert, full-floor color-keyed carpeting, day/night mirror with dual reading lamps, ETR AM/FM stereo with digital clock, Scotchgarded cloth trim, door panels and carpeting, deluxe 2-spoke black steering wheel, color-keyed padded sunshades with slider extensions.

Accessories

CODE	DESCRIPTION	DEALER	LIST
	Regular Cab		
SPA1	**Preferred Equip Group 1**	(129)	(150)
AAA2	**Preferred Equip Group 2**	NC	NC
AAA6	**Preferred Equip Group 6**		
	S10603 - S10803 w/LB4 or L35 eng	202	235
	T10603 - T10803 w/MM5 trans	202	235
	S10603 - S10803 w/LN2 eng	202	235
	T10603 - T10803 w/MX0 trans	202	235
	Extended Cab		
BAA1	**Preferred Equip Group 1**		
BAA6	**Preferred Equip Group 6**		
	S10653 w/LB4 or L35 eng	202	235
	T10653 w/MM5 trans	202	235
	S10653 w/LN2 eng	202	235
	T10653 w/MX0 trans	202	235
C60	**Air Conditioning**	671	780
ANL	**Air Dam w/Fog Lamps (Incl w/B4U)**	99	115
—	**Axles, Rear**		
GU2	2.73 ratio	NC	NC
GU4	3.08 ratio	NC	NC
GU6	3.42 ratio	NC	NC
GT4	3.73 ratio	NC	NC
GT5	4.10 ratio	NC	NC
G80	locking differential (incl w/B4U)	217	252
UA1	**Battery** — HD w/o V10 cold climate	48	56
	w/V10 cold climate	NC	NC
VF6	**Bumper Equip** — rear step w/B4U SS pkg or SPA1	47	55
	w/o B4U SS pkg	NC	NC
—	**Chassis Pkg**		
ZR2	wide stance, sport performance	1449	1685
Z85	increased capacity		
	CS10653/CS10803/CT10653	NC	NC
	CS10603	55	64
	CT10*03	187	217

CODE	DESCRIPTION	DEALER	LIST
ZM6	off-road (T10 only)		
	CT10603	414	481
	CT10803	359	417
	CT10653	282	328
Z83	solid smooth ride	NC	NC
ZQ8	sport (S10*03 only)		
	CS10603	272	316
	CS10803	217	252
V10	**Cold Climate Pkg**	94	109
V08	**Cooling System** — HD w/Z82	NC	NC
	w/MX0	170	198
	w/MM5	116	135
—	**Convenience Group**		
ZQ6	power door locks, windows & ext elec remote mirrors	409	475
ZQ3	tilt steering & speed control	329	383
—	**Decor**		
YC3	LS	NC	NC
YC5	LS w/exterior appearance pkg		
	C*10803 w/AAA2/AAA6	NC	NC
	C*106*3 w/AAA2/BAA1/AAA6/BAA6	237	276
FE9	**Federal Emissions**	NC	NC
NG1	**New York Emissions**	NA	NA
YF5	**California Emissions**	NA	NA
—	**Engines**		
LN2	2.2 liter MFI L4	NC	NC
LB4	4.3 liter EFI V6		
	CS10**3	731	850
	CT10**3	NC	NC
L35	4.3 liter CPI V6		
	CS10**3	1212	1409
	CT10**3	481	559
—	**Floor Covering**		
BG9	full floor, vinyl, charcoal	NC	NC
B30	carpet, full floor (incl w/YC3 or YC5)	47	55
B32	auxiliary front floor mats	17	20
VK3	**License Plate Bracket**	NC	NC
D44	**Mirrors** — exterior, below eye-line type, black (incl w/YC3 or YC5)	45	52
—	**Paints, Exterior**		
ZY1	solid	NC	NC
ZY3	special two-tone	195	227
ZY7	sport two-tone	148	172
—	**Radio Equip**		
UT5	radio - w/SPA1	82	95
	incls AM radio w/clock		
UM7	radio - w/AAA2/BAA1	NC	NC
	w/SPA1	194	226
	incls elect tuned AM/FM stereo radio w/seek & scan & digital clock		
UM6	radio - w/AAA6/BAA6	NC	NC
	w/AAA2/BAA1	105	122
	w/SPA1	299	348
	incls elect tuned AM/FM stereo radio w/seek & scan, stereo cass tape, & digital clock		

CHEVROLET

CODE	DESCRIPTION	DEALER	LIST
UX1	radio - w/AAA6/BAA6	129	150
	w/AAA2/BAA1	234	272
	w/SPA1	428	498
	incls elect tuned AM stereo/FM stereo radio w/seek & scan, stereo cass tape w/search & repeat, digital clock & graphic equalizer		
U1C	radio - w/AAA6/BAA6	244	284
	w/AAA2/BAA1	349	406
	w/SPA1	544	632
	incls elect tuned AM/FM stereo radio w/seek-scan, compact disc player & digital clock		
UL5	radio delete - w/SPA1	NC	NC
—	**Seat Trim**		
V1	custom vinyl bench	NC	NC
C1	custom cloth bench	NC	NC
L3	deluxe cloth 60/40 reclining split bench........................	NC	NC
L6	deluxe cloth reclining high back buckets		
	C*10*03...	156	181
	C*10653..	134	156
ZM5	**Shield Pkg** — incl w/ZR2	108	126
B4U	**SS Pkg** — CS10603 only	541	629
NP5	**Steering Wheel, Leather-Wrapped** — incl w/B4U	46	54
—	**Striping**		
D88	sport..	59	69
D96	upper body side (incl w/ZY3)	47	55
U16	**Tachometer** — incl w/L35	51	59
—	**Tires**		
	All Seasons SBR		
QCE	P205/75R15 BW	NC	NC
QCF	P205/75R15 white lettered	104	121
QPP	P215/65R15 white lettered (incl in ZQ8).......................	NC	NC
QFL	P235/75R15 BW (incl in Z85).....................................	NC	NC
	On-Off Road SBR		
QJL	P205/75R15 white lettered	146	170
QEB	P235/75R15 white lettered		
	w/CT10**3 & ZM6 chassis pkg	NC	NC
	w/CT10**3 & Z85 chassis pkg	157	182
QJJ	31x10.5R15 BW (incl in ZR2)	NC	NC
Z82	**Trailering Special** — HD -w/LB4 & MX0	351	408
	w/LB4 & MM5..	297	345
	w/L35 eng	181	210
NP1	**Transfer Case** — electronic shift	106	123
—	**Transmissions**		
MX0	4-spd automatic w/overdrive	797	927
MM5	5-spd manual w/overdrive	NC	NC
—	**Wheels**		
N60	aluminum, argent -w/AAA6/BAA6 & LN2 eng or w/B4U	NC	NC
	w/YC3/YC5	213	248
N90	aluminum, cast -w/AAA6/BAA6 & MX0...........................	NC	NC
	w/YC3/YC5	241	280
A28	**Windows** — sliding rear -w/SPA1/AAA2/BAA1	97	113
	w/AAA6/BAA6	NC	NC
U89	**Wiring Harness, 5-Lead**	35	41

CODE	DESCRIPTION	DEALER	LIST

DODGE DAKOTA

DAKOTA 2WD

AN1L61	WS Regular Cab 112" WB	9160	9560
AN1L62	WS Regular Cab 124" WB	10563	11085
AN1L61	Base Regular Cab 112" WB	10425	11432
AN1L62	Base Regular Cab 124" WB	11173	12282
AN1L61	Sport Regular Cab 112" WB	10033	10742
AN1L31	Base Club Cab 131" WB	12948	14299
AN1L31	Sport Club Cab 131" WB	12722	14042

DAKOTA 4WD

AN5L61	WS Regular Cab 112" WB	13932	14704
AN5L62	WS Regular Cab 124" WB	14093	14878
AN5L61	Base Regular Cab 112" WB	14307	15798
AN5L62	Base Regular Cab 124" WB	14461	15973
AN5L61	Sport Regular Cab 112" WB	14157	15280
AN5L31	Base Club Cab 131" WB	16006	17728
AN5L31	Sport club Cab 131" WB	15779	17471
Destination Charge:		495	495

Standard Equipment

DAKOTA REGULAR CAB PICKUP - BASE: 5-speed manual transmission, manual bench seat, manual rack and pinion steering, power front disc/rear drum brakes, center high-mounted stop light, driver's air bag and knee bolster protection supplemental restraint system, ETR AM/FM stereo with seek, front door window demisters, tinted glass all windows, stainless steel exhaust system, black front bumper with integral air dam, single rectangular headlamps.

SPORT (in addition to or instead of BASE equipment): Black rear step bumper, dimensional graphics, painted body color grille, ETR AM/FM stereo with cassette, "Naples" cloth and vinyl seat trim, 60/40 split highback front bench seat, cast aluminum wheels.

SPECIAL SLT (in addition to or instead of SPORT equipment): Bright rear step bumper, bright grille, lower bodyside protective moldings, tape stripes, cab back carpet, 5" x 7" outside dual remote mirrors, "Prism" cloth and vinyl trim, full-face chrome styled steel wheels.

CODE	DESCRIPTION	DEALER	LIST

DAKOTA CLUB CAB PICKUP - BASE: 3.9 Liter V-6, 5-speed manual trans, manual bench seat, man rack and pinion steering, power front disc/rear drum brakes, center high-mounted stop light, driver's air bag and knee bolster protection, ETR AM/FM stereo with seek, front door window demisters, tinted glass all windows, stainless steel exhaust system, black front bumper w/integral air dam, seat track covers, 60/40 split highback bench seats, pass-side easy entry/exit system, rear quarter flip-out windows.

SPORT (in addition to or instead of BASE equipment): Black rear step bumper, dimensional graphics, painted body color grille, ETR AM/FM stereo with cassette, "Prism" cloth and vinyl seat trim, rear seat back and corner bolsters, split 60/40 highback bench with center arm rest, cast aluminum wheels.

SUPER SLT (in addition to or instead of SPORT equipment): Dual outside remote 5" x 7" mirrors, silencer hood pad, speed control with steering wheel switches, tilt steering column.

Accessories

—	**Quick Order Pkgs - Base Regular Cab 2WD**		
23D	**SLT Pkg** — Base Regular Cab 2WD	718	845
	w/EHC eng, add	451	531
24D	w/EHC eng & DGB trans, add	1214	1428
	incls power steering, SLT decor group, AM/FM ETR stereo radio w/cassette & 4 speakers, bright rear step bumper, sliding rear window, floor carpeting, tachometer, cloth/vinyl upholstery, 22 gal fuel tank, light group, intermittent wipers, styled steel chrome wheels [reqs 3.9L eng]		
23E	**Special SLT Pkg** — Base Regular Cab 2WD 112" WB	1199	1411
	w/EHC eng, add	451	531
24E	w/EHC eng & DGB trans, add	1214	1428
25E	w/ELF eng, add	950	1118
26E	w/ELF eng & DGB trans, add	1713	2015
	incls air conditioning, SLT quick order pkg [reqs 3.9L V6 eng or 5.2L V8 eng]		
23E	**Special SLT Pkg** — Base Regular Cab 2WD 124" WB	1199	1411
24E	w/DGB trans, add	762	897
25E	w/ELF eng, add	499	587
26E	w/ELF eng & DGB trans, add	1261	1484
	incls air conditioning, SLT quick order pkg		
—	**Quick Order Pkgs - Base Regular Cab 4WD**		
23D	**SLT Pkg** — Base Regular Cab 4WD 112" WB	694	817
24D	w/DGB trans, add	762	897
	incls cloth/vinyl upholstery, sliding rear window, bright rear step bumper, floor carpeting, intermittent wipers, SLT decor group, tachometer, 22 gal fuel tank, styled steel chrome wheels, P235/75R15XL SBR all-season BW tires (5), AM/FM ETR stereo radio w/cassette & 4 speakers		
23E	**Special SLT Pkg** — Base Regular Cab 4WD 112" WB	1117	1314
24E	w/DGB trans, add	762	897
25E	w/ELF eng, add	499	587
26E	w/ELF eng & DGB trans, add	1261	1484
	incls air conditioning, SLT quick order pkg		
23D	**SLT Pkg** — Base Regular Cab 4WD 124" WB	643	756
24D	w/DGB trans, add	762	897
	incls 22 gal fuel tank, light group, bright rear step bumper, floor carpeting, cloth/vinyl upholstery, intermittent wipers, SLT decor group, sliding rear window, tachometer, styled steel chrome wheels, P235/75R15XL SBR all-season BW tires (5), AM/FM ETR stereo radio w/cassette & 4 speakers		

DODGE

CODE	DESCRIPTION	DEALER	LIST
23E	**Special SLT Pkg** — Base Regular Cab 4WD 124" WB	1065	1253
24E	w/DGB trans, add...	762	897
25E	w/ELF eng, add..	499	587
26E	w/ELF eng & DGB trans, add...	1261	1484
	incls air conditioning, SLT quick order pkg		
—	**Quick Order Pkgs - Base Club Cab**		
23F	**Super SLT Pkg** — Base Club Cab 2WD...................................	779	917
24F	w/DGB trans, add...	762	897
25F	w/ELF eng, add..	499	587
26F	w/ELF eng & DGB trans, add...	1261	1484
	incls SLT decor group, styled steel chrome wheels, cruise control, air conditioning, sliding rear window, floor carpeting, premium cloth upholstery, power steering, P215/75R15 OWL tires (5), light group, tachometer, bright rear step bumper, intermittent wipers, 22 gal fuel tank, tilt steering column, bodyside & wheel flare moldings, premium door trim panels, 60/40 split flip-type rear bench seat, AM/FM ETR stereo radio w/cassette & 4 speakers		
23F	**Super SLT Pkg** — Base Club Cab 4WD...................................	678	798
24F	w/DGB trans, add...	762	897
25F	w/ELF eng, add..	499	587
26F	w/ELF eng & DGB trans, add...	1261	1484
	>incls 22 gal fuel tank, premium cloth upholstery, air cond, cruise control, light group, intermittent wipers, SLT decor group, styled steel chrome wheels, AM/FM stereo radio w/cassette & 4 speakers, premium door trim panels, 60/40 split flip-type rear bench seat, power steering, tilt-steering column, bright rear step bumper, floor carpeting, sliding rear window, P235/75R15XL OWL tires (5), bodyside & wheel flare moldings		
—	**Groups**		
AJK	**Deluxe Convenience Group** — Sport, Base w/SLT or special SLT pkg	300	353
	incls spt steering wheel, tilt steering col, cruise control, intermittent wipers		
AED	**Bright Group** — Sport	212	249
	incls bright rear step bumper, bright front bumper w/spt air dam, fog lights		
ADH	**Heavy Duty Electrical Group**...	102	120
	incls 750 amp battery, 120 amp HD alternator		
ADP	**Heavy Duty Suspension Group**	35	41
	incls HD front & rear gas shock absorbers, front stabilizer bar (2WD Regular Cab)		
AHH	**Snow Plow Preparation Group**		
	Regular Cab 4WD 112" WB w/man trans - WS & Base................	643	756
	w/SLT or SLT special pkg	339	399
	Regular Cab 4WD 112" WB w/auto trans - WS & Base...............	696	819
	w/SLT or SLT special pkg	393	462
	Regular Cab 4WD 124" WB w/man trans - WS & Base................	591	695
	w/SLT or SLT special pkg	339	399
	Regular Cab 4WD 124" WB w/auto trans - WS & Base...............	644	758
	w/SLT or SLT special pkg	393	462
	Club Cab 4WD w/man trans - Base	496	583
	w/super SLT pkg...	292	343
	Club Cab 4WD w/auto trans - Base	549	646
	w/super SLT pkg...	345	406
	incls maximum engine cooling, HD electrical pkg, P235/75R15XL SBR BW all-terrain tires (incl'd w/super SLT pkg), auxiliary trans, oil-to-air cooler		

CODE	DESCRIPTION	DEALER	LIST
	w/trans oil temperature warning light (included in models w/auto trans), Z25C 2000# payload pkg (Regular Cab), Z5B 1800# payload pkg (Club Cab)		
AFH	**Overhead Convenience Group**		
	Sport, Base w/quick order pkg...	239	281
	incls automatic dimming day/night rearview mirror, overhead console w/temperature display/compass/storage compartment/map-reading lights		
CCA	**Rear Seat Group** — Base Club Cab	208	245
	incls rear seat, rear seatbelts, rear seatback & corner bolsters, cloth lower backlight molding [reqs carpeting]		
—	**GVWR Payload Pkgs**		
Z1C	1800# - Regular Cab 2WD - WS & Base....................................	164	193
	w/SLT or SLT special pkg	112	132
	incls P205/75R15 SBR all-season BW tires (5) [reqs power steering]		
Z1E	2600# - Regular Cab 2WD - WS & Base....................................	472	555
	w/SLT or SLT special pkg	368	433
	incls LT 215/75R15 SBR all-season BW tires (5) [reqs power steering]		
Z5C	2000# - Regular Cab 4WD 112" WB - WS & Base......................	368	433
	w/SLT or SLT special pkg	108	127
	Regular cab 4WD 124" WB - WS & Base..................................	316	372
	w/SLT or SLT special pkg	108	127
	incls P235/75R15 SBR all-season BW tires (5)		
Z1D	2000# - Club Cab 2WD - Base...	416	489
	w/super SLT pkg..	212	249
	incls P205/75R15 SBR all-season BW tires (5) [reqs power steering]		
Z5B	1800# - Club Cab 4WD - Base	264	311
	w/super SLT pkg..	108	127
	Base incls P235/75R15 SBR all-season BW tires (5)		
AWE	**Off-Road Appearance Group** — Sport..................................	560	659
	incls fog lights, elliptical light bar, bright front bumper w/sport air dam, round off-road lights (2), bright rear step bumper w/sport air dam		
AJL	**Power Overhead Convenience Group**		
	Sport, Base w/quick order pkg...	469	552
	incls overhead convenience group, power convenience group		
ADA	**Light Group**	66	78
	incls ignition switch w/time delay, ashtray, glovebox, instrument panel courtesy, underhood		
AJP	**Power Convenience Group**		
	Sport, Base w/quick order pkg...	315	371
	incls power windows, power door locks		
ADL	**Protection Group** — 4WD	110	129
	incls frt deflector shield, skid plates for transfer case, front axle & fuel tank		
AHC	**Trailer Towing Prep Group**		
	w/man trans w/o AHH		
	WS...	235	276
	Sport Regular Cab..	230	270
	Sport Club Cab...	185	218
	Base w/o quick order pkg	279	328
	Base w/quick order pkg	185	218
	w/auto trans w/o AHH		
	WS...	288	339
	Sport Regular Cab..	283	333
	Sport Club Cab...	239	281

DODGE

DODGE

CODE	DESCRIPTION	DEALER	LIST
	Base w/o quick order pkg	332	391
	Base w/quick order pkg	239	281
	w/AHH		
	WS	84	99
	Base w/o quick order pkg	128	151
	Base w/quick order pkg	35	41
	incls 22 gal fuel tank, tachometer, HD electrical pkg, HD flashers, maximum engine cooling, 5-lead trailer tow wiring harness [NA w/2.5L 4 cyl eng]		
ASP	**SLT Decor Group** — w/quick order pkg - see pkgs		
	incls light group, analog tachometer, aero headlights, right visor vanity mirror, jack cover, bright front bumper w/air dam, bright grille & headlight bezels, cloth sunvisors w/map pockets, intermittent wipers, floor carpeting, carpeted floor mats, dual manual remote mirrors, bodyside & wheel flare moldings, door trim panels w/cloth inserts & lower carpeting, woodtone finish instrument panel applique, deluxe sound insulation,m upper bodyside & tailgate tape stripes, styled steel chrome wheels, premium cloth upholstery (Club Cab), rear seat group (Club Cab), tinted swing-out quarter windows (Club Cab)		
EHC	**Engine** — 3.9L V6 EFI		
	WS & Base Reg Cab 2WD 112" WB	451	531
	[WS reqs power steering, 22 gal fuel tank]		
ELF	**Engine** — 5.2L V8 EFI		
	Sport Reg Cab		
	2WD	950	1118
	4WD	499	587
	WS 2WD 124" WB	499	587
	WS 4WD		
	112" WB	551	648
	124" WB	499	587
	Sport Club Cab	499	587
6C	**Paint** — two-tone center band - w/quick order pkg	147	173
6D	**Paint** — two-tone lower break - w/quick order pkg	143	168
P	**Paint** — extra cost - all ex Sport	65	77
—	**Tires**		
TMD	P215/75R15 SBR all-season BW (5)		
	WS & Base Reg Cab 2WD w/o Z1C GVWR	104	122
	w/Z1C GVWR	52	61
	WS & Base Reg Cab 4WD		
	w/112" WB	104	122
	w/124" WB	52	61
	Club Cab 2WD	104	122
TME	P215/75R15 SBR all-season OWL (5)		
	Reg Cab 2WD w/quick order pkg	100	118
TSC	P235/75R15XL SBR all-season BW (5)		
	WS & Base Reg Cab 4WD		
	w/112" WB	260	306
	w/124" WB	208	245
	Sport Reg Cab	NC	NC
	Club Cab 4WD - Base w/quick order pkg	156	184
	Sport or w/super SLT pkg	NC	NC
TSK	P235/75R15XL SBR all-terrain BW (5)		

138   **EDMUND'S VAN/PICKUP/SPORT UTILITY BUYER'S GUIDE**

CODE	DESCRIPTION	DEALER	LIST
	WS		
	4WD w/112" WB	308	301
	w/124" WB	256	301
	Base Reg Cab 4WD 112" WB		
	w/o quick order pkg	308	362
	w/quick order pkg	48	56
	Base Reg Cab 4WD 124" WB		
	w/o quick order pkg	48	56
	Club Cab 4WD		
	w/o Z5B	204	240
	w/Z5B	48	56
TSM	P235/75R15XL SBR all-terrain OWL (5)		
	Base Reg Cab 4WD w/quick order pkg	152	179
HAA	**Air Conditioning**	677	797
	2WD models req power steering		
NFB	**Fuel Tank** — 22 gal - Base & Sport	44	52
MBD	**Bumper** — painted rear step - WS & Base	113	133
MB8	**Bumper** — rear step delete - Sport	NC	NC
GPP	**Mirrors** — dual bright power - w/quick order pkg	91	107
GTE	**Mirrors** — dual black manual remote	43	51
GTH	**Mirrors** — dual bright manual - WS & Base	76	89
CKE	**Carpeting** — Base Club Cab	49	58
RAL	**Radio** — WS	165	194
	incls AM/FM ETR stereo, 2 speakers & digital clock		
RAS	**Radio** — Base	179	210
	incls AM/FM ETR stereo w/cassette, 4 speakers & digital clock		
RAY	**Radio** — Sport, Base w/quick order pkg	225	300
	incls AM/FM ETR stereo w/cassette & graphic equalizer, 4 Infinity sound speakers, digital clock, seek-scan		
RCE	**Radio** — speakers, Infinity - Sport, Base w/quick order pkg	145	171
RA8	**Radio** — AM/FM radio delete - Base	(104)	(122)
NAE	**California Emissions**	87	102
NBY	**New York Emissions**	87	102
NAF	**High Altitude Emissions**	NC	NC
K38	**Moldings** — lower bodyside & wheel flares delete - Sport	NC	NC
SBA	**Power Steering** — Base 2WD, WS 2WD 112" WB	239	281
	NA w/2.5L 4 cyl eng		
SUA	**Tilt Steering Column** — WS, Base w/o quick order pkg	114	204
	Sport, Base Reg Cab w/quick order pkg	114	134
	incls intermittent wipers		
NHK	**Engine Block Heater**	29	34
DMD	**Axle** — 3.55 ratio - all ex WS 112" WB & Reg Cab 4WD	33	39
DMH	**Axle** — 3.90 ratio	33	39
DSA	**Axle** — sure grip rear	218	257
	reqs 3.55 or 3.90 ratio		
JAY	**Tachometer** — WS & Base	49	58
	NA w/2.5L 4 cyl eng		
JHA	**Intermittent Wipers** — SW & Base	60	70
WME	**Wheel Trim Rings** — brushed - WS & Base	52	61
GFD	**Brakes** — 4 wheel anti lock	425	500
E1	**Seat** — deluxe cloth/vinyl bench		
	WS & Base Reg Cab	45	53

CODE	DESCRIPTION	DEALER	LIST
C2	**Seat** — vinyl bench		
	Base Reg Cab w/SLT or SLT special pkg	NC	NC
J5	**Seat** — cloth/vinyl bucket		
	Sport Reg Cab	322	379
	Club Cab	47	55
	Base w/quick order pkg		
	Reg Cab	260	305
	Club Cab	93	109
NMC	**Cooling** — engine, maximum - w/man trans	48	57
	w/auto trans	102	120
	models w/auto trans include auxiliary trans oil cooler		
DGB	**Transmission** — 4-spd automatic overdrive	762	897
	NA w/2.5L 4 cyl eng		
CKJ	**Mat** — black rubber floor - w/quick order pkg	NC	NC
WJ2	**Wheels** — styled steel chrome - Sport	NC	NC
	NA w/P195 or P205 tires		
WJL	**Wheels** — cast aluminum predator		
	Base w/quick order pkg	NC	NC
	NA w/P195 or P205 tires		

DODGE RAM BR1500 PICKUP

BR1500 2WD PICKUP 6 CYL

BR1L61	WS Regular Cab 119" WB	11485	12534
BR1L61	LT Regular Cab 119" WB	12686	14389
BR1L62	WS Regular Cab 135" WB	11724	12806
BR1L62	LT Regular Cab 135" WB	12917	14661

BR1500 4WD PICKUP 8 CYL

BR6L61	LT Regular Cab 119" WB	15250	17376
BR6L62	LT Regular Cab 135" WB	15522	17696

Destination Charge:	595	595

Standard Equipment

RAM 1500 2WD PICKUP - WORK SPECIAL: Painted front bumper, NV3500 5-speed manual transmission, driver's air bag and knee bolsters with supplemental restraint, side door guard beams, center high-mounted stop light, power steering, power front disc/rear drum brakes with 4-wheel anti-lock braking system, air exhausters, black front bumper air dam and step pad, side window demisters, tinted glass all windows, dual manual-control outside 6" x 9" mirrors, bench seat with folding back, vinyl fusion seat trim.

LT (in addition to or instead of WORK SPECIAL equipment): Painted front grille and bumper, ETR AM/FM stereo with seek, clock and two speakers; conventional spare tire and wheel.

ST (in addition to or instead of LT equipment): Bright front bumper and bright rear step bumper, tailgate protection moldings, single aero halogen headlamps, 40/20/40 split bench seat with dual recliners, driver's manual lumbar control.

LARAMIE SLT (in addition to or instead of ST equipment): Air conditioning, sight shields, black bodyside protection moldings with bright insert, power door locks, dual note horn, overhead console with storage pocket, cloth bolster door trim, time delay interior light and extra glove box and courtesy lights, ETR AM/FM stereo with cassette, seek, Dolby sound, clock and four speakers.

RAM 1500 4WD PICKUP - WORK SPECIAL: Painted front bumper, NV3500 5-speed manual transmission, driver's air bag and knee bolsters with supplemental restraint, side door guard beams, center high-mounted stop light, power steering, power front disc/rear drum brakes with 4-wheel anti-lock braking system, link/coil front suspension, air exhausters, black front bumper air dam and step pad, side window demisters, tinted glass all windows, dual manual-control outside 6" x 9" mirrors, bench seat with folding back, vinyl fusion seat trim, front axle disconnect with shift-on-the-fly.

LT (in addition to or instead of WORK SPECIAL equipment): Painted front grille and bumper, ETR AM/FM stereo with seek, clock and two speakers; conventional spare tire and wheel.

ST (in addition to or instead of LT equipment): Bright front bumper and bright rear step bumper, tailgate protection moldings, single aero halogen headlamps, 40/20/40 split bench seat with dual recliners, driver's manual lumbar control.

LARAMIE SLT (in addition to or instead of ST equipment): Air conditioning, sight shields, black bodyside protection moldings with bright insert, power door locks, dual note horn, overhead console with storage pocket, cloth bolster door trim, time delay interior light and extra glove box and courtesy lights, ETR AM/FM stereo with cassette, seek, Dolby sound, clock and four speakers.

Accessories

CODE	DESCRIPTION	DEALER	LIST
—	**Quick Order Pkgs - 2WD**		
21C	ST Pkg — 2WD	428	504
22C	w/DGB trans, add	762	897
23C	w/ELF eng, add	499	587
24C	w/ELF eng & DGB trans, add	1261	1484
26C	w/EML eng & DGB trans, add	1491	1754
	incls deluxe cloth upholstery, dome & cargo lights, bright front & rear bumpers, wheel dress-up w/bright trim rings & hubs, behind seat storage, floor carpeting, split bench seat, tailgate protection molding		
21G	Laramie SLT Pkg — 2WD	1696	1995
22G	w/DGB trans, add	762	897
23G	w/ELF eng, add	499	587
24G	w/ELF eng & DGB trans, add	1261	1484
26G	w/ELM eng & DGB trans, add	1491	1754
	incls tachometer, leather-wrapped steering wheel, AM/FM ETR stereo radio		

w/cassette & 4 speakers, air cond, light group, deluxe convenience group, floor carpeting, premium decor group, dual front bumper sight shields, bodyside moldings, P245/75R16 SBR all-season BW tires (5), bright front & rear bumpers, power convenience group (incls power door locks & power windows), premium cloth upholstery, tailgate top protection molding, split bench seat, bodyside accent stripe, chrome wheels, behind seat storage

CODE	DESCRIPTION	DEALER	LIST
—	**Quick Order Pkgs - 4WD**		
23C	**ST Pkg** — 4WD	173	204
24C	w/DGB trans, add	762	897
26C	w/EML eng & DGB trans, add	992	1167

incls floor carpeting, behind seat storage, split bench seat, deluxe cloth upholstery, bright front & rear bumpers, dome & cargo lights, wheel dress-up w/bright trim rings & hubs, tailgate top protection molding

CODE	DESCRIPTION	DEALER	LIST
23G	**Laramie SLT Pkg** — 4WD	1704	2005
24G	w/DGB trans, add	762	897
26G	w/EML eng & DGB trans, add	992	1167

incls floor carpeting, chrome wheels, light group, air conditioning, behind seat storage, premium decor group, leather-wrapped steering wheel, tachometer, power convenience group (incls power door locks & power windows), LT245/75R16C SBR all-season BW tires (5), bodyside moldings, deluxe convenience group, split bench seat, dual front bumper sight shields, tailgate tip protection molding, AM/FM ETR stereo radio w/cassette & 4 speakers, premium cloth upholstery, bodyside accent stripe, bright front & rear bumpers

CODE	DESCRIPTION	DEALER	LIST
—	**Groups**		
AHH	**Light Duty Snow Plow Prep Group** — 4WD	NC	NC

incls HD front springs, extra-duty front suspension [reqs HD service group, trailer towing prep group, rear bumper]

CODE	DESCRIPTION	DEALER	LIST
AJK	**Deluxe Convenience Group**	300	353

incls tilt steering column, cruise control

CODE	DESCRIPTION	DEALER	LIST
AWK	**Travel Convenience Group** — WS	196	231

incls dual bright power mirrors, overhead console w/compass, full deluxe headliner, outside temperature display & reading lights, auto dimming day/night rearview mirror [reqs quick order pkg]

CODE	DESCRIPTION	DEALER	LIST
ADA	**Light Group** — all ex WS - w/quick order pkg	139	164
	w/ST pkg	107	126

incls glove box light, auxiliary 12-volt electrical receptacle, passenger assist grip, full deluxe cloth headliner, exterior cargo light, underhood light, ignition key light w/time delay, overhead console w/storage & map reading lights

CODE	DESCRIPTION	DEALER	LIST
ADJ	**Heavy Duty Service Group**		
	2WD w/std 5-spd manual trans	235	277
	2WD w/DGB trans	290	341
	4WD w/std 5-spd manual trans	273	321
	4WD w/DGB trans	327	385

incls HD 750 amp battery, HD 120 amp alternator, maximum eng cooling, auxiliary trans oil cooler (models w/4-spd auto trans), skid plate transfer case (4WD)

CODE	DESCRIPTION	DEALER	LIST
AHC	**Trailer Touring Prep Group** — all ex WS	206	242

incls HD flashers, class IV platform hitch receiver, fifth-wheel take-out provision, 7-lead wiring harness [reqs HD service group, rear bumper; NA w/3.9L V6 eng]

CODE	DESCRIPTION	DEALER	LIST
ASP	**Premium Decor Group** — see pkgs		
	incls split bench seat, full floor carpeting, bodyside tape stripes, front floor mats, black sport leather-wrapped steering wheel, bright front bumper w/step pad, premium cloth upholstery, black bodyside moldings, dual horns, map pockets on doors, black tailgate panel applique, door trim panels w/cloth inserts & carpeted lower, underhood insulation, covered right visor vanity mirror		
NAE	**California Emissions**	87	102
NAF	**High Altitude Emissions**	NC	NC
HAA	**Air Conditioning**	677	797
ELF	**Engine** — 5.2L V8 EFI - LT 2WD	244	287
EML	**Engine** — 5.9L V8 EFI - LT 2WD	473	557
	reqs DGB 4-spd auto trans		
—	**Tires**		
TYF	P245/75R16C SBR all-season BW (5) - 2WD ex WS	111	130
TYG	P245/75R16C SBR all-season OWL (5) - 2WD w/ST pkg	217	255
	w/Laramie SLT pkg	107	126
TYK	LT245/75R16C SBR all-season BW (5) - 4WD	119	140
TYL	LT245/75R16C SBR all-terrain BW (5) - 4WD		
	w/o Laramie SLT pkg	238	280
	w/Laramie SLT pkg	119	140
TYM	LT245/75R16C SBR all-terrain OWL (5) - 4WD		
	w/o Laramie SLT pkg	344	405
	w/Laramie SLT pkg	225	265
TXD	LT265/75R16C SBR all-terrain OWL (5) - 4WD - w/ST pkg	463	545
	w/Laramie SLT pkg	344	405
TBB	**Conventional Spare Tire & Wheel** — WS	136	160
B3	**Seat** — cloth bench - WS	61	72
T9	**Seat** — premium cloth split bench		
	LT w/quick order pkg	222	261
	w/ST pkg	NC	NC
TX	**Seat** — heavy duty vinyl split bench w/quick order pkg	NC	NC
JPS	**Seat** — 6-way power driver - w/Laramie SLT pkg	252	296
	reqs std Laramie SLT premium cloth trim		
BGK	**Anti-Lock Brakes**	425	500
GPP	**Mirrors** — dual bright power 6" x 9" - all ex WS	84	99
GPC	**Mirrors** — dual bright manual 7" x 10" - all ex WS	41	48
DSA	**Sure Grip Axle** — all ex WS	218	257
DM	**Rear Axle** — optional ratio	33	39
NHK	**Engine Block Heater**	29	34
MBD	**Bumper** — painted rear step	113	133
MB8	**Bumper** — bright rear step delete - w/quick order pkg	(199)	(234)
LNC	**Cab Clearance Lights**	44	52
LPE	**Cargo Lights** — WS	32	38
RAL	**Radio** — WS	162	190
	incls AM/FM ETR stereo w/2 speakers		
RAS	**Radio** — LT	179	210
	WS	340	400
	incls AM/FM ETR stereo w/cassette, 4 speakers & digital clock		
RAY	**Radio** — w/Laramie SLT pkg	281	331
	incls AM/FM ETR stereo w/cassette & graphic equalizer, 6 Infinity speakers & digital clock		

DODGE

CODE	DESCRIPTION	DEALER	LIST
RA8	**Radio** — AM/FM delete - LT	(104)	(122)
RCD	**Radio** — 2 additional speakers	43	50
RCE	**Radio** — 4 additional speakers - w/quick order pkg..........	172	202
	reqs RAS radio		
WJA	**Wheels** — chrome (4) - 2WD w/ST pkg	274	322
WDB	**Wheels** — chrome (4) - 4WD w/ST pkg	273	322
JAY	**Tachometer** — w/Laramie SLT pkg	65	76
CKQ	**Floor Carpeting** — delete - w/quick order pkg	NC	NC
K17	**Lower Bodyside Moldings** — w/ST pkg	87	102
GFD	**Window** — sliding rear	114	134
DGB	**Transmission** — 4-spd automatic	762	897
6D	**Paint** — two-tone lower break	112	132
	incls lower bodyside moldings		
6C	**Paint** — two-tone center band		
	w/o Laramie SLT pkg	207	243
	w/Laramie SLT pkg	155	182
	incls upper bodyside & rear tape stripes, secondary mid-section color,		
	lower bodyside moldings, main upper & lower body color		
P	**Paint** — extra cost	65	77
WMC	**Wheel Dress-Up** — LT	51	60
	incls bright trim rings & hubs		

DODGE RAM BR2500 PICKUP

BR2500 2WD PICKUP 8 CYL
BR2L62	LT Light Duty Regular Cab (7500 GVWR)	13984	15916
BR2L62	LT Heavy Duty Regular Cab (8800 GVWR)	14992	17102

BR2500 4WD PICKUP 8 CYL
BR7L62	LT Light Duty Regular Cab (7500 GVWR)	15945	18194
BR7L62	LT Heavy duty Regular Cab (8800 GVWR)	17172	19638

Destination Charge:	595	595

DODGE

Standard Equipment

RAM 2500 2WD PICKUP - LT BASE: Painted front grille and bumper, 5-speed manual, driver's air bag and knee bolsters with supplemental restraint, side door guard beams, center high-mounted stop light, power steering, power front disc/rear drum brakes with 4-wheel anti-lock braking system, air exhausters, black front bumper air dam and step pad, side window demisters, tinted glass all windows, dual manual control outside 6" x 9" mirrors, bench seat with folding back, vinyl fusion seat trim, ETR AM/FM stereo with seek, clock and two speakers; power take-off adapter.

ST (in addition to or instead of LT equipment): Bright front bumper and bright rear step bumper, tailgate protection moldings, single aero halogen headlamps, 40/20/40 split bench seat with dual recliners, driver's manual lumbar control.

LARAMIE SLT (in addition to or instead of ST equipment): Air conditioning, sight shields, black bodyside protection moldings with bright insert, power door locks, dual note horn, overhead console with storage pocket, cloth bolster door trim, time delay interior light and extra glove box and courtesy lights, ETR AM/FM stereo with cassette, seek, Dolby sound, clock and four speakers.

RAM 2500 4WD PICKUP - LT BASE: Painted front grille, bumper, 5-speed man, driver's air bag, knee bolsters w/supplemental restraint, side door guard beams, center high-mtd stop light, pwr steering, pwr front disc/rear drum brakes w/4-wheel anti-lock braking system, link/coil front suspension, air exhausters, black front bumper air dam and step pad, side window demisters, tinted glass all windows, dual man control outside 6" x 9" mirrors, bench seat w/folding back, vinyl fusion seat trim, ETR AM/FM stereo w/seek, clock, two speakers; power take-off adapter, front axle disconnect w/shift-on-the-fly.

ST (in addition to or instead of LT equipment): Bright front bumper and bright rear step bumper, tailgate protection moldings, single aero halogen headlamps, 40/20/40 split bench seat with dual recliners, driver's manual lumbar control.

LARAMIE SLT (in addition to or instead of ST equipment): Air conditioning, sight shields, black bodyside protection moldings with bright insert, power door locks, dual note horn, overhead console with storage pocket, cloth bolster door trim, time delay interior light and extra glove box and courtesy lights, ETR AM/FM stereo with cassette, seek, Dolby sound, clock and four speakers.

Accessories

CODE	DESCRIPTION	DEALER	LIST
—	**Quick Order Pkgs - 2WD Light Duty**		
23C	**ST Pkg** — 2WD Light Duty	343	404
24C	w/DGB transmission, add...	762	897
25C	w/EML engine, add...	230	270
26C	w/EML engine & DGB transmission, add	992	1167
	incls split bench seat, bright front & rear bumpers, behind seat storage, dome & cargo lights, floor carpeting, wheel dress-up w/bright trim rings & hubs, deluxe cloth upholstery, tailgate tip protection molding		
23G	**Laramie SLT Pkg** — 2WD Light Duty...	2265	2665
24G	w/DGB transmission, add...	762	897
25G	w/EML engine, add...	230	270
26G	w/EML engine & DGB transmission, add	992	1167
	incls AM/FM stereo radio w/cass & 4 spkrs, dlx convenience group, behind seat storage, bodyside accent stripe, light grp, premium decor grp, air cond, split bench seat, dual front bumper sight shields, tailgate top protection molding, bodyside moldings, bright front/rear bumpers, tachometer, pwr convenience grp (incls pwr door locks & pwr windows), leather-wrapped steering wheel, prem cloth upholstery, floor carpeting, chrome wheels		
—	**Quick Order Pkgs - 2WD Heavy Duty w/std 5.9L V8 Engine**		
25D	**ST Pkg** — 2WD Heavy Duty	343	404

CODE	DESCRIPTION	DEALER	LIST
26D	w/DGB transmission, add...	762	897
	incls dome & cargo lights, floor carpeting, bright front & rear bumpers, wheel dress-up w/bright trim rings & hubs, split bench seat, tailgate top protection molding, deluxe cloth upholstery, behind seat storage		
25H	**Laramie SLT Pkg** — 2WD Heavy Duty	2265	2665
26H	w/DGB transmission, add...	762	897
	incls behind seat storage, split bench seat, premium decor group, air conditioning, bodyside molding, tachometer, leather-wrapped steering wheel, tailgate top protection molding, deluxe convenience group, bright front & rear bumpers, dual front bumper sight shields, AM/FM ETR stereo radio w/cassette & 4 speakers, bodyside accent stripe, light group, floor carpeting, power convenience group includes power door locks & power windows, chrome wheels, premium cloth upholstery		
—	**Quick Order Pkgs - 2WD Heavy Duty w/EWA V10 Engine**		
—	**ST Pkg** — 2WD Heavy Duty w/std manual transmission.............................	579	681
	w/EWA engine, add...	400	470
	w/EWA engine & DGB transmission, add	1216	1431
	incls heavy duty service group, dome & cargo lights, deluxe cloth upholstery, bright front & rear bumpers, split bench seat, tailgate top protection molding, wheel dress-up w/bright trim rings & hubs, floor carpeting, behind seat storage [reqs 8.0L V10 engine]		
—	**Laramie SLT Pkg** — 2WD Heavy Duty w/std manual transmission	2501	2942
	w/EWA engine, add...	400	470
	w/EWA engine & DGB transmission, add	1216	1431
	incls premium decor group, air conditioning, dual front bumper sight shields, bodyside accent stripe, deluxe convenience group, tachometer, AM/FM ETR stereo radio w/cassette & 4 speakers, light group, bright front & rear bumpers, behind seat storage, floor carpeting, heavy duty service group, power convenience group (incls power door locks & power windows), tailgate top protection molding, bodyside moldings, split bench seat, premium cloth upholstery, leather-wrapped steering wheel, chrome wheels [reqs 8.0L V10 engine]		
—	**Quick Order Pkgs - 2WD Heavy duty w/ETB Diesel Engine**		
—	**ST Pkg** — 2WD Heavy Duty w/std manual transmission.............................	579	681
29D	w/ETB diesel engine, add...	3521	4142
2YD	w/ETB diesel engine & DGB transmission, add	4338	5103
	incls wheel dress-up w/bright trim rings & hubs, bright front & rear bumpers, behind seat storage, split bench seat, heavy duty service group, floor carpeting, dome & cargo lights, deluxe cloth upholstery, tailgate top protection molding [reqs 5.9L 6 cyl diesel Cummins engine]		
	Laramie SLT Pkg — 2WD Heavy Duty w/std manual transmission	2436	2866
29H	w/ETB diesel engine, add...	3521	4142
2YH	w/ETB diesel engine & DGB transmission, add	4338	5103
	incls dlx convenience group, light group, split bench seat, floor carpeting, behind seat storage, leather-wrapped steering wheel, air cond, bodyside moldings, dual front bumper sight shields, tachometer, heavy duty service grp, chrome whls, prem decor grp, tailgate top protection molding, pwr convenience grp (incls pwr door locks & pwr windows), prem cloth upholstery, bright front & rear bumpers, bodyside accent stripe, AM/FM ETR stereo radio w/cass & 4 speakers [reqs 5.9L 6 cyl diesel Cummins eng]		
—	**Quick Order Pkgs - 4WD Light Duty**		
23C	**ST Pkg** — 4WD Light Duty	343	404

CODE	DESCRIPTION	DEALER	LIST
24C	w/DGB transmission, add..	762	897
25C	w/EML engine, add..	230	270
26C	w/EML engine & DGB transmission, add	992	1167
	incls floor carpeting, bright front & rear bumpers, dome & cargo lights, wheel dress-up w/bright trim rings & hubs, split bench seat, behind seat storage, deluxe cloth upholstery, tailgate top protection molding		
23G	**Laramie SLT Pkg** — 4WD Light Duty..	2265	2665
24G	w/DGB transmission, add..	762	897
25G	w/EML engine, add..	230	270
26G	w/EML engine & DGB transmission, add	992	1167
	incls leather-wrapped steering wheel, behind seat storage, split bench seat, air conditioning, bodyside moldings, dual front bumper sight shields, bright front & rear bumpers, deluxe convenience group, tachometer, AM/FM ETR stereo radio w/cassette & 4 speakers, premium decor group, light group, tailgate top protection molding, bodyside accent stripe, chrome wheels, premium cloth upholstery, power convenience group (incls power door locks & power windows), floor carpeting		
—	**Quick Order Pkgs - 4WD Heavy Duty w/Std 5.9L V8 Engine**		
25D	**ST Pkg** — 4WD Heavy Duty	343	404
26D	w/DGB transmission, add..	762	897
	incls split bench seat, wheel dress-up w/bright trim rings & hubs, bright front & rear bumpers, behind seat storage, deluxe cloth upholstery, floor carpeting, dome & cargo lights, tailgate top protection molding		
25H	**Laramie SLT Pkg** — 4WD Heavy Duty..	2265	2665
26H	w/DGB transmission, add..	762	897
	incls split bench seat, tachometer, dual front bumper sight shields, air conditioning, premium decor group, leather-wrapped steering wheel, behind seat storage, light group, AM/FM ETR stereo radio w/cassette & 4 speakers, deluxe convenience group, bodyside moldings, floor carpeting, chrome wheels, premium cloth upholstery, power convenience group (incls power door locks & power windows), bodyside accent stripe, tailgate top protection molding, bright front & rear bumpers		
—	Quick Order Pkgs - 4WD Heavy duty w/EWA V10 Engine		
—	**ST Pkg** — 4WD Heavy Duty w/std manual transmission....................	616	725
	w/EWA engine, add..	400	470
	w/EWA engine & DGB transmission, add	1216	1431
	incls behind seat storage, bright front & rear bumpers, split bench seat, wheel dress-up w/bright trim rings & hubs, heavy duty service group, tailgate top protection molding, dome & cargo lights, deluxe cloth upholstery, floor carpeting [reqs 8.0L V10 engine]		
—	**Laramie SLT Pkg** — 4WD Heavy Duty w/std manual transmission	2538	2986
	w/EWA engine, add..	400	470
	w/EWA engine & DGB transmission, add	1216	1431
	incls light group, split bench seat, bodyside accent stripe, air cond, heavy duty service group, leather-wrapped steering wheel, deluxe convenience group, tachometer, bodyside moldings, prem decor grp, dual front bumper sight shields, bright front/rear bumpers, prem cloth upholstery, behind seat storage, tailgate top protection molding, pwr convenience group (incls pwr door locks & power windows), chrome whls, floor carpeting, AM/FM ETR stereo radio w/cass & 4 spkrs {reqs 8.0L V10 engine}		
—	**Quick Order Pkgs - 4WD Heavy Duty w/ETB Diesel Engine**		
—	**ST Pkg** — 4WD Heavy Duty w/std manual transmission..............................	616	725

DODGE

CODE	DESCRIPTION	DEALER	LIST
29D	w/ETB diesel engine, add...	3521	4142
2YD	w/ETB diesel engine & DGB transmission, add	4338	5103

incls heavy duty service group, floor carpeting, dome & cargo lights, deluxe cloth upholstery, bright front & rear bumpers, behind seat storage, wheel dress-up w/bright trim rings & hubs, split bench seat, tailgate top protection molding [reqs 5.9L 6 cyl diesel Cummins engine]

—	**Laramie SLT Pkg** — 4WD Heavy Duty w/std manual transmission	2474	2910
29H	w/ETB diesel engine, add...	3521	4142
2YH	w/ETB diesel engine & DGB transmission, add	4338	5103

incls split bench seat, air conditioning, premium decor group, leather-wrapped steering wheel, tachometer, floor carpeting, bodyside moldings, behind seat storage, light group, bright front & rear bumpers, deluxe convenience group, bodyside accent stripe, AM/FM ETR stereo radio w/cassette & 4 speakers, premium cloth upholstery, chrome wheels, heavy duty service group, dual front bumper sight shields, tailgate top protection molding, power convenience group (incls power door locks & power windows) [reqs 5.9L 6 cyl diesel Cummins engine]

| AHC | **Trailer Towing Prep Group** .... | 206 | 242 |

incls heavy duty flashers, 7-lead wiring harness, Class IV platform hitch receiver, fifth-wheel take-out provision [reqs heavy duty service group, rear bumper]

| AJK | **Deluxe Convenience Group** .... | 300 | 353 |

incls tilt steering column, cruise control [4WD models require ST pkg]

| ADA | **Light Group** — w/o quick order pkg .... | 139 | 164 |
| | w/ST pkg .... | 107 | 126 |

incls full deluxe cloth headliner, glove box light, passenger assist group, auxiliary 12-volt electrical receptacle, ignition key light w/time delay, underhood light, overhead console w/storage, map lights/reading lights; exterior cargo light

| AWK | **Travel Convenience Group**... | 196 | 231 |

incls dual bright power mirrors, full deluxe headliner, overhead console incls compass/outside temperature display/reading lights, automatic dimming day/night rearview mirror [reqs quick order pkg]

ADJ	**Heavy Duty Service Group**		
	w/std 5-spd manual transmission	235	277
	w/DGB transmission	290	341
	4WD w/std 5-spd manual transmission..	273	321
	w/DGB transmission	327	385

incls heavy duty 750 amp battery (two on diesel models), maximum engine cooling, heavy duty 120 amp alternator, skid plate for transfer case (4WD); [models w/4-spd automatic transmission also include auxiliary transmission oil cooler]

| AHD | **Heavy Duty Snow Plow Prep Group** — 4WD Heavy Duty.......................... | 230 | 270 |

incls heavy duty front springs, extra-duty front suspension, instrument panel warning light for auto trans oil overheat; [reqs rear bumper, conventional spare tire, heavy duty service group, trailer towing prep group]

| — | **Premium Decor Group** — see pkgs | | |

incls dual horns, bright front bumper w/step pad, door map pockets, split bench seat, front floor mats, black bodyside moldings, underhood insulation, full floor carpeting, black spt leather-wrapped steering wheel, bodyside tape stripes, door trim panels w/cloth inserts & carpeted lower, covered right visor vanity mirror, prem cloth upholstery, black tailgate panel applique

CODE	DESCRIPTION	DEALER	LIST
MXB	**Air Dam** — front	10	12
JAY	**Tachometer** — w/ST pkg	65	76
WDC	**Wheels** — chrome (4) - w/ST pkg	274	322
HAA	**Air Conditioning**	677	797
—	**Tires**		
TYD	LT245/75R16E SBR all-season BW (4) - Light Duty	153	180
TYH	LT245/75R16 SBR all-terrain BW (4) - Light Duty	248	292
	Heavy Duty	95	112
TYN	245/75R16E SBR all-season OWL (4) - Light Duty	238	280
	Heavy Duty	85	100
TYP	LT245/75R16E SBR all-terrain OWL (4) - Light Duty	333	392
	Heavy Duty	180	212
TBB	**Conventional Spare Tire & Wheel**		
	w/TWP std LT225/75R16E tire - Light Duty	246	289
	w/TYD LT245/75R16E tire	284	334
	w/TYH LT245/75R16E tire - w/quick order pkg	308	362
	w/TYN LT245/75R16E tire - w/quick order pkg	305	359
	w/TYP LT245/75R16E tire - w/quick order pkg	329	387
6D	**Paint** — two-tone lower break	112	132
	incls lower bodyside moldings		
6C	**Paint** — two-tone center band - w/o SLT Pkg	207	243
	w/SLT pkg	155	182
P	**Paint** — extra cost	65	77
EML	**Engine** — 5.9L V8 EFI - Light Duty	230	270
EWA	**Engine** — 8.0L V10 EFI - Heavy Duty	400	470
	incls maximum engine cooling, heavy duty battery & alternator, auxiliary transmission oil cooler included in 4-spd automatic transmission, skid plated for transfer case (4WD), [reqs heavy duty service group]		
ETB	**Engine** — 5.9L 6 cyl diesel Cummins - Heavy Duty	3521	4142
	incls air manifold-mounted electric heater, maximum engine cooling, extra diesel sound insulation, diesel message center includes warning lights, auxiliary transmission oil cooler (4-spd auto trans), skid plate for transfer case (4WD) [reqs heavy duty service group]		
RAS	**Radio**	179	210
	AM/FM ETR stereo w/cassette, 4 speakers & digital clock		
RAY	**Radio** — w/Laramie SLT pkg	281	331
	AM/FM ETR stereo w/cass & graphic equalizer, 6 Infinity spkrs & dig clock		
RA8	**Radio** — AM/FM delete - LT	(104)	(122)
RCD	**Radio** — 2 additional speakers	43	50
RCE	**Radio** — 4 additional speakers - w/Laramie SLT pkg	172	202
	reqs RAS radio		
NAE	**California Emissions**	87	102
NAF	**High Altitude Emissions**	NC	NC
DSA	**Axle** — sure grip	218	257
DM	**Axle** — rear, optional ratio	33	39
GPP	**Mirrors** — dual bright 6" x 9" power	84	99
GPC	**Mirrors** — dual bright 7" x 10" manual	41	48
DGB	**Transmission** — 4-spd auto	762	897
JPS	**Seats** — 6-way power driver - w/Laramie SLT pkg	252	296
	reqs std Laramie SLT premium cloth trim		
T9	**Seats** — premium cloth split bench		
	LT w/o quick order pkg	222	261

DODGE

CODE	DESCRIPTION	DEALER	LIST
	LT w/ST pkg	NC	NC
TX	**Seats** — heavy duty vinyl split bench w/quick order pkg	NC	NC
GFD	**Window** — sliding rear	114	134
BGK	**Anti-Lock Brakes**	425	500
CKQ	**Carpeting** — floor delete - w/quick order pkg....................................	NC	NC
LNC	**Cab Clearance Light**	44	52
WMC	**Wheel Dress-Up**	51	60
	incls bright trim rings & hubs		
NHK	**Engine Block Heater**	29	34
MBD	**Bumper** — painted rear step	113	133
MB8	**Bumper** — bright rear step delete - w/quick order pkg	(199)	(234)
K17	**Moldings** — lower bodyside w/ST pkg...	87	102

DODGE RAM BR3500 PICKUP

BR3500 PICKUP 8 CYL

BR3L62	2WD LT DRW 135" WB	16109	18417
BR8L62	4WD LT DRW 135" WB	18217	20867
	Destination Charge:..	595	595

Standard Equipment

RAM 3500 2WD PICKUP - LT BASE: Standard dual rear wheels, 5-speed manual, driver's air bag and knee bolsters w/supplemental restraint, side door guard beams, center high-mounted stop light, power steering, power front disc/rear drum brakes with 4-wheel anti-lock braking system, air exhausters, black front bumper air dam and step pad, side window demisters, tinted glass all windows, dual manual-control outside 6" x 9" mirrors, bench seat with folding back, vinyl fusion seat trim, ETR AM/FM stereo with seek, clock and two speakers; power take-off adapter, front axle disconnect with shift-on-the-fly.

ST (in addition to or instead of LT equipment): Bright front bumper and bright rear step bumper, tailgate protection moldings, single aero halogen headlamps, 40/20/40 split bench seat with dual recliners, driver's manual lumbar control.

LARAMIE SLT (in addition to or instead of ST equipment): Air conditioning, sight shields, black bodyside protection moldings with bright insert, power door locks, dual note horn, overhead console with storage pocket, cloth bolster door trim, time delay interior light and extra glove box and courtesy lights, ETR AM/FM stereo with cassette, seek, Dolby sound, clock and four speakers.

RAM 3500 4WD PICKUP - LT BASE: Standard dual rear wheels, 5-speed manual, driver's air bag and knee bolsters with supplemental restraint, side door guard beams, center high-mounted stop light, power steering, power front disc/rear drum brakes with 4-wheel anti-lock braking system, link/coil front suspension, air exhausters, black front bumper air dam and step pad, side window demisters, tinted glass all windows, dual manual control outside 6" x 9" mirrors, bench seat with folding back, vinyl fusion seat trim, ETR AM/FM stereo with seek, clock and two speakers; power take-off adapter, front axle disconnect with shift-on-the-fly.

ST (in addition to or instead of LT equipment): Bright front bumper and bright rear step bumper, tailgate protection moldings, single aero halogen headlamps, 40/20/40 split bench seat with dual recliners, driver's manual lumbar control.

LARAMIE SLT (in addition to or instead of ST equipment): Air conditioning, sight shields, black bodyside protection moldings with bright insert, power door locks, dual note horn, overhead console with storage pocket, cloth bolster door trim, time delay interior light and extra glove box and courtesy lights, ETR AM/FM stereo w/cass, seek, Dolby sound, clock and four speakers.

CODE	DESCRIPTION	DEALER	LIST

Accessories

Quick Order Pkgs w/Std 5.9L Engine

25C	**ST Pkg**	562	649
26C	w/DGB trans, add..	762	897

incls dome & cargo lights, bright front & rear bumpers, split bench seat, wheel dress-up, tailgate top protection molding, cloth upholstery, behind seat storage

25G	**Laramie SLT Pkg**...	2200	2588
26G	w/DGB trans, add..	762	897

incls premium decor group, split bench seat, tachometer, air conditioning, light group, floor carpeting, behind seat storage, AM/FM ETR stereo radio w/cassette & 4 speakers, dual front bumper sight shields, bodyside accent stripe, deluxe convenience group, bright front & rear bumpers, tailgate top protection molding, leather-wrapped steering wheel, wheel dress-up, power convenience group (incls power door locks/power windows), bodyside moldings, premium cloth upholstery

Quick Order Pkgs w/EVA V10 Engine

—	**ST Pkg** — 2WD w/std manual trans...	787	962
	4WD w/std manual trans....................................	825	970
	w/EWA eng, add	400	470
	w/EWA eng & DGB trans, add............................	1216	1431

incls HD service group, dome & cargo lights, floor carpeting, behind seat storage, wheel dress-up w/bright trim rings & hubs, split bench seat, bright front & rear bumpers, deluxe cloth upholstery, tailgate top protection molding [reqs 8.0L V10 eng]

	Laramie SLT Pkg — 2WD w/std manual trans...	2435	2865
	4WD w/std manual trans....................................	2473	2909
	w/EWA eng, add	400	470
	w/EWA eng & DGB trans, add............................	1216	1431

incls leather-wrapped steering wheel, light group, air cond, AM/FM ETR stereo radio w/cassette & 4 speakers, premium decor group, tailgate top protection molding, tachometer, split bench seat, HD service group, deluxe convenience group, bodyside accent stripe, behind seat storage, bodyside moldings, dual front bumper sight shields, bright front & rear bumpers, wheel dress-up, power convenience group (incls power door locks/power windows), premium cloth upholstery, floor carpeting [reqs 8.0L V10 eng]

Quick Order Pkgs w/ETB Diesel Engine

—	**ST Pkg** — 2WD w/std manual trans...	787	926
	4WD w/std manual trans....................................	825	970
29C	w/ETB diesel eng, add	3521	4142
2YC	w/ETB diesel eng & DGB trans, add...................	4338	5103

incls behind seat storage, split bench seat, floor carpeting, wheel dress-up, bright front & rear bumpers, dome & cargo lights, deluxe cloth upholstery, tailgate top protection molding, HD service group [reqs 5.9L 6 cyl diesel Cummins eng]

—	**Laramie SLT Pkg** — w/std manual trans		
	2WD w/std manual trans....................................	2371	2789
	4WD w/std manual trans....................................	2408	2833
29G	w/ETB diesel eng, add	3521	4142
2YG	w/ETB diesel eng & DGB trans, add...................	4338	5103

incls HD service group [reqs 5.9L 6 cyl diesel Cummins eng], deluxe convenience group, premium decor group, split bench seat, wheel dress-

DODGE

CODE	DESCRIPTION	DEALER	LIST

up, floor carpeting, AM/FM ETR stereo radio w/cassette & 4 speakers, air conditioning, tailgate top protection molding, behind seat storage, light group, tachometer, dual front bumper sight shields, bodyside accent stripe, bright front & rear bumpers, wheel dress-up, leather-wrapped steering wheel, bodyside moldings, power convenience group (incls power door locks/power windows), premium cloth upholstery

Code	Description	Dealer	List
—	**Groups**		
ADJ	**Heavy Duty Service Group** — 2WD		
	w/std 5-spd manual trans...	235	277
	w/DGB trans	290	341
	4WD w/std 5-spd manual trans..	273	321
	w/DGB trans	327	385

incls skid plate for transfer case (4WD), HD 120 amp alternator, auxiliary trans oil cooler (included in models w/4-spd automatic trans), HD 750-amp battery (two HD 750-amp batteries on diesel models)

Code	Description	Dealer	List
AWK	**Travel Convenience Group**..	196	231

incls full deluxe headliner, dual bright power mirrors, overhead console (incls reading lights/outside temperature display/compass, auto dimming day/night rearview mirror) [reqs quick order pkg]

Code	Description	Dealer	List
ADA	**Light Group** — w/o quick order pkg	139	164
	w/ST Pkg...	107	126

incls exterior cargo light, underhood light, passenger assist grip, full deluxe cloth headliner, auxiliary 12-volt elec receptacle, ignition key light w/time delay, glove box light, overhead console w/map/reading lights & storage

Code	Description	Dealer	List
AJK	**Deluxe Convenience Group**	300	353

incls tilt steering column, cruise control

Code	Description	Dealer	List
AHD	**Heavy Duty Snow Plow Prep Group** — 4WD....................	230	270

incls LT215/85R16E SBR all-terrain BW tires, extra-duty front suspension, instrument panel warning light for auto trans oil overheat, HD front springs [reqs trailer towing prep group, rear bumper, HD service group, conventional spare tire]

Code	Description	Dealer	List
ASP	**Premium Decor Group** — see pkgs		

incls full floor carpeting, split bench seat, black bodyside moldings, front floor mats, bright front bumper w/step pad, door map pockets, black sport leather-wrapped steering wheel, bodyside tape stripes, premium cloth upholstery, dual horns, covered right visor vanity mirror, underhood insulation, door trim panels w/cloth inserts & lower carpeting, black tailgate panel applique

Code	Description	Dealer	List
AHC	**Trailer Towing Prep Group**	206	242

incls HD flashers, class IV platform hitch receiver, fifth-wheel take-out provision, 7-lead wiring harness [reqs rear bumper, HD service group]

Code	Description	Dealer	List
MXB	**Air Dam** — front..	10	12
NAE	**California Emissions**..	87	102
NAF	**High Altitude Emissions**	NC	NC
—	**Tires**		
TVW	LT215/85R16D SBR all-terrain BW (6)................................	143	168
TMF	LT215/85R16D SBR all-season OWL (6).............................	128	150
	reqs quick order pkg		
TMG	LT215/85R16D SBR all-terrain OWL (6)..............................	270	318
	reqs quick order pkg		
TBB	**Conventional Spare Tire & Wheel**		
	w/TVW std LT215/85R16D tire..	211	248

CODE	DESCRIPTION	DEALER	LIST
	w/TVW LT215/85R16D tire	235	276
	w/TMF LT215/85R16D tire - w/quick order pkg	232	273
	w/TMG LT215/85R16D tire - w/quick order pkg	256	301
NHK	**Heater** — engine block	29	34
JAY	**Tachometer** — w/ST pkg	65	76
HAA	**Air Conditioning**	677	797
CKQ	**Carpeting** — floor delete - w/quick order pkg...................	NC	NC
MBD	**Bumper** — painted rear step	113	133
MB8	**Bumper** — bright rear step delete - w/quick order pkg	(199)	(234)
GFD	**Window** — sliding rear	114	134
DGB	**Transmission** — 4-spd automatic....................................	762	897
JPS	**Seat** — 6-way power driver - w/Laramie SLT pkg................	252	296
	reqs std Laramie SLT premium cloth trim		
T9	**Seats** — premium cloth split bench		
	w/o quick order pkg...	222	261
	w/ST pkg..	NC	NC
TX	**Seats** — HD vinyl split bench		
	w/quick order pkg..	NC	NC
WMG	**Wheel Dress-Up**	259	305
DSA	**Axle** — sure grip...	218	257
DM	**Axle** — rear, optional ratio	33	39
GPP	**Mirrors** — dual bright 6" x 9" power	84	99
GPC	**Mirrors** — dual bright 7" x 10" manual	41	48
EWA	**Engine** — 8.0L V10 EFI...	400	470
	incls HD alternator & battery, auxiliary trans oil cooler included w/4-spd		
	auto trans models, skid plate for transfer case (4WD) [reqs HD svc group]		
ETB	**Engine** — 5.9L 6 cyl diesel Cummins...............................	3521	4142
	incls tachometer, diesel message center includes warning lights, air-		
	manifold mounted electric heater, extra sound insulation, auxiliary trans oil		
	cooler (included w/4-spd auto trans), skid plate for transfer case (4WD)		
	[reqs HD service group]		
K17	**Moldings** — lower bodyside w/ST pkg..............................	87	102
RAS	**Radio**	179	210
	incls AM/FM ETR stereo w/cassette, 4 speakers & digital clock		
RAY	**Radio** — w/Laramie SLT pkg	218	331
	incls AM/FM ETR stereo w/cass & graphic equalizer, 6 Infinity spkrs &		
	digital clock		
RA8	**Radio Delete** — AM/FM - LT	(104)	(122)
RCD	**Radio** — 2 additional speakers	43	50
RCE	**Radio** — 4 additional speakers		
	w/Laramie SLT pkg...	172	202
	reqs RAS radio		
6B	**Paint** — two-tone waterfall		
	2WD, 4WD w/o Laramie SLT pkg	183	215
	4WD w/Laramie SLT pkg	131	154
	incls rear & upper bodyside tape stripes		
P	**Paint** — extra cost..	65	77

DODGE

FORD F150 PICKUP

FORD F150 2WD REGULAR CAB STYLESIDE PICKUP

Code	Description	Dealer	List
F15	117" WB S, Special	10949	12266
F15	133" WB S, Special	11394	12772
F15	117" WB XL, XLT	12018	13956
F15	133" WB XL, XLT	12208	14180

F150 4WD REGULAR CAB STYLESIDE PICKUP

Code	Description	Dealer	List
F14	117" WB S, Special	13950	15676
F14	133" WB S, Special	14239	16005
F14	117" WB XL, XLT	14080	16383
F14	133" WB XL, XLT	14385	16741

F150 2WD REGULAR CAB FLARESIDE PICKUP

Code	Description	Dealer	List
F15	117" WB	12764	14834
F14	117" WB	14800	17229

F150 2WD SUPER CAB STYLESIDE PICKUP

Code	Description	Dealer	List
X15	139" WB S, Special	12580	14119
X15	155" WB S, Special	12786	14353
X15	139" WB XL, XLT	13383	15562
X15	155" WB XL, XLT	13589	15805

F150 4WD SUPER CAB STYLESIDE PICKUP

Code	Description	Dealer	List
X14	139" WB	15341	17866
X14	155" WB	15461	18007

F150 2WD SUPER CAB FLARESIDE PICKUP

Code	Description	Dealer	List
X15	139" WB	13983	16268
X14	139" WB	15940	18571
	Destination Charge:	600	600

Standard Equipment

F150 SERIES REGULAR CAB PICKUP - S BASE: 5-speed manual transmission, driver's air bag, 75-amp alternator, side door intrusion beams, Twin I-Beam front suspension, power steering, power front disc/rear drum brakes with rear wheel anti-lock braking system, high-mount stop light, argent painted front bumpers and grille, tinted glass, aero halogen headlamps, black manual exterior mirrors, removable tailgate, bright hub caps on argent steel wheels, front carpeting, full instrumentation and gauges.

XL (in addition to or instead of BASE S equipment): Front chrome grille, carpeted back panel cover, electronic AM radio with two speakers and digital clock.

XLT (in addition to or instead of XL equipment): Black rub strip with front bumper, chrome grille, bright manual mirrors, argent headlamp/parking bezels, bright windshield moldings, color-keyed lower bodyside protection, headlights-on alert signal, vinyl door trim panel with large perforated vinyl/upper insert other accents and moldings, color-keyed speaker grilles, courtesy lamp/reflector and carpeted map pockets, color-keyed cloth headliner, ETR AM/FM stereo with four speakers and digital clock.

F150 SERIES SUPER CAB PICKUP - S BASE: 5-speed manual transmission, driver's air bag (under 8,500-lb. GVW models), 75-amp alternator, side door intrusion beams, Twin I-Beam front suspension, power steering, power front disc/rear drum brakes with rear wheel anti-lock braking system, high-mounted stop/cargo lamp, argent painted front bumpers and grille, tinted glass, aero halogen headlamps, black manual exterior mirrors, removable tailgate, bright hub caps on argent steel wheels, front carpeting, full instrumentation and gauges, windshield upper and door moldings.

XL (in addition to or instead of BASE S equipment): Front chrome grille, carpeted back panel cover, electronic AM radio with two speakers and digital clock.

XLT (in addition to or instead of XL equipment): Black rub strip with front bumper, bright manual mirrors, argent headlamp/parking bezels, bright windshield moldings, color-keyed lower bodyside protection, headlights-on alert signal, vinyl door trim panel with large perforated vinyl/upper insert other accents and moldings, color-keyed speaker grilles, courtesy lamp/reflector and carpeted map pockets, color-keyed cloth headliner, rear quarter trim panels include LH/RH open storage bins and cup holders, ETR AM/FM stereo with four speakers and digital clock.

Accessories

CODE	DESCRIPTION	DEALER	LIST
—	**Preferred Equip Pkgs** — prices include pkg discounts		
	Regular Cab Styleside		
499A	**Pkg 499A** — S	NC	NC
498A	**Pkg 498A** — S 2WD	302	356
	S 4WD	213	250
500A	**Pkg 500A** — XL	NC	NC
503A	**Pkg 503A** — XLT 2WD w/4.9L/5.0L eng	1787	2102
	XLT 2WD w/5.8L eng	1872	2202
	XLT 4WD w/4.9L/5.0L eng	1654	1946
	XLT 4WD w/5.8L eng	1739	2046
507A	**Pkg 507A** — XLT 2WD w/4.9L/5.0L eng	1918	2256
	XLT 2WD w/5.8L eng	2428	2856
	XLT 4WD w/4.9L/5.0L eng	1785	2100
	XLT 4WD w/5.8L eng	2295	2700
	Regular Cab Flareside		
512A	**Pkg 512A** — XL 2WD	NC	NC
	XL 4WD	NC	NC
515A	**Pkg 515A** — XLT 2WD w/4.9L/5.0L eng	1711	2013
	XLT 2WD w/5.8L eng	2221	2613
	XLT 4WD w/4.9L/5.0L eng	1579	1857
	XLT 4WD w/5.8L eng	2089	2457
	Super Cab Styleside		
519A	**Pkg 519A** — S 2WD	NC	NC
518A	**Pkg 518A** — Special 2WD	190	224
520A	**Pkg 520A** — XL	NC	NC

CODE	DESCRIPTION	DEALER	LIST
523A	**Pkg 523A** — XLT w/4.9L/5.0L eng...............................	1782	2096
	XLT w/5.8L eng	1867	2196
527A	**Pkg 527A** — XLT w/4.9L/5.0L eng...............................	1913	2250
	XLT w/5.8L eng	2423	2850
	Super Cab Flareside		
532A	**Pkg 532A** — XL...	NC	NC
535A	**Pkg 535A** — XLT w/4.9L/5.0L eng...............................	1706	2007
	XLT w/5.8L eng	2216	2607
—	**Combined PEP & Manual Transmission Special Value Pkgs**		
	prices include pkg discounts		
500A	**Pkg 500A** — F150 Regular Cab Styleside/Flareside	620	729
512A	**Pkg 512A** — F150 2WD Regular Cab Styleside/Flareside	620	729
	F150 4WD Regular Cab Styleside/Flareside......................	620	729
520A	**Pkg 520A** — F150 Super Cab Styleside/Flareside	556	654
532A	**Pkg 532A** — F150 Super Cab Styleside/Flareside	556	654
—	**Payload Pkgs**		
—	pkg 1	STD	STD
—	pkg 2	39	46
—	pkg 3	79	93
99Y	**Engine** — 4.9L EFI I-6	STD	STD
99N	**Engine** — 5.0L EFI V8	541	637
99H	**Engine** — 5.8L EFI V8	729	857
44M	**Transmission** — 5-spd manual overdrive........................	STD	STD
44U	**Transmission** — electronic automatic overdrive	786	924
	bonus discount	(145)	(171)
44E	**Transmission** — electronic 4-spd automatic	786	924
—	**Limited Slip Axle**	215	252
—	**Optional Axle Ratio (Upgrade)**	37	44
422	**California Emissions**	85	100
428	**High Altitude Emissions**	NC	NC
—	**Tires** — Regular Cab 2WD		
T74	P215/75R15SL steel radial BSW all-season - 2WD..................	STD	STD
T77	P235/75R15XL steel radial BSW all-season - 2WD..................	133	156
T78	P235/75R15XL steel radial WSW all-season - 2WD..................	220	258
	credit w/PEP's w/P235 BSW A-S tires - 2WD	(133)	(156)
T7Q	P235/75R15XL steel radial OWL all-season - 2WD..................	239	282
	credit w/ PEP's w/P235 BSW A-S tires - 2WD	(133)	(156)
T7P	P235/75R15XL steel radial OWL all-terrain - 2WD.................	350	412
	(5) all-terrain all-around		
	credit w/PEP's w/P235 BSW A-S tires - 2WD	(133)	(156)
—	**Tires** — Regular Cab 4WD		
T77	P235/75R15XL steel radial BSW - 4WD............................	STD	STD
T78	P235/75R15XL steel radial WSW all-season - 4WD..................	87	102
T7Q	P235/75R15XL steel radial OWL all-season - 4WD..................	107	126
T7P	P235/75R15XL steel radial OWL all-terrain - 4WD.................	218	256
	(5) all-terrain all-around		
T7W	P265/75R15XL steel radial OWL all-terrain - 4WD.................	506	595
	(5) all-terrain all-around		
—	**Tires** — Super Cab 2WD		
T77	P235/75R15XL steel radial BSW all-season - 2WD..................	STD	STD
T78	P235/75R15XL steel radial WSW all-season - 2WD..................	87	102
T7Q	P235/75R15XL steel radial OWL all-season - 2WD..................	107	126

FORD

CODE	DESCRIPTION	DEALER	LIST
T7P	P235/75R15XL steel radial OWL all-terrain - 2WD	218	256
	(5) all-terrain all-around		
—	**Tires** — Super Cab 4WD		
T77	P235/75R15XL steel radial BSW all-season - 4WD	STD	STD
T78	P235/75R15XL steel radial WSW all-season - 4WD	87	102
T7Q	P235/75R15XL steel radial OWL all-season - 4WD	107	126
T7P	P235/75R15XL steel radial OWL all-terrain- 4WD	218	256
	(5) all-terrain all-around		
T7W	P265/75R15XL steel radial OWL all terrain - 4WD	506	595
	(5) all-terrain all-around		
—	**Seats** — Regular Cab		
A	vinyl bench - S, XL	STD	STD
B	knitted vinyl bench - S, XL	60	70
C	cloth & vinyl bench - S, XL	85	100
D	cloth flight bench (w/power lumbar) - XLT	STD	STD
B	knitted vinyl bench - XLT	(83)	(98)
J	40/20/40 bench (w/power lumbar) - XLT	445	523
—	**Seats** — Super Cab		
B	knitted vinyl bench - XL	STD	STD
C	cloth & vinyl bench - XL	NC	NC
F	cloth captain's chairs (w/power lumbar) - XL	640	752
G	cloth bench - XLT	STD	STD
B	knitted vinyl bench - XLT	NC	NC
F	cloth captain's chairs (w/power lumbar) - XLT	503	591
J	40/20/40 bench (w/power lumbar) - XLT	528	621
90P	power driver seat, 40/20/40 - XLT	247	290
572	**Air Conditioning**	685	806
522	**Axle, Limited Slip Front/Rear**	254	299
632	**Battery, Heavy Duty**	48	56
76C	**Bumper, Argent Rear Step**	111	130
768	**Bumper, Chrome Rear Step**	202	238
532	**Camper Pkg**	308	362
	credit w/off-road pkg	(102)	(120)
183	**Chrome Appearance Pkg** — Styleside XL	153	180
624	**Cooling, Super Engine**	86	101
903	**Door Locks/Windows, Power**	312	367
213	**Electric Shift 4x4, Touch Drive**	105	123
166	**Floor Mat in Lieu of Carpet**	(16)	(18)
85D	**4x4 Decal Not Included**	NC	NC
651	**Fuel Tank, Single**	(98)	(116)
684	**Handling Pkg**	102	120
533	**Headliner & Insulation Pkg**	64	76
41H	**Heater, Engine Block**	28	33
21M	**Hubs, Manual Locking**	(51)	(60)
153	**License Plate Bracket**	NC	NC
61A	**Light/Convenience Group A**	172	202
593	**Light/Convenience Group B**	109	128
545	**Mirrors, Bright Low-Mount Swingaway** — S or XL		
	w/o chrome appearance pkg	38	45
	w/all others	NC	NC
543	**Mirrors, Bright Electric**	84	99
55R	**Off-Road Pkg**	281	330

FORD

CODE	DESCRIPTION	DEALER	LIST
952	**Paint, Deluxe Two-Tone** — w/XLT trim	234	276
954	**Paint, Lower Accent Two-Tone** — w/XL trim	216	254
	w/XLT trim	155	183
879	**Seat, Rear Bench (Vinyl)** — Super Cab only		
	use w/XL trim	177	209
	use w/XLT trim	NC	NC
873	**Seat, Rear Jump (Vinyl)** — Super Cab XLT only	(177)	(209)
55S	**Security Group**	216	254
52N	**Speed Control/Tilt Steering Wheel**	325	383
674	**Suspension Pkg, Heavy Duty** — front	84	99
683	**Suspension Pkg, Heavy Duty** — rear	80	94
152	**Tachometer**	50	59
535	**Trailer Towing Pkg**	308	362
	credit w/off-road pkg	(102)	(120)
648	**Wheels, Argent Styled Steel**	174	205
	w/PEP which incls chrome styled steel wheels	(150)	(177)
64C	**Wheels, Chrome Styled steel**	324	382
	w/PEP which incls argent styled steel wheels	150	177
649	**Wheels, Forged Aluminum (Deep Dish)**	324	382
	w/PEP which incls argent styled steel wheels	150	177
	w/PEP which incls chrome styled steel wheels	NC	NC
433	**Window, Sliding Rear**	96	113
—	**Radio Systems**		
583	electronic AM w/clock - "S" model only	104	122
587	electronic AM/FM stereo w/clock	125	148
589	electronic AM/FM stereo w/cassette/clock	219	257
	w/PEP which incls AM/FM stereo	93	110
588	premium AM/FM stereo w/cassette over AM	295	348
588	premium AM/FM stereo w/cassette over AM/FM	170	200
588	premium AM/FM stereo w/cassette over Midline cassette	77	90
582	premium AM/FM stereo w/CD over AM	536	630
582	premium AM/FM stereo w/CD over AM/FM	410	483
582	premium AM/FM stereo w/CD over Midline cassette	317	373
58Y	radio credit option	(52)	(61)

FORD F250 PICKUP
(Under 8,500# GVWR)

F250 PICKUP 6 CYL

F25	Regular Cab 2WD 133" WB	12907	15002
Destination Charge:		600	600

Standard Equipment

F250 SERIES (UNDER 8,500-LB. GVW) - BASE XL: 5-speed manual transmission, driver's air bag, 75-amp alternator, side door intrusion beams, Twin I-Beam front suspension, power steering, power front disc/rear drum brakes with rear wheel anti-lock braking system, high-mounted stop/cargo lamp, chrome grille, tinted glass, four LT215/85R16D steel belted radials, 3,900-lb. front axle/5,300-lb. rear axle capacity, aero halogen headlamps, black manual exterior mirrors, removable tailgate, bright hub caps on argent steel wheels, front carpeting, full instrumentation and gauges, windshield upper and door moldings, carpeted back panel cover, electronic AM radio with two speakers and digital clock.

CODE	DESCRIPTION	DEALER	LIST

XLT (in addition to or instead of BASE XL equipment): Black rub strip with front bumper, bright manual mirrors, argent headlamp/parking bezels, bright windshield moldings, color-keyed lower bodyside protection, headlights-on alert signal, vinyl door trim panel with large perforated vinyl/upper insert other accents and moldings, color-keyed speaker grilles, courtesy lamp/reflector and carpeted map pockets, color-keyed cloth headliner, rear quarter trim panels include LH/RH open storage bins and cup holders, ETR AM/FM stereo with four speakers and digital clock.

Accessories

CODE	DESCRIPTION	DEALER	LIST
—	**Preferred Equip Pkgs** — prices include pkg discounts		
540A	XL Pkg	NC	NC
543A	XLT Pkg	1998	2351
—	Payload Pkg 1	STD	STD
—	**Combined PEP & Manual Transmission Value Pkg** prices include pkg discounts		
540A	Pkg 540A	620	729
99Y	Engine — 4.9L EFI I-6	STD	STD
99N	Engine — 5.0L EFI V8	541	637
99H	Engine — 5.8L EFI V8	729	857
44M	Transmission — 5-spd manual overdrive	STD	STD
44E	Transmission — electronic 4-spd automatic	786	924
—	Limited Slip Axle	215	252
—	Optional Axle Ratio (Upgrade)	37	44
422	California Emissions	85	100
428	High Altitude Emissions	NC	NC
—	**Tires**		
T33	LT215/85R16D steel radial BSW all-season	STD	STD
T3C	LT215/85R16D steel radial BSW all-terrain	70	83
	(2) all-season for front, (2) all-terrain for rear		
T35	LT235/85R16E steel radial BSW all-season	149	175
	w/5.0L engine, 5-spd man trans & high altitude emissions	NC	NC
T3M	LT235/85R16E steel radial BSW all-terrain	212	249
	(2) all-season for front, (2) all-terrain for rear		
512	**Spare Tire & Wheel**		
	LT215/85R16D steel radial BSW all-season	210	248
	LT235/85R16E steel radial BSW all-season	227	267
513	Wheel, Spare Rear	114	134
—	**Seats**		
A	vinyl bench - XL	STD	STD
B	knitted vinyl bench - XL	60	71
C	cloth & vinyl bench - XL	85	100
D	cloth flight bench (w/power lumbar) - XLT	STD	STD
B	knitted vinyl bench - XLT	(83)	(98)
J	40/20/40 bench (w/power lumbar) - XLT	445	523
572	Air Conditioning	685	806
632	Battery, Heavy Duty	48	56
76C	Bumper, Argent Rear Step	111	130
768	Bumper, Chrome Rear Step	202	238
532	Camper Pkg	308	362
183	Chrome Appearance Pkg — XL	153	180
624	Cooling, Super Engine	86	101
166	Floor Mat in Lieu of Carpet	(16)	(18)
651	Fuel Tank, Single	(98)	(116)

FORD

PICKUPS

CODE	DESCRIPTION	DEALER	LIST
684	Handling Pkg	102	120
533	Headliner & Insulation Pkg	64	76
41H	Heater, Engine Block	28	33
153	License Plate Bracket	NC	NC
61A	Light/Convenience Group A	172	202
593	Light/Convenience Group B	109	128
543	Mirrors, Bright Electric	84	99
545	Mirrors, Bright Low-Mount Swingaway		
	XL w/o chrome appearance pkg	38	45
	w/all other	NC	NC
952	Paint, Deluxe Two-Tone — w/XLT trim	234	276
55S	Security Group	216	254
52N	Speed Control/Tilt Steering Wheel	325	383
683	Suspension Pkg, Heavy Duty Rear	110	129
152	Tachometer	50	59
535	Trailer Towing Pkg	308	362
644	Wheel Covers, Sport	70	83
433	Window, Sliding Rear	96	113
—	Radio Systems		
587	electronic AM/FM stereo w/clock	125	148
589	electronic AM/FM stereo w/cassette/clock - w/XL	219	257
	w/PEP which incls AM/FM stereo	93	110
588	premium AM/FM stereo w/cassette over AM	295	348
588	premium AM/FM stereo w/cassette over AM/FM	170	200
588	premium AM/FM stereo w/cassette over midline cassette	77	90
582	premium AM/FM stereo w/CD over AM	536	630
582	premium AM/FM stereo w/CD over AM/FM	410	483
582	premium AM/FM stereo w/CD over midline cassette	317	373
58Y	radio credit option	(52)	(61)

FORD F250 HD PICKUP
(Over 8500# GVWR)

F250 HD PICKUP

F25	Regular Cab 2WD 133" WB	13389	15569
F26	Regular Cab 4WD 133" WB	16302	18996
X25	Super Cab 2WD S 155" WB	14734	16567
X25	Super Cab 2WD XL 155" WB	15540	18100
X25	Super Cab 2WD XLT 155" WB	15540	18100
X25	Super Cab 4WD XL 155" WB	17625	20552
X25	Super Cab 4WD XLT 155" WB	17625	20552
	Destination Charge	600	600

Standard Equipment

F250 HD SUPER CAB (OVER 8,500-LB. GVW) - BASE XL: 5-speed heavy-duty manual transmission, 95-amp alternator, side door intrusion beams, Twin I-Beam front suspension, power steering, power front disc/rear drum brakes with rear wheel anti-lock braking system, high-mounted stop/cargo lamp, chrome grille, tinted glass, four LT235/85R16E steel belted radials, 4,200-lb. front axle/6,250-lb. rear axle capacity, aero halogen headlamps, black manual exterior mirrors, removable tailgate, bright hub caps on argent steel wheels, front carpeting, full instrumentation and gauges, windshield upper and door moldings, carpeted back panel cover, electronic AM radio with two speakers and digital clock.

XLT (in addition to or instead of BASE XL equipment): Black rub strip with front bumper, bright manual mirrors, argent headlamp/parking bezels, bright windshield moldings, black lower bodyside protection, headlights-on alert signal, vinyl door trim panel with large perforated vinyl/upper insert other accents and moldings, color-keyed speaker grilles, courtesy lamp/reflector and carpeted map pockets, color-keyed cloth headliner, rear quarter trim panels include LH/RH open storage bins and cup holders, ETR AM/FM stereo with four speakers and digital clock.

Accessories

CODE	DESCRIPTION	DEALER	LIST
—	**Preferred Equip Pkgs** — prices include pkg discounts		
	Regular Cab		
600A	**Pkg 600A** — XL	NC	NC
603A	**Pkg 603A** — XLT	1998	2351
	Super Cab		
609A	**Pkg 609A** — S	NC	NC
610A	**Pkg 610A** — XL	NC	NC
613A	**Pkg 613A** — XLT	2126	2501
—	**Combined PEP & Manual Transmission Special Value Pkgs**		
600A	**Pkg 600A** — Regular Cab Styleside	620	729
610A	**Pkg 610A** — Super Cab Styleside	556	654
99Y	**Engine** — 4.9L EFI I-6 - use w/Regular Cab 4x2 models	STD	STD
	use w/Super Cab 4x2 models	(729)	(857)
99H	**Engine** — 5.8L EFI V8 - use w/Regular Cab 4x2 models	729	857
	use w/Regular Cab 4x4 & all Super Cab models	STD	STD
99G	**Engine** — 7.5L EFI V8 - use w/Regular Cab 4x2 models	1140	1341
	use w/Regular Cab 4x4 & all Super Cab models	412	484
99M	**Engine** — 7.3 diesel V8 (non-turbo) - use w/ Regular Cab 4x2 models	2611	3072
	use w/ Regular Cab 4x4 & all Super Cab models	1882	2215
99K	**Engine** — 7.3L diesel V8 (turbo) - use w/Regular Cab 4x2 models	3941	4637
	use w/Regular Cab 4x4 & all Super Cab models	3212	3779
44W	**Transmission** — 5-spd manual overdrive heavy duty	STD	STD
44C	**Transmission** — 5-spd manual overdrive heavy duty (w/diesel eng)	NC	NC
44G	**Transmission** — automatic	592	696
44E	**Transmission** — electronic 4-spd automatic	786	924
—	**Limited Slip Axle**	215	252
—	**Optional Axle Ratio (Upgrade)**	37	44
422	**California Emissions**	NC	NC
428	**High Altitude Emissions**	NC	NC
—	**Tires — Regular Cab**		
T35	LT235/85R16E steel radial BSW all-season - 2WD	STD	STD
T3N	LT235/85R16E steel radial BSW all-terrain - 2WD	48	56
	(2) all-season for front, (2) all-terrain for rear		
T35	LT235/85R16E steel radial BSW all-season 4WD	STD	STD
T3N	LT235/85R16E steel radial BSW all-terrain - 4WD	95	111
	(4) all-terrain all-around		
—	**Tires - Super Cab**		
T35	LT235/85R16E steel radial BSW all-season 2WD	STD	STD
T3N	LT235/85R16E steel radial BSW all-terrain - 2WD	48	56
	(2) all-season for front, (2) all-terrain for rear		
T35	LT235/85R16E steel radial BSW all-season - 4WD	STD	STD

CODE	DESCRIPTION	DEALER	LIST
T3N	LT235/85R16E steel radial BSW all-terrain - 4WD	95	111
	(4) all-terrain all-around		
512	**Spare Tire & Wheel**	227	267
	LT235/85R16E steel radial BSW all-season		
513	**Wheel, Spare Rear**	114	134
515	**Spare Tire & Wheel** — all-terrain - 4WD	251	295
	LT235/85R16E steel radial BSW all-terrain		
—	**Seats - Regular Cab**		
A	vinyl bench - XL	STD	STD
B	knitted vinyl bench - XL	60	71
C	cloth & vinyl bench - XL	85	100
D	cloth flight bench (w/power lumbar) - XLT	STD	STD
B	knitted vinyl bench - XLT	(83)	(98)
J	40/20/40 bench (w/power lumbar) - XLT	445	523
—	**Seats - Super Cab**		
B	knitted vinyl bench - XL	STD	STD
C	cloth & vinyl bench - XL	NC	NC
F	cloth captain's chairs (w/power lumbar) - XL	640	752
G	cloth bench - XLT	STD	STD
B	knitted vinyl bench - XLT	NC	NC
F	cloth captain's chairs (w/power lumbar) - XLT	503	591
J	40/20/40 bench (w/power lumbar) - XLT	528	621
90P	power driver seat 40/20/20 - XLT	247	290
572	**Air Conditioning**	685	806
632	**Battery, Heavy-Duty**	48	56
76C	**Bumper, Argent Rear Step**	111	130
768	**Bumper, Chrome Rear Step**	202	238
532	**Camper/Trailer, Towing Pkg**	308	362
	credit w/off-road pkg	(102)	(120)
	credit w/7.3L non-turbo	(48)	(56)
	credit w/7.3L IDI turbo	(134)	(157)
	credit w/super engine cooling	(86)	(101)
183	**Chrome Appearance Pkg** — XL	153	180
592	**Clearance Lights, Roof**	45	52
624	**Cooling, Super Engine**	86	101
166	**Floor Mat in Lieu of carpet**	(16)	(18)
85D	**4x4 Decal Not Included**	NC	NC
651	**Fuel Tank, Single**	(98)	(116)
435	**Fuel Tap, Auxiliary**	26	30
684	**Handling Pkg**	102	120
533	**Headliner & Insulation Pkg**	64	76
41H	**Heater, Engine Block**		
	use w/4.9L or 5.8L engine (single element)	28	33
	use w/7.5L engine (dual element)	56	66
21M	**Hubs, Manual Locking**	(51)	(60)
153	**License Plate Bracket**	NC	NC
61A	**Light/Convenience Group A**	172	202
593	**Light/Convenience Group B**	109	128
543	**Mirrors, Bright Electric**	84	99
545	**Mirrors, Bright Low-Mount Swingaway** — S or XL		
	w/o chrome appearance pkg	38	45
545	**Mirrors, Bright Low-Mounted Swingaway** — w/all others	NC	NC

CODE	DESCRIPTION	DEALER	LIST
548	**Mirrors, Bright Swing-Out Rec** — XL w/o chrome appearance pkg	46	54
548	**Mirrors, Bright Swing-Out Rec** — w/all others	7	9
55R	**Off-Road Pkg**	257	302
	w/7.3L 4x4	182	215
952	**Paint, Deluxe Two-Tone** — w/XLT trim	234	276
879	**Seat, Rear Bench (Vinyl)** — Super Cab only w/XL trim	177	209
	w/XLT trim	NC	NC
873	**Seats, Rear Jump (Vinyl)** — Super Cab XLT only	177	209
55S	**Security Group**	216	254
686	**Soft Ride 4x4 Suspension**	NC	NC
52N	**Speed Control/Tilt Steering Wheel**	325	383
674	**Suspension Pkg, Heavy Duty Front**	60	71
683	**Suspension Pkg, Heavy Duty Rear**	110	129
152	**Tachometer**	50	59
535	**Trailer Towing Pkg**	308	362
	credit w/off-road pkg	(102)	(120)
	credit w/7.3L non-turbo	(48)	(56)
	credit w/7.3L IDI turbo	(134)	(157)
	credit w/super engine cooling	(86)	(101)
644	**Wheel Covers, Sport**	70	83
433	**Window, Sliding Rear**	96	113
—	**Radio Systems**		
583	electronic AM radio w/clock - "S" model only	104	122
587	electronic AM/FM stereo w/clock	125	148
589	electronic AM/FM stereo w/cassette/clock	219	257
	w/PEP which incls AM/FM stereo	93	110
588	premium AM/FM stereo w/cassette over AM	295	348
588	premium AM/FM stereo w/cassette over AM/FM	170	200
588	premium AM/FM stereo w/cassette over midline cassette	77	90
582	premium AM/FM stereo w/CD over AM	536	630
582	premium AM/FM stereo w/CD over AM/FM	410	483
582	premium AM/FM stereo w/CD over midline cassette	317	373
58Y	radio credit option	(52)	61)

FORD F350 PICKUP

FORD F350 PICKUP

F35	Regular Cab DRW 2WD 133" WB	15318	17839
F36	Regular Cab SRW 4WD 133" WB	16719	19486
W35	Crew Cab SRW 2WD 168" WB	16595	19341
W35	Crew Cab DRW 2WD 168" WB	17093	19927
W36	Crew Cab SRW 4WD 168" WB	19171	22372
F37	Regular Chassis Cab SRW 2WD 133" WB	13277	15437
F37	Regular Chassis Cab DRW 2WD 137" WB	13813	16068
F37	Regular Chassis Cab DRW 2WD 161" WB	13944	16222
F38	Regular Chassis Cab SRW 4WD 133" WB	16497	19225
F38	Regular Chassis Cab DRW 4WD 137" WB	17692	20631
F38	Regular Chassis Cab DRW 4WD 161" WB	17806	20765
X35	Super Cab DRW 2WD 155" WB	17097	19932
Destination Charge:		600	600

FORD

CODE	DESCRIPTION	DEALER	LIST

Standard Equipment

F350 SERIES REGULAR CAB PICKUP - BASE XL: 5-speed heavy-duty manual transmission, 95-amp alternator, side door intrusion beams, Twin I-Beam front suspension, power steering, power front disc/rear drum brakes with rear wheel anti-lock braking system, high-mounted stop/cargo lamp, chrome grille, tinted glass, four LT215/85R16D steel belted radials, 4,200-lb. front axle/6,250-lb. rear axle capacity, aero halogen headlamps, black manual exterior mirrors, removable tailgate, bright hub caps on argent steel wheels, front carpeting, full instrumentation and gauges, windshield upper and door moldings, carpeted back panel cover, electronic AM radio with two speakers and digital clock.

XLT (in addition to or instead of BASE XL equipment): Black rub strip with front bumper, bright manual mirrors, argent headlamp/parking bezels, bright windshield moldings, black lower bodyside protection, headlights-on alert signal, vinyl door trim panel with large perforated vinyl/upper insert other accents and moldings, color-keyed speaker grilles, courtesy lamp/reflector and carpeted map pockets, color-keyed cloth headliner, rear quarter trim panels include LH/RH open storage bins and cup holders, ETR AM/FM stereo with four speakers and digital clock.

F350 CREW CAB PICKUP - BASE XL: 5-speed heavy-duty manual transmission, 95-amp alternator, side door intrusion beams, Twin I-Beam front suspension, power steering, power front disc/power rear drum brakes with rear wheel anti-lock braking system, high-mounted stop/cargo lamp, chrome grille, tinted glass, LT235/85R16E steel belted radials, 5,000-lb. front axle/6,250-lb. rear axle capacity, aero halogen headlamps, bright recreational swing-out mirrors, removable tailgate, bright hub caps on argent steel wheels, front carpeting, full instrumentation and gauges, windshield upper and door moldings, "B" and "C" pillar trim panels and upper rear window moldings, carpeted back panel cover, color-keyed cloth headliner, electronic AM radio with two speakers and digital clock.

XLT (in addition to or instead of BASE XL equipment): Black rub strip with front bumper, argent headlamp/parking bezels, bright windshield moldings, black lower bodyside protection, headlights-on alert signal, vinyl door trim panel with large perforated vinyl/upper insert other accents and moldings, color-keyed speaker grilles, courtesy lamp/reflector and carpeted map pockets, color-keyed cloth headliner, rear quarter trim panels include LH/RH open storage bins and cup holders, ETR AM/FM stereo with four speakers and digital clock.

F350 CHASSIS CAB PICKUP - BASE XL: 5-speed heavy-duty manual transmission, 95-amp alternator, side door intrusion beams, Twin I-Beam front suspension, power steering, power front disc/rear drum brakes with rear wheel anti-lock braking system, high-mounted stop/cargo lamp, chrome grille, tinted glass, LT235/85R16E steel belted radials, 5,000-lb. front axle/8,250-lb. rear axle capacity, aero halogen headlamps, black manual exterior mirrors, removable tailgate, bright hub caps on argent steel wheels, front carpeting, full instrumentation and gauges, windshield upper and door moldings, carpeted back panel cover, electronic AM radio with two speakers and digital clock.

XLT (in addition to or instead of BASE XL equipment): Separate light housings with integral side markers and license plate lamp, five cab roof clearance/identification lights, bright RV swing-out mirrors, headlamp/parking bezels, bright windshield moldings, black lower bodyside protection, headlights-on alert signal, vinyl door trim panel with large perforated vinyl/upper insert other accents and moldings, color-keyed speaker grilles, courtesy lamp/reflector and carpeted map pockets, color-keyed cloth headliner, rear quarter trim panels include LH/RH open storage bins and cup holders, ETR AM/FM stereo with four speakers and digital clock.

F350 SUPER CAB PICKUP - BASE XL: 5-speed heavy-duty manual transmission, 95-amp alternator, side door intrusion beams, Twin I-Beam front suspension, power steering, power front disc/rear drum brakes with rear wheel anti-lock braking system, high-mounted stop/cargo lamp, chrome grille, tinted glass, LT235/85R16E steel belted radials, 5,000-lb. front axle/6,250-lb. rear axle capacity, aero halogen headlamps, bright recreational swing-out mirrors, removable tailgate, bright hub caps on argent steel wheels, front carpeting, full instrumentation and gauges, windshield upper and door moldings, carpeted back panel cover, electronic AM radio with two speakers and digital clock.

CODE	DESCRIPTION	DEALER	LIST

XLT (in addition to or instead of BASE XL equipment): Black rub strip w/front bumper, argent headlamp/parking bezels, bright windshield moldings, black lower bodyside protection, headlights-on alert signal, vinyl door trim panel w/large perforated vinyl/upper insert other accents, moldings, color-keyed spkr grilles, courtesy lamp/reflector and carpeted map pockets, color-keyed cloth headliner, rear quarter trim panels include LH/RH open storage bins/cup holders, ETR AM/FM stereo w/four spkrs, digital clock.

Accessories

CODE	DESCRIPTION	DEALER	LIST
—	**Preferred Equipment Pkgs** — prices include pkg discounts		
	Regular Cab		
650A	**XL DRW Pkg 650A** — 2WD	NC	NC
651A	**XLT DRW Pkg 651A** — 2WD	1928	2268
640A	**XL SRW Pkg 640A** — 4WD	NC	NC
642A	**XLT SRW Pkg 642A** — 4WD	1998	2351
	Crew Cab		
660A	**XL SRW Pkg 660A** — 2WD & 4WD	NC	NC
661A	**XLT SRW Pkg 661A** — 2WD & 4WD	2147	2527
670A	**XL DRW Pkg 670A** — 2WD	NC	NC
671A	**XLT DRW Pkg 671A** — 2WD	2077	2444
	Regular Chassis Cab		
620A	**XL SRW Pkg 620A**	NC	NC
630A	**XL DRW Pkg 630A**	NC	NC
632A	**XLT DRW Pkg 632A**	1793	2110
	Super Cab		
617A	**XL DRW Pkg 617A**	NC	NC
618A	**XLT DRW Pkg 618A**	2055	2418
—	**Combined PEP & Manual Transmission Special Value Pkgs**		
	prices include pkg discounts		
640A/650A	**Pkg 640A/650A** — Regular Cab Styleside................................	620	729
617A	**Pkg 617A** — Super Cab Styleside	556	654
660A/670A	**Pkg 660A/670A** — Crew Cab Styleside..................................	556	654
—	**Payload Pkgs**		
—	**Pkg 1**	STD	STD
—	**Pkg 2** — Regular Chassis Cab..	27	32
—	**Tires** — Regular Cab/Crew Cab/Regular Chassis Cab SRW		
T35	LT235/85R16E SBR BSW all-season - 2WD	NC	NC
T3N	LT235/85R16E SBR BSW all-terrain - 2WD	48	56
	(2) all-season for front, (2) all-terrain for rear		
T35	LT235/85R16E SBR BSW all-season - 4WD	NC	NC
T3N	LT235/85R16E SBR BSW all-terrain - 4WD	95	111
—	**Tires** — Regular Cab/Crew Cab/Regular Chassis Cab DRW/Super Cab		
T63	LT215/85R16D SBR BSW all-season - 2WD	NC	NC
T6C	LT215/85R16D SBR BSW all-terrain - 2WD	95	111
	(2) all-season for front, (2) all-terrain for rear		
TE5	LT235/85R16E SBR BSW all-season - 4WD	NC	NC
TEE	LT235/85R16E SBR BSW all-terrain - 4WD	143	167
	(6) all-terrain all-around		
—	**Tires** — all models		
512	spare tire & wheel		
	LT215/85R16D SBR BSW all-season..	210	248
	LT235/85R16E SBR BSW all-season..	227	267
513	spare rear wheel...	114	134
515	spare tire & wheel, all-terrain		

FORD

FORD
PICKUPS

CODE	DESCRIPTION	DEALER	LIST
	LT235/85R16E SBR BSW	251	295
99Y	**Engine** — 4.9L EFI I-6 (Chassis Cab 4x2 models)	STD	STD
99H	**Engine** — 5.8L EFI V8 - use w/Chassis Cab 4x2 models	729	857
	use w/all other models (ex Chassis Cab 4x4 & Super Cab 4x2 models)	STD	STD
99G	**Engine** — 7.5L EFI V8 - use w/Chassis Cab 4x2 models	1140	1341
	use w/Chassis Cab 4x4 & Super Cab 4x2 models	STD	STD
	use w/ all other models	412	484
99M	**Engine** — 7.3L diesel V8 (non-turbo)		
	use w/Chassis Cab 4x2 models	2611	3072
	use w/Chassis Cab 4x4 & Super Cab 4x2 models	1471	1730
	use w/all other models	1882	2215
99K	**Engine** — 7.3L diesel V8 (turbo)		
	use w/Chassis Cab 4x2 models	3941	3779
	use w/Chassis Cab 4x4 & Super Cab 4x2 models	2801	3295
	use w/all other models	3212	37779
44W	**Transmission** — 5-spd manual overdrive HD	STD	STD
44C	**Transmission** — 5-spd manual overdrive HD (w/diesel eng)	NC	NC
44G	**Transmission** — automatic	592	696
44E	**Transmission** — electronic 4-spd automatic	786	924
—	**Limited Slip Axle**	215	252
—	**Optional Axle Ratio (Upgrade)**	37	44
422	**California Emissions**	NC	NC
428	**High Altitude Emissions**	NC	NC
—	**Seats - Regular Cab**		
A	vinyl bench - XL	STD	STD
B	knitted vinyl bench - XL	60	71
C	cloth & vinyl bench - XL	85	100
D	cloth flight bench - XLT	STD	STD
B	knitted vinyl bench - XLT	(83)	(98)
J	40/20/40 bench (w/power lumbar) - XLT	445	523
—	**Seats - Crew Cab**		
A	vinyl bench - XL	STD	STD
B	knitted vinyl bench - XL	60	71
G	cloth bench - XL	85	100
G	cloth bench - XLT	STD	STD
D	cloth flight bench - XLT	NC	NC
B	knitted vinyl bench - XLT	NC	NC
J	40/20/40 bench (w/power lumbar) - XLT	528	621
—	**Seats - Super Cab**		
B	knitted vinyl bench - XL	STD	STD
C	cloth & vinyl bench - XL	NC	NC
F	cloth captain's chairs (w/power lumbar) - XL	640	752
G	cloth bench - XLT	STD	STD
B	knitted vinyl bench - XLT	NC	NC
F	cloth captain's chairs (w/power lumbar) - XLT	503	591
J	40/20/40 bench (w/power lumbar) - XLT	528	621
90P	power driver seat 40/20/40 - XLT	247	290
572	**Air Conditioning**	685	806
632	**Battery, Heavy Duty**	48	56
76C	**Bumper, Argent Rear Step**	111	130
768	**Bumper, Chrome Rear Step**	202	238
532	**Camper/Trailer, Towing Pkg**	308	362

CODE	DESCRIPTION	DEALER	LIST
	credit w/off-road pkg	(102)	(120)
	credit w/7.3L non-turbo	(48)	(56)
	credit w/7.3L IDI turbo	(134)	(157)
	credit w/super engine cooling	(86)	(101)
183	**Chrome Appearance Pkg — XL**	153	180
592	**Clearance Lights, Roof**	45	52
624	**Cooling, Super Engine**	86	101
166	**Floor Mat in Lieu of Carpet**	(16)	(18)
85D	**4x4 Decal Not Included**	NC	NC
651	**Fuel Tank, Single**	(98)	(116)
435	**Fuel Tap, Auxiliary**	26	30
684	**Handling Pkg**	102	120
533	**Headliner & Insulation Pkg**	64	76
41H	**Heater, Engine Block**		
	use w/ 4.9L or 5.8L eng (single element)	28	33
	use w/7.5L eng (dual element)	56	66
21M	**Hubs, Manual Locking**	(51)	(60)
153	**License Plate Bracket**	NC	NC
61A	**Light/Convenience Group A**	172	202
593	**Light/Convenience Group B**	109	128
543	**Mirrors, Bright Electric**	84	99
545	**Mirrors, Bright Low-Mount Swingaway**		
	XL w/o chrome appearance pkg	38	45
	w/all others	NC	NC
548	**Mirrors, Bright Swing-Out Recreational**		
	XL w/o chrome appearance pkg	46	54
	w/all others	7	9
55R	**Off-Road Pkg**	220	259
	w/7.3L 4x4	145	171
952	**Paint, Deluxe Two-Tone — w/XLT trim**	234	276
	use w/Styleside dual rear wheel models	141	166
879	**Seat, Rear Bench (Vinyl)** - Super Cab only - w/XL trim	177	209
	w/XLT trim	NC	NC
873	**Seats, Rear Jump (Vinyl) — Super Cab only**	(177)	(209)
55S	**Security Group**	216	254
52N	**Speed Control/Tilt Steering Wheel**	325	383
674	**Suspension Pkg, HD — front**	23	27
152	**Tachometer**	50	59
644	**Wheel Covers, Sport**	70	83
649	**Wheels, Forged Aluminum**	708	833
433	**Window, Sliding Rear**	96	113
—	**Radio Systems**		
587	electronic AM/FM stereo w/clock	125	148
589	electronic AM/FM stereo w/cassette/clock	219	257
	w/PEP which incls AM/FM stereo	93	110
588	premium AM/FM stereo w/cassette over AM	295	348
588	premium AM/FM stereo w/cassette over AM/FM	170	200
588	premium AM/FM stereo w/cassette over Midline cassette	77	90
582	premium AM/FM stereo w/CD over AM	536	630
582	premium AM/FM stereo w/CD over AM/FM	410	483
582	premium AM/FM stereo w/CD over Midline cassette	317	373
58Y	radio credit option	(52)	(61)

FORD RANGER

RANGER REGULAR CAB

CODE	DESCRIPTION	DEALER	LIST
R10	XL 2WD 108" WB	8753	9389
R10	XL 2WD 114" WB	9097	9763
R11	XL 4WD 108" WB	12865	13858
R11	XL 4WD 114" WB	13173	14193
R10	XLT 2WD 108" WB	9892	11111
R10	XLT 2WD 114" WB	10377	11661
R11	XLT 4WD 108" WB	13690	15426
R11	XLT 4WD 114" WB	14217	16025
R10	STX 2WD 108" WB	10763	12100
R10	STX 2WD 114" WB	11249	12652
R11	STX 4WD 108" WB	14426	16262
R11	STX 4WD 114" WB	14953	16861
R10	Splash 2WD 108" WB	11418	12845
R11	Splash 4WD 108" WB	15702	17713

RANGER SUPER CAB

CODE	DESCRIPTION	DEALER	LIST
R14	XL 2WD 125" WB	10527	11832
R15	XL 4WD 125" WB	13671	15405
R14	XLT 2WD 125" WB	10964	12328
R15	XLT 4WD 125" WB	14818	16708
R14	STX 2WD 125" WB	11791	13268
R15	STX 4WD 125" WB	15416	17387
R14	Splash 2WD 125" WB	12711	14314
R15	Splash 4WD 125" WB	16508	18628
	Destination Charge:	460	460

Standard Equipment

RANGER REGULAR CAB 2WD & 4WD PICKUP - BASE XL / XL SPORT: 5-speed manual transmission, 95-amp alternator, 58-amp battery, Twin I-Beam front suspension, 2,400-lb. front/2,750-lb. rear axles, power steering, power front disc/rear drum brakes with 4-wheel anti-lock braking, side door guard beams, high-mounted stop light, tinted glass, gray painted grille, black sail-mounted mirrors, argent styled wheels with hub cabs, color-keyed hardboard headliner, vinyl bench seat, trip odometer, tachometer.

FORD

CODE	DESCRIPTION	DEALER	LIST

XLT (in addition to or instead of BASE XL / XL SPORT equipment): Front gray-painted bumpers, rear chrome step (4WD), cargo box light, bright surround grille molding, chrome plated grille (4WD), tape stripe, full face steel wheels, cargo cover, color-keyed carpeting, color-keyed cloth and vinyl door trim, light group (includes glove box, headlights-on warning, engine compartment, map lights), ETR AM/FM stereo with digital clock.

STX (in addition to or instead of XLT equipment): Handling package (2WD), STX striping, dual cloth captain's chairs with floor console, leather-wrapped deluxe steering wheel.

SPLASH (in addition to or instead of STX equipment): Front color-keyed bumper, rear-step color-keyed bumper, color-keyed grille, color-keyed exterior mirrors Splash striping, full-face chrome wheels (2WD) and deep-dish cast aluminum wheels (4WD), floor consolette with dual cupholders, 60/40 cloth split bench seat with storage armrest, black steering wheel.

RANGER SUPER CAB 2WD & 4WD PICKUP - BASE XL: 5-speed manual transmission, 95-amp alternator, 58-amp battery, Twin I-Beam front suspension, 2,400-lb. front/2,750-lb. rear axles, power steering, power front disc/rear drum brakes with 4-wheel anti-lock braking, side door guard beams, high-mounted stop light, tinted glass, gray painted grille, black sail-mounted mirrors, argent styled wheels with hub cabs, color-keyed hardboard headliner, vinyl bench seat, trip odometer, tachometer.

XLT (in addition to or instead of BASE XL equip): Front gray-painted bumpers, rear chrome step (4WD), cargo box light, bright surround grille molding, chrome plated grille (4WD), tape stripe, full face steel wheels, cargo cover, color-keyed carpeting, color-keyed cloth & vinyl door trim, light group (includes glove box, headlights-on warning, eng compartment, map lights), ETR AM/FM stereo with digital clock.

STX (in addition to or instead of XLT equipment): Handling package (2WD), STX striping, dual cloth captain's chairs with floor console, leather-wrapped deluxe steering wheel.

SPLASH (in addition to or instead of XLT equipment): Front color-keyed bumper, rear-step color-keyed bumper, color-keyed grille, color-keyed exterior mirrors Splash striping, full-face chrome wheels (2WD) and deep-dish cast aluminum wheels (4WD), floor consolette with dual cupholders, 60/40 cloth split bench seat with storage armrest, black steering wheel.

Accessories

Code	Description	Dealer	List
—	**Preferred Equip Pkgs - (Regular Cab)** — prices include pkg discounts		
861A	**XL 2WD Pkg 861A**	NC	NC
861A	**XL 4WD Pkg 861A**	NC	NC
862A	**XL Sport 2WD Pkg 862A**	532	625
862A	**XL Sport 4WD Pkg 862A**	450	529
864A	**XLT Special Value 2WD Pkg 864A** — w/man trans	144	169
	w/auto trans	470	552
864A	**XLT Special Value 4WD Pkg 864A** — w/man trans	690	812
	w/auto trans	689	811
866A	**Splash 2WD Pkg 866A**	NC	NC
866A	**Splash 4WD Pkg 866A**	NC	NC
865A	**STX 2WD Pkg 865A** — w/man trans	117	138
	w/auto trans	329	388
865A	**STX 4WD Pkg 865A** — w/man trans	290	341
	w/auto trans	503	591
—	**Preferred Equip Pkgs - (Super Cab)** — prices include pkg discounts		
850A	**XL 2WD Pkg 850A**	NC	NC
850A	**XL 4WD Pkg 850A**	NC	NC
853A	**XLT Special Value 2WD Pkg 853A** — w/man trans	400	471
	w/auto trans	579	682
853A	**XLT Special Value 4WD Pkg 853A** — w/man trans	367	433

CODE	DESCRIPTION	DEALER	LIST
	w/auto trans	567	667
854A	**STX 2WD Pkg 854A** — w/man trans	390	459
	w/auto trans	602	709
854A	**STX 4WD Pkg 854A** — w/man trans	562	662
	w/auto trans	775	912
855A	**Splash 2WD Pkg 855A**	NC	NC
855A	**Splash 4WD Pkg 855A**	NC	NC
—	**Tires - (2WD) Regular Cab/Super Cab**		
T83	P195/70Rx14SL steel BSW all-season (ex STX & Splash)	STD	STD
T85	P215/70Rx14SL steel BSW all-season	82	96
T80	P225/70Rx14SL OWL all-season	203	239
	use w/XL Sport & "Comfort Cab" pkg	121	143
	use w/STX	STD	STD
T73	P235/60Rx15 steel RBL all-season - Splash	STD	STD
—	**Tires - (4WD) Regular Cab/Super Cab**		
T74	P215/75Rx15SL BSW all-season (ex STX & Splash)	STD	STD
T7F	P215/75Rx15SL steel OWL all-terrain	197	232
	use w/STX	STD	STD
T7R	P235/75Rx15SL steel OWL all-terrain	255	300
	use w/Splash	STD	STD
T7S	P265/75Rx15SL steel OWL all-terrain	348	410
	use w/XLT & STX PEP	93	110
	use w/Base STX	151	178
—	**Payload Pkgs** — all models		
—	**Pkg 1** — all models	STD	STD
—	**Pkg 2** — all models	50	59
—	**Engines**		
99A	2.3L EFI I-4 (ex SuperCab 4x4/Splash 4x4 & all STX)	STD	STD
99U	3.0L EFI V-6 - use w/4x2 XL/XLT/Splash models	416	489
	use w/4x4 XL/XLT Regular Cab models (incl skid plates)	514	605
	use w/all other models	STD	STD
99X	4.0L EFI V-6 - use w/all 4x2 XL/XLT/Splash models	568	668
	use w/4x4 XL/XLT Regular Cab models (incl skid plates)	667	784
	use w/all other models	152	179
44M	**Transmission** — 5-spd manual overdrive	STD	STD
44T	**Transmission** — automatic overdrive	842	990
—	**Performance Axle (Limited Slip Axle)**	215	252
422	**California Emissions**	85	100
428	**High Altitude Emissions**	NC	NC
—	**Seats - Regular Cab**		
H	vinyl bench - XL	STD	STD
E	60/40 cloth split bench - XL	218	256
E	60/40 cloth split bench - XLT/Splash	STD	STD
G	cloth sport bucket/floor console - Splash	307	361
F	cloth captain's chairs/floor console - STX	STD	STD
G	cloth sport bucket/floor console - STX	NC	NC
	use w/Base STX	41	49
E	60/40 cloth split bench - STX	(265)	(312)
—	**Seats - Super Cab**		
I	60/40 knitted vinyl split bench - XL	STD	STD
E	60/40 cloth split bench - XL	NC	NC
F	cloth captain's chairs/floor console - XL	265	312

FORD

CODE	DESCRIPTION	DEALER	LIST
E	60/40 cloth split bench - XLT/Splash	STD	STD
I	60/40 knitted vinyl split bench - XLT/Splash	NC	NC
F	cloth captain's chairs/floor console - XLT/Splash	265	312
G	cloth sport bucket/floor console - XLT/Splash	307	361
F	cloth captain's chairs/floor console - STX	STD	STD
G	cloth sport bucket/floor console - STX	NC	NC
	use w/Base STX	41	49
E	60/40 cloth split bench - STX	(265)	(312)
572	**Air Conditioning**	685	806
768	**Bumper, Chrome Rear Step**	84	99
76D	**Bumper, Painted Rear Step, Delete** — w/Regular Cab XL SWB	NC	NC
624	**Cooling, Super Engine**	47	55
188	**Comfort Cab (Super Cab) Pkg**	NC	NC
416	**Floor Consolette**	26	30
166	**Floor Mat in Lieu of Carpet**	NC	NC
—	**Fog Lamps, Delete Credit - w/STX**	(158)	(185)
595	**Fog Lamps**	158	185
652	**Fuel Tank, High Capacity**	21	24
684	**Handling Pkg**		
	use w/Regular Cab 4x2 models w/4-cyl eng & man str	98	116
	use w/Regular cab 4x2 models w/4-cyl eng & pwr str	66	78
	use w/Regular Cab 4x2 models w/V-6 eng	34	40
	use w/Super Cab	NC	NC
21M	**Hubs, Manual Locking**	(88)	(104)
153	**License Plate Bracket**	NC	NC
543	**Mirrors, Power**	119	140
965	**Moldings, Bodyside Protection**	103	121
—	**Paint, Clearcoat** — use w/XL trim	72	84
	use w/ all other trims	NC	NC
601	**Performance Pkg** — XLT/STX 4x4	460	541
—	**Performance Pkg Credit**	(93)	(110)
903	**Power Window/Lock Group**	322	379
873	**Seat, Rear Jump**	192	226
52N	**Speed Control/Tilt Steering Wheel**	336	395
52H	**Steering, Power**	233	274
152	**Tachometer**	47	55
85K	**Tape Stripe, Accent (Narrow)**	47	55
—	**Tape Stripe, Accent (Narrow) Delete**	(16)	(18)
851	**Tape Stripe, Sport**	85	100
—	**Tape Stripe - Sport/STX/Splash, Delete**	(55)	(65)
954	**Two-Tone, Deluxe**	199	234
	use w/Base XLT	235	277
649	**Wheels, Cast Aluminum (Deep Dish) (Set of 4)**		
	use w/XL trim	300	352
	use w/XLT trim (w/o man trans) w/"Comfort Cab" & w/Base STX	214	251
	use w/STX 4x4 or XLT trim (w/man trans)	NC	NC
	credit when deleted from XLT man trans special value pkg	(214)	(251)
642	**Wheels, Full Face Steel**	86	101
433	**Windows, Sliding Rear**	96	113
43H	**Windows, Pivoting Quarter**	41	49
—	**Radio Systems**		
587	electronic AM/FM stereo w/clock	150	177

FORD

CODE	DESCRIPTION	DEALER	LIST
589	electronic AM/FM stereo w/cassette/clock	267	315
	use w/Base XLT/STX/Splash	117	138
—	electronic AM/FM stereo w/cassette/clock		
	downgrade to electronic AM/FM stereo w/clock (XLT/Splash)	(117)	(138)
588	electronic prem AM/FM stereo w/cassette/clock	63	74
	use w/Base XLT/STX/Splash	180	212
582	electronic prem AM/FM stereo w/CD player	314	370
	use w/Base XLT/STX/Splash	431	507
632	**Battery Heavy Duty** — (650 C.C.A.)...	46	54
41H	**Heater, Engine Block**	26	30

GMC SIERRA CREW CAB

SIERRA CREW CAB 8 CYL

TC30943 2WD 4-Dr Crew Cab 168.5" WB			
w/E63 Wideside Body		16939	19359
w/ZW9 Chassis Cab Body		16262	18585
TK30943 4WD 4-Dr Crew Cab 168.5" WB			
w/E63 Wideside Body		19619	22422
w/ZW9 Chassis Cab Body		18952	21659
Destination Charge:		600	600

Standard Equipment

SIERRA 3500 SERIES CREW CAB PICKUP - BASE SL: 5.7-liter V-8, 5-speed heavy-duty manual transmission with deep low gear and overdrive, power front disc/rear drum with rear-wheel anti-lock system, power steering, chrome bumpers, RH and LH below-eyeline 9" x 6.5" mirrors, four steel belted radials (single rear wheel models), argent painted steel wheels, side impact guard beams, full instrumentation and gauges, tinted Solar Ray glass all windows, heavy-duty heater/defogger, electronic AM/FM stereo with seek-scan and digital clock, Scotchgarded carpeting cloth and door panels, full-width front bench seat in vinyl trim and matching rear seat, center high-mounted stop light.

SLE (in addition to or instead of BASE SL equipment): Chrome front and black rear bumper guards, chrome grille and front lamp bezels, dual RH and LH composite dual halogen headlamps, color-keyed door trim panels with map pockets, carpet trim and padded armrests, full color-keyed carpeting, auxiliary lighting all door-operated, full-width three-passenger front cloth bench and cloth rear seats (optional buckets include console).

Accessories

—	**Decor**		
R9S	**SL Decor**	NC	NC
	incls molded F & R black vinyl mats, 4-spoke custom steering wheel, RH & LH black below-eye-line mirrors		
YE9	**SLE Decor** — w/o rear wheels R05................................	782	909
	w/rear wheels R05	797	927
	incls V22 deluxe frt appearance pkg, carpeting, color-keyed floor mats, sport steering wheel, auxiliary lighting & P01 wheel covers w/R04 & P06 wheel trim rings w/R05		
—	**Option Pkgs** — decor price incl'd in pkgs		
1SA	**Pkg 1SA** — w/R9S SL decor	NC	NC

CODE	DESCRIPTION	DEALER	LIST
	incls vehicle w/std equip		
1SB	**Pkg 1SB** — w/YE9 SLE decor	1908	2219
	incls pkg 1SA plus air conditioning, tilt wheel & speed control, UM6 radio (AM/FM w/seek-scan, cass, clock; radio may be upgraded to UX1)		
—	**Body**		
E63	wideside body	NC	NC
ZW9	chassis cab body	NC	NC
—	**GVW Pkgs**		
C6U	9000 lb.	NC	NC
C6W	9200 lb.	NC	NC
C6Y	9600 lb.	NC	NC
C7A	10000 lb.	NC	NC
—	**Rear Wheels**		
R04	single rear wheels (reqs GVW C6U or C6Y or C6W)	NC	NC
R05	dual rear wheels (reqs GVW C7A) - w/body E63	737	857
	w/body ZW9	585	680
	incls U01 roof marker lamps		
Z82	**HD Trailering Equip** — w/body E63	181	210
	incls platform hitch, wiring harness, HD hazard flasher (reqs V43 or VB3 bumpers)		
Z81	**Camper Equipment** — w/eng L65	85	99
	w/o eng L65	200	233
F60	**HD Front Torsion Bars** — w/model TK30943	54	63
NZZ	**Off-Road Skid Plates** — w/model TK30943	82	95
	incls differential, transfer case, fuel tank and engine shields		
V76	**Tow Hooks** — w/model TC30943	33	38
	std on TK30943		
—	**Emissions**		
FE9	federal	NC	NC
YF5	California	NA	NA
NG1	New York	NC	NC
—	**Engines**		
L05	5.7L (350 CID) V8 EFI gas	NC	NC
L19	7.4L (454 CID) V8 gas	404	470
L65	6.5L (395 CID) V8 turbo diesel	2430	2825
	incls dual batteries, hydraulic brakes, HD radiator, engine oil cooler, extra sound insulation, engine block heater, glow plugs, integral two-stage fuel filter & water separator w/instrument panel warning light & fuel filter change signal		
—	**Transmissions**		
MT8	5-spd manual trans w/overdrive	NC	NC
MT1	4-spd automatic trans w/overdrive	765	890
—	**Rear Axles**		
GT4	3.73 ratio	NC	NC
GT5	4.10 ratio	NC	NC
HC4	4.56 ratio	NC	NC
G80	**Locking Rear Differential**	217	252
KNP	**Cooling** — w/trans MT1	NA	NA
	incls HD auxiliary trans cooling system		
V10	**Cold Climate Pkg**	28	33
	incls engine block heater & special insulation (reqs engines L05 or L19)		
TP2	**Battery** — auxiliary, 600 cold cranking amp	115	134

CODE	DESCRIPTION	DEALER	LIST
	incl'd w/Z81 camper equip; reqs engines L05 or L19		
—	**Wheel Equip**		
P01	wheel covers (4, bright metal)	36	42
	reqs rear wheels R04		
P06	trim rings & hub caps (4, bright metal)		
	w/decor YE9 & rear wheels R04	15	18
	w/decor R9S	52	60
P13	spare wheel & tire carrier	NC	NC
	reqs rear wheels R04 & body E63 and NA w/bedliner BZY		
—	**Front Tires**		
XHP	LT225/75R16D all season BW SBR	(60)	(70)
XHR	LT225/75R16D on-off road BW SBR	(41)	(48)
XHH	LT245/75R16E all season BW SBR	NC	NC
XGK	LT245/75R16E on-off road BW SBR	19	22
—	**Rear Tires**		
YHP	LT225/75R16D all season BW SBR	368	428
YHR	LT225/75R16D on-off road BW SBR	406	472
YHH	LT245/75R16E all season BW SBR	NC	NC
YGK	LT245/75R16E on-off road BW SBR	19	22
—	**Spare Tires**		
ZHP	LT225/75R16D all season BW SBR	258	300
ZHR	LT225/75R16D on-off road BW SBR	267	311
ZHH	LT245/75R16E all season BW SBR	288	335
ZGK	LT245/75R16E on-off road BW SBR	298	346
C60	**Air Conditioning** — incl'd in pkg 1SB	692	805
—	**Convenience Pkgs**		
R7V	power locks & windows not desired	NC	NC
	reqs decor YE9		
ZQ2	power locks & windows (reqs decor YE9)	466	542
R7W	tilt wheel & speed control not desired - reqs pkg 1SA	NC	NC
ZQ3	tilt wheel & speed control (incl'd in pkg 1SB)	329	383
TR9	**Auxiliary Lighting** — incl'd w/decor YE9	52	61
UM7	**Radio**	NC	NC
	incls AM/FM w/seek-scan & clock (std), 4 spkrs [reqs pkg 1SA]		
UP4	**Radio**	(146)	(170)
	incls AM radio (reqs decor R9S & pkg 1SA)		
UM6	**Radio**	105	122
	incls AM/FM stereo w/seek-scan, cass, clock & 4 spkrs (incl'd w/pkg 1SB)		
UX1	**Radio**	234	272
	incls AM stereo/FM stereo w/seek-scan, cass, equalizer, dig clock, 4 spkrs		
UL5	**Radio Delete** — reqs pkg 1SA & decor R9S	(247)	(287)
—	**Seats**		
A52	front bench seat	NC	NC
	incls center fold down armrest w/YE9 and custom cloth trim		
AE7	front 40/60 reclining split bench seat	150	174
	incls 3-pass folding rear bench seat; reqs decor YE9		
A95	front high back reclining bucket seats	464	540
	incls inboard & outboard armrests, roof & floor console and 3-pass folding rear bench seat (reqs decor YE9)		
AG9	**6-Way Power Seat Adjuster** — driver's side	206	240
	reqs seats AE7 or A95		
U16	**Tachometer**	51	59

CODE	DESCRIPTION	DEALER	LIST
V22	**Deluxe Front Appearance Pkg**..	164	191
	incls color-keyed grille, composite halogen headlamps & dual horns (incl'd w/decor YE9)		
BZY	**Bedliner**..	194	225
	NA w/P13 spare wheel & tire carrier; reqs body E63		
—	**Bumpers**		
V43	painted rear step bumper...	112	130
	reqs decor R9S & body E63		
VB3	chromed rear step bumper	197	229
	reqs body E63		
U01	**Roof Marker Lamps** — five..	45	52
	incl'd w/R05 dual rear wheels; NA w/YF5		
VK3	**License Plate Bracket**...	NC	NC
—	**Mirrors**		
D48	dual electric control exterior, black below-eye-line	84	98
	reqs YE9 decor & ZQ2; NA w/Z81 camper equip		
DF2	camper type exterior, stainless steel		
	incl'd w/Z81 camper equip		
C49	**Rear Electric Window Defogger** — NA w/A28...	132	154
A28	**Sliding Rear Window** — NA w/rear electric window defogger		
AJ1	**Deep Tinted Solar Ray Glass**	155	180
	excludes windshield and driver & front passenger windows (incls light tinted solar-ray rear window w/A28 sliding rear window)		
—	**Paint**		
ZY1	solid	NC	NC
ZY2	conventional two-tone paint (NA w/body ZW9)	114	132
ZY4	deluxe two-tone (NA w/body ZW9)	209	243

GMC SIERRA C-K 1500 PICKUPS

SIERRA C1500 2WD PICKUPS

	DEALER	LIST
TC10703/E63/881 Special Wideside (6.5 ft)...	11244	12424
TC10703/E63 Wideside Regular Cab (6.5 ft)	12484	14267
TC10703/E62 Sportside Regular Cab (6.5 ft)...	13064	14930

GMC

CODE	DESCRIPTION	DEALER	LIST
TC10903/E63/X81	Special Wideside (8 ft)	11244	12424
TC10903/E63	Wideside Regular Cab (8 ft)	12729	14547
TC10753/E63	Wideside Club Coupe (6.5 ft)	14803	16094
TC10753/E62	Sportside Club Coupe (6.5 ft)	14443	16506
TC10953	Wideside Club Coupe (8 ft)	14820	16937

SIERRA K1500 4WD PICKUPS

CODE	DESCRIPTION	DEALER	LIST
TK10703/E63/X81	Special Wideside (6.5 ft)	14042	15516
TK10703/E63	Wideside Regular Cab (6.5 ft)	14620	16709
TK10703/E62	Sportside Regular Cab (6.5 ft)	15112	17271
TK10903/E63/X81	Special Wideside (8 ft)	14042	15516
TK10903/E63	Wideside Regular Cab (8 ft)	14882	17008
TK10753/E63	Wideside Club Coupe (6.5 ft)	16117	18419
TK10753/E62	Sportside Club Coupe (6.5 ft)	16477	18831
TK10753	Wideside Club Coupe (8 ft)	16794	19193
Destination Charge:		600	600

Standard Equipment

SIERRA 1500 REGULAR CAB PICKUP - BASE SL: 5-speed manual transmission, power front disc/rear drum brakes with rear-wheel anti-lock system, power steering, chrome bumpers and painted argent grille, black RH and LH below-eyeline mirrors, side impact door guard beams, full gauges and instrumentation, tinted Solar Ray glass all windows, color-keyed headliner, deluxe heater with windshield and side window defoggers, heavy-duty radiator, electronic AM radio w/fixed-mast antenna, Scotchgarded carpeting and cloth trim, three-passenger all-vinyl front bench seat with folding backrest.

SLE (in addition to or instead of BASE SL equipment): Bumpers with black rub strip and bright trim, deluxe front appearance grille, dual composite halogen headlamps, black bodyside moldings with bright trim, Rally wheel trim, rear quarter swing-out windows, color-keyed carpeting, electronic AM/FM stereo with seek-scan and digital clock, three-passenger front seat with choice of vinyl or custom cloth front bench with headrest and folding backrest, sport steering wheel.

SIERRA 1500 CLUB COUPE PICKUP - BASE SL: 5-speed manual transmission, power front disc/rear drum brakes with rear-wheel anti-lock system, chrome bumper and painted argent grille, black RH and LH below-eyeline mirrors, side impact door guard beams, full gauges and instrumentation, tinted Solar Ray glass all windows, color-keyed headliner, deluxe heater with windshield and side window defoggers, heavy-duty radiator, electronic AM radio with fixed mast antenna, Scotchgarded carpeting and cloth trim, 60/40 vinyl split bench seat includes folding rear seat, power steering.

SLE (in addition to or instead of BASE SL equipment): Chrome front bumpers with black rub strip and bright trim, deluxe front appearance grille, dual composite halogen headlamps, black bodyside moldings with bright trim, Rally wheel trim, rear quarter swing-out windows, color-keyed carpeting, electronic AM/FM stereo with seek-scan and digital clock, 60/40 split bench seat, sport steering wheel.

Accessories

—	**Body**		
E63	Wideside	NC	NC
	incl in pkg 1SA, 1SB, 1SC, 1SE, 1SF, 1SL, 1ST		
E62	Sportside	NC	NC
	NA w/special pkg X81		
—	**Decor**		
R9S	SL Decor	NC	NC
	incls std equip		
YE9	SLE Decor	686	798

176   **EDMUND'S VAN/PICKUP/SPORT UTILITY BUYER'S GUIDE**

	incls V22 deluxe frt appearance, wheel trim rings, sport steering wheel, color-keyed frt bumper w/rub strip & bright body side & wheel opening moldings (incls A20 swing-out windows on Club Coupe) (reqs ZQ2 or ZQ3 & R7V or R7W)		
—	**Special Pkgs**		
BYP	**Sport Pkg**		
	w/model TC10703 or TC10753 & chassis equip ZQ8	159	185
	w/model TC10703 & w/o chassis equip ZQ8	408	474
	w/model TK10703	588	654
	w/model TC10753 & w/o chassis equip ZQ8	347	404
	w/model TK10753	439	511
	incls body colored F & R bumpers, black below-eye-line mirrors, GT sport decals (incls fog lamps on 2WD models) (incls N90 wheels w/o ZQ8 on 2WD models) (incls PF4 wheels on 4WD models) (incl'd in pkg 1SE, 1SF) (reqs model TC10703 or TC10753 or TK10703 or TK10753 & decor YE9, and paint scheme ZY1 and pkg 1SE or 1SF)		
X81	**X81 Special Pkg**	NC	NC
	incl'd in model listings (incl'd in pkg 1SL, 1ST)		
—	**Option Pkgs** — decor price included in pkgs		
	w/X81 Special Pkg		
1SL	**Pkg 1SL**	NC	NC
	incls R9S SL decor, X81 special pkg, E63 wideside body & 4.3L (262 CID) V6 EFI gas engine		
1ST	**Pkg 1ST** — 2WD Regular Cab w/R9S SL decor	139	162
	4WD Regular Cab w/R9S SL decor...	192	223
	incls pkg 1SL plus P06 trim rings & hub caps, V43 painted rear step bumper, UP4 AM radio (may be upgraded to UM7 or UM6 radio), ZET P225/75R15 all season spare tire (2WD; may be upgraded), ZHE LT225/75R16C all season spare tire (4WD; may be upgraded)		
	w/BYP Sport Pkg		
1SE	**Pkg 1SE** — 2WD Regular Cab w/YE9 SLE decor...	750	872
	4WD Regular Cab w/YE9 SLE decor	900	1047
	2WD Club Coupe w/YE9 SLE decor..	1034	1202
	4WD Club Coupe w/YE9 SLE decor..	1124	1307
	incls YE9 SLE decor, BYP sport pkg, E63 Wideside body		
1SF	**Pkg 1SF** — 2WD Regular Cab w/YE9 SLE decor...	1699	1976
	4WD Regular Cab w/YE9 SLE decor	1850	2151
	2WD Club Coupe w/YE9 SLE decor..	2241	2606
	4WD Club Coupe w/YE9 SLE decor..	2331	2711
	incls pkg 1SE plus ZQ3 tilt wheel & speed control, c60 air conditioning, UM6 AM/FM radio w/seek-scan, cass, clock (may be upgraded to UX1 radio), TR9 auxiliary lamps		
	w/Regular Cab & Club Coupe		
1SA	**Pkg 1SA** — Regular Cab w/R9S SL decor	NC	NC
	Club Coupe w/R9S SL decor	NC	NC
	incls Wideside body (may be substituted w/Sportside body on models TC10703, TC10753, TK10703 or TK10753), R9S SL decor		
1SB	**Pkg 1SB** — Regular Cab w/R9S SL decor	348	405
	Club Coupe w/R9S SL decor	348	405
	incls pkg 1SA plus air conditioning		
1SC	**Pkg 1SC** — Regular Cab w/YE9 SLE decor	939	1092
	Club Cab w/YE9 SLE decor...	939	1092

CODE	DESCRIPTION	DEALER	LIST
	incls Wideside body (may be substituted w/Sportside body on models TC10703, TC10753, TK10703 or TK10753), YE9 SLE decor, air conditioning, TR9 auxiliary lamps, D45 below-eye-line exterior mirrors		
1SD	**Pkg 1SD** — Regular Cab w/YE9 SLE decor...	1474	1714
	Club Coupe w/YE9 SLE decor..	1474	1714
	incls pkg 1SC plus UM6 AM/FM radio w/seek-scan, cass, clock (may be upgraded to UX1 radio), pwr locks & windows, tilt wheel & speed control		
—	**GVW Pkgs**		
C5G	5600 lb..	NC	NC
C5M	6100 lb..	NC	NC
Q4B	6200 lb..	NC	NC
C5S	6600 lb..	NC	NC
C5U	6800 lb..	NC	NC
Z71	**Off-Road Chassis Equip Pkg**	232	270
	incls NZZ skid plate & Bilstein gas shocks (reqs XGL or XGM tires) (NA w/F51 chassis equip) (reqs model TK10703 or TK10753 or TK10903 or TK10953 and NA w/special pkg X81)		
ZQ8	**Sport Handling Pkg** — w/decor YE9	838	974
	w/decor R9S...	916	1065
	incls Bilstein shocks & N83 chrome wheels (reqs XCN tires) (NA w/F51 chassis equip or P13 spare wheel & tire carrier) (reqs model TC10903 & GVW C5M or model TC10703 or TC10753 or TC10953 and NA special pkg X81 or engines L49 or L56)		
F44	**Heavy Duty Chassis Equip**	198	230
	incl'd w/L49, L56 engine on TK10753, TK10953 (reqs model TK10753 & GVW C5S or model TK10953 & GVW C5S or C5U)		
F51	**Heavy Duty Shock Absorbers** — front & rear	34	40
	incl'd w/VYU snow plow prep pkg & Z82 trailering (NA chassis equip ZQ8 or Z71)		
Z82	**Heavy Duty Trailering Equip**		
	w/o chassis equip ZQ8 or Z71 or snow plow pkg VYU	215	250
	w/chassis equip ZQ8 or Z71 or snow plow pkg VYU	181	210
	incls trailer hitch & wiring harness, F51 shock absorbers (F51 shocks are replaced by Bilstein shocks w/Z71 or ZQ8) (reqs VB3 or V43 bumper w/o TC/K10703-53) (reqs V08 cooling w/LB4, L03, L05 & M30 & GT4, GU4, GU6) (reqs KC4 cooling w/L05 & MT8), (reqs LB4, L03, L05, L49 & MT8 & GT4) or (reqs L56 & MT1) or (reqs L05 & MT8) (NA w/LB4 & GU4) (NA w/specialty pkgs X81 or BYP)		
VYU	**Snow Plow Prep Pkg** — w/model TK10703 or TK10903............................	136	158
	w/model TK10703 or TK10903 & chassis equip Z71	47	55
	incls F60 HD frt torsion bars, F51 HD shocks, HD pwr steering cooler, two electric relays & special forward lamp wiring harness (deletes F51 shocks & F60 torsion bars w/Z71 chassis equip) (reqs V08 cooling w/M30) (reqs DC4 cooling w/MG5, MT8) (NA w/special pkg BYP or engines L49 or L56)		
F60	**Heavy Duty Torsion Bars**	54	63
	incl'd w/VYU snow plow prep pkg (reqs model TK10703 or TK10753 or TK10903 or TK10953 and NA w/engines L49 or L56 or chassis equip Z71)		
NZZ	**Off-Road Skid Plates**	82	95
	incls differential, transfer case & eng shield (incl'd w/Z71 chassis equip) (reqs model TK10703 or TK10753 or TK10903 or TK10953 and NA w/special pkg Z81)		
V76	**Tow Hooks**	33	38

CODE	DESCRIPTION	DEALER	LIST
	std on 4WD (reqs model TC10703 or TC10752 or TC10903 or TC10953 and NA w/special pkg BYP)		
—	**Emissions**		
FE9	federal	NC	NC
NA6	high altitude	NC	NC
YF5	California	NC	NC
NG1	New York w/GVW Q4B or C5M or C5S or C5U	NC	NC
	w/GVW C5G	86	100
—	**Engines**		
LB4	4.3L (262 CID) V6 EFI gas	NC	NC
	incl'd in pkg 1SL, 1ST		
L03	5.0L (305 CID) V8 EFI gas - w/model TC10953 or TK10953	NC	NC
	w/model TC10703 or TC10753 or TK10703 or TK10753 or TC10903 or TK10903	495	575
L05	5.7L (350 CID) V8 EFI gas - w/model TC10953 or TK10953	232	270
	w/model TC10703 or TC10753 or TK10703 or TK10753 or TC10903 or TK10903	727	845
L49	6.5L (395 CID) 155 HP V8 diesel w/model TC10753 or TK10753 or TC10903 or TK10903	2468	2870
	w/model TC10953 or TK10953	1974	2295
	incls dual batteries, hydraulic brakes, HD radiator, eng oil cooler, extra sound insulation, eng block heater, glow plugs, integral two-stage fuel filter, fuel & water separator w/instrument panel warning light & fuel filter change signal		
L56	6.5L (395 CID) 108 HP V8 turbo diesel w/model TC10703 or TK10753 or TC10903 or TK10903	3156	3670
	w/model TC10953 or TK10953	2662	3095
	incls dual batteries, hydraulic brakes, HD radiator, engine oil cooler, extra sound insulation, eng block heater, glow plugs, integral two-stage fuel filter, fuel & water separator w/instrument panel warning light & fuel filter change signal		
—	**Transmissions**		
MG5	5-spd manual w/overdrive (New Venture, 4.02 1st)	NC	NC
MT8	5-spd manual w/overdrive (Deep Low, New Venture, 6.34 1st)		
	w/diesel engine L49	NC	NC
	w/engine L05 or LB4	84	98
M30	4-spd automatic w/overdrive (4L60E)	765	890
M31	4-spd automatic w/overdrive (4L80E)	765	890
—	**Rear Axles**		
GU4	3.08 ratio	NC	NC
GU6	3.42 ratio	NC	NC
GT4	3.73 ratio	NC	NC
GT5	4.10 ratio	NC	NC
G80	**Locking Rear Differential** — NA w/rear axle GU4	217	252
KC4	**Engine Oil Cooler**	116	135
	incls engines LB4 or L03 or L05 & trans MT8 or MG5 & GU4 or GU6 or GT4		
V08	**Heavy Duty Cooling**	170	198
	reqs engines LB4, L03 or L05 & trans M30 & rear axles GU4 or GU6 or GT4 and NA w/cooling KC4		
KNP	**Heavy Duty Transmission Cooling System** — auxiliary	NA	NA
	reqs trans MT1 or M30 & NA w/rear axles GU4 & NA w/engines L03 or LB4		
TP2	**Battery** — 600 amp cold cranking, auxiliary HD	115	134

CODE	DESCRIPTION	DEALER	LIST
	reqs engines L03 or L05 and NA w/model TC10703 or TC10753 and special pkg BYP		
V10	**Cold Climate Pkg**	28	33
	incls eng block heater & special insulation (reqs eng LB4 or L03 or L05)		
—	**Wheel Equip**		
N90	aluminum cast wheels (4) - w/decor YE9	215	250
	w/decor R9S	267	310
	incls (4) 15" x 7" wheels & special hub caps; spare wheel is steel (incl'd w/BYP sport pkg w/o chassis equip ZQ8) (reqs model TC10703 or TC10903 or TC10753 or TC10953 and NA chassis equip ZQ8 or special pkg X81)		
PF4	aluminum cast wheels (4) - w/decor YE9	215	250
	w/decor R9S	267	310
	incls (4) 16" x 7" wheels & special hub caps; spare wheel is 16" x 6.5" base steel (incl'd w/BYP sport pkg) (reqs model TK10703 or TK10753 or TK10903 or TK10953 and NA w/special pkg X81)		
N83	chrome wheels (4) - w/decor YE9	206	239
	w/decor R9S	257	299
	incls (4) 15" x 7" wheels (incl'd w/ZQ8 sport handling pkg) (reqs model TC10703 or TC10903 or TC10753 or TC10953 and NA w/special pkg BYP w/o ZQ8 and NA w/special pkg X81)		
P01	wheel covers, bright metal	36	42
	reqs decor R9S and NA w/chassis equip ZQ8 or special pkg BYP or wheels N90, PF4 or N83		
P06	trim rings & hub caps, bright metal	52	60
	NA w/chassis equip ZQ8 or special pkg BYP or wheels fn90, PF4 or N83 (incl'd w/YE9 decor)		
P13	**Spare Wheel & Tire Carrier**	NC	NC
	NA w/BZY bedliner (NA w/special pkg X81 or BYP or chassis equip ZQ8 or model TC10753 or TK10753 or TC10703 or TK10703)		
R6G	**Air Conditioning Delete**	NC	NC
	reqs pkg 1SA or 1SE or 1SL or 1ST		
C60	**Air Conditioning**	692	805
	incl'd in pkg 1SB, 1SC, 1SD, 1SF		
—	**Convenience Pkg I**		
R7V	power locks & window delete	NC	NC
	reqs decor YE9 and NA w/1SD		
ZQ2	power locks & windows	316	367
	incl'd in pkg 1SD (NA w/special pkg X81)		
—	**Convenience Pkg II**		
R7W	tilt wheel & speed control delete	NC	NC
	reqs decor YE9 and NA w/pkg 1SD or 1SF		
ZQ3	tilt wheel & speed control	329	383
	incl'd in pkg 1SD, 1SF (NA w/special pkg X81)		
BG9	**Color-Keyed Rubber Floor Covering**		
	w/model TC10703 or TC10903 or TK10703 or TK10903	(17)	(20)
	w/model TC10753 or TC10953 or TK10753 or TK10953	(31)	(36)
TR9	**Auxiliary Lamps** — incl in 1SC, 1SD, 1SF	81	94
	NA w/special pkg X81		
C95	**Dome & Reading Lamps**	28	33
	incl'd w/TR9 lighting (NA w/special pkg X81)		
—	**Radio Equipment**		
UM7	radio - w/o special pkg X81	NC	NC

CODE	DESCRIPTION	DEALER	LIST
	w/special pkg X81	286	332
	incls AM/FM stereo w/seek-scan & clock, 4 spkrs (std w/o X81) (NA w/pkg 1SD or 1SF)		
UP4	radio - w/special pkg X81	139	162
	w/o special pkg X81 or decor YE9	(146)	(170)
	incls AM radio (reqs pkg 1SA or 1SB or 1SL or 1ST) (reqs decor R9S)		
UM6	radio - w/special pkg X81	390	454
	w/o special pkg X81	105	122
	incls AM/FM stereo w/seek-scan, cass, clock, 4 spkrs (incl'd in pkg 1SD & 1SF)		
UX1	radio	234	272
	incls AM stereo/FM stereo w/seek-scan, cass, equalizer, clock, 4 spkrs (NA w/special pkg X81)		
UL5	radio delete - w/o special pkg X81	(247)	(287)
	w/special pkg X81	NC	NC
	reqs decor R9S & pkg 1SA or 1SB or 1SL		
—	**Seats**		
A52	front bench seat..	NC	NC
	incls center fold down armrest w/YE9 SLE decor & custom cloth trim (reqs model TC10703 or TC10903 or TK10703 or TK10903)		
AE7	front 40/60 reclining split bench seat		
	w/model TC10703 or TC10903 or TK10703 or TK10903	150	174
	w/model TC10753 or TC10953 or TK10753 or TK10953	NC	NC
	incls easy entry feature on Club Coupe models (NA w/special pkg X81)		
A50	front low back reclining bucket seats		
	w/model TC10703 or TC10903 or TK10703 or TK10903	249	289
	w/model TC10753 or TC10953 or TK10753 or TK10953	99	115
	incls center floor console (incls easy entry feature on Club Coupe models) (NA w/special pkg X81)		
A95	front high back reclining bucket seats		
	w/model TC10703 or TC10903 or TK10703 or TK10903	421	490
	w/model TC10753 or TC10953 or TK10753 or TK10953	250	291
	incls inboard armrests, center floor console (incls easy entry feature on Club Coupe models) (reqs decor YE9)		
YG4	rear seat delete..	(340)	(395)
	reqs model TC10703 or TK10753 or TC10953 or TK10953 & decor R9S & seats A50 or AE7		
AG9	**Six-Way Power Seat Adjuster** — driver's side only	206	240
	reqs decor YE9 & model TC10953 or TK10953 or TC10753 or TK10753 & seats AE7 or A95		
U16	**Tachometer** — NA w/special pkg X81	51	59
V22	**Deluxe Front Appearance Pkg**..	164	191
	incls color-keyed grille, composite halogen headlamps & dual horns (incl'd w/YE9 decor) (NA w/special pkg X81)		
BZY	**Bedliner**..	194	25
	NA w/spare wheel & tire carrier P13 or body/chassis E62		
—	**Bumpers**		
V43	painted, rear step bumper..	112	130
	reqs special pkg BYP or body/chassis E63 (incl'd w/BYP sport truck) (incl'd in pkg 1ST)		
VB3	chrome rear step bumper w/rub strip................................	197	229
	reqs VG3 bumper guards (NA w/body/chassis E63 & decor R9S or special		

CODE	DESCRIPTION	DEALER	LIST
	pkg BYP or X81)		
—	**Bumper Guards**		
VG3	front bumper rub strip	22	26
	incl'd w/YE9 decor (reqs V27 bumper guards w/L49 or L56 eng) (NA w/decor R9S & body/chassis E63 or special pkg X81 or BYP)		
V27	black front bumper guards	28	32
	reqs bumper guards VG3 (incl'd w/YE9 decor & L49, L56)		
U01	**Roof Marker Lamps** — five	45	52
	NA w/emissions YF5 or special pkg X81 or BYP		
VK3	**Front License Plate Bracket**	NC	NC
—	**Mirrors**		
D45	below-eye-line exterior, stainless steel, 9" x 6.5"	39	45
	incl'd in pkg 1SC, 1SD (NA w/special pkg X81 or BYP)		
DF2	camper type exterior mirrors, stainless steel, 7.5" x 10.5"	46	53
	NA special pkg X81 or BYP		
B85	**Bright Exterior Molding** — w/body E62 or chassis equip ZQ8	65	76
	w/body E63 & w/o chassis equip ZQ8	92	107
C49	**Electric Rear Window Defogger**	132	154
	NA w/A28 sliding rear window (NA w/pkg BYP & TC10752) (reqs model TC10753 or tC10953 or TK10753 or TK10953 & decor YE9)		
A28	**Sliding Rear Window**	97	113
	NA w/rear window defogger C49 or special pkg X81		
A20	**Swing-Out Quarter Windows**	37	43
	incl'd w/TE9 decor & AJ1 tinted glass (reqs model TC10753 or TC10953 or TK10753 or TK10953 and NA w/special pkg X81)		
AJ1	**Deep Tinted Solar Ray Glass** — w/decor R9S & window A28	99	115
	w/decor R9S & w/o window A28	129	150
	w/decor YE9 & rear window defogger C49 or window A28	62	72
	w/decor YE9 & w/o rear window defogger C49 or window A28	92	107
	reqs model TC10753 or TC10953 or TK10753 or TK10953 and NA w/special pkg X81 (w/C49 rear window defogger or A28 sliding rear window incls light tinted rear window) (incls A20 swing-out windows)		
—	**Paint**		
ZY1	solid	NC	NC
ZY2	two-tone conventional paint	114	132
	NA w/special pkg X81 or BYP		
ZY4	deluxe two-tone paint	209	243
	NA w/special pkg X81 or BYP or body E63		
—	**Front Tires** — SBR		
XFL	P235/75R15 all season BW		
	w/model TC10703 & special pkg BYP	NC	NC
	w/model TC10703 or TC10903 & w/o engines L49 or L56	24	28
	w/model TC10903 & engines L49 or L56 or TC10753 or TC10953	NC	NC
XFM	P235/75R15 all season white stripe		
	w/model TC10703 or TC10903 & w/o engines L49 or L56	55	64
	w/model TC10903 & engines L49 or L56 or TC10753 or TC10903	31	36
XFN	P235/75R15 all season white lettered		
	w/model TC10703 or TC10903 & w/o engines L49 or L56	67	78
	w/model TC10903 & engines L49 or L56 or TC10753 or TC10953	43	50
XCN	P275/60R15 all season BW	NC	NC
XHE	LT225/75R16C all season BW	NC	NC
XHJ	LT225/75R16C on-off road BW	19	22

CODE	DESCRIPTION	DEALER	LIST
XHN	LT225/75R16C on-off road white lettered OWL	62	72
XBK	LT245/75R16C all season BW	NC	NC
XBN	LT245/75R16C on-off road BW	20	23
XBX	LT245/75R16C on-off road white lettered	63	73
XGL	LT245/75R16C on-off road BW		
	w/model TK10703 or TK10753 & special pkg BYP	NC	NC
	w/model TK10703 or TK10903 & w/o special pkg X81	115	134
	w/model TK10753 or TK10953	65	76
XGM	LT265/75R16C on-off road white letter		
	w/model TK10703 or TK10903 & w/o special pkg X81	158	184
	w/model TK10753 or TK10953	108	126
—	**Rear Tires**		
YET	P225/75R15 all season BW	NC	NC
YEV	P225/75R15 all season white lettered	43	50
YFL	P235/75R15 all season BW		
	w/model TC10703 or TC10753 & special pkg BYP	NC	NC
	w/model TC10703 or TC10903 & w/o engines L49 or L56	24	28
	w/model TC10903 & engines L49 or L56 or TC10753 or TC10953	NC	NC
YFM	P235/75R15 all season white stripe		
	w/model TC10703 or TC10903 & w/o engines L49 or L56	55	64
	w/model TC10903 & engines L49 or L56 or TC10753 or TC10953	31	36
YFN	P235/75R15 all season white lettered		
	w/model TC10703 or TC10903 & w/o engines L49 or L56	67	78
	w/model TC10903 & engines L49 or L56 or TC10753 or TC10953	43	50
YCN	P275/60R15 all season BW	NC	NC
YHE	LT225/75R16C all season BW	NC	NC
YHJ	LT225/75R16C on-off road BW	19	22
YHN	LT225/75R16C on-off road white lettered	62	72
YBK	LT245/75R16C all season BW	NC	NC
YBN	LT245/75R16C on-off road BW	20	23
YBX	LT245/75R16C on-off road white lettered outline	63	73
YGL	LT265/75R16C on-off road BW		
	w/model TK10703 or TK10753 & special pkg BYP	NC	NC
	w/model TK10703 or TK10903 & w/o special pkg X81	115	134
	w/model TK10753 or TK10953	65	76
YGM	LT265/75R16C on-off road white lettered		
	w/model TK10703 or TK10903 & w/o special pkg X81	158	184
	w/model TK10753 or TK10953	108	126
—	**Spare Tires** — SBR		
ZET	P225/75R15 all season BW		
	w/model TC10703 or TC10903 & special pkg X81	138	160
	w/model TC10703 or TC10903	NC	NC
ZEV	P225/75R15 all season white lettered		
	w/model TC10703 or TC10903 & special pkg X81	159	185
	w/model TC10703 or TC10903	22	25
ZFL	P235/75R15 all season BW		
	w/model TC10703 or TC10903 & special pkg X81 & w/o eng L49 or L56	150	174
	w/model TC10703 or TC10753 & special pkg BYP	NC	NC
	w/model TC10703 or TC10903 & w/o engines L49 or L56	12	14
	w/model TC10903 & engines L49 or L56 or TC10753 or TC10953	NC	NC
ZFM	P235/75R15 all season white stripe		
	w/model TC10703 or TC10903 & special pkg X81 & w/o eng L49 or L56	165	192

CODE	DESCRIPTION	DEALER	LIST
	w/model TC10703 or TC10903 & w/o engines L49 or L56	28	32
	w/model TC10903 & engines L49 or L56 or TC10753 or TC10953..............	15	18
ZFN	P235/75R15 all season white lettered		
	w/model TC10703 or TC10903 & special pkg X81 & w/o eng L49 or L56.....	171	199
	w/model TC10703 or TC10903 & w/o engines L49 or L56	34	39
	w/model TC10903 & engines L49 or L56 or TC10753 or TC10953..............	22	25
ZCN	P275/60R15 all season BW..	NC	NC
ZHE	LT225/75R16C all season BW		
	w/model TK10703 or TK10903 & special pkg X81	190	221
	w/model TK10703 or TK10903	NC	NC
ZHJ	LT225/75R16C on-off road BW		
	w/model TK10703 or TK10903 & special pkg X81	200	232
	w/model TK10703 or TK10903	9	11
ZHN	LT225/75R16C on-off road white lettered		
	w/model TK10703 or TK10903 & special pkg X81	221	257
	w/model TK10703 or TK10903	31	36
ZBK	LT245/75R16C all season BW..	NC	NC
	LT245/75R16C on-off road BW	9	11
ZBX	LT245/75R16C on-off road white lettered	31	36
ZGL	LT245/75R16C on-off road BW		
	w/model TK10703 or TK10753 & special pkg BYP	NC	NC
	w/model TK10703 or TK10903 & w/o special pkg X81.............................	58	67
	w/model TK10753 or TK10953	33	38
ZGM	LT265/75R16C on-off road white lettered		
	w/model TK10703 or TK10903 & w/o special pkg X81.............................	79	92
	w/model TK10753 or TK10953	54	63

GMC SIERRA C-K 2500 PICKUPS

SIERRA C2500 2WD PICKUPS

TC20903 Wideside Regular Cab (8 ft.)		13435	15354
TC20903/C6P Heavy Duty Wideside Regular Cab (8 ft.)..............................		14895	17023
TC20753 Wideside Club Coupe (6.5 ft.)		15647	17882
TC20953 Wideside Club Coupe (8 ft.)		16424	18770

SIERRA K2500 4WD PICKUPS

TK20903 Wideside Regular Cab (8 ft.)		15210	17383
TK20903/C6P Heavy Duty Wideside Regular Cab (8 ft.)..............................		17041	19475
TK20753 Wideside Club Coupe (6.5 ft.)		17237	19699
TK20953 Wideside Club Coupe (8 ft.)		18587	21242
Destination Charge:		600	600

Standard Equipment

SIERRA 2500 REGULAR CAB PICKUP - BASE SL: 5-speed manual transmission, black air dam (7200 GVW only), 600-amp battery, power front disc/rear drum brakes with rear-wheel anti-lock system, power steering, chrome front bumper and painted argent grille, heavy duty radiator, LT225/75R16D all-season radials with 7,200-lb. GVW, LT245/75R16E all season radials with 8,600-lb. GVW, side door guard beams, full gauges, tinted Solar Ray glass all windows, deluxe heater with windshield and side window defoggers, electronic AM radio with fixed-mast antenna, Scotchgarded carpeting, cloth trim and door panels, three-passenger all-vinyl trim front bench seat with head restraints and folding backrest.

SLE (in addition to or instead of BASE SL equipment): Bumpers with black rub strip and bright trim, deluxe front appearance grille, dual composite halogen headlamps, black bodyside moldings with bright trim and bright wheel openings, Rally wheel trim, color-keyed carpeting, electronic AM/FM stereo with seek-scan and digital clock, three-passenger front seat with choice of custom vinyl or custom cloth front bench with folding backrest (optional bucket seats include console).

SIERRA 2500 CLUB COUPE PICKUP - BASE SL: 5-speed manual transmission, black air dam (7200 GVW only), 600-amp battery, power front disc/rear drum brakes with rear-wheel anti-lock system, power steering, chrome front bumper and painted argent grille, heavy duty radiator, LT225/75R16D all-season radials with 7,200-lb. GVW, LT245/75R16E all-season radials with 8,600-lb. GVW, side door guard beams, full gauges, tinted Solar Ray glass all windows, deluxe heater with windshield and side window defoggers, electronic AM radio with fixed-mast antenna, Scotchgarded carpeting, cloth trim and door panels, 60/40 vinyl reclining split bench seats with driver and passenger easy entry feature.

SLE (in addition to or instead of BASE SL equipment): Bumpers with black rub strip and bright trim, deluxe front appearance grille, dual composite halogen headlamps, black bodyside moldings with bright trim and bright wheel openings, Rally wheel trim, color-keyed carpeting, electronic AM/FM stereo with seek-scan and digital clock, custom vinyl reclining 60/40 split bench seat with easy entry feature.

Accessories

CODE	DESCRIPTION	DEALER	LIST
—	**Body/Chassis**		
E63	Wideside - incl'd in pkg 1SA, 1SB, 1SC, 1SD	NC	NC
—	**GVW Pkgs**		
C5Z	7200 lb.	NC	NC
C6P	8600 lb.	NC	NC
—	**Decor**		
R9S	**SL Decor**	NC	NC
	incls std equip		
YE9	**SLE Decor**	686	798
	incls V22 deluxe frt appearance, wheel trim rings, sport steering wheel, color-keyed frt bumper w/rub strip & bright body side & wheel opening moldings (incls A20 swing out windows on Club Coupe) (reqs ZQ2 or R7V convenience group I or ZQ3 or R7W convenience group II)		
—	**Option Pkgs** — includes decor pricing		
1SA	**Pkg 1SA** — w/R9S SL decor	NC	NC
	incls vehicle w/standard equip & SL decor R9S		
1SB	**Pkg 1SB** — w/R9S SL decor	348	405
	incls pkg 1SA plus air conditioning		
1SC	**Pkg 1SC** — Regular Cab w/YE9 SLE decor	1068	1242
	Club Coupe w/YE9 SLE decor	982	1142
	incls pkg 1SB plus TR9 auxiliary lamps & D45 below-eye-line exterior mirrors (may be upgraded to DF2)		
1SD	**Pkg 1SD** — Regular Cab w/YE9 SLE decor	1646	1914
	Club Coupe w/YE9 SLE decor	1474	1714
	incls pkg 1SC plus UM6 AM/FM radio w/seek-scan, cass, clock (may be upgraded to UX1 radio), pwr locks, pwr windows, tilt wheel & speed control		
Z81	**Camper Equipment** — w/diesel engine L65	85	99
	w/engines LB4 or L03 or L05 or L19	200	233
	incls DF2 stainless steel mirrors & wiring harness (incls TP2 battery w/o L65) (reqs KC4 cooling w/C5Z & MG5, MT8) (reqs KC4 cooling w/C6P & L05 /MT8 & GT4, GU6) (reqs V08 w/M30, MT1 & GU6, GT4) (NA w/L49 or L56) (NA w/MG5)		
Z82	**Heavy Duty Trailering Equip**	181	210
	incls trailer hitch & wiring harness (reqs VB3 or V43 bumper w/o TC20753		

CODE	DESCRIPTION	DEALER	LIST
	or TK20753) (reqs KC4 cooling w/L05 & MT8 & GT4, GU6) (reqs V08 cooling w/LB4, L03, L05 & M30 & GT4, GU6) (NA w/TC20753 & L05 & MT8 & GT4) (NA w/TC20903, TK20903 & LB4 & MT8) (NA w/MG5)		
VYU	**Snow Plow Prep Pkg** — TK20903	101	118
	incls F60 HD frt torsion bars, HD pwr steering cooler, two elec relays & special forward wiring harness (reqs KC4 cooling w/C5Z & MG5, MT8) (reqs KC4 cooling w/C6P & L05 & MT8 and GT4, GU6) (reqs V08 cooling w/C5Z & M30 & GT4, GU6) (NA w/L49 or L56)		
F60	**Heavy Duty Front Torsion Bars**...	54	63
	reqs model TK20753 or TK20903 or TK20953 and NA w/engines L49 or L56 (incl'd w/VYU snow plow pkg)		
NZZ	**Off-Road Skid Plate**	82	95
	incls differential, transfer case & engine shield (reqs model TK20753 or TK20903 or TK20953)		
V76	**Tow Hooks**	33	38
	standard on 4WD models; reqs model TC20753 or TC20903 or TC20953)		
—	**Emissions**		
FE9	federal	NC	NC
NA6	high altitude (NA on TC20953 or TK20953)	NC	NC
YF5	California	NA	NA
NG1	New York	NC	NC
—	**Engines**		
LB4	4.3L (262 CID) V6 EFI gas	NC	NC
	L035.0L (305 CID) V8 EFI gas - model TC20753 or TK20753 ..	NC	NC
	model TC20903 or TK20903	495	575
	reqs GVW C5Z		
L05	5.7L (350 CID) V8 EFI gas		
	w/model TC20753 or TK20753 & GVW C5Z..........................	232	270
	w/model TC20903 or TC20953 or TK20903 or TK20953 & GVW C6P	NC	NC
	w/model TC20903 or TK20903 & GVW C5Z..........................	727	845
L19	7.4L (454 CID) V8 EFI gas	520	605
L49	6.5L (395 CID) 155 HP V8 diesel		
	w/model TC20903 or TK20903 & GVW C5Z..........................	2468	2870
	w/model TC20753 or TK20753 & GVW C5Z..........................	1974	2295
	incls dual batteries, hydraulic brakes, HD radiator, eng oil cooler, extra sound insulation, engine block heater, glow plugs, integral two-stage fuel filter, fuel & water separator w/instrument panel warning light & fuel filter change signal		
L56	6.5L (395 CID) 180 HP V8 turbo diesel		
	w/model TC20903 or TK20903 & GVW C5Z..........................	3156	3670
	w/model TC20753 or TK20753 & GVW C5Z..........................	2662	3095
	incls dual batteries, hydraulic brakes, HD radiator, eng oil cooler, extra sound insulation, eng block heater, glow plugs, integral two-stage fuel filter, fuel & water separator w/instrument panel warning light & fuel filter change signal		
L65	6.5L (395 CID) 190 HP V8 turbo diesel	2430	2825
	incls dual batteries, hydraulic brakes, HD radiator, eng oil cooler, extra sound insulation, eng block heater, glow plugs, integral two-stage fuel filter, fuel & water separator w/instrument panel warning light & fuel filter change signal		
—	**Transmissions**		
MG5	5-spd manual w/overdrive (4.02 1st)	NC	NC
MT8	5-spd manual w/overdrive (6.34 1st)		
	w/GVW C6P or diesel engines L49 or L65..............................	NC	NC
	w/engines LB4 or L05 or L19 & w/o GVW C6P........................	84	98

CODE	DESCRIPTION	DEALER	LIST
M30	4-spd automatic w/overdrive (4L60E)..	765	890
MT1	4-spd automatic w/overdrive (4L80E)..	765	890
—	**Rear Axles**		
GU6	3.42 ratio..	NC	NC
GT4	3.73 ratio..	NC	NC
GT5	4.10 ratio..	NC	NC
HC4	4.56 ratio..	NC	NC
G80	**Locking Rear Differential**	217	252
KC4	**Engine Oil Cooler**..	116	135
	reqs engine LB4 or L03 & trans MT8 or MG5 and rear axles GU6 or GT4		
V08	**Heavy Duty Cooling**..	170	198
	reqs engine LB4 or L03 or L05 and trans MT1 or M30 and rear axles GU6 or GT4 and NA w/cooling KC4		
KNP	**Auxiliary HD Transmission Cooling System**.............................	NA	NA
	reqs trans MT1 or M30 and NA w/engines L03 or LB4		
TP2	**Battery** — auxiliary HD, 600 cold cranking amp...........................	115	134
	reqs engine LB4 and camper equip Z81 or engines L03 or L05 or L19 (incl'd w/Z81 camper equip)		
V10	**Cold Climate Pkg**..	28	33
	incls eng block heater & special insulation (reqs eng LB4 or L03 or L05 or L19)		
—	**Wheels**		
P01	bright metal, wheel covers (reqs decor R9S)	36	42
P06	trim rings & hub caps, bright metal (incl'd w/YE9 decor)	52	60
P13	**Spare Wheel & Tire Carrier**...	NC	NC
	side mounted on driver's side (NA w/BZY bedliner) (NA w/model TC20753 or TK20753)		
—	**Front Tires**		
XBK	LT245/75R16C all season BW SBR	NC	NC
XBN	LT245/75R16C on-off road BW SBR..	20	23
XBX	LT245/75R16C white lettered on-off road SBR...............................	63	73
XHP	LT225/75R16D all season BW SBR	NC	NC
XHR	LT225/75R16D on-off road BW SBR..	19	22
XHH	LT245/75R16E all season BW SBR		
	w/GVW C5Z - w/GVW C6P...	NC	NC
XGK	LT245/75R16E on-off road BW SBR		
	w/model TK20903 & GVW C5Z...	98	114
	w/model TK20903 or TK20953 & GVW C6P...................................	19	22
—	**Rear Tires**		
YBK	LT245/75R16C all season BW SBR	NC	NC
YBN	LT245/75R16C on-off road BW SBR..	20	23
	YBXLT245/75R16C on-off road white lettered outline SBR..............	63	73
YHP	LT225/75R16D all season BW SBR	NC	NC
YHR	LT225/75R16D on-off road BW SBR..	19	22
YHH	LT245/75R16E all season BW SBR		
	w/model TC20753 or TC20903 or TC20953 or TC20903 & w/GVW C5Z	79	92
	w/GVW C6P..	NC	NC
YGK	LT245/75R16E on-off road BW SBR		
	w/model TC20753 or TC20903 or TK20903 & w/GVW C5Z	98	114
	w/model TC20903 or TC20953 or TK20903 or TK20953 & w/GVW C6P	19	22
—	**Spare Tires**		
ZBK	LT245/75R16C all season BW SBR	259	301
ZBN	LT245/75R16C on-off road BW SBR..	268	312

GMC

CODE	DESCRIPTION	DEALER	LIST
ZBX	LT245/75R16C on-off road white letter SBR..	290	337
ZHP	LT225/75R16D all season BW SBR	249	289
ZHR	LT225/75R16D on-off road BW SBR..	258	300
ZHH	LT245/75R16E all season BW SBR...	288	335
ZGK	LT245/75R16E on-off road BW SBR	298	346
R6G	**Air Conditioning Delete**..	NC	NC
	reqs pkg 1SA		
C60	**Air Conditioning** — incl'd in pkg 1SB, 1SC, 1SD	692	805
—	**Convenience Pkg I**		
R7V	power locks & windows delete..	NC	NC
	reqs decor YE9 and NA w/pkg 1SD		
ZQ2	power locks & windows (incl'd in pkg 1SD)..	316	367
—	**Convenience Pkg II**		
R7W	tilt wheel & speed control delete	NC	NC
	reqs decor YE9 and NA w/pkg 1SD		
ZQ3	tilt wheel & speed control (incl'd in pkg 1SD).......................................	329	383
BG9	**Color-Keyed Rubber Floor Covering** — w/model TC20903 or TK20903....	(17)	(20)
	w/model TC20753 or TC20953 or TK20753 or TK20953.........................	(31)	(36)
	replaces carpet & floor mats (reqs decor YE9)		
TR9	**Auxiliary Lamps** — incl'd in 1SC, 1SD	81	94
C95	**Lamps** — dome & reading (incl'd w/TR9 lighting)	28	33
UM7	**Radio**	NC	NC
	incls AM/FM stereo w/seek-scan w/4 spkrs (NA w/pkg 1SD)		
UP4	**Radio**	(146)	(170)
	incls AM radio, reqs decor R9S and pkg 1SA or 1SB		
UM6	**Radio**	105	122
	incls AM/FM stereo w/seek-scan, cass, clock (incl'd in 1SD)		
UX1	**Radio**	234	272
	incls AM stereo/FM stereo w/seek-scan, cass, equalizer, clock & 4 spkrs		
UL5	**Radio Delete** — reqs decor R9S and pkg 1SA or 1SB	(247)	(287)
—	**Seats**		
A52	front bench	NC	NC
	incls center fold down armrest w/YE9 SLE decor & custom cloth trim (reqs model TC20903 or TK20903)		
AE7	front 40/60 reclining split bench - w/model TC20903 or TK20903	150	174
	w/model TC20753 or TC20953 or TK20753 or TK20953............................	NC	NC
A50	front low back reclining buckets - w/model TC20903 or TK20903	249	289
	w/model TC20753 or TC20953 or TK20753 or TK20953............................	99	115
	incls center floor console (incls easy entry feature on Club Coupe)		
A95	front high back reclining buckets - w/model TC20903 or TK20903	421	490
	w/model TC20753 or TC20953 or TK20753 or TK20953............................	250	291
	incls inboard armrests, center floor console (incls easy entry feature on Club Coupe) (reqs decor YE9)		
YG4	rear seat delete..	(340)	(395)
	reqs model TC20953 or TC20753 or TK20953 or TK20753 and decor R9S and seats A50 or AE7		
AG9	**6-Way Power Seat Adjuster**	206	240
	reqs decor YE9 and model TC20753 or TK20753 or TC20953 or TK20953 and seats AE7 or A95		
U16	**Tachometer**	51	59
V22	**Deluxe Front Appearance Pkg**		
	incls color-keyed grille, composite halogen headlamps & dual horns		

CODE	DESCRIPTION	DEALER	LIST
	(incl'd w/YE9 decor)		
BZY	**Bedliner** — NA w/P13 spare wheel & tire carrier	194	225
—	**Bumpers**		
V43	painted rear step..	112	130
	VB3chromed rear step bumper w/rub strip (reqs decor YE9)	197	229
V27	**Bumper Guards** — front, black		
	incl'd w/YE9 decor w/L49, L56, L65 (reqs YE9 decor)		
U01	**Roof Marker Lamps** — NA w/YF5 emissions...................................	45	52
VK3	**Front License Plate Bracket**	NC	NC
—	**Mirrors**		
D45	below-eye-line, stainless steel..	39	45
	incl'd in pkg 1SC, 1SD		
DF2	camper type, stainless steel...	46	53
	incl'd w/Z81 camper equip		
B85	**Bright Exterior Moldings** — w/model TC20903 or TC20753 or TC20953...	92	107
	w/model TC20753 or TK20903 and GVW C5Z	92	107
	w/model TC20903 or TK20953 and GVW C6P	65	76
	incls wheel opening moldings w/o K2500 & C6P (incls body side moldings)		
	(incl'd w/YE9 decor) (NA w/camper equip Z81)		
C49	**Rear Window Electric Defogger**	132	154
	reqs model TC20753 or TC20953 or TK20753 or TK20953 and decor YE9		
	(NA w/A28 sliding rear window)		
A28	**Sliding Rear Window** — NA w/rear window elec defogger	97	113
A20	**Swing-Out Quarter Windows**..	37	43
	reqs model TC20753 or TC20953 or TK20753 or TK20953		
	(incl'd w/YE9 decor & AJ1 deep tinted glass)		
AJ1	**Deep Tinted Solar Ray Glass** — w/decor R9S & window A28	99	115
	w/decor R9S & w/o window A28...	129	150
	w/decor YE9 & rear defogger C49 or window A28....................................	62	72
	w/decor YE9 & w/o rear defogger C49 or window A28	92	107
	reqs model TC20753 or TC20953 or TK20753 or TK20953		
—	**Paint**		
ZY1	solid	NC	NC
ZY2	conventional two-tone	114	132
ZY4	deluxe two-tone..	209	243

CODE	DESCRIPTION	DEALER	LIST

GMC SIERRA C-K 3500 PICKUPS

SIERRA C3500 2WD PICKUPS 8 CYL

TC30903	Wideside Regular Cab (8 ft)	14893	17020
TC30953	Wideside Club Coupe (8 ft)	17731	20264

SIERRA K3500 4WD PICKUPS 8 CYL

TK30903	Wideside Regular Cab (8 ft)	17177	19631
TK30953	Wideside Club Coupe (8 ft)	19654	22462
Destination Charge:		600	600

Standard Equipment

SIERRA 3500 REGULAR CAB PICKUP - BASE SL: 7 liter V-8, 5-speed manual transmission with deep low gear and overdrive, 600-amp battery, power front disc/rear drum brakes with rear-wheel anti-lock system, chrome front bumper and argent painted grille, single rectangular halogen headlamps, RH and LH below-eyeline black painted mirrors, heavy-duty radiator, LT245/75R16-E all-season radial tires, silver painted steel wheels, side door guard beams, full gauges and instrumentation, tinted Solar Ray glass all windows, deluxe heater with windshield and side window defoggers, electronic AM radio with fixed-mast antenna, Scotchgarded carpeting, cloth trim and door panels, three-passenger all-vinyl trim front bench seat with head restraints and folding backrest.

SLE (in addition to or instead of BASE SL equipment): Bumpers with black rub strip and bright trim, deluxe front appearance grille, dual composite halogen headlamps, black bodyside moldings with bright trim, Rally wheel trim, swing-out rear quarter windows, color-keyed carpeting, electronic AM/FM radio with seek-scan and digital clock, three-passenger seats with choice of custom vinyl or custom cloth front bench with head restraint and folding backrest.

SIERRA 3500 CLUB COUPE PICKUP - BASE SL: 5.7 liter V-8, 5-speed manual transmission with deep low gear and overdrive, 600-amp battery, power front disc/rear drum brakes with rear-wheel anti-lock system, chrome front bumper and argent painted grille, single rectangular halogen headlamps, RH and LH below-eyeline black painted mirrors, heavy-duty radiator, LT245/75R16-E all-season radial tires, silver painted steel wheels, side door guard beams, full gauges and instrumentation, tinted Solar Ray glass all windows, deluxe heater with windshield and side window defoggers, electronic AM radio with fixed-mast antenna, Scotchgarded carpeting, cloth trim and door panels, three-passenger all-vinyl trim front 60/40 reclining split bench seat with driver and passenger easy entry.

CODE	DESCRIPTION	DEALER	LIST

SLE (in addition to or instead of BASE SL equipment): Bumpers with black rub strip and bright trim, deluxe front appearance grille, dual composite halogen headlamps, black bodyside moldings with bright trim, Rally wheel trim, swing-out rear quarter windows, color-keyed carpeting, electronic AM/FM radio with seek-scan and digital clock, three-passenger seats with choice of custom vinyl or custom cloth front bench with head restraint and folding backrest.

Accessories

CODE	DESCRIPTION	DEALER	LIST
—	**Decor**		
R9S	**SL Decor**	NC	NC
	incls vehicle w/std equip		
YE9	**SLE Decor**	686	798
	incls V22 deluxe frt appearance, sport steering wheel, color-keyed frt bumper w/rub strip, bright metal trim rings w/single rear wheels (incls A20 swing-out windows on Club Coupe)		
—	**Option Pkgs** — decor price incl'd in pkgs		
1SA	**Pkg 1SA** — w/R9S SL decor	NC	NC
	incls vehicle w/std equip		
1SB	**Pkg 1SB** — w/R9S SL decor	348	405
	incls pkg 1SA plus air conditioning		
1SC	**Pkg 1SC** — Regular Cab w/YE9 SLE decor	1154	1342
	Club Coupe w/YE9 SLE decor	982	1142
	incls pkg 1SB plus auxiliary lamps and D45 below-eye-line exterior mirrors (may be upgraded to DF2 mirrors)		
1SD	**Pkg 1SD** — Regular Cab w/YE9 SLE decor	1689	1964
	Club Coupe w/YE9 SLE decor	1474	1714
	incls pkg 1SC plus UM6 radio (AM/FM w/seek-scan, cass, clock) (radio may be upgraded to UX1 radio), pwr windows, pwr door locks, tilt wheel & speed control		
—	**GVW Pkgs**		
C6U	9000 lb	NC	NC
C6W	9200 lb	NC	NC
C7A	10000 lb	NC	NC
—	**Rear Wheels**		
R04	single rear wheels (reqs GVW C6U or C6W)	NC	NC
R05	dual rear wheels (std on TC30953, TK30953)	821	955
	incls U01 roof marker lamps; reqs GVW C7A		
Z81	**Camper Equip** — w/engine L65	85	99
	w/engines L05 or L19	200	233
	incls DF2 stainless steel mirrors & wiring harness		
Z82	**Heavy Duty Trailering Equipment**	181	210
	incls trailer hitch & wiring harness; reqs VB3 or V43 bumpers		
VYU	**Snow Plow Prep Pkg** — TK30903	101	118
	incls F60 HD frt torsion bars, HD pwr steering cooler, two elec relays & special forward wiring harness		
F60	**Heavy Duty Front Torsion Bars** — TK30903 or TK30953	54	63
	incl'd w/VYU snow plow prep pkg		
NZZ	**Off-Road Skid Plates** — TK30903 or TK30953	82	95
	incls differential, transfer case & engine shields		
V76	**Tow Hooks** — std on 4WD models	33	38
—	**Emissions**		
FE9	federal	NC	NC
YF5	California	NA	NA

CODE	DESCRIPTION	DEALER	LIST
NG1	New York	NC	NC
—	**Engines**		
L05	5.7L (350 CID) V8 EFI gas	NC	NC
L19	7.4L (454 CID) V8 EFI gas	404	470
L65	6.5L (395 CID) V8 turbo diesel	2430	2825
	incls dual batteries, hydraulic brakes, HD radiator, eng oil cooler, extra sound insulation, eng block heater, glow plugs, integral two-stage fuel filter, fuel & water separator w/instrument panel warning light & fuel filter change signal		
—	**Transmissions**		
MT8	5-spd manual w/overdrive	NC	NC
MT1	4-spd automatic w/overdrive	765	890
—	**Rear Axles**		
GT4	3.73 ratio	NC	NC
GT5	4.10 ratio	NC	NC
HC4	4.56 ratio	NC	NC
G80	**Locking Rear Differential**	217	252
	NA w/rear wheels RO4 & rear axle GT4		
KNP	**Cooling** — w/trans MT1	NA	NA
	incls HD auxiliary trans cooling system		
TP2	**Battery** — auxiliary, 600 cold cranking amp	115	134
	incl'd w/Z81 camper equip; reqs L05 or L19 eng		
V10	**Cold Climate Pkg**	28	33
	incls eng block heater & special insulation (reqs engines L05 or L19)		
—	**Wheel Equip**		
P01	wheel covers (4, bright metal)...	36	42
	reqs decor R9S & rear wheels RO4		
P06	trim rings & hub caps (4, bright metal)....................................	52	60
	incl'd w/decor YE9 & RO4 wheels		
P13	spare wheel & tire carrier..	NC	NC
	reqs rear wheels RO4; NA w/BZY bedliner		
—	**Front Tires**		
XHE	LT225/75R16C all season BW SBR w/model TC30953	NC	NC
	w/model TC30903	(89)	(104)
XHP	LT225/75R16D all season BW SBR w/model TK30953	NC	NC
	w/model TC30953	29	34
	w/model TC30903 or TK30903	(60)	(70)
XHR	LT225/75R16D on-off road BW SBR w/model TK30953	19	22
	w/model TK30903	(41)	(48)
XHH	LT245/75R16E all season BW SBR..	NC	NC
XGK	LT245/75R16E on-off road BW SBR	19	22
—	**Rear Tires**		
YHP	LT225/75R16D all season BW SBR		
	w/model TC30953 or TK30953	NC	NC
	w/model TC30903 or TK30903	368	428
YHR	LT225/75R16D on-off road BW SBR		
	w/model TC30953 or TK30953	38	44
	w/model TC30903 or TK30903	406	472
YHH	LT245/75R16E all season BW SBR..	NC	NC
YGK	LT245/75R16E on-off road BW SBR	19	22
—	**Spare Tires**		
ZHP	LT225/75R16D all season BW SBR	258	300

CODE	DESCRIPTION	DEALER	LIST
ZHR	LT225/75R16D on-off road BW SBR..	267	311
ZHH	LT245/75R16E all season BW SBR..	288	335
ZGK	LT245/75R16E on-off road BW SBR..	298	346
C60	**Air Conditioning** — incl'd in 1SB, 1SC, 1SD..	692	805
—	**Convenience Pkgs**		
R7V	power locks & windows not desired..	NC	NC
ZQ2	power locks & windows (incl'd in 1SD)...	316	367
R7W	tilt wheel & speed control not desired..	NC	NC
	reqs decor YE9 & NA w/1SD		
ZQ3	tilt wheel & speed control (incl'd in 1SD)...	329	383
BG9	**Color-Keyed Rubber Floor Covering** — w/model TC30903 or TK30903	(17)	(20)
	w/model TC30953 or TK30953	(31)	(36)
	replaces carpet & floor mats (reqs decor YE9)		
TR9	**Auxiliary Lamps**...	81	94
	incls C95 dome & reading lamps, courtesy, ashtray, glovebox & underhood lamps (incl'd in 1SC, 1SD)		
C95	**Dome & Reading Lamps** — incl'd w/TR9 lighting	28	33
UM7	**Radio**	NC	NC
	incls AM/FM stereo w/seek-scan & clock & 4 spkrs (NA w/1SD)		
UP4	**Radio**	(146)	(170)
	incls AM radio (reqs decor R9S & 1SA or 1SB)		
UM6	**Radio**	105	122
	incls AM/FM stereo w/seek-scan, cass, clock (incl'd in 1SD)		
UX1	**Radio**	234	272
	incls AM stereo/FM stereo w/seek-scan, cass, equalizer, clock & 4 spkrs		
UL5	**Radio Delete** — reqs decor R9S & 1SA or 1SB	(247)	(287)
—	**Seats**		
A52	front bench seat..	NC	NC
	incls center fold down armrest w/YE9 SLE decor & custom cloth trim; reqs model TC30903 or TK30903		
AE7	front 40/60 reclining split bench seat		
	w/model TC30953 or TK30953	NC	NC
	w/model TC30903 or TK30903	150	174
	incls easy entry feature on Club Coupe models		
A50	front low back reclining bucket seats		
	w/model TC30903 or TK30903	249	289
	w/model TC30953 or TK30953	99	115
	incls center floor console (incls easy entry feature on Club Coupe models)		
A95	front high back reclining bucket seats		
	w/model TC30903 or TK30903	421	490
	w/model TC30953 or TK30953	250	291
	incls inboard armrests, center floor console (incls easy entry feature on Club Coupe models)		
YG4	rear seat delete - models TC30953 or TK30953..	(340)	(395)
	reqs decor R9S & seats AE7 or A50		
AG9	**6-Way Power Seat Adjuster** — driver's side	206	240
	reqs decor YE9 & model TC30953 or TK30953 & seats AE7 or A95		
U16	**Tachometer**	51	59
V22	**Deluxe Front Appearance Pkg**..	164	191
	incls color-keyed grille, composite halogen headlamps, dual horns (incl'd w/decor YE9)		
BZY	**Bedliner**	194	225

CODE	DESCRIPTION	DEALER	LIST
	NA w/P13 spare wheel & tire carrier		
—	**Bumpers**		
V43	painted rear step bumper...	112	130
VB3	chromed rear step bumper w/rub strip..	197	229
	reqs decor YE9		
V27	black front bumper guards..	28	32
	reqs decor YE9; incl'd w/YE9 decor & L65		
U01	**Roof Marker Lamps** — five...	45	52
	incl'd w/R05 dual rear wheels; NA w/YF5 emissions & R04 rear wheels [std on TC30953 & TK30953]		
VK3	**Front License Plate Bracket**	NC	NC
—	**Mirrors**		
D45	below-eye-line exterior mirrors, stainless steel	39	45
	incl'd in 1SC, 1SD; NA w/camper equip Z81		
DF2	camper type exterior, stainless steel	46	53
	incl'd w/Z81 camper equip		
B85	**Molding** — bright exterior - w/model TC30903...........................	92	107
	w/model TK30903	65	76
	NA w/R05 wheels; incl'd w/YE9 decor		
C49	**Electric Rear Window Defogger**	132	154
	reqs model TC30953 or TK30953 & decor YE9 (NA w/A28 sliding rear window)		
—	**Window Options**		
A28	sliding rear window	97	113
	NA w/electric rear window defogger		
A20	swing-out quarter windows	37	43
	reqs model TC30953 or TK30953; incl'd w/YE9 decor & AJ1 deep tinted glass		
AJ1	deep tinted solar ray glass		
	w/decor YE9 & rear window defogger or A28 windows	62	72
	w/decor YE9 & w/o rear window defogger or A28 windows.........	92	107
	w/decor R9S and A28 windows	99	115
	w/decor R9S & w/o A28 windows	129	150
	reqs model TC30953 or TK30953 (w/rear window defogger C49 or A28 sliding rear window - incls light tinted rear window)		
—	**Paint**		
ZY1	solid	NC	NC
ZY2	conventional two-tone paint...	114	132
ZY4	deluxe two-tone paint..	209	243

CODE	DESCRIPTION	DEALER	LIST

GMC

GMC SONOMA PICKUPS

SONOMA PICKUPS 2WD

TS10603 2WD Regular Cab (6.1 ft) 108.3" WB

w/R9S decor (SL)	9267	9806
w/YC3 decor (SLS)	10080	11138

TS10803 2WD Regular Cab (7.4 ft) 117.9" WB

w/R9S decor (SL)	9550	10106
w/YC5 decor (SLE)	10570	11680
TS10653 2WD Club Coupe (6.1 ft) 122.9" WB	10962	12113

SONOMA PICKUPS 4WD

TT10603 4WD Regular Cab (6.1 ft) 108.3" WB

w/R9S decor (SL)	13519	14306
w/YC3 decor (SLS)	14152	15638

TT10803 4WD Regular Cab (7.4 ft) 117.9" WB

w/R9S decor (SL)	13803	14606
w/YC5 decor (SLE)	14643	16180
TT10653 4WD Club Coupe (6.1 ft.) 122.9" WB	15035	16613
Destination Charge:	470	470

Standard Equipment

SONOMA REGULAR CAB PICKUP - BASE SL: 5-speed manual transmission, 100-amp alternator, air dam, 525-amp battery, power front disc/rear drum brakes with rear-wheel anti-lock braking on 4-cylinder engine and 4-wheel anti-lock braking system on V-6, power steering, front and rear step bumpers, tinted Solar Ray glass windows, halogen headlamps, full-sized spare (mounted under bed), center high-mounted stop light, coil spring front suspension 2WD and torsion bar on 4WD models, semi-floating rear axle and 2-stage multi-leaf springs, P205/75R15 all-season radials, 15" x 7" steel argent painted wheels, deluxe heater with windshield and side window defoggers, full instrumentation and gauges, ETR AM radio with digital clock and two speakers, Scotchgarded cloth trim, color-keyed seat and shoulder belts, deluxe steering wheel, door-operated interior lamps, dark gray vinyl floor covering.

SLS (in addition to or instead of BASE SL equipment): Chrome grille with halogen headlamps, door trim panels with LH and RH molded pockets, molded plastic with soft cloth upper insert, full-floor color-keyed carpeting, day/night mirror with dual reading lamps, ETR AM/FM stereo with digital clock, Scotchgarded

GMC

cloth trim, door panels and carpeting, deluxe 2-spoke black steering wheels, color-keyed padded sunshades with slider extensions.

SONOMA CLUB COUPE PICKUP - BASE SLS: 5-speed manual transmission, 100-amp alternator, air dam, 525-amp battery, power front disc/rear drum brakes with rear-wheel anti-lock braking on 4-cylinder engine and 4-wheel anti-lock braking system on V-6, power steering, front and rear step bumpers, tinted Solar Ray glass windows, full-sized spare, center high-mounted stop light, coil spring front suspension 2WD and torsion bar on 4WD models, P205/75R15 all-season radials, 15" x 7" steel argent painted wheels, deluxe heater with windshield and side window defoggers, full instrumentation and gauges, chrome grille with halogen headlamps, door trim panels with LH and RH molded pockets, and cloth upper insert, full-floor color-keyed carpeting, day/night mirror with dual reading lamps, ETR AM/FM stereo with digital clock, Scotchgarded cloth trim, door panels and carpeting, deluxe 2-spoke black steering wheels, color-keyed padded sunshades with slider extensions.

Accessories

CODE	DESCRIPTION	DEALER	LIST
—	**Decor**		
R9S	**SL Decor**..	NC	NC
	incls A52 frt bench seat, BG9 full floor vinyl covering, painted gray F & R bumper and steel wheels w/hub caps (incl'd in pkg 1SA, 1SB) (reqs model TS10603 or TS10803 or TT10603 or TT10803)		
YC3	**SLS Sport Decor**...	NC	NC
	incls dual illuminated visor mirrors w/extenders, interior rearview mirror w/illuminated entry feature & dual reading lamps, AV5 reclining bucket seats w/floor console, B30 full floor carpeting, vinyl floor mats, D44 black painted mirrors, painted body color F & R step bumper, steel wheels w/hub caps trim rings, lower body & bumper stripe, two dash mounted pwr outlets, and composite headlamps (incl'd in pkg 1SC, 1SD) (reqs model TS10603 or TS10653 or TT10603 or TT10653)		
YC5	**SLE Comfort Decor** — w/model TS10803 or TT10803	NC	NC
	w/model TS10603 or TS10653 or TT10603 or TT10653	230	267
	incls dual illuminated visor mirrors w/extenders, interior rearview mirror w/illuminated entry feature & dual reading lamps, AM6 frt 60/40 reclining split bench seat, B30 full floor carpeting, vinyl floor mats, D44 black painted mirrors, painted gray F & R step bumpers, steel wheels w/hub caps & trim rings, ZY2 conventional two-tone paint, gray body side moldings w/bright accent, two dash mounted pwr outlets and composite headlamps (incl'd in pkg 1SC, 1SD w/models TS10803 or TT10803)		
—	**Body**		
E63	**Wideside**...	NC	NC
	incls pkg 1SA, 1SB, 1SC, 1SD		
—	**Option Pkgs - Regular Cab**		
1SA	**Pkg 1SA** — Regular Cab	NC	NC
	incls vehicle w/std R9S SL decor		
1SB	**Pkg 1SB** — Regular Cab	(242)	(281)
	incls pkg 1SA plus UL5 radio delete & VF7 bumper delete		
1SC	**Pkg 1SC** — Regular Cab w/o bonus value pkg	NC	NC
	Regular Cab w/bonus value pkg...............................	NC	NC
	incls vehicle w/YC3 SLS decor or YC5 SLE decor (N60 aluminum wheels incl'd on 2WD w/LN2 eng when ordered w/bonus value pkg) (N90 alum wheels incl'd on 4WD w/M30 trans when ordered w/bonus value pkg)		
1SD	**Pkg 1SD** — Regular Cab w/o bonus value pkg	105	122
	Regular Cab w/bonus value pkg...............................	105	122

CODE	DESCRIPTION	DEALER	LIST
	incls pkg 1SC plus UM6 AM/FM w/seek-scan, cass, clock		
—	**Option Pkgs - Club Coupe**		
1SC	**Pkg 1SC** — Club Coupe w/o bonus value pkg	NC	NC
	Club Coupe w/bonus value pkg	NC	NC
	incls vehicle w/YC3 SLS decor (N90 aluminum wheels incl'd on 2WD w/LN2 eng when ordered w/bonus value pkg), (N90 aluminum wheels incl'd on 4WD w/M30 trans when ordered w/bonus value pkg)		
1SD	**Pkg 1SD** — Club Coupe w/o bonus value pkg	105	122
	Club Coupe w/bonus value pkg	105	122
	incls pkg 1SC plus UM6 AM/FM radio w/seek-scan, cass, clock (may be upgraded to UX1 or U1C radio)		
—	**GVW Pkgs**		
C5T	4200 lb.	NC	NC
C5D	4600 lb.	NC	NC
C5X	4650 lb.	NC	NC
C5A	4900 lb.	NC	NC
C6F	5150 lb.	NC	NC
Z82	**HD Trailering Equip** — w/eng LB4 & trans M30	351	408
	w/eng LB4 & trans MY2	297	345
	w/eng L35	181	210
	incls 7-lead wiring harness, weight - distribution hitch platform & HD flasher (incls V08 cooling w/LB4 eng) (reqs LB4 or L35 eng) (NA on 2WD & GU2) (reqs model TS10603 or TS10653 & GVWR C5D or model TS10803 & GVWR C5A or model TT10603 or TT10803 or TT10653 & GVWR C6F)		
Z83	**Solid Smooth Ride Suspension Pkg**	NC	NC
	incls HD shocks & QCE tires (std on TS10603, TT10603, TT10803) (reqs model TS10603 & GVWR C5T or model TT10603 or TT10803 & GVWR C5X)		
Z85	**Heavy Duty Suspension Pkg** — w/model TS10603	55	64
	w/model TT10603 or TT10803	187	217
	incls HD rear springs & HD F & R shocks (incls QFL tires on 4WD) (reqs GVWR C5D or C5A or C6F)		
ZQ8	**Sport Suspension Pkg** — w/model TS10603	272	316
	w/model TS10803	217	252
	incls HD rear springs, HD F & R shocks & QPP tires (reqs model TS10603 & decor YC3 or YC5 & GVWR C5D or model TS10803 & decor YC5 & GVWR C5A or C5D)		
ZR2	**Highrider Suspension Pkg**	1449	1685
	incls F & R wheel opening flares, Bilstein shocks, HD springs, QJJ tires, ZM5 shield pkg & additional chassis enhancements for increased width/ height (reqs GT4 rear axle) (reqs mdl TT10603 & decor YC3 & GVWR C5X)		
ZM6	**Off-Road Suspension Pkg** — w/model TT10603	414	481
	w/model TT10803	359	417
	w/model TT10653	282	328
	incls special Bilstein gas shocks, upsized torsion bar, jounce bumpers, stabilizer bar, QEB tires & HD springs		
ZM5	**Underbody Shield Pkg**	108	126
	incls transfer case shield, frt differential skid plates, fuel tank shield & steering linkage shields (reqs model TT10603 or TT10803 or TT10653)		
U89	**Wiring Harness**	35	41
	incls 5-lead wiring harness (NA w/Z82 trailering equip)		
—	**Emissions**		
FE9	federal	NC	NC

CODE	DESCRIPTION	DEALER	LIST
YF5	California	100	100
NG1	New York	86	100
—	**Engines**		
LN2	2.2L (133 CID) MPI 4 cyl gas	NC	NC
LB4	4.3L (262 CID) EFI V6 gas		
	w/model TT10603 or TT10653 or TT10803..	NC	NC
	w/model TS10653 or TS10803	731	850
L35	4.3L (262 CID) CPI V6 gas		
	w/model TT10603 or TT10653 or TT10803..	481	559
	w/model TS10603 or TS10653 or TS10803..	1212	1409
—	**Transmissions**		
MW1	5-spd manual trans w/overdrive	NC	NC
	incls Borg Warner, 4.03 1st		
MY2	5-spd manual trans w/overdrive	NC	NC
	incls New Venture, 4.02 1st		
M30	4-spd automatic trans w/overdrive...	797	927
	incls electronic control		
—	**Rear Axles**		
GU2	2.73 ratio..	NC	NC
GU4	3.08 ratio..	NC	NC
GU6	3.42 ratio..	NC	NC
GT4	3.73 ratio..	NC	NC
GT5	4.10 ratio..	NC	NC
G80	**Locking Rear Differential**	217	252
	reqs models TT10603 or TT10653 or TT10803 and rear axles GU6 or GT4 (reqs models TS10603 or TS10653 or TS10803 and trans MY2 and rear axle GU4 or trans M30 and rear axles GU6 and NA w/LN2 eng)		
NP1	**Transfer Case** — electronic shift..	106	123
	reqs model TT10603 or TT10653 or TT10803 and decor YC3 or YC5		
V08	**Heavy Duty Cooling** — w/engine LB4 & trans M30	170	198
	w/engine LB4 & trans MY2	116	135
	incls eng oil cooler (incls trans oil cooler w/M30 trans) (incl'd w/Z82 trailering w/LB4 eng) (reqs LB4 eng)		
V10	**Cold Climate Pkg**	94	109
	incls UA1 battery, eng block heater & anti-freeze protection to -34 degrees fahrenheit		
UA1	**Heavy Duty Battery** - 690 cold cranking amp	48	56
	incl'd w/V10 cold climate pkg		
N60	**Aluminum Wheels** — (4), 15" x 7"..	213	248
	reqs model TS10603 or TS10803 or TS10653 and NA w/decor R9S		
N90	**Aluminum Wheels** — (4), 15" x 7"..	241	280
	reqs model TT10603 or TT10653 or TT10803 and NA w/decor R9S		
—	**Tires** — includes front, rear and full-size spare		
QCE	P205/75R15 all season BW SBR	NC	NC
	incl'd w/Z85 susp'n pkg on 2WD models; incl'd w/Z83 susp'n pkg		
QCF	P205/75R15 all season white lettered SBR	104	121
QJL	P205/75R15 on-off road white lettered SBR..	146	170
QPP	P215/65R15 highway white lettered low profile "sport"	NC	NC
	incl'd w/ZQ8 susp'n pkg		
QEB	P235/75R15 on-off road white lettered SBR..	157	182
	incl'd w/ZM6 susp'n pkg		
QFL	P235/75R15 all season BW SBR	NC	NC

CODE	DESCRIPTION	DEALER	LIST
	std on TT10653; incl'd w/Z85 susp'n pkg on 4WD models		
QJJ	31x10.5R15 on-off road BW SBR	NC	NC
	incl'd w/ZR2 susp'n pkg		
R6G	**Air Conditioning Delete**..	NC	NC
C60	**Air Conditioning**	671	780
—	**Convenience Pkgs**		
ZQ6	power locks, windows & dual electric mirrors	409	475
	reqs decor YC3 or YC5		
ZQ3	tilt wheel & speed control	329	383
—	**Floor Covering**		
BG9	full floor black vinyl covering..	(17)	(20)
	replaces carpeting; incl'd w/R9S decor		
B30	full floor carpeting	65	75
	incls vinyl floor mats; incl'd w/YC3 SLS or YC5 SLE decor		
UM7	**Radio**	NC	NC
	incls AM/FM stereo w/seek-scan & clock, 4 spkrs (NA w/1SB or 1SD)		
UM6	**Radio**	105	122
	incls AM/FM stereo w/seek-scan, cass, clock, 4 spkrs (NA w/1SB)		
UX1	**Radio**	234	272
	incls AM stereo/FM stereo w/seek-scan, cass, clock, 4 spkrs (NA w/pkg 1SB)		
U1C	**Radio**	349	406
	incls AM/FM stereo w/seek-scan, CD player, clock, 4 coaxial spkrs (NA w/pkg 1SB)		
UL5	**Radio Delete**...	(194)	(226)
	reqs decor R9S and NA w/pkg 1SA		
—	**Seats**		
A52	front bench seat (reqs decor R9S)	NC	NC
AM6	front 60/40 reclining split bench seat - w/decor YC5	NC	NC
	w/model TS10603 or TT10603 & decor YC3	(156)	(181)
	w/model TS10653 or TT10653 & decor YC3	(134)	(156)
AV5	front high back reclining bucket seats - w/decor YC3.......................	NC	NC
	w/model TS10603 or TS10803 or TT10603 or TT10803 & decor YC5	156	181
	w/model TS10653 or TT10653 & decor YC5	134	156
NP5	**Leather-Wrapped Steering Wheel** — reqs decor YC3 or YC5	46	54
U16	**Tachometer** — incl'd w/L35 engine	51	59
ANL	**Air Deflector & Fog Lamps**	99	115
	reqs model TS10603 or TS10653 or TS10803 & decor YC3 or YC5		
VF7	**Bumper Delete** — deletes rear bumper.......................................	(47)	(55)
	reqs decor R9S		
VK3	**Front License Plate Bracket**	NC	NC
D44	**Mirrors** — below-eye-line, black	47	52
	incl'd w/YC3 SLS or YC5 SLE decor; NA w/convenience pkg ZQ6		
A28	**Sliding Rear Window**	97	113
—	**Paint**		
ZY1	solid (reqs decor R9S or YC3)..	NC	NC
ZY2	conventional two-tone (reqs decor YC5)...	NC	NC
ZY3	special two-tone	225	297
	incls upper graduated stripe; reqs decor YC3		
D96	**Striping** — upper body stripe...	47	55
	reqs decor R9S and paint ZY1		

ISUZU PICKUPS

Code	Description	Dealer	List
Q16	2WD 2.3L S Regular Cab Std Bed (5-spd)	8506	9399
Q46	2WD 2.3L S Regular Cab Long Bed (5-spd)	9620	10809
S14	2WD 2.6L S Regular Cab Std Bed (auto)	10679	11999
S75	2WD 2.6L S Spacecab (5-spd)	11311	12709
T15	4WD 2.6L S Regular Cab Std Bed (5-spd)	11897	13519
U15	4WD 3.1L S Regular Cab Std Bed (5-spd)	12654	14379
Destination Charge:		350	350

Standard Equipment

S PICKUP: Cigarette lighter, cut-pile carpeting, molded headliner, dome lamp, day/night rearview mirror, remote hood opener, special instrumentation gauges [water temp, oil pressure (4WD), voltmeter (4WD), tachometer (4WD), trip odometer], warning/indicator lamps [oil pressure, battery, brake system, 4WD engagement (4WD), low fuel], 3-passenger bench seat (Regular Cab), reclining buckets seats (Spacecab), forward facing jump seats (Spacecab), see-thru headrests, 3-spoke steering wheel, dual sunvisors, semi-concealed 2-speed windshield wiper/washer with mist wipe, retractable cargo cover (Spacecab), assist grip, glove box with lock, automatic transmission interlock, power front disc brakes, rear disc brakes (4WD), rear wheel ABS, manual locking front hubs (4WD), power assisted recirculating ball steering (except 2.3L models), fuel tank skid plate (4WD), transfer case skid plate (4WD), radiator skid plate (4WD), oil pan skid plate (4WD), maintenance-free battery, single note horn.

Accessories

Code	Description	Dealer	List
C2	**California/New York Emissions** — w/2.3L engine	225	250
C3	**California/New York Emissions** — w/2.6L engine	135	150
A2/AF	**Air Conditioning** — NA on 2WD 2.6L models	706	830
M1	**Tire/Wheel Pkg** — 4WD	974	1145
	incls 31-10.5R15 off-road tires, alum wheels, mud flaps and fender flares		
GRP	**Brush/Grille Guard** — 4WD	216	305
G2	**Power Steering** — 2WD Reg Cab w/2.3L engine	276	325
ID	**Black Rear Step Bumper**	116	165
FBP	**AM/FM ETR Radio w/Cassette**	284	405
P1	**Bright Pkg** — 2WD	447	525

ISUZU

CODE	DESCRIPTION	DEALER	LIST
	incls bright grille/trim rings/mirrors/bumpers/door handles		
P2	**Bright Pkg — 4WD**..	1421	1670
	incls tire/wheel pkg plus bright bumpers/grille/wheel opening moldings/ dual mirrors		

MAZDA PICKUPS

B2300	2WD Base Short Bed (5-spd)...	8652	9390
B2300	2WD SE Short Bed (5-spd)	9875	11210
B2300	2WD Base Cab Plus (5-spd)	10588	12020
B3000	2WD SE Long Bed (5-spd)..	10857	12325
B3000	2WD SE Long Bed (auto)	12240	13895
B3000	2WD SE Cab Plus (5-spd)	11601	13170
B4000	2WD SE Long Bed (5-spd)	11011	12500
B4000	2WD LE Cab Plus (auto)	13526	15355
B4000	4WD SE Short Bed (5-spd)	14469	16425
B4000	4WD SE Cab Plus (5-spd)	15235	17295
B4000	4WD LE Cab Plus (auto)	17177	19500

Destination Charge:Alaska & Hawaii		600	600
Other States..		460	460

Standard Equipment

2WD TRUCK - BASE: 2.3L SOHC 8-valve 4 cylinder engine, electronic fuel injection, 5-speed manual transmission w/overdrive, power assisted front disc/rear drum brakes, rear wheel anti-lock braking system (ABS), steel wheels, P195/70R14 radial tires, double-wall cargo bed w/one-touch tailgate release, tinted glass, rear step bumper, high-mount rear stop light, dual side mirrors, full-size spare tire, rear mud guards, 3-passenger bench seat, 60/40 split reclining bench seat w/fold-down armrest (Cab Plus), vinyl upholstery, full instrumentation includes coolant temperature/voltmeter/oil pressure, trip odometer, AM/FM electronically tuned stereo (Cab Plus), floor console w/dual cupholders (Cab Plus).

SE 2WD TRUCK (in addition to or instead of BASE 2WD TRUCK equipment): Variable power assisted steering, full-faced styled steel wheels, P225/70R14 radial tires, flip-open rear quarter window (Cab

Plus), dual aero-style mirrors, 3-passenger bench seat deleted, reclining bucket seats, 60/40 split reclining bench seat w/fold-down armrest deleted, cloth upholstery, fold-down rear jump seats (Cab Plus), full carpeting, AM/FM cass stereo w/digital clock, tachometer, leather-wrapped steering wheel.

LE 2WD TRUCK (in addition to or instead of SE 2WD TRUCK equipment): 4.0L 12-valve V6 engine, 4-speed automatic transmission w/overdrive, sliding rear window, dual aero-style power mirrors, reclining bucket seats deleted, 60/40 split reclining bench seat w/fold-down armrest, Premium AM/FM cassette stereo w/digital clock, rear cargo cover (Cab Plus), tilt steering, cruise control, power windows and locks.

4WD TRUCK - SE: 4.0L 12-valve V6 engine, elec fuel injection, 5-speed manual trans, shift-on-the fly 2-speed transfer case w/auto locking front hubs, variable power assisted steering, power assisted front disc/rear drum brakes, rear wheel anti-lock braking system (ABS), protective underbody skid plates, styled steel wheels, P235/75R15 all terrain radial tires, double-wall cargo bed with one-touch tailgate release, tinted glass, flip-open rear quarter window (Cab Plus), rear step bumper, high-mount rear stop light, dual aero-style mirrors, front/rear mud guards, reclining sport bucket seats w/thigh & lumbar support, cloth upholstery, fold-down rear jump seats (Cab Plus), full carpeting, full instrumentation includes coolant temperature/voltmeter/oil pressure gauges, trip odometer, AM/FM cass stereo w/digital clock, floor console w/dual cupholders, tachometer, leather-wrapped steering wheel, sliding rear window.

LE 4WD TRUCK (in addition to or instead of SE 4WD TRUCK equip): 4-speed auto trans w/overdrive, dual aero-style power mirrors, reclining sport bucket seats with thigh and lumbar support deleted, Premium AM/FM cass stereo w/digital clock, tilt steering, cruise control, power windows and locks.

Accessories

CODE	DESCRIPTION	DEALER	LIST
AC1	**Air Conditioning**	656	800
AW1	**Alloy Wheels** — NA on Base models	205	250
BLN	**Bed Liner**	150	250
PS1	**Power Steering** — Base Short Bed	226	275
FLM	**Floor Mats**	42	60
CE1	**California Emissions**	NC	NC
HA1	**High Altitude Emissions**	NC	NC
JCP	**Two-Tone Paint** — LE	230	280
RA1	**AM/FM Radio w/Clock** — Base Short Bed	144	175
CD1	**Compact Disc Player** — LE	242	295
1VP	**Value Pkg** — 2WD Base Cab Plus	NC	NC
	incls P215/70R14 all-season tires, styled steel wheels, fold-down center armrest, map pockets, 60/40 split bench seat, upgraded door trim, LE cloth upholstery, carpeting		
1PP	**Performance Pkg** — Long Bed	205	250
	2WD SE Cab Plus	287	350
	2WD Short Bed	287	350
1WP	**Alloy Wheel Pkg** — 4WD Cab Plus	500	610
	incls alloy wheels, P265/75R15 all-terrain tires, performance axle		
1LU	**LE Upgrade Pkg** — 4WD LE Cab Plus w/o alloy wheel pkg	500	610
	incls sport bucket seats and performance axle		
2LU	**LE Upgrade Pkg** — 4WD LE Cab Plus w/alloy wheel pkg	295	360
	incls sport bucket seats		
1SU	**SE Upgrade Pkg**		
	2WD SE Long Bed	558	680
	incls sport bucket seats, dual power mirrors, power windows, power door locks and sliding rear window		
	2WD SE Cab Plus	599	730
	incls sport bucket seats, dual power mirrors, power windows, power door		

	locks, sliding rear window and cargo cover		
	4WD SE Short Bed	631	770
	incls performance axle, dual pwr mirrors, power windows & pwr door locks		
	4WD SE Cab Plus w/o alloy wheels	672	820
	incls performance axle, dual power mirrors, power windows, power door locks and cargo cover		
2SU	**SE Upgrade Pkg** — 4WD SE Cab Plus w/alloy wheels.................	467	570
	incls dual power mirrors, power windows, power door locks & cargo cover		

MITSUBISHI MIGHTY MAX PICKUPS

TK27-G	2WD Regular Cab (5-spd)..	8512	9429
TK27-G	2WD Regular Cab (auto)..	9109	10349
TK27-J	2WD Macrocab (5-spd)..	9595	10899
TK27-J	2WD Macrocab (auto)	10192	11579
TF27-G	4WD Regular Cab (5-spd)..	12510	14219
Destination Charge:		420	420

Standard Equipment

MIGHTY MAX 2WD REGULAR CAB: Bench seat, full face cloth seat trim, adjustable head restraints, full carpeting, color-coordinated headliner, behind-seat storage area, bi-level heating/ventilation system, side window defoggers, remote hood release, tilt steering column, 2-speed windshield wipers, dual sunvisors, one-touch keyless locking doors, fuel level gauge, tripmeter, coolant temperature gauge, sport-type steering wheel, warning lights for: brakes/battery charge/low fluid/seatbelts/low oil pressure; front air dam extension, welded double-wall cargo box, steel tie-down hooks, one-hand tailgate release, chrome grille, black front bumper, rectangular headlamps, tinted glass, dual sideview mirrors, passenger-side convex mirror, P195/75R14 radial tires, 2.4L SOHC 4 cylinder engine, dual engine stabilizers, electronic ignition system, automatic valve lash adjusters, stainless steel exhaust system, 5-speed manual overdrive transmission, independent front suspension, front stabilizer bar, rigid rear axle

CODE	DESCRIPTION	DEALER	LIST

with leaf springs, recirculating ball steering, power assisted vented front disc/rear drum brakes, self-adjusting rear brakes, load sensing brake proportion valve, sealed brake fluid reservoir, underhood service item I.D., on-board diagnostic system, 13.7 gallon fuel tank.

MIGHTY MAX 2WD MACROCAB (in addition to or instead of 2WD REGULAR CAB equipment): Split bench seat w/adjustable seat back, concealed storage compartment, cargo strap, lower section cab back trim, rear quarter windows, P205/75R14 radial tires, 18.2 gallon fuel tank.

MIGHTY MAX 4WD MACROCAB (in addition to or instead of 2WD MACROCAB equipment): Bench seat, concealed storage compartment deleted, cargo strap deleted, lower section cab back trim deleted, passenger assist grips, rear anti-lock braking system (ABS), 4WD engaged warning light, ABS warning light, large flared fenders, front and rear mudguards, skid plates: front end/transfer case/fuel tank; front towing hook, rear quarter windows deleted, P225/75R15 all terrain M & S radial tires, 3.0L SOHC V6 engine, dual engine stabilizers deleted, automatic locking front hubs, part-time 4WD system, 2-speed transfer case, power assist steering, anti-lock braking system ABS (2-wheel rear), 15.7 gallon fuel tank.

Accessories

CODE	DESCRIPTION	DEALER	LIST
DC	**Digital Clock**	60	92
AC	**Air Conditioning**	598	729
RA	**Radio Accommodation Pkg** — w/4 speakers - Macrocab	53	76
RT	**Radio Accommodation Pkg** — w/2 speakers - 2WD Regular Cab	33	47
EVPK	**Port Installed Value Pkg** — 2WD	759	759
	incls color-keyed rear step bumpers, digital clock, air conditioning, bodyside stripes, AM/FM ETR stereo radio w/cassette (req's Sport Pkg)		
SP	**Sport Pkg** — 2WD	356	445
	incls day/night rearview mirror, bright windshield molding, halogen head-lights, door map pockets, cut-pile carpeting, color-keyed front bumpers, full door trim panel w/large armrests & lower carpeting, chrome grille, sliding rear window, full instrumentation, cloth bench seat, tachometer, Radio Accommodation Pkg (RT - Regular Cab, RA - Macrocab) (req's Port Installed Value Pkg)		
SW	**Sliding Rear Window** — 4WD	71	89
ER	**AM/FM ETR Radio** — 2WD	210	321
EQ	**AM/FM ETR Radio** — w/cassette	327	481
NB	**Black Rear Step Bumper**	113	162
BB	**Color-Keyed Front Bumper** — 4WD	30	38
CB	**Color-Keyed Rear Bumper** — 4WD	143	204
	req's color-keyed front bumper		
FM	**Floor Mats**	34	52
SM	**Bodyside Molding** — 2WD	72	111
TR	**Wheel Trim Rings** — 4WD	49	76
SC	**Chrome Rear Bumper**	141	201
	NA w/Sport Pkg on 2WD models		
CM	**Dual Chrome Sport Mirrors** — 4WD	77	118
LD	**Limited Slip Differential** — 4WD	181	226
PS	**Power Steering** — 2WD	232	290

CODE	DESCRIPTION	DEALER	LIST

NISSAN 2WD PICKUPS

Code	Description	Dealer	List
33054	Standard (5-spd)	8782	9359
33554	XE Reg Cab (5-spd)	9401	10129
33514	XE Reg Cab (auto)	10622	11444
43554	Standard Long Bed V6 (5-spd)	10271	11189
53554	XE King Cab (5-spd)	10484	11679
53514	XE King Cab (auto)	11664	12994
53454	SE-V6 King Cab (5-spd)	12671	14279
53414	SE-V6 King Cab (auto)	13559	15279
	Destination Charge:	375	375

Standard Equipment

2WD STANDARD PICKUP: 2.4L SOHC 4 cyli eng, sequential multi-point electronic fuel injection, 5-speed manual overdrive transmission, power vented front disc/rear drum brakes, independent front suspension with stabilizer bar/solid rear axle with leaf springs, double-wall cargo box with removable tailgate, tinted glass, halogen headlamps, bench seat, vinyl seat trim and floor covering, side window defoggers, steel side-door guard beams, 3-point front manual seatbelt system, energy-absorbing steering column.

2WD XE PICKUP: 2.4L SOHC 4 cyl eng, sequential multi-point elec fuel injection, 5-speed manual overdrive trans, power vented front disc/rear drum brakes, independent front suspension with stabilizer bar/solid rear axle with leaf springs, double-wall cargo box with removable tailgate, tinted glass, black painted rear step bumper, halogen headlamps, dual outside mirrors w/passenger-side convex mirror, styled steel wheels with trim rings, sliding rear window, cloth seat trim and full carpeting, front door map pockets, reclining front bucket seats (King Cab), bench seat (Reg Cab), side window defoggers, steel side-door guard beams, 3-point front manual seatbelt system, energy-absorbing steering column.

2WD STANDARD LONG BED: 3.0L SOHC V6 eng, sequential multi-point elec fuel injection, 5-speed manual overdrive trans, power recirculating ball steering, power vented front disc/rear drum brakes, independent front suspension w/stabilizer bar/solid rear axle w/leaf springs, double-wall cargo box with removable tailgate, tinted glass, halogen headlamps, dual outside mirrors with passenger-side convex mirror, bench seat, vinyl seat trim and floor covering, front door map pockets, side window defoggers, steel side-door guard beams, 3-point front manual seatbelt system, energy-absorbing steering column.

2WD SE KING CAB: 3.0L SOHC V6 eng, sequential multi-point elec fuel injection, 5-speed manual

NISSAN

overdrive trans, power recirculating ball steering, power vented front disc/rear drum brakes, independent front suspension with stabilizer bar/solid rear axle with leaf springs, double wall cargo box with removable tailgate, pop-up tie-down hooks, bedliner, tinted glass, chrome rear step bumper, halogen headlamps, chromed dual outside mirrors, chromed steel wheels, sliding rear window, reclining front bucket seats, multi-adjustable driver's seat with 2-way head restraints/front seat cushion tilt/seatback recline/3-position lumbar support and fore/aft adjustments, rear jump seats, cloth seat trim and full carpeting, front door map pockets, cruise control, tilt steering column, 2-speed variable intermittent windshield wipers, side window defoggers, passenger-side vanity mirror, lockable glove box, center console, map lights, tachometer, trip odometer, digital quartz clock, 100-watt (peak) electronically tuned AM/FM/cassette stereo audio system with auto reverse/diversity antenna system/Dolby noise reduction, steel-side-door guard beams, 3-point front manual seatbelt system, energy-absorbing steering column, Chrome Package (chrome grille, chrome front and rear bumpers, chrome door handles, chrome windshield moldings, chrome side marker lamp bezels, chrome dual outside mirrors, chrome wheels and body side graphics), Jump Seat Package (jump seats with seatbelts).

Accessories

Code	Description	Dealer	List
A01	**Air Conditioning** — Standard, XE, SE-V6 King Cab	843	995
H01	**AM/FM Cassette Stereo** — Standard	228	500
	std on SE-V6 King Cab		
K05	**Power Pkg** — SE-V6 King Cab	423	500
	incls power windows and door locks		
S02	**Sport/Power Pkg** — SE-V6 King Cab	1219	1440
	incls power windows and door locks, flip-up sunroof, alloy wheels		
P06	**Power Steering** — std on Standard Long Bed V6 & SE-V6 King Cab	266	315
E08/E09	**Metallic or Pearl Paint** — Standard	85	100
T07	**Value Truck Pkg** — XE	843	995
	incls air cond, AM/FM cass w/2 spkrs, chrome wheels, chrome molding, chrome grille, chrome bumper, bodyside graphics, power mirrors, variable intermittent wipers, locking glove box, ashtray, cigar lighter & glove box lights, tachometer, trip odometer, digital clock, map lights (King Cab), center console (King Cab), visor vanity mirror (King Cab), 4 spkrs (King Cab)		
C01	**California Emissions**	128	150
L30/L31	**Bedliner** — std on SE-V6 King Cab	128	280
G01	**Convenience Pkg** — XE Reg Cab	254	300
	incls dual power outside mirrors, locking glove box/map/glove box/ cigarette lighter/ashtray lamps, variable intermittent wipers, tilt steering wheel		
W04	**Chrome Pkg** — XE Reg Cab	423	500
	incls chrome grille, chrome front and rear bumpers, chrome door handles, chrome windshield moldings, chrome dual outside mirrors, chrome wheels and bodyside graphics		
U03	**Jump Seat Pkg** — XE King Cab (std on SE-V6)	191	225
	incls jump seats w/seatbelts		
V03	**Sport Pkg** — SE-V6 King Cab	1101	1300
	incls flip-up sunroof, alloy wheels		

CODE	DESCRIPTION	DEALER	LIST

NISSAN 4WD PICKUPS

33754	XE Reg Cab (5-spd)	12225	13619
53754	XE King Cab (5-spd)	13390	15089
53954	XE-V6 King Cab (5-spd)	14091	15879
53914	XE-V6 King Cab (auto)	14979	16879
53854	SE-V6 King Cab (5-spd)	14368	16379
53814	SE-V6 King Cab (auto)	15245	17379
Destination Charge:		375	375

Standard Equipment

4WD XE PICKUP: 2.4L SOHC 12-valve 4 cylinder engine, sequential multi-point electronic fuel injection, 5-speed manual overdrive transmission, power recirculating ball steering, power vented front disc/rear drum brakes, rear-wheel anti-lock braking system (ABS), independent front suspension with stabilizer bar/solid rear axle with leaf springs, manual locking front hubs, double-wall cargo box with removable tailgate, tinted glass, black painted rear step bumper, halogen headlamps, dual outside mirrors with passenger-side convex mirror, triple skid plates and tow hook, titanium finish steel wheels, sliding rear window, bench seat (Reg Cab), reclining front bucket seats (King Cab), cloth seat trim and full carpeting, front door map pockets, side window defoggers, steel side-door guard beams, 3-point manual front seatbelt system, energy-absorbing steering column.

4WD XE-V6 KING CAB: 3.0L SOHC V6 engine, sequential multi-point electronic fuel injection, 5-speed manual overdrive transmission, power recirculating ball steering, power vented front disc/rear drum brakes, rear-wheel anti-lock braking system (ABS), independent front suspension with stabilizer bar/solid rear axle with leaf springs, automatic locking front hubs, double-wall cargo box with removable tailgate, bedliner, tinted glass, black painted rear step bumper, halogen headlamps, dual outside mirrors with passenger-side convex mirror, fender flares, triple skid plates and tow hook, titanium finish steel wheels, sliding rear window, reclining front bucket seats, rear jump seats, cloth seat trim and full carpeting, front door map pockets, side window defoggers, steel side-door guard beams, 3-point manual front seatbelt system, energy-absorbing steering column, Jump Seat Package (includes jump seats with seatbelts).

4WD SE-V6 KING CAB (in addition to or instead of 4WD XE-V6 KING CAB): Pop-up tie-down hooks, chromed rear step bumper, chromed dual outside mirrors, chromed steel wheels, multi-adjustable driver's seat w/2-way head restraints/front-seat cushion tilt/seatback recline/3-position lumbar support & fore/aft adjustments, cruise control, tilt steering col, 2-speed variable intermittent windshield wipers, pass-side

CODE	DESCRIPTION	DEALER	LIST

vanity mirror, lockable glove box, center console, map lamps, tachometer, trip odometer, digital quartz clock, 100-watt (peak) elec-tuned AM/FM/cass stereo audio system w/auto reverse/ diversity antenna system/Dolby noise reduction, Value Truck Pkg (air cond, AM/FM cass w/2 speakers, chrome wheels, chrome molding, chrome grille, chrome bumper, body side graphics, power mirrors, variable intermittent wipers, locking glove box, ashtray, cigar lighter, glove box lights, tachometer, trip odometer, digital clock, fender flares, full size spare tire, map lights, center console, visor vanity mirror, 4 speakers).

Accessories

Code	Description	Dealer	List
A01	**Air Conditioning**	843	995
L30/31	**Bedliner** — XE (std on XE-V6 & SE-V6)	128	280
W04	**Chrome Pkg** — XE Reg Cab..	423	500
	incls chrome grille, chrome front/rear bumpers, chrome door handles, chrome windshield molding, chrome dual outside mirrors, fender flares & bodyside graphics		
G01	**Convenience Pkg** — XE Reg Cab	254	300
	incls dual pwr outside mirrors, locking glove box, map/glove box/cigar lighter/ashtray lamps, variable intermittent wipers and P235/75R15 spare tire		
V03	**Sport Pkg** — SE-V6..	1587	1875
	incls flip-up sunroof, alloy wheels, limited slip differential, 31x10.5 R15 tires, P235/75R15 spare tire		
K05	**Power Pkg** — SE-V6	423	500
	incls power windows and door locks		
S02	**Sport/Power Pkg** — SE-V6	1672	1975
	incls alloy wheels, flip-up sunroof, power windows, power locks, limited slip differential, 31x10.5 R15 tires and P235/75R15 spare tire		
V03	**Jump Seat Pkg** — XE King Cab (std on XE-V6, SE-V6)........................	191	225
	incls jump seats w/seatbelts		
C01	**California Emissions**	128	150
T07	**Value Truck Pkg** — XE, XE-V6..	843	995
	incls air conditioning, AM/FM cassette w/2 speakers, chrome wheels, chrome molding, chrome grille, chrome bumper, body side graphics, power mirrors, variable intermittent wipers, locking glove box, ashtray, cigar lighter and glove box lights, tachometer, trip odometer, digital clock, fender flares, full size spare, tilt steering wheel (XE-V6 King Cab), cruise control (XE-V6 King Cab), map lights (King Cab), center console (King Cab), visor vanity mirror (King Cab), 4 speakers (King Cab)		

TOYOTA

TOYOTA COMPACT PICKUPS

2WD

Code	Description	Dealer	List
8100	Standard 4 Cyl Reg Cab (5-spd)	8836	9818
8113	DX 4 Cyl Reg Cab (5-spd)	9654	10908
8104	DX 4 Cyl Reg Cab (auto)	10291	11628
8116	DX 4 Cyl Xtracab (5-spd)	10838	12458
8123	DX 4 Cyl Xtracab (auto)	11465	13178
8154	DX V6 Xtracab (5-spd)	11839	13608
8153	DX V6 Xtracab (auto)	12674	14568
8157	SR5 V6 Xtracab (5-spd)	13302	15558
8158	SR5 V6 Xtracab (auto)	14123	16518

4WD

Code	Description	Dealer	List
8503	DX 4 Cyl Reg Cab (5-spd)	12642	14448
8504	DX 4 Cyl Reg Cab (auto)	13429	15348
8524	DX 4 Cyl Xtracab (5-spd)	13750	15988
8513	DX V6 Reg Cab (5-spd)	13736	15698
8554	DX V6 Xtracab (5-spd)	14807	17218
8553	DX V6 Xtracab (auto)	15865	18448
8557	SR5 V6 Xtracab (5-spd)	16180	19148
8558	SR5 V6 Xtracab (auto)	17211	20368
Destination Charge:		400	400

Standard Equipment

PICKUP - STANDARD REGULAR CAB: Vinyl upholstery, power front disc/rear drum brakes, cargo tie-down hooks, vinyl floor mats, intermittent wipers, tilt forward bench seat, double-wall cargo bed, one-touch tailgate release, styled steel wheels, 2.4L 4 cylinder EFI engine, left black mirror, front stabilizer bar, P195/75R14 SBR all-season BW tires, full-size spare tire.

DX REGULAR CAB (in addition to or instead of STANDARD REGULAR CAB equipment): Cloth upholstery, passenger assist grip, door trim panels w/cloth inserts, skid plates (4WD), P225/75R15 SBR mud & snow tires (4WD), tinted windshield, dual black mirrors (right convex), day/night rearview mirror, full wheel covers (2WD), cut-pile carpeting, manual locking front hubs (4WD), front and rear mud guards (4WD), 3.0L V6 EFI engine (V6), power steering (V6).

TOYOTA

PICKUPS

CODE	DESCRIPTION	DEALER	LIST

DX XTRACAB (in addition to or instead of DX REGULAR CAB equipment): Reclining front bucket seats, flip-out rear quarter windows, front and rear mud guards (4WD), rear mudguards (2WD), P205/75R14 SBR all-season BW tires (2WD), P225/75R15 SBR mud & snow tires (4WD), dual rear quarter storage.

SR5 (in addition to or instead of DX XTRACAB equipment): Digital clock, halogen headlights, lower door trim panel carpeting, trip odometer, tilt steering column, manual locking front hubs (4WD) deleted, 60/40 split fold-down front bench seats, dual forward-facing rear jump seats, right visor vanity mirror, door map pockets, tachometer, power front disc/anti-lock rear drum brakes, variable intermittent wipers, AM/FM ETR stereo radio w/2 speakers.

Accessories

CODE	DESCRIPTION	DEALER	LIST
PX	**Metallic Paint** — Standard	76	120
	Pickup except Standard	NC	NC
SX	**Sports Pkg** — SR5	248	310
	incls 7-way adjustable cloth sport seats, gray privacy glass on quarter windows, rear storage console (reqs Chrome Pkg or Value Pkg)		
VP	**Value Pkg** — (DX w/4 cyl engine)		
	2WD Reg Cab	373	414
	4WD Reg Cab	418	464
	Xtracab Models...	481	534
	incls pwr steering, sliding rr window, chrome rear bumper, carpeted floor mats, exterior stripes, AM/FM ETR radio w/2 spkrs, Chrome Pkg (Xtracab also incls rear jump seats w/seatbelts, 60/40 split front bench seat)		
VP	**Value Pkg** — (DX w/V6 engine)		
	4WD Reg Cab	202	244
	Xtracab Models...	310	344
	incls chrome rr bumper, sliding rear window, carpeted floor mats, AM/FM ETR stereo radio w/2 speakers, Chrome Pkg, exterior stripes (Xtracab also includes rear jump seats w/seatbelts, 60/40 split front bench seat)		
VP	**Value Pkg** — SR5..	365	405
	incls chrome rear bumper, sliding rear window, carpeted floor mats, deluxe AM/FM ETR stereo radio w/cassette & 4 speakers, Chrome Pkg		
BG	**Cloth Pkg** — 2WD Standard	84	105
	incls cut-pile carpeting, cloth bench seat, cigarette lighter, day/night rearview mirror		
PW	**Window Pkg**	160	200
	incls sliding rear window, front vent windows		
CK	**All Weather Guard Pkg**	55	65
	incls large windshield washer, heavy-duty starter, front and rear mud guards. (4 cylinder models also incl distributor & coil cover) (V6 models also incl heavy-duty battery) (Standard also incls heavy-duty heater)		
TP	**Touring Pkg** — (DX w/man trans)		
	2WD, 4WD V6 models..	92	115
	4WD 4 cyl models...	124	155
	incls trip odometer, halogen headlights, tachometer. (4WD DX w/4 cyl also incls front and rear gas shock absorbers)		
CM	**Comfort Pkg** — DX Xtracab...	216	270
	incls rear jump seats w/seatbelts, 60/40 split fold-down front bench seat		
PO	**Power Pkg** — SR5...	588	735
	incls power door locks, power antenna, power windows w/driver side express down, dual chrome power mirrors (req's Cruise Control Pkg)		
TO	**Towing Pkg** — (2WD w/auto trans)		

CODE	DESCRIPTION	DEALER	LIST
	w/4-cyl engine...	40	50
	w/V6 engine...	52	65
	incls larger radiator		
CH	**Chrome Pkg** — 2WD DX, 4WD	144	180
	2WD SR5	128	160
	incls chrome grille/front bumper/door handles/windshield moldings		
CL	**Cruise Control Pkg** — SR5	308	385
	incls intermittent windshield wipers w/timer, cruise control, leather-		
	wrapped steering wheel		
CL	**Cruise Control Pkg** — DX except 2WD w/4 cyl engine	212	265
	incls 3-spoke urethane-wrapped steering wheel, cruise control,		
	intermittent windshield wipers		
CA	**California Emissions**..	130	153
PS	**Power Steering** — std V6 models	246	290
RA	**AM/FM ETR Radio** — std SR5	180	240
	incls 2 speakers		
EX	**Deluxe AM/FM ETR Radio** — w/cassette		
	Standard & DX Reg Cab	341	455
	DX Xtracab...	416	555
	SR5 Xtracab..	236	315
	incls 2 speakers (Reg Cab), 4 speakers (Xtracab)		
CE	**Premium AM/FM ETR Radio w/Cassette** — SR5	472	630
	incls 4 speakers		
SV	**Styled Steel Wheels** — DX Regular Cab 4WD V6.........................	464	580
	incls five 10.5 R15 tires, wheel opening moldings, five silver steel wheels		
AW	**Aluminum Wheels** — 2WD SR5	612	765
	incls aluminum wheels w/center caps, chrome wheel opening moldings,		
	P215/65R15 tires (reqs Value Pkg or Chrome Pkg)		
AW	**Aluminum Wheels** — 4WD SR5	708	885
	incls aluminum wheels, 10.5 R15 tires, large wheel opening moldings (reqs		
	Valve Pkg or Chrome Pkg)		
LK	**Anti-Lock Rear Brakes** — std SR5	255	300
	models w/4 cyl engine req Power Steering or Value Pkg		
SR	**Pop-Up Moonroof** — SR5	304	380
	4WD models req Value Pkg or Chrome Pkg		
VW	**Front Vent Windows**	52	65
FD	**Four-Wheel On Demand System** — DX 4WD V6............................	178	210
TW	**Tilt Steering Column** — DX..	132	155
	incls intermittent wipers w/timer		

TOYOTA T100 PICKUPS

Code	Description	Dealer	List
8713	DX Half-Ton 2WD (5-spd)	12787	14698
8712	DX Half-Ton 2WD (auto)	13570	15598
8813	DX Half-Ton 4WD (5-spd)	15624	18168
8812	DX Half-Ton 4WD (auto)	16398	19068
8717	DX One-Ton 2WD (5-spd)	13431	15438
8716	DX One-Ton 2WD (auto)	14214	16338
8715	SR5 Half-Ton 2WD (5-spd)	14504	16768
8714	SR5 Half-Ton 2WD (auto)	15283	17668
8815	SR5 Half-Ton 4WD (5-spd)	17252	20178
8814	SR5 Half-Ton 4WD (auto)	18022	21078
	Destination Charge: approximate	400	400

Standard Equipment

T100 - DX: Power steering, driver side airbag, double-wall cargo bed, cloth upholstery, tinted glass, full carpeting, P215/75R15 all-season SBR tires (2WD Half-Ton), P235/75R15 mud & snow SBR tires (One-Ton & 4WD Half-Ton), front and rear mud guards, skid plates (4WD), styled steel wheels (4WD), digital clock, center armrest, cargo tie-down hooks, full wheel covers (2WD), door map pockets, front stabilizer bar (heavy-duty on One-Ton), 3.0L V6 EFI engine, dual black mirrors (right convex), intermittent wipers, 3-passenger bench seat, power front disc/rear drum brakes (heavy-duty on One-Ton).

SR5 (in addition to or instead on DX equip): Trip odometer, center armrest w/storage, chrome front bumper, 60/40 split bench seat, right visor vanity mirror, tachometer, chrome grille, variable intermittent wipers, tool storage & cover, power brakes w/anti-lock rr, overhead map lights, tilt steering column, sliding rear window, P235/75R15 SBR mud & snow tires, door trim panels w/cloth inserts, deluxe AM/FM ETR radio w/5 speakers.

Accessories

Code	Description	Dealer	List
CQ	**Convenience Pkg** — DX	367	445
	incls sliding rear window, tilt steering column, oil pressure and voltmeter gauges, tachometer, variable intermittent wipers		
QL	**Convenience Pkg** — DX	595	730

CODE	DESCRIPTION	DEALER	LIST
	incls sliding rear window, tilt steering column, oil pressure and voltmeter gauges, tachometer, variable intermittent wipers, cruise control		
RR	**Radio Prep Pkg** — DX	37	50
	incls antenna, wiring harness		
CH	**Chrome Pkg** — DX	120	150
	incls chrome grille, door handles and front bumper		
PO	**Power Pkg** — SR5	588	735
	incls power antenna, power door locks, power windows w/driver side express down, dual chrome power mirrors (reqs Cruise Control Pkg, VP Value Pkg or VK Value Pkg/Two-Tone)		
VP	**Value Pkg** — DX Half-Ton 2WD	298	331
	incls Chrome Pkg, bodyside moldings, carpeted floor mats, chrome rear bumper, P235/75R15 tires		
VP	**Value Pkg** — DX One-Ton; DX Half-Ton 4WD	185	206
	incls Chrome Pkg, bodyside mldgs, carpeted floor mats, chrome rr bumper		
VP	**Value Pkg** — SR5	1261	1401
	incls bodyside moldings, carpeted floor mats, chrome rear bumper, cruise control, Power Pkg, air conditioning, variable intermittent wipers, upgraded 5-speed shift knob (manual trans only), leather-wrapped steering wheel		
CL	**Cruise Control Pkg** — DX	279	345
	incls 3-spoke urethane-wrapped steering wheel, upgraded 5-spd shift knob (man trans only), cruise control, variable intermittent wipers		
CL	**Cruise Control Pkg** — SR5	288	360
	incls leather-wrapped steering wheel, upgraded 5-spd shift knob (man trans), variable intermittent wipers, cruise control		
HT	**Chrome Pkg/Two-Tone** — DX	384	480
	incls two-tone paint, Chrome Pkg		
VK	**Value Pkg/Two-Tone** — DX Half-Ton 2WD	505	561
	DX Half-Ton 4WD, DX One-Ton	392	436
	SR5	1468	1631
	incls VP Value Pkg and two-tone paint; bodyside moldings deleted		
WR	**Sliding Rear Window** — DX 4WD	108	135
CA	**California Emissions**	130	153
RA	**AM/FM ETR Radio - DX**	180	240
	incls 2 speakers		
EX	Deluxe AM/FM ETR Radio w/Cassette — DX	461	615
	incls 3 speakers		
EX	Deluxe AM/FM ETR Radio w/Cassette — SR5	127	170
	incls 5 speakers		
CE	Premium AM/FM ETR Radio w/Cassette — SR5	394	525
	incls programmable equalization, 7 speakers		
DC	Premium 3-In-1 Combo Radio — SR5	994	1325
	incls 7 speakers, programmable equalization, premium AM/FM ETR stereo w/cassette, compact disc		
PX	**Metallic Paint**	NC	NC
TT	**Two-Tone Paint** — DX	320	400
	incls chrome front bumper		
TU	**Tire Upgrade** — DX Half-Ton	100	125
	incls P235/75R15 tires		
LK	**Rear Brakes** — anti-lock - DX	255	300
ST	**Styled Steel Wheels** — DX 4WD	212	265
	incls 31-10.5 tires, styled steel wheels		

TOYOTA

CODE	DESCRIPTION	DEALER	LIST
AW	**Aluminum Wheels** — SR5 2WD	472	590
	incls chrome wheel opening moldings, aluminum wheels, P235/75R15 tires, aluminum wheel ornament		
AW	**Aluminum Wheels** — SR5 4WD	588	735
	incls chrome wheel opening moldings, aluminum wheels, 31-10.5 tires, aluminum wheel ornament		

TOYOTA

SPORT UTILITY

CONTENTS

SPORT UTILITY

CODE	DESCRIPTION	DEALER	LIST

CHEVROLET S/T BLAZER

4.3 LITER EFI 6 CYL
S10 SERIES 2WD

		DEALER	LIST
CS10516 E55 Tailgate 2-Dr 100.5" WB		13971	15438
CS10506 E55 Tailgate 4-Dr 100.5" WB		15139	16728

T10 SERIES 4WD

		DEALER	LIST
CT10516 E55 Tailgate 2-Dr 100.5" WB		15597	17234
CT10506 E55 Tailgate 4-Dr 100.5" WB		17161	18962
Destination Charge:		475	475

Standard Equipment

BLAZER COMPACT S10 2-DOOR - BASE: 5-speed manual overdrive transmission, power steering, power disc front/rear drum brakes, 4-wheel anti-lock braking, independent front suspension, Solar-Ray tinted glass all windows, side guard door beams, center high-mount stop light, full-sized spare tire, side-window defogger, color-keyed front carpeting, ETR AM radio with digital clock and two speakers, vinyl front bucket seats, body-colored bumpers, black grille, black below-eyeline mirrors, 15" x 6" wheels.

TAHOE (in addition to or instead of BASE equipment): Chromed grilles, chromed bumpers, floor console (seat divider), color-keyed deluxe cloth door inserts and carpeted lower inserts, color-keyed carpeting front and rear, carpeted tailgate, lower quarter panels and rear quarter area; dual front lighted visor mirrors, bright aluminum wheel openings and bodyside black moldings with bright accents. Some equipment such as AM/FM with seek-scan, cassette player and digital clock required.

TAHOE LT (in addition to or instead of TAHOE equipment): Power door locks, power windows, leather upper door inserts and carpeted lower inserts and map pockets, leather seating on high-back front bucket seats with 6-way power driver's seat, folding rear bench seat, 4-spoke leather-wrapped steering wheel, remote keyless entry, black luggage carrier. Some equipment such as speed control, adjustable tilt steering wheel and AM/FM stereo with cassette player, graphic equalizer and digital clock required.

BLAZER COMPACT S10 4-DOOR - BASE TAHOE: 5-speed manual overdrive transmission, power steering, power disc front/rear drum brakes, 4-wheel anti-lock braking, independent front suspension, Solar-Ray tinted glass all windows, side guard door beams, center high-mount stop light, full-sized spare tire, side-window defogger, deluxe cloth interiors, chromed grilles, chromed bumpers, floor console (seat divider), color-keyed carpeting front and rear, carpeted tailgate, lower quarter panels and rear quarter area; dual front lighted visor mirrors, bright aluminum wheel openings and bodyside black moldings with bright accents. Some equipment such as AM/FM with seek-scan, cassette player and digital clock required.

TAHOE LT (in addition to or instead of BASE TAHOE equipment): Power door locks, power windows, leather upper door inserts and carpeted lower inserts, map pockets, leather seating on high-back front bucket seats with 6-way power driver's seat, folding rear bench seat, 4-spoke leather-wrapped steering wheel, remote keyless entry, black luggage carrier. Some equip such as speed control, adjustable tilt steering wheel and AM/FM stereo with cassette player, graphic equalizer and digital clock required.

Accessories

CODE	DESCRIPTION	DEALER	LIST
CAA1	**Preferred Equip Group 1**	NC	NC
DAA1	**Tahoe Preferred Equip Group 1**	NC	NC
—	**Tahoe Preferred Equip Group 2**		
CAA2	S10516	1185	1378
CAA2	T10516	1158	1346
DAA2	S10506	560	651
DAA2	T10506	163	190
—	**Tahoe Preferred Equip Group 3**		
CAA3	S10516	2531	2943
CAA3	T10516	2531	2943
DAA3	S10506	2034	2365
DAA3	T10506	1687	1962
—	**LT Preferred Equip Group 1**		
LTB1	S10516	3651	4245
LTB1	T10516	3793	4410
LTA1	S10506	3247	3776
LTA1	T10506	3043	3538
C60	**Air Conditioning** — w/CAA1/DAA1 or CAA2/DAA2	671	780
	w/CAA3/DAA3 or LTB1/LTA1	NC	NC
ANL	**Air Dam w/Fog Lamps**	99	115
ZQ9	**Appearance Pkg, Blackout**	11	13
—	**Axles, Rear**		
GU4	3.08 ratio	NC	NC
GU6	3.42 ratio	NC	NC
G80	locking differential	217	252
UA1	**Battery** — HD w/o V10	48	56
	w/V10	NC	NC
E55	**Body Code** — tailgate	NC	NC
—	**Carriers**		
PNV	outside spare tire carrier not desired	NC	NC
P16	spare wheel & tire	137	159
V10	**Cold-Climate Pkg** — w/CAA1	154	179
	w/o CAA1	94	109
D55	**Console** — seat separator, incl w/YC2 or YC9	125	145
DK6	**Console: Overhead** (Incl w/YC9)	71	83
V08	**Cooling System** — HD, incl w/Z82 or Z72 w/MX0	116	135
—	**Driver Convenience**		
ZQ2	operating convenience pkg -w/CAA3/DAA3 or LTB1/LTA1	NC	NC
	w/CAA1 or CAA2	316	367
	w/DAA1 or DAA2	466	542

CODE	DESCRIPTION	DEALER	LIST
ZQ3	tilt-wheel & speed control -w/CAA1 or DAA1	329	383
	w/o CAA1 or DAA1	NC	NC
ZM8	rear window convenience pkg		
	w/CAA1/DAA1 or CAA2/DAA2	169	197
	w/CAA3/DAA3 or LTB1/LTA1	NC	NC
FE9	**Federal Emissions**	NC	NC
NG1	**New York Emissions** — w/L35 eng	NC	NC
	w/o L35 eng	NC	NC
YF5	**California Emissions** — w/R8Y	NA	NA
	w/o R8Y	NA	NA
LB4	**Engine** — gasoline, 4.3 liter EFI V6	NC	NC
R8Y	**Enhanced Powertrain**	997	1160
—	**Floor Covering**		
BG9	full floor, rubber, charcoal	NC	NC
—	mats, color-keyed, removable (incl w/YC2 or YC9)		
B32	front w/CAA1	22	25
B33	rear w/CAA1	17	20
—	**Glass**		
AA3	deep tinted w/light tinted rear window -w/CAA1/DAA1	124	144
	w/CAA2/DAA2 or CAA3/DAA3 or LTB1/LTA1	NC	NC
AJ1	deep tinted -w/CAA1/DAA1	194	225
	w/CAA2/DAA2 or CAA3/DAA3 or LTB1/LTA1	70	81
U52	**Instrumentation, Electronic**	168	195
AX3	**Keyless Entry, Remote (Incl w/YC9)**	116	135
V54	**Luggage Carrier** — w/CAA1/DAA1 or CAA2/DAA2	108	126
	w/CAA3/DAA3 or LTB1/LTA1	NC	NC
D48	**Mirrors** — exterior, electric remote	71	83
B74	**Moldings** — wheel opening, black incl w/ZQ9		
	w/CAA1	37	43
	w/o CAA1	11	13
—	**Paints, Exterior**		
ZY1	solid	NC	NC
ZY3	special two-tone	195	227
ZY8	custom two-tone -w/o LTB1/LTA1	237	275
	w/LTB1/LTA1	NC	NC
—	**Radio Equip**		
UM7	radio - w/CAA1/DAA1	113	131
	w/CAA2/DAA2	NC	NC
	incls elect tuned AM/FM stereo radio w/seek & scan & digital clock		
UM6	radio - w/CAA1/DAA1	218	253
	w/CAA2/DAA2	105	122
	w/CAA3/DAA3 or LTB1/LTA1	NC	NC
	incls elect tuned AM/FM stereo radio w/seek & scan, stereo cass tape & digital clock		
UX1	radio - w/CAA1/DAA1	347	403
	w/CAA2/DAA2	234	272
	w/CAA3/DAA3 or LTB1/LTA1	129	150
	incls elect tuned AM stereo/FM stereo radio w/seek & scan, stereo cass tape w/search & repeat, digital clock & graphic equalizer		
U1C	radio - w/CAA1/DAA1	462	537
	w/CAA2/DAA2	349	406
	w/CAA3/DAA3 or LTB1/LTA1	244	284

CODE	DESCRIPTION	DEALER	LIST
	incls elect tuned AM/FM stereo radio w/seek-scan compact disc player & digital clock		
UL5	radio delete..	(82)	(95)
—	**Seat Trim**		
X6	custom vinyl reclining high back buckets	NC	NC
D6	deluxe cloth reclining high back buckets w/manual lumbar adjustment		
	w/CAA1	190	221
	w/DAA1	181	211
	w/CAA2/DAA2 or CAA3/DAA3	NC	NC
D3	deluxe cloth 60/40 reclining split folding bench - w/DAA1	NC	NC
	w/DAA2/DAA3	(204)	(237)
D8	deluxe cloth reclining high back buckets w/power lumbar adjustment &		
	6-way power driver seat - w/CAA1	315	366
	w/DAA1	431	501
	w/CAA2/DAA2 or CAA3/DAA3	249	290
	w/LTB1 or LTA1	(559)	(650)
A8	ultrasoft leather reclining high back buckets		
	w/power lumbar adjustment & 6-way power driver seat w/LTB1 or LTA1.....	NC	NC
—	**Seats**		
AM7	folding rear - w/CAA2/DAA2 or CAA3/DAA3...........................	NC	NC
	w/DAA1	374	435
	C*10516 w/vinyl trim	352	409
	C*10516w/cloth trim	374	435
YG4	rear seat not desired..	NC	NC
RYJ	**Security Shade** — cargo	59	69
ZM5	**Shield Pkg**	65	75
F51	**Shock Absorbers** — HD, F & R - w/o F60	34	40
	w/F60	NC	NC
F60	**Springs** — front, HD	54	63
ZM6	**Suspension Equip** — off-road -w/CAA1	157	182
	w/CAA2 or CAA3	105	122
—	**Tires**		
	C*10516 - C*10506		
	All Seasons SBR		
QCE	P205/75R15 BW	NC	NC
QCF	P205/75R15 white lettered -w/CAA1/DAA1	105	121
	w/CAA2/DAA2 or CAA3/DAA3 or LTB1/LTA1	NC	NC
QFN	P235/75R15 white lettered (T10 only) -w/CAA1/DAA1	246	286
	w/CAA2/DAA2 or CAA3/DAA3...	142	165
	w/LTB1/LTA1	NC	NC
	On-Off Road SBR		
QJL	P205/75R15 white lettered -w/CAA1/DAA1	146	170
	w/CAA2/DAA2 or CAA3/DAA3...	42	49
QEB	P235/75R15 white lettered (T10 only) -w/CAA1/DAA1	288	335
	w/CAA2/DAA2 or CAA3/DAA3...	184	214
—	**Trailering Special**		
Z72	light duty w/R8Y enhanced powertrain................................	94	109
	w/MM5 trans	258	300
Z82	heavy duty -w/R8Y enhanced powertrain	181	210
	w/MM5 trans	297	345
NP1	**Transfer Case** — electronic shift................................	106	123
MM5	**Transmission** - 5-spd manual w/overdrive	NC	NC

CHEVROLET

CODE	DESCRIPTION	DEALER	LIST
P06	**Wheel Trim** — trim rings -w/CAA1 & w/o ZJ7	52	60
	w/CAA2 or CAA3 or W/ZJ7	NC	NC
—	**Wheels**		
ZJ7	rally (incl w/ YC2)	79	92
PA3	aluminum, cast -w/CAA1	292	340
	w/DAA1, CAA2 or DAA2	213	248
	W/CAA3/DAA3 or LTB1/LTA1	NC	NC
5P2	aluminum, special -w/CAA1	292	340
	w/DAA1 or CAA2/DAA2	241	280
	w/CAA3/DAA3 or LTB1/LTA1	NC	NC
AD5	**Window** - sliding side	221	257
C25	**Wiper System** — rear window wiper/washer		
	w/CAA1/DAA1 or CAA2/DAA2	108	125
	w/CAA3/DAA3 or LTB1/LTA1	NC	NC

CHEVROLET K BLAZER

5.7 LITER (350 CID) EFI 8 CYL
K1500 SERIES 4WD

CK10516 E55 Utility 111.5" WB	18481	21125
Destination Charge:	600	600

Standard Equipment

BLAZER FULL-SIZED 2-DOOR - BASE CHEYENNE: 5-speed manual transmission, black air dam, power front disc/rear drum brakes, 4-wheel anti-lock brake system, front and rear chromed bumpers, molded painted argent grille, 16" x 6.5" painted argent wheel trim, padded armrests, cupholders, side door guard beams, full gauges, deluxe heater with windshield and side window defoggers, 10" rearview mirror, electronically-tuned AM/FM stereo with seek-scan and digital clock, vinyl bucket front seats with sliding driver and passenger for easy entry, color-keyed sunshades, 4-spoke steering wheel.

SILVERADO (in addition to or instead of CHEYENNE equipment): Air conditioning, convenience group (Comfortilt steering and speed control), power door locks and windows, deep-tinted glass, AM/FM stereo with tape player and clock, aluminum wheels, deluxe front appearance package with dark argent chrome grille and bright trim, dual composite halogen headlamps, chrome RH and LH below-eyeline mirrors, Rally trim wheels, color-keyed door trim panels with padded armrests, map pockets and carpet trim, color-keyed front compartment carpeting, color-keyed molded plastic floor console, auxiliary lighting with front and rear map lights, Scotchgard fabric protector, 40/60 custom cloth split front bench seats, simulated leather steering wheel.

SPORT (in addition to or instead of SILVERADO equipment): AM/FM stereo with tape, clock and graphic equalizer; front bumper rubber strip and rear bumper with step pad, Sport decals, gunmetal gray grille, composite halogen headlamps, black RH and LH below-eyeline 9.0" x 6.5" mirrors, two-tone paint, floor and roof console with bucket seats, rear electric lift glass release, color-keyed carpeted rear quarter trim panels, 40/60 custom cloth split front bench seats and three-passenger folding rear bench seat.

Accessories

CODE	DESCRIPTION	DEALER	LIST
K5A1	**Cheyenne Preferred Equip Group**	NC	NC
K5A2	**Silverado Preferred Equip Group**	1595	1855
K5A3	**Silverado Preferred Equip Group**	2070	2407
K5A4	**Silverado Preferred Equip Group - Sport Blazer**	2628	3056
C60	**Air Conditioning** — w/PEGS K5A2, K5A3 or K5A4	NC	NC
	w/PEG K5A1	727	845
V22	**Appearance Pkg** — w/PEG K5A1	164	191
—	**Axles**		
GU6	3.42 ratio	NC	NC
GT4	3.73 ratio	NC	NC
G80	locking differential	217	252
E55	**Body Code** — tailgate	NC	NC
V54	**Carrier, Roof, Painted Black**	108	126
Z71	**Chassis Equip, Off Road Pkg**	344	400
V10	**Cold-Climate Pkg**	28	33
—	**Convenience Group**		
ZQ2	power door locks & front door power windows		
	w/PEGS K5A3 or K5A4	NC	NC
	w/PEG K5A2	316	367
ZQ3	tilt wheel & speed control		
	w/PEGS K5A2, K5A3 or K5A4	NC	NC
	w/PEG K5A1	329	383
—	**Cooling Systems**		
KC4	engine oil -w/Z82	NC	NC
	w/o Z82	116	135
V08	engine oil & transmission -w/Z82	NC	NC
	w/o Z82	170	198
FE9	**Federal Emissions**	NC	NC
NA6	**High Altitude Emissions**	NC	NC
YF5	**California Emissions**	86	100
NG1	**New York Emissions**	NC	NC
—	**Engines**		
L05	gasoline, 5.7 liter (350 cu.in.) EFI V8	NC	NC
L56	diesel 6.5 liter (395 cu. in.) turbo	2430	2825
AJ1	**Glass** — deep tinted -w/PEGS K5A3 or K5A4	NC	NC
	w/PEGS K5A1 or K5A2	185	215
VK3	**License Plate Bracket**	NC	NC
—	**Mirrors, Exterior**		

CODE	DESCRIPTION	DEALER	LIST
D48	below eye-line, electric remote, painted		
	w/PEGS K5A3 or K5A4	NC	NC
	w/PEG K5A2	84	98
DF2	camper type, stainless steel	46	53
B71	**Molding** — w/PEG K5A4	NC	NC
	w/PEGS K5A1, K5A2 or K5A3	155	180
—	**Paints, Exterior**		
ZY1	solid	NC	NC
ZY2	conventional two-tone -w/PEG K5A4	NC	NC
	w/PEGS K5A1, K5A2 or K5A3	155	180
ZY4	deluxe two-tone	249	290
—	**Radio Equip**		
UM6	radio - w/PEG K5A3	NC	NC
	w/PEGS K5A1 or K5A2	105	122
	incls elect tuned AM/FM stereo radio w/seek & scan, stereo cass tape & digital clock		
UX1	radio - w/PEG K5A4	NC	NC
	w/PEG K5A3	129	150
	w/PEGS K5A1 or K5A2	234	272
	incls elect tuned AM stereo/FM stereo radio w/seek & scan, stereo cass tape w/search & repeat, graphic equalizer & digital clock		
UL5	radio delete	(247)	(287)
—	**Rear Window Equip**		
ZP6	wiper/washer system w/defogger	240	279
C25	wiper/washer system w/o defogger	108	125
AG9	**Seat, Power Driver's Seat**	206	240
—	**Seat Trim**		
V4	vinyl reclining low back buckets	NC	NC
L3	custom cloth reclining split bench	NC	NC
L6	custom cloth reclining high back buckets	293	341
NZZ	**Skid Plate Pkg** — w/Z71	NC	NC
	w/o Z71	194	225
BYP	**Sport Pkg**	NC	NC
F60	**Springs** — front, heavy duty	54	63
U16	**Tachometer**	51	59
—	**Tires - All Seasons SBR**		
QIT	LT245/75R16C BW	NC	NC
	On-Off Road SBR		
QBN	LT245/75R16C BW	47	57
QBX	LT245/75R16C white outlined	155	182
QIX	LT265/75R16C BW	163	191
QIY	LT265/75R16C white outlined lettered	271	316
Z82	**Trailering Special Equip** — w/diesel	181	210
	w/o diesel	351	408
—	**Transmissions**		
MM5	5-spd manual	NC	NC
MX0	4-spd automatic w/overdrive	765	890
P06	**Wheel Trim** — rally w/PEG K5A2	NC	NC
	w/PEG K5A1	52	60
PF4	**Wheels** — aluminum cast -w/PEGS K5A3 or K5A4	NC	NC
	w/PEG K5A2	215	250
	w/PEG K5A1	267	310

CODE	DESCRIPTION	DEALER	LIST

CHEVROLET C-K 1500 SUBURBAN

5.7 LITER (350 CID) EFI 8 CYL
C1500 SERIES 2WD

CC10906 ZW9 Panel Doors 129.5" WB		17645	20166

K1500 SERIES 4WD

CK10906 ZW9 Panel Doors 129.5" WB		19615	22417
Destination Charge:		640	640

Standard Equipment

C/K 1500 SUBURBAN FULL-SIZED 4-DOOR - BASE CHEYENNE: 4-speed automatic transmission, power front disc/rear drum brakes with 4-wheel anti-lock braking, side guard door beams, front and rear chromed bumpers, single rectangular halogen headlamps, full-sized spare tire and wheel, mounted inside behind LR wheelhouse, argent painted steel wheels, full gauge instrumentation, tinted Solar-Ray glass windows, electronic AM/FM stereo with seek-scan and digital clock, Scotchgard fabric protector, three-passenger full bench front seat with custom vinyl trim and 4-spoke steering wheel.

SILVERADO (in addition to or instead of CHEYENNE equipment): Air conditioning, tilt wheel and speed control, power door locks and windows, remote outside electric mirror, deep tinted glass, AM/FM stereo with tape and clock, aluminum wheels, dual composite halogen headlamps, three-passenger front bench seat with textured velour custom cloth, auxiliary lighting all door-actuated.

Accessories

CODE	DESCRIPTION	DEALER	LIST
N1A1	**Cheyenne Preferred Equip Group**	NC	NC
N1A2	**Silverado Preferred Equip Group**		
	w/ZW9 body	3333	3876
	w/E55 body	3278	3812
N1A3	**Silverado Preferred Equipment Group**		
	w/ZW9 body	4800	5581
	w/E55 body	4745	5517
—	**Air Conditioning**		
C60	front - w/PEGS N1A2 or N1A3 or C69	NC	NC
	w/PEG N1A1	727	845
C69	front & rear - w/PEG N1A3	NC	NC

CODE	DESCRIPTION	DEALER	LIST
	w/PEG N1A2	387	450
	w/PEG N1A1	1114	1295
V22	**Appearance Pkg**	164	191
—	**Axles, Rear**		
GU6	3.42 ratio	NC	NC
GT4	3.73 ratio	NC	NC
G80	locking differential	217	252
—	**Body Codes**		
ZW9	panel doors	NC	NC
E55	tailgate	NC	NC
V54	**Carrier, Roof Luggage**	108	126
V10	**Cold Climate Pkg**	28	33
—	**Convenience Group**		
ZQ2	power door locks & power windows for side doors		
	w/PEGS N1A2 or N1A3	NC	NC
ZQ3	tilt wheel & speed control		
	w/PEGS N1A2 or N1A3	NC	NC
	w/PEG N1A1	329	383
V08	**Cooling Engine & Transmission Oil** — w/Z82	NC	NC
	w/o Z82	170	198
FE9	**Federal Emissions**	NC	NC
NA6	**High Altitude Emissions**	NC	NC
NG1	**New York Emissions**	NC	NC
YF5	**California Emissions**	86	100
L05	**Engine** — gasoline, 5.7 liter (350 cu. in.) EFI V8	NC	NC
AJ1	**Glass** — deep tinted, Solar-Ray -w/PEG N1A3	NC	NC
	w/PEGS N1A1 or N1A2	262	305
C36	**Heater, Auxiliary, Rear Passenger**	176	205
U01	**Lamps** — roof marker, (5)	45	52
VK3	**License Plate Bracket, Front**	NC	NC
—	**Mirrors, Exterior**		
D48	below eye-line, electric remote, painted	NC	NC
DF2	camper type, stainless steel -w/PEG N1A1	46	53
	w/PEGS N1A2 or N1A3	(39)	(45)
B71	**Molding - Wheel Flares**	155	180
—	**Paints, Exterior**		
ZY1	solid	NC	NC
ZY2	conventional two-tone	155	180
ZY4	deluxe two-tone	249	290
—	**Radio Equip**		
UM6	radio - w/PEG N1A3	NC	NC
	w/PEGS N1A1 or N1A2	105	122
	incls elec tuned AM/FM stereo radio w/seek & scan, stereo cass tape & digital clock		
UX1	radio - w/PEG N1A3	129	150
	w/PEGS N1A1 or N1A2	234	272
	incls elect tuned AM stereo/FM stereo radio w/seek & scan, stereo cass tape w/search & repeat, graphic equalizer & digital clock		
UL5	radio delete	(247)	(287)
U88	speakers - premium speaker system	73	85
—	**Rear Window Equip**		
C49	defogger, rear window, electric- w/ZP6	NC	NC

CODE	DESCRIPTION	DEALER	LIST
	w/o ZP6	132	154
ZP6	wiper-washer system w/defogger	240	279
C25	wiper-washer system w/o defogger -w/ZP6	NC	NC
	w/o ZP6	108	125
AG9	**Seat** — power driver's	206	240
—	**Seating**		
AT5	center folding - w/PEGS N1A2 or N1A3 or AS3	NC	NC
	w/PEG N1A1 or w/o AS3	503	585
AS3	center & rear w/PEG N1A3	NC	NC
	w/PEG N1A2	497	578
	w/PEG N1A1	942	1095
YG4	optional seat not desired	NC	NC
—	**Seat Trim**		
V1	vinyl bench	NC	NC
L1	custom cloth bench	NC	NC
L3	custom cloth reclining split bench	150	174
L6	custom cloth reclining bucket	464	540
A6	custom leather reclining high back buckets - w/AT5	1337	1555
	w/AS3	1651	1920
NZZ	**Skid Plate Pkg**	194	225
F60	**Springs** — front, HD	54	63
U16	**Tachometer**	51	59
—	**Tires**		
	All Seasons SBR		
QHA	P235/75R15XLS BW - C10906 only	NC	NC
QHB	P235/75R15XLS white stripe - C10906 only	82	95
QHP	LT225/75R16D BW - K10906 only	NC	NC
QIZ	LT245/75R16E BW - CC10906	391	460
	CK10906	194	230
QIT	LT245/75R16C BW - K10906 only	47	59
	On-Off Road SBR		
QHR	LT/225/75R16D BW - K10906 only	47	55
QBN	LT245/75R16C BW - K10906 only	95	116
QBX	LT245/75R16C WOL - K10906 only	202	241
QIW	LT245/75R16E BW	241	285
V76	**Tow Hooks**	33	38
Z82	**Trailering Special Equip** — w/diesel	181	210
	w/o diesel	351	408
MX0	**Transmission** — 4-spd auto w/overdrive	NC	NC
P06	**Wheel Trim** — rally -w/PEG N1A2	NC	NC
	w/PEG N1A1	52	60
—	**Wheels**		
N90	aluminum, cast - C1500 only		
	w/PEG N1A3	NC	NC
	w/PEG N1A2	215	250
	w/PEG N1A1	267	310
PF4	aluminum, cast - K1500 only		
	w/PEG N1A3	NC	NC
	w/PEG N1A2	215	250
	w/PEG N1A1	267	310

CHEVROLET C-K 2500 SUBURBAN

5.7 LITER (350 CID) EFI 8 CYL
C2500 SERIES 2WD
CC20906 ZW9 Panel Doors 131.5" WB 18720   21399

K2500 SERIES 4WD
CK20906 ZW9 Panel Doors 131.5" WB 20661   23618

Destination Charge: 640   640

Standard Equipment

C/K 2500 SUBURBAN FULL-SIZED 4-DOOR - BASE CHEYENNE: 4-speed automatic transmission, power front disc/rear drum brakes with 4-wheel anti-lock braking, side guard door beams, front and rear chromed bumpers with black rub strip, single rectangular halogen headlamps, full-sized spare tire and wheel, mounted inside behind LR wheelhouse, argent painted steel wheels, full gauge instrumentation, tinted Solar-Ray glass windows, electronic AM/FM stereo with seek-scan and digital clock, Scotchgard fabric protector, three-passenger full bench front seat w/custom vinyl trim and 4-spoke steering wheel.

SILVERADO (in addition to or instead of CHEYENNE equipment): Air conditioning, tilt wheel and speed control, power door locks and windows, remote outside electric mirror, deep tinted glass, AM/FM stereo with tape and clock, aluminum wheels, dual composite halogen headlamps, three-passenger front bench seat with textured velour custom cloth, auxiliary lighting all door-actuated.

Accessories

CODE	DESCRIPTION	DEALER	LIST
N2A1	**Cheyenne Preferred Equip Group**	NC	NC
N2A2	**Silverado Preferred Equip Group**		
	w/ZW9 body	3333	3876
	w/E55 body	3278	3812
N2A3	**Silverado Preferred Equip Group**		
	w/ZW9 body	4585	5331
	w/E55 body	4530	5267
—	**Air Conditioning**		
C60	front - w/PEGS N2A2, N2A3 or C69	NC	NC
	w/PEG N2A1	727	845

CHEVROLET

CODE	DESCRIPTION	DEALER	LIST
C69	front & rear - w/PEG N2A3	NC	NC
	w/PEG N2A2	387	450
	w/PEG N2A1	1114	1295
V22	**Appearance Pkg**	164	191
—	**Axles, Rear**		
GT4	3.73 ratio	NC	NC
GT5	4.10 ratio	NC	NC
G80	locking differential	217	252
—	**Body Codes**		
ZW9	panel doors	NC	NC
E55	tailgate	NC	NC
V54	**Carrier, Roof Luggage**	108	126
V10	**Cold-Climate Pkg**	28	33
—	**Convenience Group**		
ZQ2	power door locks & power windows for side doors	NC	NC
ZQ3	tilt wheel & speed control -w/PEGS N2A2 or N2A3	NC	NC
	w/PEG N2A1	329	383
V08	**Cooling** — engine & transmission oil -w/Z82	NC	NC
	w/o Z82	170	198
FE9	**Federal Emissions**	NC	NC
YF5	**California Emissions**	86	100
NG1	**New York Emissions**	NC	NC
—	**Engines**		
	gasoline		
L05	5.7 liter (350 cu. in.) EFI V8	NC	NC
L19	7.4 liter (454 cu. in.) EFI V8	520	605
	diesel		
L65	6.5 liter (395 cu. in.) V8 turbo diesel	2430	2825
AJ1	**Glass** — deep tinted -w/PEG N2A3	NC	NC
	w/PEGS N2A1 or N2A2	262	305
C36	**Heater, Auxiliary, Rear Passenger**	176	205
U01	**Lamps** — roof marker (5)	45	52
VK3	**License Plate Bracket**	NC	NC
—	**Mirrors, Exterior**		
D48	dual elec remote control below eye-level, painted	NC	NC
DF2	camper type, stainless steel -w/PEG N2A1	46	53
	w/PEGS N2A2 or N2A3	(39)	(45)
—	**Paints, Exterior**		
ZY1	solid	NC	NC
ZY2	conventional two-tone	155	180
ZY4	deluxe two-tone	249	290
—	**Radio Equip**		
UM6	radio - w/PEG N2A3	NC	NC
	w/PEGS N2A1 or N2A2	105	122
	incls elect tuned AM/FM stereo radio w/seek & scan, stereo cass tape & digital clock		
UX1	radio - w/PEG N2A3	129	150
	w/PEGS N2A1 or N2A2	234	272
	incls elect tuned AM stereo/FM stereo radio w/seek & scan, stereo cass tape w/search & repeat, graphic equalizer & digital clock		
UL5	radio delete	(247)	(287)
U88	speakers - premium speaker system	(73)	(85)

CODE	DESCRIPTION	DEALER	LIST
—	**Rear Window Equip**		
C49	defogger, rear window, electric -w/ZP6	NC	NC
	w/o ZP6	132	154
ZP6	wiper-washer system w/defogger	240	279
C25	wiper-washer system w/o defogger - w/ZP6	NC	NC
	w/o ZP6	108	125
AG9	**Seat** — power driver's seat	206	240
—	**Seats**		
AT5	center, folding - w/PEGS N2A2, N2A3 or AS3	NC	NC
	w/PEG N2A1 w/o AS3	503	585
AS3	center & rear - w/PEGS N2A2 or N2A3	497	578
	w/PEG N2A1	942	1095
YG4	optional seat not desired	NC	NC
—	**Seat Trim**		
V1	vinyl bench	NC	NC
L1	custom cloth	NC	NC
L3	custom cloth reclining split bench	150	174
L6	custom cloth reclining high back buckets	464	540
A6	custom leather reclining high back buckets -w/AT5	1337	1555
	w/AS3	1651	1920
NZZ	**Skid Plate Pkg**	194	225
6Y4	**Spare Tire & Wheel Delete**	(243)	(283)
F60	**Springs** — front, HD	54	63
U16	**Tachometer**	51	59
—	**Tires**		
	All Seasons SBR		
QIZ	LT245/75R16E black lettered	NC	NC
	On-Off Road SBR		
QIW	LT245/75R16E black lettered	47	55
V76	**Tow Hooks**	33	38
Z82	**Trailering Special Equip** — w/diesel or L19	181	210
	w/o diesel or L19	351	408
MX0	**Transmission** — 4-spd automatic w/overdrive	NC	NC
P06	**Wheel Trim** — rally - w/PEGS N2A2 or N2A3	NC	NC
	w/PEG N2A1	52	60

FORD BRONCO

BRONCO 8 CYL

Code	Description	Dealer	List
U15	XL 4WD	18497	21515
U15	XLT 4WD	20402	23755
U15	Eddie Bauer 4WD	22812	26590
	Destination Charge:	600	600

Standard Equipment

FULL-SIZED BRONCO - BASE XL: 5-speed manual transmission, power steering, Twin Traction Beam suspension, power front disc/rear drum brakes and four-wheel anti-lock braking system, 15" x 6" styled steel wheels and tires, front side window demisters, tinted glass, high-mounted stop light, driver's air bag, vinyl bucket seats, swing-down tailgate with power window and electronic AM/FM stereo with digital clock.

XLT (in addition to or instead of XL equipment): Chrome front bumper with black rub strip, bright manual mirrors, argent styled steel wheels, rear cargo light, color-keyed carpeting, full-length color-keyed cloth headliner, tachometer and trip odometer, cloth captain's chairs with recline and power lumbar controls, three-passenger rear flip/fold bench, tilt steering wheel and speed control.

EDDIE BAUER (in addition to or instead of XLT equipment): Privacy glass, bright wheel lip molding, dual bodyside accent paint stripe, two-tone rocker panel paint, forged aluminum deep-dish wheels, air conditioning, overhead console with compass and temperature display, rear window defroster and light convenience groups A and B.

Accessories

Code	Description	Dealer	List
—	**Preferred Equip Pkgs** — prices include pkg discounts		
680A	**XL Pkg 680A**	846	995
683A	**XLT Pkg 683A**	413	485
684A	**XLT Pkg 684A**	824	970
686A	**Eddie Bauer Pkg 686A**	229	270
99N	**Engine** — 5.0L EFI V-8	STD	STD
99H	**Engine** — 5.8L EFI V-8	187	220
44M	**Transmission** — 5-spd manual overdrive	STD	STD

FORD

SPORT UTILITY

CODE	DESCRIPTION	DEALER	LIST
44E	**Transmission** — electronic 4-spd automatic	787	926
XH9	**Limited Slip Axle**	213	250
422	**California Emissions**	85	100
428	**High Altitude Emissions**	NC	NC
—	**Tires**		
T77	P235/75Rx15XL steel radial - BSW all-season	STD	STD
T7X	P235/75Rx15XL steel radial - BSW all-terrain	47	55
T7Q	P235/75Rx15XL steel radial - OWL all-season	107	125
T7P	P235/75Rx15XL steel radial - OWL all-terrain	170	200
T7W	P265/75Rx15SL OWL all-terrain		
	use w/Base XLT or Base Eddie Bauer model	680	800
	use w/PEP 684 or 686	540	635
—	**Seats**		
S	vinyl bucket - XL	STD	STD
U	cloth & vinyl bench - XL	85	100
V	cloth captain's chairs - XLT	STD	STD
U	cloth & vinyl bench - XLT	(298)	(350)
X	captain's chairs w/leather seating surface - XLT	548	645
W	cloth captain's chairs - Eddie Bauer	STD	STD
X	captain's chairs w/leather seating surface	548	645
601	**Climate Control Group**	838	985
213	**Electric Shift 4X4, Touch Drive**	107	125
41H	**Heater, Engine Block**	30	35
21M	**Hubs, Manual Locking**	(51)	(60)
153	**License Plate Bracket**	NC	NC
55L	**Luxury Group** — use w/PEP 684	838	985
	use w/PEP 686	514	605
545	**Mirrors, Bright Low-Mount Swing-Away**	NC	NC
—	**Spare Tire Carrier, O/S Swing-Away, Credit**	(140)	(165)
535	**Trailer Towing Pkg** — use w/Eddie Bauer	259	305
	use w/P265 tires	272	320
	use w/Eddie Bauer w/P265 tires	225	265
911	**Cargo Cover** -w/PEP 683, 684	68	80
912	**Cargo Net** -w/PEP 683, 684	26	30
55S	**Security Group**	217	255
61A	**Light & Convenience Group A** -w/PEP 684	174	205
952	**Two-Tone, Deluxe**	208	245
65W	**Wheel Group** — use w/XL	263	310
	use w/XLT	340	400
	use w/Eddie Bauer	140	165
649	**Wheels, Forged Aluminum (Deep Dish)** — use w/PEP 684	NC	NC
—	**Radio Systems**		
588	premium AM/FM stereo cassette -w/PEP 683	182	215
588	premium AM/FM stereo cassette -w/PEP 684, 686	67	80
582	premium AM/FM stereo CD -w/PEP 683	433	510
582	premium AM/FM stereo CD -w/PEP 684, 686	318	375

CODE	DESCRIPTION	DEALER	LIST

FORD EXPLORER

EXPLORER 2-DOOR 6 CYL

Code	Description	Dealer	List
U22	XL 2WD	15361	17240
U24	XL 4WD	16902	18990
U22	Sport 2WD	16286	18290
U24	Sport 4WD	17790	20000
U22	Eddie Bauer 2WD	18891	21250
U24	Eddie Bauer 4WD	20387	22950

EXPLORER 4-DOOR 6 CYL

Code	Description	Dealer	List
U32	XL 2WD	16145	18130
U34	XL 4WD	17702	19900
U32	XLT 2WD	18327	20610
U34	XLT 4WD	19911	22410
U32	Eddie Bauer 2WD	20782	23400
U34	Eddie Bauer 4WD	22370	25205
U32	Limited 2WD	23717	26735
U34	Limited 4WD	25301	28535
	Destination Charge:	485	485

Standard Equipment

EXPLORER COMPACT 2-DOOR - XL: 5-speed man trans, Twin I-beam suspension, pwr steering, pwr front disc/rear drum brakes w/four-whl anti-lock braking, 15" x 6" whls & tires, bright front/rear bumpers w/3,500-lb trailer-tow, tinted glass windows, flip-open opera windows, one-piece liftgate, color-keyed lower rocker panels, high-mounted rear stoplight, dlx styled steel wls, full-length color-keyed carpeting, light group, elec AM/FM stereo w/digital clock, two additional spkrs in doors, vinyl front bucket seats.

SPORT (in addition to or instead of XL equipment): Black grille, blk wheel lip molding, black/orange body-side molding insert, deep dish cast alum wheels, rear window washer/defroster, color-keyed instrument cluster applique, leather- wrapped steering wheel and LH/RH illuminated visor vanity and auxiliary visors.

EDDIE BAUER (in addition to or instead of SPORT equipment): Electric remote control mirrors, mocha/bright bodyside insert moldings, two-tone mocha paint stripes, roof rack, luxury cast aluminum wheels, color-keyed soft vinyl door trim and carpeted lower portion of panels, garment bag and duffle bag, power windows, power door locks, cloth sport bucket seats with power seat and matching split/folding rear seat, floor console and tilt steering column with speed control.

FORD

SPORT UTILITY

CODE	DESCRIPTION	DEALER	LIST

EXPLORER COMPACT 4-DOOR - XL: 5-speed manual transmission, Twin I-beam suspension, power steering, power front disc/rear drum brakes with four-wheel anti-lock braking, 15" x 6" wheels and tires, bright front and rear bumpers with 3,500-lb. trailer-tow, tinted glass windows, one-piece liftgate, color-keyed lower rocker panels, high-mounted rear stoplight, deluxe styled steel wheels, full-length color-keyed carpeting, light group, electronic AM/FM stereo with digital clock and two additional speakers in doors, cloth captain's chairs, rear split/folding rear seat, floor console.

EDDIE BAUER (in addition to or instead of XL equipment): Mocha bright/bright bodyside molding inserts, two-tone paint treatment with mocha tape stripe, roof rack, garment bag and duffle bag, cloth sport bucket seats with power seat and matching split/folding rear seat, floor console.

LIMITED (in addition to or instead of EDDIE BAUER equipment): Color-keyed front bumper with color-coordinated rub strip and front fascia, color-keyed rear trailer tow bumper (3,500-lb. capacity), black grille, heated outside mirrors, color-keyed bodyside molding inserts, special tape striping, cast aluminum wheels with skirted spokes, air conditioning, color-keyed leather/cloth door panel accents and carpeted lower portion with map pocket in front door and courtesy light/reflectors, luxury bucket seats with leather surface, power seat and matching split/fold rear seat, driver's 3-position memory switch, 2-way adjustable head restraints, floor console, leather-wrapped steering wheel.

Accessories

CODE	DESCRIPTION	DEALER	LIST
—	**Preferred Equipment Pkgs**		
930A	XL 2-Dr Pkg 930A	NC	NC
931A	Sport 2-Dr Pkg 931A	NC	NC
932A	Eddie Bauer 2-Dr Pkg 932A	85	100
940A	XL 4-Dr Pkg 940A	NC	NC
941A	XLT 4-Dr Pkg 941A	378	445
	special bonus discount w/manual transmission	NC	NC
942A	Eddie Bauer 4-Dr Pkg 942A	214	251
943A	Limited 4-Dr Pkg 943A	336	395
—	**Seats - 2-Door XL**		
A	knitted vinyl bucket - XL	STD	STD
J	cloth captain's chairs w/console - XL	238	280
—	**Seats - 2-Door Sport**		
A	knitted vinyl bucket - Sport	STD	STD
J	cloth captain's chairs w/console - Sport	238	280
K	cloth sport bucket - Sport	867	1020
—	upgrade from captain's chairs - Sport	638	750
F	sport bucket w/leather seating surfaces - Sport	1360	1600
—	upgrade from captain's chairs - Sport	1127	1326
—	**Seats - 2-Door Eddie Bauer**		
Z	cloth Eddie Bauer sport bucket - Eddie Bauer	STD	STD
F	sport bucket w/leather seating surface - Eddie Bauer	NC	NC
—	**Seats - 4-Door XL**		
A	knitted vinyl bucket - XL	STD	STD
J	cloth captain's chairs - XL	238	280
M	cloth 60/40 split bench - XL	217	255
—	**Seats - 4-Door XLT**		
J	cloth captain's chairs - XLT	STD	STD
K	cloth sport bucket - XLT	812	955
M	cloth 60/40 split bench - XLT	(17)	(20)
F	sport bucket w/leather seating surfaces - XLT	1301	1530
—	**Seats - 4-Door Eddie Bauer**		
Z	cloth Eddie Bauer sport bucket - Eddie Bauer	STD	STD

FORD

CODE	DESCRIPTION	DEALER	LIST
F	sport bucket w/leather seating surface - Eddie Bauer	NC	NC
99X	**Engine** — 4.0L EFI V6	STD	STD
44M	**Transmission** — 5-spd manual overdrive	STD	STD
44T	**Transmission** — automatic overdrive	757	890
—	**Rear Axle** — performance 3.27 axle (limited slip)	217	255
—	**Rear Axle** — performance 3.75 axle & trailer tow	306	360
—	**Rear Axle** — optional axle ratio (upgrade)	38	45
422	**California Emissions**	85	100
428	**High Altitude Emissions**	NC	NC
—	**Tiers**		
T7H	P225/70Rx15SL RBL all-season	STD	STD
T7R	P235/75Rx15SL OWL all-terrain	196	230
572	**Air Conditioning**	663	780
	w/man trans & PEP 930 or 940	NC	NC
416	**Consolette, Floor Mounted**	26	30
624	**Cooling, Super Engine**	47	55
167	**Floor Mats, Color-Keyed, Front/Rear**	38	45
595	**Fog Lamps**	158	185
924	**Glass, Privacy**	187	220
41H	**Heater, Engine Block**	30	35
21M	**Hub, Manual Locking** — 4WD	(89)	(105)
153	**License Plate Bracket**	NC	NC
965	**Molding, Bodyside**	102	120
903	**Power Equip Group** — 2-Dr XL	765	900
	4-Dr XL	1050	1235
—	**Power Equip Group, Credit**	(162)	(190)
151	**Electronics Group**	413	485
615	**Rack, Luggage** — w/man trans & PEP 941	NC	NC
43B	**Roof, Tilt-Up Open Air**	238	280
186	**Running Boards** — 4-Dr	336	395
—	**Running Boards** — 4-Dr credit (Limited)	(336)	(395)
186	**Running Boards** — 2-Dr	208	245
558	**Special Appearance Pkg**	243	285
52N	**Speed Control/Tilt Steering Wheel**	328	385
	w/man trans & PEP 931	NC	NC
85C	**Tape Stripe, Deluxe** — 4-Dr	47	55
534	**Trailer Towing Pkg**	89	105
952	**Two-Tone Paint, Deluxe**	102	120
649	**Wheels, Cast Aluminum (Deep Dish)** — XL, Sport	213	250
	XLT Eddie Bauer	NC	NC
644	**Wheels, Luxury Aluminum** — Sport	NC	NC
17C	**Wipers/Washer/Defroster, Rear Window**	238	280
—	**Radio Systems**		
587	electronic AM/FM stereo w/clock	STD	STD
588	electronic premium AM/FM stereo w/cassette/clock	178	210
	w/man trans & PEP 931	NC	NC
916	Ford JBL audio system w/cassette	595	700
—	upgrade from premium cassette	417	490
917	Ford JBL audio system w/CD player	850	1000
—	upgrade from premium cassette	672	790
58Y	w/Limited	255	300

GEO TRACKER

TRACKER 2WD 4 CYL

CE10367	2-Dr Convertible	10343	10865

TRACKER 4WD 4 CYL

CJ10316	2-Dr	11705	12295
CJ10367	2-Dr Convertible	11553	12135
CJ10316/B2Z	LSi 2-Dr	13104	13765
CJ10367/B2Z	LSi 2-Dr Convertible	12852	13500
Destination Charge:		300	300

Standard Equipment

TRACKER: Radio antenna, power front disc/rear drum brakes, rear-wheel anti-lock brakes, front/rear bumpers w/integral black rub strip, 1.6 liter single overhead camshaft 4-cylinder electronic fuel injection engine (available w/FE9 Federal Emission only), 1.6 liter single overhead camshaft 16-valve 4-cylinder multi-port fuel injection engine (available with YF5 California or NG1 New York Emission only), stainless steel muffler and tailpipe exhaust, composite halogen headlights, front manual locking hubs, dual outside black mirrors, spare tire cover, full-size outside rear-mounted lockable spare tire and wheel, front MacPherson strut suspension, rear solid axle coil spring suspension, swing-open right-hand hinged door tailgate with lock, P195/75R15 all-season SBR BW tires (2WD), P205/75R15 all-season SBR BW tires (4x4), front and rear tow hooks, transfer case, 5-speed manual transmission w/5th gear overdrive, styled steel wheels w/center caps, fixed intermittent wipers, front/rear passenger assist grips, cargo area trim, full carpeting including cargo area, center console with cupholders and storage tray, rear window defogger (NA - Convertible), tachometer (4x4), trip odometer, 3-position dome light, lighter/power socket, inside day/night rearview mirror, restraint system (front lap/shoulder belts, rear outboard lap/shoulder belts), Scotchgard fabric protection on seats, fold-and-stow rear bench seat (4x4), driver and passenger easy-entry seats, high-back reclining front bucket seats w/integral head restraints, cloth bolsters and vinyl seatbacks, self-aligning steering wheel, driver and passenger door storage bins.

LSi (in addition to or instead of Tracker equipment): Tinted glass,LSi styled steel wheels, front and rear floor mats, power steering, body side moldings, rear window wiper/washer (except Convertible), automatic locking hubs, AM/FM ETR stereo radio with digital clock, color-keyed bumpers, fold-down rear bucket seats, color-keyed dual OS mirrors.

CODE	DESCRIPTION	DEALER	LIST

Accessories

CODE	DESCRIPTION	DEALER	LIST
—	**Tracker 2WD Convertible Base Equipment Group 1** — CE10367	NC	NC
UL1	w/UL1 radio, add	272	306
UL0	w/UL0 radio, add	446	501
UP0	w/UP0 radio, add	798	897
	incls standard equipment		
—	**Tracker 2WD Convertible Preferred Equipment Group 2** — CE10367	517	581
UL0	w/UL0 radio, add	174	195
UP0	w/UP0 radio, add	526	591
	incls standard equipment, electronically tuned AM/FM stereo radio with seek, digital clock and four speakers, power steering		
—	**Tracker 4WD & Tracker 4WD Convertible Base Equipment Group 1** — CJ10316 & CJ10367	NC	NC
UL1	w/UL1 radio, add	272	306
UL0	w/UL0 radio, add	446	501
UP0	w/UP0 radio, add	798	897
	incld w/model		
—	**Tracker 4WD & Tracker 4WD Convertible Preferred Equipment Group 2** — CJ10316 & CJ10367	517	581
UL0	w/UL0 radio, add	174	195
UP0	w/UP0 radio, add	526	591
	incls standard equipment, electronically tuned AM/FM stereo radio with seek, digital clock and four speakers		
—	**Tracker 4WD LSi & Tracker 4WD LSi Convertible Base Equipment Group 1** — CJ10316/B2Z & CJ10367/B2Z	NC	NC
UL0	w/UL0 radio, add	174	195
UP0	w/UP0 radio, add	526	591
	incld w/model		
—	**Radio Equipment** — see pkgs		
UL1	radio - see pkgs		
	ncls electronically tuned AM/FM stereo radio with seek, digital clock and four speakers		
UL0	radio - see pkgs		
	incls electronically tuned AM/FM stereo radio with seek and scan, tone select, stereo cassette tape, digital clock, theft deterrent and four speakers		
UP0	radio - see pkgs		
	incls electronically tuned AM/FM stereo radio with seek and scan, tone select, stereo cassette tape, compact disc player, digital clock, theft deterrent and four speakers		
—	**Interior Trim**		
L2	linear cloth bucket seats	NC	NC
E2	expressive cloth bucket seats	NC	NC
C2	custom cloth bucket seats - LSi & Tracker 4x4 LSi Convertible	NC	NC
—	**Exterior Color** — paint, solid	NC	NC
—	**Engines**		
LS5	1.6 liter SOHC L4 EFI (w/FE9 Emissions only)	NC	NC
LO1	1.6 liter SOHC 16-valve L4 MFI (w/YF5 or NG1 Emissions only)	NC	NC
C60	**Air Conditioning** — CFC free	663	745
YF5	**California Emission Requirements**	62	70
FE9	**Federal Emission Requirements**	NC	NC
NG1	**New York State Emission Requirements**	62	70
B37	**Floor Mats** — front & rear - std on LSi models	25	28

GEO

GEO / GMC

CODE	DESCRIPTION	DEALER	LIST
B84	**Moldings** — bodyside - CJ10316 model (std on Tracker LSi)	53	59
	Convertible models (std on LSi Convertible)	76	85
—	**Seating**		
AP6	rear not desired - CE10367 model only	NC	NC
AM7	rear folding bench - CE10367 model only (std on 4x4 models)	396	445
NY7	**Skid Plates** — front differential & transfer case	67	75
N33	**Steering Wheel** — tilt	102	115
—	**Transmissions**		
MM5	5-speed manual w/5th gear overdrive	NC	NC
MX1	3-speed automatic	530	595
QA4	**Wheels** — 15" alloy w/steel spare	298	335

GMC JIMMY

JIMMY 2WD 6 CYL

TS10516	2-Dr Tailgate 100.5" WB	14153	15639
TS10506	4-Dr Tailgate 107" WB	15332	16941

JIMMY 4WD 6 CYL

TT10516	2-Dr Tailgate 100.5" WB	15890	17558
TT10506	4-Dr Tailgate 107" WB	17465	19298
Destination Charge:		475	475

Standard Equipment

S-JIMMY COMPACT 2-DOOR - BASE SL: 5-speed manual overdrive transmission, power steering, power disc front/rear drum brakes, 4-wheel anti-lock braking, independent front suspension, Solar-Ray tinted glass all windows, side guard door beams, center high-mount stop light, full-sized spare tire, side-window defogger, color-keyed front carpeting, ETR AM/FM stereo with seek-scan, digital clock and fixed-mast antenna; vinyl front bucket seats, gray painted bumpers and 15" x 6" wheels.

SLS (in addition to or instead of BASE SL equipment): Door panels with deluxe cloth upper inserts, carpeted lower inserts with map pockets, floor console, color-keyed full-length floor carpeting and mats, color-keyed cowl kick panels, carpeted lower rear quarter and endgate panels, 10-inch rearview mirror

236   **EDMUND'S VAN/PICKUP/SPORT UTILITY BUYER'S GUIDE**

with dual reading lamps, high-back reclining bucket seats with folding backs and deluxe cloth trim, and molded plastic grille painted lower body color.

SLE (in addition to or instead of SLS equipment): Power door locks, power windows, leather upper door inserts and carpeted lower inserts and map pockets, leather seating on high-back front bucket seats with 6-way power driver's seat, folding rear bench seat, 4-spoke leather-wrapped steering wheel, remote keyless entry, black luggage carrier.

SLT (in addition to or instead of SLE equipment): Color-keying packages for grille, insert moldings, trim and wheels.

S-JIMMY COMPACT 4-DOOR - BASE SL, TAHOE: 5-speed manual overdrive transmission, power steering, power disc front/rear drum brakes, 4-wheel anti-lock braking, independent front suspension, Solar-Ray tinted glass all windows, side guard door beams, center high-mount stop light, full-sized spare tire, side-window defogger, deluxe cloth interiors, chromed grilles, chromed bumpers, floor console (seat divider), color-keyed carpeting front and rear, carpeted tailgate and lower quarter panels and rear quarter area, dual front lighted visor mirrors, bright aluminum wheel openings and bodyside black moldings with bright accents. Some equipment such as AM/FM w/seek-scan, cassette player and digital clock required.

SLS (in addition to or instead of SL equipment): Power door locks, power windows, leather upper door inserts and carpeted lower inserts and map pockets, leather seating on high-back front bucket seats with 6-way power driver's seat, folding rear bench seat, 4-spoke leather-wrapped steering wheel, remote keyless entry, black luggage carrier.

SLE (in addition to or instead of SLS equipment): Power door locks, power windows, leather upper door inserts and carpeted lower inserts and map pockets, leather seating on high-back front bucket seats with 6-way power driver's seat, folding rear bench seat, 4-spoke leather-wrapped steering wheel, remote keyless entry, black luggage carrier.

SLT (in addition to or instead of SLE equipment): Color-keying packages for grille, insert moldings, trim and wheels.

Accessories

CODE	DESCRIPTION	DEALER	LIST
C60	**Air Conditioning**	671	780
V08	**Heavy Duty Cooling**	116	135
	incls engine oil cooler [reqs 4.3 liter V6 engine]		
UA1	**Heavy Duty Battery**	48	56
AJ1	**Deep Tinted Glass**	194	225
	reqs tailgate/defroster convenience pkg		
AA3	**Deep Tinted Glass w/Light Tinted Rear Window**	124	144
YF5	**California Emissions**	NA	NA
NG1	**New York Emissions**	NA	NA
C25	**Rear Window Wiper Washer**	108	125
	reqs tailgate/defroster convenience pkg		
F51	**Heavy Duty Shock Absorbers — F & R - 4-Dr 2WD**	34	40
F60	**Heavy Duty Front Springs — 4WD**	54	63
	incls HD shock absorbers		
G80	**Axle — locking differential**	217	252
	reqs 3.42 optional rear axle ratio		
GU6	**Optional Axle Ratio — 3.42**	NC	NC
RYJ	**Retractable Cargo Security Shade — 4-Dr**	59	69
	reqs spare tire & wheel carrier		
D96	**Upper Body Stripes**	47	55
U52	**Electronic Instrumentation**	168	195
	incls speedometer, tachometer, oil pressure, fuel & temperature gauges,		

GMC

CODE	DESCRIPTION	DEALER	LIST
	voltmeter & trip odometer		
ANL	**Air Deflector w/Fog Lights** — 2WD	99	115
—	**Tires** — steel belted radials		
QCF	P205/75R15 all-season white letter	104	121
QJL	P205/75R15 on-off road white letter	146	170
QEB	P235/75R15 on-off road white letter	288	335
QFL	P235/75R15 BW	132	153
QFN	P235/75R15 all-season white letter - 4WD w/YC9	114	133
	4WD w/o YC9	246	286
P06	**Wheel Trim Rings** — std on 4-Dr 4WD	52	60
ZJ7	**Rally Wheels** — incls wheel trim rings - 2WD	79	92
N60	**Aluminum Wheels** — 2-Dr 2WD w/YC2	213	248
	2-Dr 2WD w/o YC2	292	340
	4-Dr 2WD	213	248
N90	**Aluminum Wheels** — 2-Dr 4WD w/YC2	241	280
	2-Dr 4WD w/o YC2	292	340
	4-Dr 4WD	241	280
P16	**Spare Wheel & Tire Carrier**	137	159
D55	**Floor Console** — reqs bucket seats	125	145
DK6	**Overhead Console** — reqs YC2 or YC3	71	83
—	**Trailering Equipment**		
Z72	light duty - w/o R8Y	258	300
	w/R8Y	94	109
	incls 5-lead wiring harness & trailer hitch; models w/4.3 liter engine also include HD cooling		
Z82	heavy duty - w/o R8Y	297	345
	w/R8Y	181	210
	incls 7-lead wiring harness, HD flasher, weight distributing hitch platform; models w/4.3 liter engine also include HD cooling [models w/4.3 liter engine req optional axle ratio]		
AD5	**Sliding Side Window** — 2-Dr	221	257
ZM4	**Luggage Rack**	108	126
D48	**Power Mirrors** — dual	71	83
AX3	**Remote Keyless Entry System**	116	135
	reqs bucket seats, pwr convenience group, tailgate/defroster convenience pkg & floor console		
ZM6	**Off Road Suspension Pkg** — 2-Dr 4WD	105	122
	incls Bilstein gas shock absorbers, stabilizer bar, jounce bumpers, upgraded torsion bar, upsized tow hooks [reqs P235/75R15 tires]		
FE1	**Soft Ride Suspension Pkg** — 4-Dr 4WD w/QFL tires	194	225
	4-Dr 4WD w/QFN tires	308	358
	incls Bilstein gas shock absorbers		
B74	**Wheel Opening Moldings** — 2-Dr	37	43
R8V	**Electronic Transfer Case Delete** — 4WD	(106)	(123)
—	**Radio Equipment**		
UM6	AM/FM ETR stereo w/cassette	105	122
	incls 4 speakers, digital clock & seek/scan		
UX1	AM/FM ETR stereo radio w/cassette & graphic equalizer	234	272
	incls 4 speakers, digital clock & seek/scan		
U1C	AM/FM ETR stereo radio w/CD player	349	406
UT5	AM ETR radio w/clock	(113)	(131)
	incls 2 speakers		

CODE	DESCRIPTION	DEALER	LIST
UL5	**AM/FM ETR Radio Delete**..	(194)	(226)
ZM5	**Underbody Shield Pkg** — 4WD..	65	75
	incls transfer case & differential skid plates, fuel tank & steering linkage shields		
—	**Mats**		
B32	color-keyed, front (std on 4-Dr)...	22	25
B33	color-keyed, rear (std on 4-Dr)..	17	20
BG9	black rubber, full — 2-Dr...	NC	NC
R8Y	**Enhanced Powertrain Pkg**...	998	1160
	incls 4.3 liter CPI V6 engine, 4-spd automatic overdrive transmission, coolers for engine, oil & transmission		
ZY2	**Paint** — conventional two-tone..	148	172
ZY3	**Paint** — special two-tone...	148	172
—	**Seats**		
AM0	6-way pwr driver's seat..	249	290
	reqs pwr convenience pkg & bucket seats; 2-Dr also reqs YC2 or YC3 pkg		
AM7	fold-down rear bench seat (std on 4-Dr 4WD)		
	w/custom vinyl trim..	352	409
	w/deluxe cloth trim..	347	435
AV5	reclining highback front bucket seats — 2-Dr w/deluxe cloth trim..........	65	76
	4-Dr w/custom vinyl trim..	NC	NC
	4-Dr w/deluxe cloth trim..	181	211
—	**Decor Pkgs**		
YC2	**SLE Comfort** — 2-Dr 2WD..	774	900
	2-Dr 4WD...	746	868
	incls reclining highback front bucket seats, color-keyed floor mats, chrome grille, dual illuminated visor vanity mirrors, illuminated entry system, floor console, deluxe cloth upholstery cloth inserts on door panels, dual reading lights, grey bodyside & wheel opening moldings [pkg std on 4-Dr models; 2WD models also incl rally wheels; 4WD models incl wheel trim rings]		
YC3	**SLS Sport Equipment** — 2-Dr..	1034	1202
	incls dual reading lights, dual illuminated visor vanity mirrors, leather-wrapped steering wheel, color-keyed wheel opening moldings, illuminated entry system, passenger assist grips (4WD), aluminum wheels, grey bodyside molding, door trim panels w/cloth inserts, floor console, color-keyed f & r bumpers w/rub strips, reclining highback bucket seats, color-keyed carpeted floor mats		
YC3	**SLS Sport Equipment** — 4-Dr 2WD w/split bench seat	260	302
	4-Dr 2WD w/bucket seats...	458	533
	4-Dr 4WD w/split bench seat...	287	334
	4-Dr 4WD w/ bucket seats..	486	565
	incls aluminum wheels, leather-wrapped steering wheel, color-keyed grille & wheel opening moldings		
YC9	**SLT Touring Equipment** — 2-Dr 2WD...	2860	3325
	2-Dr 4WD...	3053	3550
	incls pwr convenience group, leather-wrapped steering wheel, P205/75R15 SBR all-season tires (2WD), P235/75R15 SBR all-season tires (4WD), 6-way pwr driver's seat, illuminated entry system, conventional two-tone paint, aluminum wheels, leather highback reclining bucket seats, floor & overhead consoles, door trim panels w/leather inserts, dual reading lights, keyless remote entry system, chrome grille, color-keyed bumpers, dual illuminated visor vanity mirrors, color-keyed floor mats, fold-down rear		

CODE	DESCRIPTION	DEALER	LIST
	seat w/center armrest, driver & passenger lumbar support adjuster, grey bodyside & wheel opening moldings, passenger assist grips		
YC9	**SLT Touring Equipment** — 4-Dr 2WD..	2456	2844
	4-Dr 4WD	2293	2666
	incls pwr convenience group, leather-wrapped steering wheel, leather highback reclining bucket seats, keyless remote entry system, passenger assist grips (4WD), 6-way pwr driver's seat, floor & overhead consoles, P205/75R15 SBR all-season tires (2WD), P235/75R15 SBR all-season tires (4WD), conventional two-tone paint, driver & passenger lumbar support adjusters, door trim panels w/leather inserts, aluminum wheels, Bilstein shock absorbers (4WD), fold-down rear seat w/center armrest		
V10	**Cold Climate Pkg** — 2-Dr w/o YC2, YC3 or YC9	154	179
	2-Dr w/YC2, YC3 or YC9	94	109
	4-Dr..	94	109
	incls engine block heater, HD battery, special insulation & -34 degree protection anti-freeze		
ZQ2	**Convenience Pkg** — power - 2-Dr	316	367
	4-Dr..	466	542
	incls pwr windows & pwr door locks		
ZQ3	**Convenience Pkg**	329	383
	incls tilt steering wheel & cruise control		
ZM8	**Convenience Pkg**	169	197
	incls elec rear window defroster & pwr tailgate		
—	**Option Pkgs — 2-Dr Models**		
1SB	**SL Group 2** — 2-Dr	588	684
	incls luggage rack, deep tinted glass w/light tinted rear window, fold-down rear seat, tilt steering wheel, cruise control, AM/FM ETR stereo radio w/cassette, seek/scan & digital clock		
1SB	**SLS Sport Group 2** — 2-Dr	1214	1412
	incls 1SB SL group 2 equipment plus SLS sport decor pkg		
1SB	**SLE Comfort Group 2** — 2-Dr 2WD	1127	1310
	2-Dr 4WD	1099	1278
	incls 1SB SL group 2 equipment plus SLE comfort decor pkg		
1SC	**SLS Sport Group 3** — 2-Dr	2289	2662
	incls SLS sport decor pkg, convenience pkg, pwr convenience pkg, air conditioning, luggage rack, power tailgate, electric rear window defroster, aluminum wheels, deep tinted glass, rear window wiper/washer, tilt steering wheel, cruise control, fold-down rear seat, AM/FM ETR stereo radio w/cassette, seek/scan & digital clock		
1SC	**SLE Comfort Group 3** — 2-Dr	2329	2708
	incls SLE comfort decor pkg, pwr convenience pkg, air conditioning, rear window wiper/washer, luggage rack, deep tinted glass, power tailgate, elec rear window defroster, tilt steering wheel, cruise control, fold-down rear seat, AM/FM ETR stereo radio w/cassette, seek/scan & digital clock		
1SD	**SLT Touring Group 1** — 2-Dr 2WD..	3626	4216
	2-Dr 4WD	3819	4441
	incls SLT touring decor pkg, deep tinted glass, air conditioning, dual pwr mirrors, pwr tailgate, elec rear window defroster, luggage rack, rear window wiper/washer, tilt steering wheel, cruise control, AM/FM ETR radio w/cassette, graphic equalizer, seek/scan & digital clock		
—	**Option Pkgs — 4-Dr Models**		
1SB	**SLE Comfort Group 2** — 4-Dr 2WD	353	410

CODE	DESCRIPTION	DEALER	LIST
	incls SLE comfort decor pkg, fold-down rear seat, tilt steering wheel, cruise control, deep tinted glass w/light tinted rear window, luggage rack, AM/FM ETR stereo radio w/cassette, seek/scan & digital clock		
1SB	**SLE Comfort Group 2** — 4-Dr 4WD	(22)	(25)
	incls deep tinted glass w/light tinted rear window, tilt steering wheel, cruise control, AM/FM ETR stereo radio w/cassette, seek/scan & digital clock, luggage rack		
1SC	**SLS Sport Group 3** — 4-Dr 2WD	1950	2268
	4-Dr 4WD	1604	1865
	incls SLS sport decor pkg, pwr convenience pkg, aluminum wheels, air conditioning, pwr tailgate, elec rear window defroster, deep tinted glass, rear window wiper/washer, luggage rack, tilt steering wheel, cruise control, reclining highback front bucket seats, fold-down rear seat, AM/FM ETR stereo radio w/seek/scan & digital clock		
1SC	**SLE Group 3** — 4-Dr 2WD	1887	2194
	incls SLE comfort decor pkg, pwr convenience pkg, floor console, aluminum wheels, pwr tailgate, elec rear window defroster, luggage rack, deep tinted glass, rear window wiper/washer, air conditioning, AM/FM ETR stereo radio w/cassette seek/scan & digital clock, fold-down rear seat		
1SC	**SLE Group 3** — 4-Dr 4WD	1576	1833
	incls deep tinted glass, pwr convenience pkg, aluminum wheels, floor console, air conditioning, reclining highback front bucket seats, tilt steering wheel, cruise control, rear window wiper/washer, luggage rack, power tailgate, elec rear window defroster, AM/FM ETR stereo radio w/cassette, seek/scan & digital clock		
1SD	**SLT Group 1** — 4-Dr 2WD	3212	3735
	4-Dr 4WD	3059	3557
	incls SLT touring equip pkg, deep tinted glass, air conditioning, dual power mirrors, rear window wiper/washer power tailgate, elec rear window defroster tilt steering wheel, cruise control, AM/FM ETR radio w/cassette, seek/scan, graphic equalizer & digital clock		

GMC SUBURBAN

SUBURBAN 8 CYL

C1500 2WD SERIES
TC10906 Panel doors 131.5" WB 17707   20236

K1500 4WD SERIES
TK10906 Panel Doors 131.5" WB 19676   22487

C2500 2WD SERIES
TC20906 Panel Doors 131.5" WB 18786   21469

K2500 4WD SERIES
TK20906 Panel Doors 131.5" WB 20728   23688

Destination Charge: 640   640

Standard Equipment

1500 SERIES SUBURBAN 4-DOOR - BASE SL: 4-speed automatic transmission, power front disc/rear drum brakes with 4-wheel anti-lock braking, front and rear chromed bumpers, single rectangular halogen headlamps, full-sized spare tire and wheel, mounted inside behind LR wheelhouse, argent painted steel wheels, full gauge instrumentation, tinted Solar-Ray glass windows, electronic AM/FM stereo with seek-scan and digital clock, Scotchgard fabric protector, three-passenger full bench front seat with custom vinyl trim, 4-spoke steering wheel.

SLE (in addition to or instead of SL equipment): Air conditioning, tilt wheel and speed control, power door locks and windows, remote outside electric mirror, deep tinted glass, AM/FM stereo with tape and clock, aluminum wheels, dual composite halogen headlamps, three-passenger front bench seat with textured velour custom cloth, auxiliary lighting all door-actuated.

2500 SERIES SUBURBAN - BASE SL: 4-speed automatic transmission, power front disc/rear drum brakes with 4-wheel anti-lock braking, side guard door beams, front and rear chromed bumpers with black rub strip, single rectangular halogen headlamps, full-sized spare tire and wheel, mounted inside behind LR wheelhouse, argent painted steel wheels, full gauge instrumentation, tinted Solar-Ray glass windows, electronic AM/FM stereo with seek-scan and digital clock, Scotchgard fabric protector, three-passenger full bench front seat with custom vinyl trim and 4-spoke steering wheel.

SLE (in addition to or instead of SL equipment): Air conditioning, tilt wheel and speed control, power door locks and windows, remote outside electric mirror, deep tinted glass, AM/FM stereo with tape and clock, aluminum wheels, dual composite halogen headlamps, three-passenger front bench seat with textured velour custom cloth, auxiliary lighting all door-actuated.

Accessories

CODE	DESCRIPTION	DEALER	LIST
—	**Option Pkgs**		
1SA	**Pkg 1SA — SL**	NC	NC
	SLE	1656	1926
	incls vehicle w/std equip		
1SB	**Pkg 1SB**	3423	3980
	incls SLE decor, C60 air conditioning, pwr windows, pwr locks, pwr mirrors, UM6 radio, folding center seat, tilt wheel & speed control		
1SC	**Pkg 1SC**	4569	5313
	incls SLE decor, C69 air cond, deep tint glass, UM6 radio, pwr windows, pwr locks, pwr mirrors, tilt wheel, speed control, center & rear seats		
—	**Decor Pkgs**		
R9S	**SL**	STD	STD
	incls models w/std equip		
YE9	**SLE** — see option pkgs 1SB & 1SC		
	incls SL equip plus F & R floor mats, carpeting, full wheel covers, deluxe frt appearance pkg, deluxe moldings, deluxe bumpers w/bumper guards, aux lighting, sport steering wheel, spare tire cover, rear cargo net, illuminated visor mirrors, frt split bench seat, center seat, upgraded door trim panels, extra insulation [reqs ZQ2, ZQ3 or R7V]		
—	**Body Codes**		
ZW9	panel doors	STD	STD
E55	tailgate	NC	NC
—	**GVW Pkgs**		
C5U	6800 lb - 1500 2WD (reqs L05 eng)	NC	NC
C5Z	7200 lb - 1500 4WD (reqs L05 eng)	NC	NC
C3F	7700 lb - 1500 2WD (reqs L65 eng)	NC	NC
C51	8050 lb - 1500 4WD (reqs L65 eng)	NC	NC
C6P	8600 lb - 2500	NC	NC
—	**Exterior Paint**		
ZY1	solid	STD	STD
ZY2	conventional two-tone	155	180
ZY4	deluxe two-tone	249	290
—	**Tires**		
	1500 Models w/Gasoline Engine		
—	P235/75R15XL all seasons radial		
QHA	BSW - 2WD	STD	STD
QHB	WSW - 2WD	82	95
—	LT225/75R16D BSW radial		
QHP	all seasons - 4WD	STD	STD
QHR	on-off road - 4WD	47	55
—	LT245/75R16C radial		
QIT	all seasons BSW - 4WD	51	59
QBN	on-off road BSW - 4WD	101	116
QBX	on-off road OWL - 4WD	208	241
	1500 Models w/Diesel Engine		
—	LT245/75R16E radial		
QIZ	all season BSW - 2WD	396	460

GMC

CODE	DESCRIPTION	DEALER	LIST
	4WD	198	230
QIW	on-off road OWL - 4WD	246	285
	2500 Models		
—	LT245/75R16E BSW radial		
QIZ	all season BSW	STD	STD
QIW	on-off road BSW - 4WD	48	55
6Y4	spare tire delete - 2500	(243)	(283)
—	**Engines**		
L05	5.7L EFI V8	STD	STD
L19	7.4L EFI V8 - 2500	520	605
L65	6.5L V8 turbo diesel - 1500	NA	NA
	2500	2430	2825
	incls HD radiator, eng block heater, extra sound insulation, dual batteries, eng oil cooler, hydraulic brakes, glow plugs, two-stage fuel filter, fuel & water sep [reqs B71 on 1500 4WD models; NA w/high altitude emissions]		
—	**Air Conditioning**		
C60	front	727	845
C69	front & rear	1114	1295
—	**Transmissions**		
M30	4-spd auto w/overdrive - 1500 gas models	STD	STD
MT1	4-spd auto w/overdrive - 1500 diesel models	STD	STD
	2500	STD	STD
—	**Rear Axles**		
GU6	3.42	NC	NC
GT4	3.73	NC	NC
GT5	4.10	NC	NC
G80	**Locking Rear Differential**	217	252
U16	**Tachometer**	51	59
VK3	**Front License Plate Bracket**	NC	NC
V76	**Tow Hooks** — 2WD	33	38
—	**Emissions**		
FE9	Federal	NC	NC
NA6	high altitude	NC	NC
YF5	California	NA	NA
NG1	New York	NC	NC
R7V	**Power Locks & Window Delete**— w/SLE decor	NC	NC
C36	**Auxiliary Rear Heater**	176	205
C49	**Electric Defogger**	132	154
ZP6	**Intermittent Washer/Wiper w/Defogger** — reqs E55	240	279
C25	**Intermittent Washer/Wiper** — reqs E55	108	125
V54	**Roof Mounted Luggage Carrier**	108	126
—	**Radio Equip**		
UP4	radio - w/pkg 1SA	(146)	(170)
	incls AM ETR w/digital clock		
UM6	radio	105	122
	incls AM/FM stereo ETR w/seek-scan, cass, dual rear spkrs & digital clock		
UX1	radio	234	272
	incls AM stereo/FM stereo w/seek-scan, search & repeat, cass, graphic equalizer & digital clock		
UL5	radio delete - w/1SA	(247)	(287)
U88	speaker system - 6 speakers	73	85
	reqs SLE decor, convenience group & UX1 radio		

GMC

CODE	DESCRIPTION	DEALER	LIST
ZQ2	**Operating Convenience Group** — w/ZW9..	521	606
	w/E55	466	542
	incls pwr windows & pwr locks [reqs SLE decor]		
ZQ3	**Convenience Group**..	329	383
	incls speed control & tilt wheel		
AG9	**Power Driver's Seat** — 6-way power..	206	240
—	**Seating**		
	Front		
A52	bench	STD	STD
AE7	40/60 reclining split bench (reqs SLE decor)	150	174
A95	high back reclining buckets	464	540
	incls floor & overhead consoles & folding rear seat [reqs SLE decor]		
	Rear		
AT5	center, folding...	503	585
AS3	center & rear - w/SL decor...	942	1095
	w/SLE decor	497	578
YG2	**Leather Seat Pkg** — w/rear seat..	1187	1380
	w/center seat...	873	1015
	incls ultra-soft leather seat trim & leather wrapped steering wheel [reqs high back reclining bucket seats & SLE decor]		
Z82	**Trailering Equip Pkg**	181	210
	incls platform hitch, HD wiring harness, HD flashers [reqs V08 w/L05 eng & M30 trans] [reqs GT5 on 2500 2WD w/L05 eng]		
V08	**Heavy Duty Cooling**..	170	198
	incl'd w/Z82		
KNP	**Heavy Duty Auxiliary Cooling** — trans	NA	NA
V10	**Cold Climate Pkg**	28	33
	incls eng block heater & special insulation (NA w/L65 eng)		
AJ1	**Deep Tint Glass**..	262	305
D48	**Mirrors** — power...	84	98
	reqs SLE decor & operating convenience group		
DF2	**Mirrors** — camper type, stainless steel	46	53
	reqs pkg 1SA		
V22	**Front End Appearance Pkg**..	164	191
	incls color-keyed grille, composite halogen headlamps & dual horns		
U01	**Roof Marker Lamps** — NA w/YF5..	45	52
NZZ	**Off Road Skid Plates** — 4WD models	194	225
	incls differential transfer case, fuel tank & eng shields		
P06	**Trim Rings & Hub Caps (4)** — bright metal - w/SL decor............................	52	60
	w/SLE decor	15	18
	NA w/N90 or PF4		
—	**Wheels**		
PF4	cast aluminum, 16" x 7" incls spare		
	1500 4WD w/SL decor..	267	310
	1500 4WD w/SLE decor	230	268
	reqs L05 eng		
N90	cast aluminum, 15" x 7", incls spare		
	1500 2WD w/SL decor..	267	310
	1500 2WD w/SLE decor	230	268
B71	**Wheel Flares** — 1500 4WD	155	180
	NA w/QHP or QHR tires		

GMC

GMC YUKON

YUKON 4WD 8 CYL

		DEALER	LIST
TK10516 Yukon 111.5" WB		18545	21195
Destination Charge:		600	600

Standard Equipment

YUKON FULL-SIZED 2-DOOR - BASE SL: 5-speed manual transmission, power front disc/rear drum brakes, 4-wheel anti-lock brake system, front and rear chromed bumpers with black rub strips and rear black step pad, molded plastic light argent grille, 16" x 6.5" silver painted steel wheels, padded armrests, cupholders, side door guard beams, full gauges, deluxe heater with windshield and side window defoggers, elec-tuned AM/FM stereo with seek-scan and digital clock, vinyl bucket front seats w/sliding driver and passenger for easy entry, color-keyed sunshades, 4-spoke steering wheel.

SLE (in addition to or instead of SL equipment): Air conditioning, Comfortilt steering and speed control, power door locks and windows, deep-tinted glass, AM/FM stereo with tape player and clock, aluminum wheels, deluxe front appearance package with dark argent chrome grille and bright trim, auxiliary lighting with front and rear map lights, Scotchgard fabric protector, 40/60 custom cloth split front bench seats, simulated leather steering wheel, floor and roof console with bucket seats, rear electric lift glass release, color-keyed, carpeted rear quarter trim panels, 40/60 custom cloth split front bench seats and three-passenger folding rear bench seat.

Accessories

		DEALER	LIST
—	**Option Pkgs**		
1SA	**Pkg 1SA** — w/SL decor	NC	NC
	incls vehicles w/std equip		
1SB	**Pkg 1SB** — w/SLE decor	1700	1977
	incls air conditioning, UM6 radio, speed control & tilt wheel		
1SC	**Pkg 1SC** — w/SLE decor	2113	2457
	incls pkg 1SB equip plus deep tint glass, pwr windows, pwr locks, dual elec mirrors & aluminum wheels		
1SD	**Pkg 1SD** — w/SLE decor	2344	2726
	incls pkg 1SC equip plus BYP sport pkg		
—	**Decor**		
R9S	**SL Decor**	NC	NC

CODE	DESCRIPTION	DEALER	LIST
	incls pwr liftgate release, 4-spoke custom steering wheel, RH & LH blk below eye-line mirrors		
YE9	**SLE Decor**....................	797	927
	incls deluxe frt appearance pkg, carpeting, aux lighting, cargo net, color-keyed F & R floor mats & sport steering wheel [models w/o BYP sport pkg also incl deluxe bumpers, deluxe moldings & wheel trim rings]		
—	**Body**		
E55	tailgate - incls elec tailgate release.................	NC	NC
	incl'd in 1SA, 1SB, 1SC, 1SD		
—	**GVW Pkg**		
C5P	6250 lb..................	NC	NC
C71	6450 lb..................	NC	NC
Z82	**HD Trailering Equip**.............	180	210
	incls platform hitch, wiring harness & HD flasher [reqs V08 HD cooling w/L05 eng & M30 trans; NA w/MG5 trans]		
Z71	**Off-Road Equip Pkg**..............	344	400
	incls skid plates & Bilstein gas shocks [reqs QIX or QIY tires]		
F60	**HD Torsion Bars**...............	54	63
	incls HD F & R shocks [reqs C5P]		
NZZ	**Skid Plates**..................	194	225
	incls differential, transfer case, fuel tank & eng shields		
—	**Emissions**		
FE9	Federal	NC	NC
NA6	high altitude...............	NC	NC
YF5	California	NA	NA
NG1	New York	NC	NC
—	**Engines**		
L05	5.7L (350 CID) V8 gas	NC	NC
L56	6.5L (395 CID) V8 turbo diesel	2429	2825
	incls electronic fuel injection, dual batteries, hydraulic brakes, HD radiator, eng oil cooler, extra sound insulation, eng block heater, glow plugs, internal two-stage fuel filter, fuel & water separator w/instrument panel warning light & fuel filter change signal		
—	**Transmissions**		
MG5	5-spd manual w/overdrive	NC	NC
M30	4-spd automatic w/overdrive	765	890
MT1	4-spd automatic w/overdrive	765	890
—	**Rear Axles**		
GU6	3.42...................	NC	NC
GT4	3.73...................	NC	NC
G80	**Locking Rear Differential**	217	252
—	**Cooling**		
KC4	engine oil cooler (reqs L05 eng & MG5 trans)......	116	135
V08	HD cooling (reqs L05 eng & M30 trans).........	170	198
KNP	HD auxiliary transmission cooling system........	NA	NA
	reqs M30 or MT1		
V10	**Cold Climate Pkg**	28	33
	incls eng block heater & special insulation		
P06	**Trim Rings & Hub Caps (4)**	52	60
	NA w/BYP sport pkg or PF4		
PF4	**Wheels** — cast aluminum, 16" x 7" (4) - w/YE9 decor...	215	250
	w/R9S decor	267	310

CODE	DESCRIPTION	DEALER	LIST
—	**Tires** — incls spare		
QIT	LT245/75R16/C all season BW SBR	NC	NC
QBN	LT245/75R16/C on-off road BW SBR	49	57
QBX	LT245/75R16/C on-off road white letter SBR	156	182
QIX	LT265/75R16/C on-off road BW SBR	164	191
QIY	LT265/75R16/C on-off road white letter SBR	272	316
R6G	**Air Conditioning Delete** — reqs 1SA	NC	NC
C60	**Air Conditioning** — incl'd in 1SB, 1SC, 1SD	727	845
R7V	**Convenience Pkg 1 Delete**	NC	NC
	pwr locks & windows deleted [reqs YE9 decor & 1SB]		
ZQ2	**Convenience Pkg 1**	316	367
	incls pwr locks & windows [reqs YE9 decor]		
R7W	**Convenience Pkg 2 Delete**	NC	NC
	tilt wheel & speed control deleted [reqs 1SA]		
ZQ3	**Convenience Pkg 2**	329	383
	incls tilt wheel & speed control [incl'd in 1SB, 1SC, 1SD]		
—	**Radio Equip**		
UM7	radio	NC	NC
	incls AM/FM stereo w/seek-scan & clock & 4 spkrs [reqs 1SA]		
UP4	radio	(146)	(170)
	incls AM radio [reqs 1SA]		
UM6	radio	104	122
	incls AM/FM stereo w/seek-scan, cass, clock & 4 spkrs		
UX1	radio	234	272
	incls AM stereo/FM stereo w/seek-scan, cass, equalizer, digital clock & 4 spkrs		
UL5	radio delete - reqs 1SA	(247)	(287)
—	**Seats**		
A50	low back reclining buckets	NC	NC
	incls 3-pass folding rear bench & easy entry feature [reqs R9S]		
AE7	front 40/60 reclining split bench	NC	NC
	incls 3-pass folding rear bench seat, easy entry feature [reqs YE9]		
A95	front high back reclining buckets	293	341
	incls inboard armrests, roof & floor console, 3-pass folding rear bench seat, easy entry feature [reqs YE9]		
—	**Seats**		
AG9	6-way power seat adjuster (driver's side)	206	240
	reqs AE7 or A95 seats		
U16	**Tachometer**	51	59
V22	**Front End Appearance Pkg**	164	191
	incls color-keyed grille, composite halogen headlamps & dual horns		
VK3	**Front License Plate Bracket**	NC	NC
V54	**Roof Mounted Luggage Carrier** — black	108	126
D48	**Mirrors**	84	98
	incls dual elec control exterior mirrors, blk below eye-line, 8.5" x 5" [reqs ZQ2 & YE9 decor]		
D42	**Mirrors**	46	53
	incls camper type exterior mirrors, stainless steel, 7.5" x 10.5" [reqs 1SA or 1SB]		
B71	**Wheel Flares** — F & R	155	180
	deletes wheel opening moldings		
ZP6	**Rear Window Equip Pkg**	240	279
	incls rear window washer/intermittent wiper & defogger		

CODE	DESCRIPTION	DEALER	LIST
C25	**Rear Window Washer/Intermittent Wiper**	108	125
AJ1	**Deep Tinted Solar Ray Glass**	185	215
—	**Paint**		
ZY1	solid	NC	NC
ZY2	conventional two-tone (NA w/BYP sport pkg)...................................	155	180
ZY4	deluxe two-tone (NA w/BYP sport pkg)...	249	290

ISUZU *(vertical side tab)*

ISUZU AMIGO

B15	2WD S (5-spd)	13067	14849
B25	2WD XS (5-spd)	13639	15499
C15	4WD S (5-spd)	14783	16799
C25	4WD XS (5-spd)	15135	17199
	Destination Charge:	350	350

Standard Equipment

AMIGO S: Cargo area mat, center console, cigarette lighter, floor mats, dome lamp, day/night rearview mirror, remote hood opener, reclining front bucket seats with see-thru headrests, rear bench seat with headrests, gauges (water temp, oil pressure, battery, brake system, low fuel, trip odometer), 3-spoke steering wheel, dual sunvisors, 2-speed wiper/washer with mist, power brakes with ventilated discs, rear wheel ABS, front manual locking hubs (4WD), power black OS mirrors, recirculating ball steering with power assist, fuel tank skid plate, transfer case skid plates (4WD), radiator skid plate (4WD), oil pan skid plate (4WD), maintenance-free battery, single note horn, 3/4 molded resin door/side trim, warning/indicator lamps, assist grips.

XS (in addition to or instead of S equipment): Full molded vinyl covered door/side trim, sporty shift knob, oil pressure gauge, voltmeter, tachometer, tilt steering wheel, 2-speed intermittent wiper/washer.

Accessories

AA	**Air Conditioning**	706	830
H1	**Sunroof**..	256	300

CODE	DESCRIPTION	DEALER	LIST
B1	**California Emissions**	135	150
C1	**New York Emissions**	135	150
FBA	**AM/FM Stereo Radio w/Cassette**	284	405
	incls 2 speakers		
FCA	**AM/FM Stereo Radio w/Cassette**	376	520
	incls 4 speakers		

ISUZU RODEO

Code	Description	Dealer	List
E45	2WD S (5-spd)	13472	14969
G45	2WD S V6 (5-spd)	15311	17499
G44	2WD S V6 (auto)	16099	18399
G64	2WD LS V6 (auto)	19887	22729
H45	4WD S V6 (5-spd)	16746	19249
H44	4WD S V6 (auto)	17703	20349
H65	4WD LS V6 (5-spd)	20705	23799
H64	4WD LS V6 (auto)	21662	24899
	Destination Charge:	375	375

Standard Equipment

RODEO S: Child-safe rear door locks, cigarette lighter, console (V6), cut-pile carpeting, carpeted floor mats (V6), lockable glove box, dome lamps, cargo lamps, day/night rearview mirror, remote hood opener, front bench seat with headrest and center armrest (4 cyl), front bucket seats with recliner and headrest (V6), tachometer (V6), trip odometer, gauges [fuel, water, oil (V6), volt (V6)], warning/indicator lamps, 3-spoke steering wheel, dual sunvisors, passenger assist grips, automatic transmission interlock, power assisted front ventilated disc brakes, rear drum brakes (4 cyl), rear ventilated disc brakes (V6), rear wheel anti-lock, 2-speed transfer case (4WD), automatic locking front hubs (4WD), manual black OS mirrors, rear defogger, rear intermittent wiper/washer (V6), gas pressurized shock absorbers, radiator

CODE	DESCRIPTION	DEALER	LIST

skid plate (V6), exhaust cross-over pipe and transmission oil pan skid plates (V6), fuel tank skid plate, transfer case skid plate (4WD), inside mounted spare tire (4 cyl), outside spare tire carrier (V6), power recirculating ball steering, 2-speed windshield wiper with mist control, maintenance-free battery, single note horn.

LS (in addition to or instead of S equipment): Illuminated cigarette lighter, digital clock (in radio), cargo area convenience net, carpeted floor mats, map light, rear hatch opener, bucket seats with recliner and headrest, rear bench seat with split back and headrest, sport type shift knob, leather-wrapped steering wheel, tilt steering column, passenger side vanity mirror, illuminated instrument panel ashtray, air conditioning, AM/FM ETR stereo radio w/cass & four speakers, rear ventilated disc brakes, cruise control, bright power OS mirrors with defogger, intermittent rear wiper/washer, radiator skid plate, exhaust cross-over pipe and transmission oil pan skid plate, outside spare tire carrier, 2-speed windshield wiper/washer w/intermittent feature, power windows, power door locks, dual note horn, center console.

Accessories

Code	Description	Dealer	List
B4	**California Emissions**	135	150
C4	**New York Emissions**	135	150
A3/AN	**Air Conditioning — S**	722	850
H2	**Sunroof — LS**	255	300
L1	**Limited Slip Differential — 4WD LS**	210	260
E1	**Rear Window Wiper/Washer — 2WD S 4-Cyl**	158	185
HR	**Aero Luggage Rack — S**	137	195
R1	**Outside Spare Tire Carrier — 2WD S 4-Cyl**	234	275
M2	**Wheel Pkg — 4WD S**	847	990
	incls limited slip differential and 16" aluminum wheels		
GRR	**Brush/Grille Guard**	216	305
JRG	**Floor Mats — 2WD S 4-Cyl**	39	55
FDY	**CD Player — LS**	385	550
FBY	**AM/FM Stereo Radio w/Cassette — S**	410	585
P3	**Preferred Equipment Pkg — S V6**	1690	1990
	incls air conditioning, power windows, roof luggage rack, cruise control, power door locks, AM/FM stereo radio w/cassette and 4 speakers, cargo net, intermittent rear window wiper/washer		

ISUZU TROOPER

L45	4WD S 4-Dr (5-spd)	18381	21250
L44	4WD S 4-Dr (auto)	19376	22400
M65	4WD LS 4-Dr (5-spd)	22822	26850
M64	4WD LS 4-Dr (auto)	23800	28000
M05	4WD RS 2-Dr (5-spd)	21120	24000
M04	4WD RS 2-Dr (auto)	22132	25150
	Destination Charge:	400	400

Standard Equipment

TROOPER S: Roof-mounted air deflector, mast type antenna, rear step bumper with pad, blue tinted glass, dual passenger side convex mirrors, clearcoat paint, chip-resistant coating, full-size spare tire, spare tire vinyl cover, styled steel wheels, tie-down hooks, center console, rear seat heater ducts, cut-pile carpeting, carpeted floor mats, storage compartment under rear seat, lockable glove box with lamp, full instrumentation (tachometer, water temp, oil pressure and volt gauges, trip odometer, low fuel warning lamp, 4WD engagement lamp), room lamp, cargo lamp, cigarette lighter and ashtray, day/night rearview mirror, driver and passenger visor vanity mirrors with lid, remote hood opener, remote fuel door opener, passenger assist grips headlamps-on reminder, reclining bucket seats with adjustable headrests and passenger seatback storage pocket, rear folding bench seat, height adjustable headrests, soft grip steering wheel, tilt steering column, full door trim with cloth insert, front door storage pockets, molded felt headliner, four speakers, maintenance-free battery, power assisted 4-wheel ventilated disc brakes with rear wheel anti-lock, rear defogger, part-time 4WD, automatic locking front hubs, dual note horn, skid plates (radiator, exhaust cross-over pipe and transmission, oil pan, fuel tank, transfer case, catalytic converter), recirculating ball power steering.

LS (in addition to or instead of S equip): Power antenna, fog lamps, bronze tinted glass, privacy tint glass (rear, side, back & quarter windows), elec remote mirrors w/defogger, bright window surround moldings, rocker moldings with integral mud flaps, aluminum wheels, retractable cargo cover, convenience net, floor rails, rear seat foot rest, dual map lights, inboard folding armrests, 60/40 split folding/reclining rear seat with center armrest, leather-wrapped steering wheel, carpeted lower doors, air conditioning, 75 amp alternator, anti-theft device, premium high power AM/FM stereo cassette system with six speakers, 4-wheel ABS, cruise control, rear defogger with auto cancel timer, headlamp wiper/washer, limited slip differential, power windows and power door locks.

ISUZU / JEEP

CODE	DESCRIPTION	DEALER	LIST

RS (in addition to or instead of LS equipment): Flip-out quarter windows, bright window surround molding deleted, two-tone paint, storage compartment under rear seat deleted, rear seat foot rest deleted, passenger side walk-in device, rear folding/reclining seat with center armrest, 4-wheel ABS deleted, gas pressurized shock absorbers.

Accessories

CODE	DESCRIPTION	DEALER	LIST
B5	**California Emissions**	135	150
C5	**New York Emissions**	135	150
A3	**Air Conditioning** — S	720	900
Z1	**Two-Tone Paint** — LS...	225	280
P5	**Appearance Pkg** — S	600	750
	incls color-keyed bumpers and 16" aluminum wheels w/locks and bright grille (req's Preferred Equipment Pkg)		
H3	**Power Sunroof** — LS	880	1100
L2	**Limited Slip Differential** — S	210	260
	req's Preferred Equipment Pkg		
L3	**Anti-Lock Brakes** — S & RS	880	1100
RC	**Retractable Cargo Cover** — S	84	120
J2	**Seats** — split fold-down rear - S	200	250
J3	**Seats** — heated leather power - LS	1915	2250
P4	**Preferred Equipment Pkg** — S	1600	1880
	incls AM/FM ETR stereo radio w/cassette and 6 speakers, air conditioning, power windows, cruise control, split fold-down rear bench seat, power door locks, cargo cover, power mirrors, convenience net		

JEEP CHEROKEE

CHEROKEE SE 4 CYL

		DEALER	LIST
XJTL72	2WD 2-Dr Wagon...	12355	13077
XJTL74	2WD 4-Dr Wagon...	13289	14087
XJJL72	4WD 2-Dr Wagon...	13721	14562
XJJL74	4WD 4-Dr Wagon...	14661	15572

JEEP

CODE	DESCRIPTION	DEALER	LIST

CHEROKEE SPORT 6 CYL

Code	Description	Dealer	List
XJTL72	2WD 2-Dr Wagon	13861	15234
XJTL74	2WD 4-Dr Wagon	14765	16244
XJJL72	4WD 2-Dr Wagon	15183	16719
XJJL74	4WD 4-Dr Wagon	16092	17729

CHEROKEE COUNTRY 6 CYL

Code	Description	Dealer	List
XJTL72	2WD 2-Dr Wagon	15301	16871
XJTL74	2WD 4-Dr Wagon	16205	17881
XJJL72	4WD 2-Dr Wagon	16623	18356
XJJL74	4WD 4-Dr Wagon	17532	19366
	Destination Charge:	495	495

Standard Equipment

CHEROKEE COMPACT 4-DOOR - BASE SE: 5-speed manual transmission, center high-mounted stop light, side impact protection door beams, power steering, power front disc/rear drum brakes with rear wheel anti-lock braking, black bumpers, black fender flares and air dam, black bodyside moldings, child protection door locks, full stainless steel exhaust system, tinted glass all windows, vinyl color-keyed door trim, dual outside black mirrors, ETR AM/FM stereo with clock and two speakers, front reclining bucket seats with headrest, folding rear bench seat, stabilizer bars front and rear.

SPORT (in addition to or instead of SE equipment): Lower two-tone paint, bodyside moldings with red inserts, vinyl color-keyed spare tire cover, dual man outside remote control mirrors, reclining bucket seats, "Jamaica" cloth seat trim, tie-down hooks in cargo area, full-faced stl wheels w/bright hub cover.

COUNTRY (in addition to or instead of SPORT equip): Air cond, champagne or argent bumpers, lower bodyside cladding, grille/headlight bezels, accent stripes, flr console w/cupholder, blk luggage roof rack folding remote control outside mirrors, ETR AM/FM stereo cass w/our speakers, high wingback reclining bucket seats, gas pressure shock absorbers, machined face lattice alum whls w/champagne inserts.

Accessories

Code	Description	Dealer	List
B	**Pkg B — SE**	418	492
	incls floor console w/armrest, cloth reclining bucket seats, visibility group		
E	**Pkg E — Sport**	994	1169
	incls sport decor group, air conditioning, floor console w/armrest, frt floor mats, black roof rack, tilt steering column, leather-wrapped steering wheel, rear window wiper/washer		
H	**Pkg H — Country**	700	824
	incls country decor group, air conditioning, AM/FM stereo radio w/cass & 4 spkrs, speed control, tilt steering column		
HAA	**Air Conditioning** — incls ADH	711	836
ADH	**Heavy Duty Alternator/Battery Group**	115	135
	w/air conditioning	NC	NC
	w/rear window defroster	54	63
DSA	**Rear Axle** — traction-lok differential (req's TBB)	242	285
BGK	**Brakes** — anti-lock (NA w/2.5L eng on SE)	509	599
AED	**Bright Group** — Country (req's AWH)	172	202
CSC	**Cargo Area Cover**	61	72
CUF	**Floor Console w/Armrest** — SE, Sport	125	147
CUN	**Overhead Console** — req's AWH - Sport, Country	173	203
GFA	**Rear Window Defroster**	137	161
	req's ADH or HAA; reqd in NY State		
NHK	**Engine Block Heater** — avail in Alaska only	26	31

CODE	DESCRIPTION	DEALER	LIST
CLC	**Floor Mats** — front - SE, Sport	17	20
LNJ	**Fog Lamps** — req's ADH or HAA - Sport, Country	94	110
GAF	**Sunscreen Deep Tinted Glass** — 2-Dr w/qtr vent - Sport, Country	259	305
GAL	side window only - 4-Dr Sport & Country	122	144
ADA	**Light Group** — SE, Sport	166	195
AJD	**Leather Seats** — 4-Dr Country	706	831
GTZ	**Mirrors** — SE, Sport	19	22
	incls dual manual remote (break away)		
GTK	**Mirrors** — Country	85	100
	incls dual elec remote (req's AWH; NA w/AED)		
AWH	**Power Windows & Door Locks** — 2-Dr Sport & Country	371	437
	4-Dr Sport & Country	495	582
RAF	**Radio** — SE, Sport	247	291
	Country	171	201
	incls AM/FM stereo radio, cass w/4 spkrs		
RCG	**Radio Speaker** — 6 premium (req AWH) - Country	109	128
MWG	**Roof Rack** — SE, Sport	118	139
JPS	**Seat** — power driver's - Country	252	296
ADL	**Skid Plate Group** — 4WD models	122	144
NHM	**Speed Control** — req AWJ on SE	196	230
SUA	**Tilt Steering Column** — req AWJ on SE	112	132
SCG	**Leather-Wrapped Steering Wheel** — SE, Sport	41	48
AWE	**Off-Road Suspension** — SE 4WD (req ADH, GTZ)	647	761
	Sport 4WD (req ADH, GTZ)	381	448
	Country (req ADH)	306	360
	incls F & R high pressure gas shocks, P225/75R15 OWL tires, conventional spare tire, F & R tow hooks, skid plate group, max eng cooling, auxiliary fan (w/4.0L 6 cyl eng), auxiliary auto trans oil cooler (w/4.0L 6 cyl eng & auto trans)		
TBB	**Tire** — conventional spare - SE w/P215/75R15 blk tires	60	71
	SE w/P225/75R15 OWL tires	99	116
	Sport	99	116
	Country	119	140
AHT	**Trailer Tow Group** — SE w/o AWE	304	358
	SE w/AWE	206	242
	Sport	304	358
	Sport 4WD w/AWE	206	242
	Country	304	358
	Country 4WD w/AWE	206	242
	incls equalizing hitch receptacle, 7-wire harness, max eng cooling, auxiliary fan, auxiliary auto trans oil cooler [req's 4.0L 6 cyl eng & auto trans & HD alternator/HD battery & conventional spare tire]		
DHP	**"Selec-Trac" Transfer Case** — 4WD SE & Country	335	394
	req's auto trans		
AWJ	**Visibility Group** — SE	177	208
	incls intermittent windshield wipers & rear wiper/washer		
WJH	**Wheels** — SE	370	435
	Sport	282	332
	Country	74	87
	incls 10-hole aluminum 15" x 7" (req TBB)		
WKB	**Wheel** — Sport	22	26
	Country	74	87
	incls matching 5th aluminum wheel (req TBB)		

CODE	DESCRIPTION	DEALER	LIST
GEC	**Windows** — front door vent	77	91
JHB	**Rear Window Wiper/Washer** — Sport	125	147
NAE	**California Emissions**	105	124
NBY	**New York Emissions**	105	124
NAF	**High Altitude Emissions**	NC	NC
MDA	**Front License Plate Bracket**	NC	NC
EPE	**Engine** — 2.5L MPI 4 cyl - SE	STD	STD
ERH	**Engine** — 4.0L MPI 6 cyl - SE	520	612
	Sport	STD	STD
	Country	STD	STD
DDQ	**Transmission** — 5-spd manual	STD	STD
DGB	**Transmission** — 4-spd auto w/overdrive	762	897
—	**Vinyl Bucket Seats** — SE	STD	STD
—	**Cloth Bucket Seats** — SE w/o pkg B	116	137
	SE w/pkg B	NC	NC
	Sport	NC	NC
	Country	NC	NC
—	**Leather Bucket Seats** — 4-Dr Country	706	831
	req's AJD; incls JPS		

JEEP GRAND CHEROKEE

GRAND CHEROKEE 6 CYL

ZJTL74	SE 2WD 4-Dr Wagon	19242	21156
ZJJL74	SE 4WD 4-Dr Wagon	20109	22096
ZJJL74	Limited 4WD 4-Dr Wagon	26729	29618
Destination Charge:		495	495

Standard Equipment

GRAND CHEROKEE 4-DOOR - BASE SE: 5-speed manual transmission (automatic transmission standard on 2WD models), side door impact guard beams, power steering, power brakes, 15" x 7" full-faced cast aluminum wheels, manual control air conditioning, accent stripes and color-keyed bodyside molding, black exterior mirrors, electric rear window defroster, stainless steel exhaust, tinted glass windshield and front doors, aero halogen headlamps, floor console with cupholders and storage bin, leather-wrapped steering wheel, roof luggage rack, ETR AM/FM stereo with cassette, clock and four speakers; speed control and tilt steering wheel.

LAREDO (in addition to or instead of BASE SE equipment): Gold bodyside accents, argent lower bodyside cladding, rocker panel covers and fascias, power door locks, "Bishop" cloth interior door trim, color-keyed carpeting and door trim, dual outside electric mirrors, wingback reclining bucket seats, sport aluminum wheels.

LIMITED (in addition to or instead of LAREDO equipment): Automatic temperature control air conditioning, body colored exterior mirrors and trim, illuminated entry system, remote keyless entry system, dual outside electric heated mirrors, ETR AM/FM stereo with cassette, 5-band equalizer and clock; Highland leather trim seats, vehicle information center, luxury aluminum lattice spoke wheels with gold painted pockets.

Accessories

CODE	DESCRIPTION	DEALER	LIST
E	**Laredo Pkg E** — SE	668	786
	incls Laredo decor group, dual elec mirrors, pwr group, protection group, 15" x 7" sport aluminum wheels		
F	**Laredo Pkg F** — SE 2WD	2355	2770
	SE 4WD	2732	3214
	incls Laredo decor group, dual elec mirrors, pwr group, protection group, 15" x 7" sport aluminum wheels, overhead console, sunscreen deep tinted glass, luxury group, AM/FM stereo radio w/cass, 6 spkrs & graphic equalizer, security group, "Quadra-Trac" transfer case (SE 4WD only)		
DGB	**Automatic Transmission** — 4-spd - 2WD models	STD	STD
	4WD SE & Laredo	762	897
	Limited	STD	STD
DDQ	**Manual Transmission** — 5-spd - 4WD SE & Laredo	STD	STD
ERH	**Engine** — 4.0L MPI 6 cyl	STD	STD
ELF	**Engine**— 5.2L MPI V8 - 4WD SE & Laredo	1000	1176
	Limited	622	732
DSA	**Rear Axle** — traction-lok differential - Limited	242	285
	SE & Laredo (NA w/5-spd trans)	242	285
CUN	**Overhead Console** — models w/Laredo pkg E	197	232
NHK	**Engine Block Heater**	26	31
AWL	**Fog Lamps** — 2WD SE & Laredo	94	110
AWL	**Fog Lamps/Skid Plate Group** — 4WD SE & Laredo w/o AWE	216	254
	4WD SE & Laredo w/AWE	94	110
	Limited w/6 cyl eng	122	144
GEG	**Sunscreen Deep Tinted Glass** — SE & Laredo	192	226
	incl'd in Laredo pkg F		
AFF	**Luxury Group** — 4WD models w/Laredo pkg E & 5-spd trans	504	593
	models w/Laredo pkg E & auto trans	585	688
	incls day/night rearview mirror, auto headlamp system, chime warning system, 6-way pwr frt seat, vehicle information center (NA w/manual trans)		
GTK	**Mirrors** — dual electric - SE	81	95
GTM	**Mirrors** — heated, dual electric - SE	119	140

CODE	DESCRIPTION	DEALER	LIST
	Laredo	38	45
AWH	**Power Group** — SE	524	616
	incls pwr windows, pwr door locks, keyless entry system w/2 transmitters, chime warning system		
ADB	**Protection Group** — SE	124	146
	incls floor mats (4), retractable rear cargo cover, convenience area net		
RAY	**Radio** — SE models, w/Laredo pkg E	524	617
	incls AM/FM cass ET stereo radio w/graphic equalizer, 6 premium sound Infinity spkrs, 120 watt pwr amplifier, pwr antenna & clock		
RBC	**Radio** — SE, models w/Laredo pkg E	669	787
	models w/Laredo pkg F	145	170
	Limited	145	170
	incls AM/FM ET stereo radio w/graphic equalizer, compact disc player, 6 premium sound Infinity spkrs, 120 watt pwr amplifier, pwr antenna, clock		
AJB	**Security Group** — SE, models w/Laredo pkg E	192	226
	incls vehicle theft security system & illuminated entry sys [req's pwr grp]		
AWE	**Up Country Suspension Group** — 4WD SE	612	720
	4WD Laredo	428	504
	Limited	297	349
	incls skid plate group, tow hooks (deleted w/trailer tow), P245/70R15 OWL tires, high pressure gas shocks (F & R), unique springs (F & R), conventional spare tire, matching 5th whl [incls gold luxury aluminum wheels on Ltd]		
TRT	**Tires** — P225/75R15 OWL all weather (4) - SE	209	246
TRN	**Tires** — P225/75R15 OWL all terrain (4) - SE	266	313
	Laredo	57	67
	Limited	NC	NC
TBB	**Tire** — conventional spare & steel wheel - SE	111	130
	Laredo	136	160
TBB	**Tire** — conventional spare - Limited	136	160
	incls matching 5th wheel		
NAE	**California Emissions**	105	124
NBY	**New York Emissions**	105	124
NAF	**High Altitude Emissions**	NC	NC
AHC	**Trailer Tow Prep Group** — w/6 cyl eng & auto trans		
	(SE & Laredo)	85	100
	Limited	85	100
	incl'd w/V8 eng		
AHT	**Trailer Tow Group III** — models w/6 cyl eng & auto trans	304	358
AHX	**Trailer Tow Group IV**		
4WD	SE & Laredo models w/V8 eng & auto trans	206	242
	Limited w/V8 eng & auto trans	206	242
DHP	**"Select Trac" Transfer Case**		
	4WD SE	335	394
	4WD models w/Laredo pkg E	335	394
	4WD models w/Laredo pkg F	NC	NC
	Limited	NC	NC
	req's 6 cyl eng & auto trans		
DHR	**"Quadra-Trac" Transfer Case**		
	4WD SE	377	444
	4WD models w/Laredo pkg E	377	444
	req's 6 cyl eng & auto trans		
—	**Seats** — SE & Laredo	NC	NC

CODE	DESCRIPTION	DEALER	LIST
	incls cloth & vinyl highback bucket seats		
—	**Seats** — Laredo..	490	576
	incls leather & vinyl low-back bucket seats [req's luxury group]		
—	**Seats** — Limited...	NC	NC
	incls leather & vinyl low-back bucket seats		
—	**Seats** — Limited...	255	300
	incls luxury leather & vinyl low-back bucket seats		

JEEP WRANGLER

WRANGLER 4WD 4 CYL

YJJL77	S Soft Top..	10988	11390

WRANGLER 4WD 6 CYL

YJJL77	SE Soft Top..	13115	14454
YJJL77	Sahara Soft Top	13115	14454
YJJL77	Renegade Soft Top	13115	14454
	Destination Charge:..	495	495

Standard Equipment

WRANGLER 2-DOOR - BASE S: 5-speed manual, center high-mounted stop light, black front bumpers, fender flares, locking half-doors, stainless steel exhaust system, tinted windshield and quarter windows with hard top, halogen headlamps, left outside swing-away mirror, highback non-reclining vinyl bucket seats, front and rear sport bar, hinged locking tailgate, argent styled steel wheels.

SE (in addition to or instead of BASE S equipment): Black rear bumperettes, swing-away dual outside mirrors, ETR AM/FM stereo with clock and two speakers, non-reclining vinyl bucket seats, rear fold-and-tumble seat, padded side bars, silver styled steel wheels with black hubs.

SAHARA (in addition to or instead of SE equipment): Front bumper extensions with tow bars, front bumper extensions with tow hooks, spare tire cover with Sahara graphics, round foglights, locking glove box, front and rear interior carpeting, reclining bucket seats with tailcloth fabric, gas charged shocks, 3-spoke leather-wrapped steering wheel, full faced color-keyed steel wheels with bright hubs.

RENEGADE (in addition to or instead of SAHARA equipment): Sculptured lower body panels, color-keyed body color front and rear fascias and bumpers, rectangular halogen headlamps, highline front and rear interior trim, reclining trail cloth fabric seats, sound insulation package, conventional locking spare tire and wheel, five-spoke aluminum wheels.

Accessories

Code	Description	Dealer	List
B	**Wrangler S Pkg B** — S	876	1030
	incls rear bumperettes, floor carpet, right o/s mirror, pwr steering, frt reclining vinyl bucket seats, rear seat		
D	**Wrangler SE Pkg D** — SE	827	973
	incls floor carpet, pwr steering, convenience group, extra capacity fuel tank (20 gal), tilt steering column, conventional spare tire		
F	**Wrangler Sport Pkg** — SE	1394	1640
	incls floor carpet, pwr steering, convenience group, extra capacity fuel tank (20 gal), tilt steering column, conventional spare tire, sound bar, sport tape stripe, bodyside body color steps, P215/75R15 OWL all terrain tires, 5-spoke full face steel wheels		
H	**Wrangler Sahara Pkg H** — Sahara	2060	2423
	incls Sahara decor group, AM/FM stereo cass radio, sound bar, tilt steering column, conventional spare tire		
K	**Wrangler Renegade Pkg K** — Renegade	3614	4252
	incls Renegade decor group, AM/FM stereo cass radio, sound bar, tilt steering wheel		
HAA	**Air Conditioning** — SE (incls ADH)	746	878
	Sahara, Renegade	746	878
ADH	**Heavy Duty Alternator/Battery Group** — S, SE	115	135
DSA	**Rear Axle** — trac-lok differential - SE	236	278
	Sahara, Renegade	236	278
	reqs conventional spare tire & P215 or P225 tires		
BGK	**Brakes** — anti-lock - SE, Sahara, Renegade	509	599
MCF	**Rear Bumperettes** — black - S	31	36
AEC	**"Bright" Exterior Group** — SE	167	197
	incls bright frt bumpers, bright rear bumperettes, bright grille overlay, bright headlamp bezels		
CKC	**Floor Carpet** — S, SE	116	137
	reqs CFM rear seat		
ADC	**Convenience Group** — w/o tilt steering column (S, SE)	198	233
	w/tilt steering column (S, SE),	145	170
	incls courtesy lights w/door switches, eng compartment light, intermittent wipers, glove box lock, center console w/cupholder		
GFA	**Rear Window Defroster** — w/hardtop	139	164
NHK	**Engine Block Heater** — avail in Alaska only	26	31
NFA	**Extra Capacity Fuel Tank** — 20 gals - S, SE	53	62
GTV	**Mirror** — right outside, black - S	23	27
	std w/hardtop		
AWE	**Off-Road Group** — SE	110	129
	incls F & R HD gas filled shocks, draw bar, tow hooks (2)		
RAB	**Radio** — S	230	270
	incls AM/FM stereo w/2 spkrs		
RAF	**Radio** — S w/o sound group	454	534
	S w/sound group	224	264
	SE	224	264

CODE	DESCRIPTION	DEALER	LIST
	incls AM/FM stereo cass w/2 spkrs		
CFM	**Rear Seat** — S	387	455
	reqs CKC carpeting; frt reclining seats w/S		
RCD	**Sound Bar** — SE	173	204
	incls 2 spkrs mounted on sport bar		
AAX	**Sound Group** — S	420	494
	incls AM/FM ET stereo radio, sound bar, sport bar main bar padding		
SBA	**Power Steering** — S, SE	255	300
SCG	**Leather-Wrapped Steering Wheel**	41	48
MRJ	**Steps** — bodyside body-color - SE	62	73
SUA	**Tilt Steering Column** — S, SE	164	193
TMW	**Tires** — P215/75R15 OWL all terrain (5) - S	231	272
	SE w/o pkg D	194	228
	SE w/pkg D	99	117
	Sahara	99	117
TRN	**Tires** — P225/75R15 OWL all terrain (5) - S	394	463
	SE w/o pkg D	356	419
	SE w/pkg D	262	308
	models w/Sport pkg	162	191
	Sahara	262	308
TBB	**Tire** — conventional spare - S, SE	94	111
JKC	**Add-A-Trunk Lockable Storage**	106	125
	reqs CKC on S, SE & models w/Sport pkg		
WJD	**Wheels** — styled steel 15" x 7" (5) - SE	STD	STD
WJ5	**Wheels** — 5-spoke full face steel 15" x 7" (5) SE	87	102
	(5) - SE	109	128
	(5) tires reqs conventional spare		
WJN	**Wheels** — 5-spoke aluminum 15" x 7" (5) - S, SE	288	339
	models w/Sport pkg	179	211
	Sahara	201	237
	S & SE req TBB & P215 or P225 tires		
NAE	**California Emissions**	109	128
NBY	**New York Emissions**	109	128
NAF	**High Altitude Emissions**	NC	NC
EPE	**Engine** — 2.5L MPI 4 cyl - S	STD	STD
ERH	**Engine** — 4.0L MPI 6 cyl - SE	STD	STD
	Sahara, Renegade	STD	STD
DDQ	**Transmission** — 5-spd manual overdrive	STD	STD
DGA	**Transmission** — 3-spd automatic	530	624
—	**Hardtop** — S, SE & models w/Sport pkg	642	755
	Sahara, Renegade	785	923
	incls full doors w/vent window, dome light, dual o/s mirrors, rear wiper/ washer, rear qtr glass (std tint on S & SE; deep tint on Sahara & Renegade)		
—	**Vinyl Bucket Seats** — non reclining - S	STD	STD
—	**Vinyl Bucket Seats** — reclining - S	64	75
	reqs rear seat & floor carpet		
—	**Vinyl Bucket Seats** — reclining w/rear bench - SE, Sport	STD	STD
—	**Cloth Bucket Seats** — reclining w/rear bench - SE, Sport	91	107
	Sahara, Renegade	STD	STD

LAND ROVER DEFENDER 90

DEFENDER 90 8 CYL

	DEALER	LIST
4WD 2-Dr (5-spd)	25100	27900
Destination Charge:	595	595

Standard Equipment

DEFENDER 90: 3.9 liter (241 CID) V8 OHV engine, EFI Lucas/Bosch multi-point fuel injection, 14 gauge boxed steel ladder frame, aluminum body, 5-speed manual transmission, front suspension (dual rate coil springs, radius arms and Panhard rod, anti-sway bar), rear suspension (single rate coil springs, lower links, "A" frame location arms, anti-sway bar), telescopic double acting non-adjustable hydraulic shocks, power assisted worm and roller steering, power 4-wheel disc brakes, 15.6 gallon fuel tank, LT265/75R16 B.F. Goodrich radial mud terrain T/A tires, permanent 4WD, unique styled steel wheels, rear-mounted swing-away spare tire, reclining bucket seats with twill-effect upholstery, AM/FM stereo cassette entertainment system with four weather-resistant speakers, lockable security cover, center console, floor mats, tachometer, intermittent windshield wipers.

Accessories

CODE	DESCRIPTION	DEALER	LIST
AAW	**Aluminum Alloy Wheels**	750	900
AC	**Air Conditioning**	1530	1800
PTP	**Soft Top**	1680	1975

LAND ROVER RANGE ROVER

		DEALER	LIST
SXVC	County 4-Dr (auto)	41000	46900
SXLB	County LWB (auto)	43700	50200
	Destination Charge:	625	625

Standard Equipment

RANGE ROVER COUNTY: 3.9 liter 182 horsepower V8 OHV eng, Lucas/Bosch multi-point elec fuel injection, 4-spd auto trans w/overdrive, 4WD, front suspension (variable rate air springs, auto self leveling, radius arms, Panhard rod, 25mm anti-sway bar), rear suspension (variable rate air springs, auto self leveling, trailing links, 18.5 mm anti-sway bar), Michelin XM + S 244 all-purpose 205R16 tubeless tires, 7.0 x 16" alloy wheels, power assisted worm & roller steering, power four-wheel disc brakes w/anti-lock braking system, 23.4 gallon fuel tank, air cond, power tilt/slide glass sunroof w/sunshade, 3-spoke alloy wheels, leather seating, Pioneer ETR AM/FM stereo radio w/cass & CD changer, diversity antenna, cruise control, 8-way power heated front bucket seats, split fold-down rear seat, electronic traction control, alarm system with keyless entry, power windows with one-touch feature on front windows, rear loadspace cover, integral trailer tow hitch receiver, tinted glass, automatic dimming rearview mirror, dual power/heated OS mirrors, central locking system, remote fuel filler door release, burl walnut trim on fascia/door cappings/center console; rear window washer/wiper, rear window defroster, side window defoggers, full instrumentation including tachometer, removable carpeting, halogen headlights.

RANGE ROVER COUNTY LWB (in addition to or instead of RANGE ROVER COUNTY equipment): 4.2 liter 200 horsepower V8 OHV engine, dual preset memory driver's seat, mediterranean poplar wood trim on fascia/door cappings/center console; "cyclone"-style alloy wheels with "Quicksilver" finish.

Accessories

—	**California Emissions System**	100	100
—	**Paint** — Beluga Black - County	250	250
BSE	**Black Sable Edition** — County LWB	875	1050
	incls Beluga Black paint and Dark Sable Connolly leather seats		
LSE	**Light Stone Edition** — County LWB	625	750
	incls Brooklands Green or Cornish Cream paint and Light Stone Connolly leather seats		
MSE	**Montpellier Sable Edition** — County LWB	625	750
	incls Montpellier Red paint and Dark Sable Connolly leather seats		

MAZDA NAVAJO

NAVAJO 6 CYL

	DEALER	LIST
DX 2WD 2-Dr (5-spd)	15658	17775
LX 2WD 2-Dr (5-spd)	16733	18995
DX 4WD 2-Dr (5-spd)	17234	19565
LX 4WD 2-Dr (5-spd)	18309	20785
Destination Charge: Alaska	600	600
Other States	490	490

Standard Equipment

NAVAJO DX: 4.0L OHC V6 engine with electronic fuel injection, 5-speed manual transmission with overdrive, shift-on-the-fly 4-wheel drive system (4WD), rear-wheel anti-lock braking system (ABS), 15-inch styled steel wheels, P225/70R15 all-season tires, intermittent windshield wipers, rear liftgate with lift-up window, engine compartment light, reclining front bucket seats, tip-and-slide front seats for easy access to rear seats, articulated split fold-down rear seat with fold-flat feature, cloth upholstery, rear storage pocket, AM/FM stereo sound system with four speakers.

LX (in addition to or instead of DX equipment): Aluminum alloy wheels, protective bodyside molding, dual power mirrors, privacy tint rear window glass, lower carpeting on door trim panels, retractable cargo cover, cargo tie down net, power windows and door locks, AM/FM/cassette stereo sound system, leather-wrapped steering wheel, auxiliary sun visors, illuminated vanity mirrors, glovebox and ashtray.

Accessories

CODE	DESCRIPTION	DEALER	LIST
CE1	**California Emissions**	85	100
HA1	**High Altitude Emissions**	NC	NC
FLM	**Floor Mats** — DX	45	65
AT1	**Automatic Transmission** — 4-speed w/overdrive - LX	757	890
CD1	**Compact Disc Player** — LX	255	300
1DX	**Special Equipment Pkg** — DX	251	295
	incls air cond, console, AM/FM ETR stereo radio w/cass, bodyside moldings		
1LE	**Leather Pkg** — LX	3396	3995
	incls premium equipment pkg plus 4-speed auto transmission, leather seats, towing pkg and power driver's seat		

CODE	DESCRIPTION	DEALER	LIST
1LX	**Premium Equipment Pkg**		
	incls moonroof, air conditioning, tilt steering wheel, luggage rack, speed		
	control, floor mats, sport bucket seats, console, rear window defroster, rear		
	window wiper/washer, all-terrain tires, AM/FM ETR stereo radio w/cassette		
1TP	**Towing Pkg — LX**	298	350
	incls limited slip differential, performance gear ratio, upgraded engine		
	cooling, trailer wiring harness, heavy duty flashers		

MITSUBISHI MONTERO

	DEALER	LIST
MP45-N LS 4WD 4-Dr (5-spd)	20505	23975
MP45-N LS 4WD 4-Dr (auto)	21219	24825
MP45-W SR 4WD 4-Dr (auto)	26290	31475
Destination Charge:	445	445

Standard Equipment

MONTERO LS: Sport type reclining front bucket seats, adjustable/see-thru headrests, reclining 2nd row seat w/headrests, fold down/tumble forward 2nd row bench seat, folding 3rd row seats w/headrests, full passenger compartment carpeting, cargo area carpeting, full interior trim, dual bi-level heating/vent system, rear-seat heater ducts, tilt steering column, sport-style steering wheel, Power Package includes: power window with auto down/power door locks/cruise control; center console w/storage and cupholders, cargo tie-down hooks, front and rear passenger assist grips, locking glove box, map/spot lights, inspection lamp w/front 12V auxiliary socket, dual sunvisors w/passenger visor vanity mirror, 2-speed intermittent windshield wiper/washer, rear window defroster w/timer, intermittent rear wiper/washer, side window defoggers, rear door mounted tool kit, driver side airbag, height adjustable front shoulder belts, four-wheel disc brakes, warning and indicator lights for: brakes/battery charge/door ajar/seatbelt reminder/cruise "on"/active trac 4WD mode indicator/low oil pressure/low fuel/low fluid/high beam indicator/parking brake on/hazard; resettable tripmeter, inclinometer, oil pressure gauge, voltmeter, digital quartz clock, ETR AM/FM stereo cassette w/6 speakers, fixed length whip antenna, skid plates: front end/transfer case/fuel tank; locking fuel filler door w/remote, side-opening rear door, front

MITSUBISHI

and rear tow hooks, front and rear mudguards, halogen headlamps, tinted glass, dual power sideview mirrors, convex passenger-side mirror, 15 x 6 styled-steel wheels w/center cap, 235/75R15 all season SBR tires, rear-mounted full-size spare tire w/lock, 3.0L SOHC V6 engine, automatic valve lash adjusters, ECI electronic multi-point fuel injection, stainless steel exhaust system, 5-speed manual overdrive transmission, Active Trac 4WD system, 2-speed transfer case, independent front suspension, front and rear stabilizer bars, coil spring rear suspension, clutch/starter override (for M/T only), power assisted recirculating ball steering.

SR (in addition to or instead of LS equipment): Driver's suspension seat, CFC-free refrigerant air cond, lighted driver's side visor vanity mirror, side window defoggers deleted, remote keyless entry, multi-mode anti-lock braking system (ABS), Multi-meter: LCD compass/interior & exterior thermometer/inclinometer/altimeter; ETR AM/FM stereo cassette w/EQ and 6 speakers, power and diversity antenna, wide body fender flares, headlamp washers, aluminum alloy wheels w/locks, 265/70R15 all-weather radial tires, spare tire cover, 3.5L DOHC V6 engine, 4-speed automatic overdrive transmission.

Accessories

Code	Description	Dealer	List
—	**Pkg A** — LS	754	754
	incls air conditioning, AM/FM stereo radio w/cassette and CD, luggage rack, remote control keyless entry, cargo mat, spare tire cover		
—	**Pkg B** — LS	1337	1337
	incls Pkg A plus power antenna and CD auto changer, graphic equalizer		
LP	**Leather & Wood Pkg** — SR	1398	1748
PI	**Power Sunroof**	550	688
AB	**Anti-Lock Brakes** — LS	950	1188
KC	**Cargo Cover** — LS	70	108
QW	**Sliding Rear Window**	100	125
RL	**Locking Rear Differential** — SR	320	400
AW	**Alloy Wheels** — LS	264	331
CW	**Chrome Wheels** — SR	500	625
RB	**Side Step**	219	335
FK	**Fog Lights**	148	228
EA	**CD Auto Changer** — SR	598	899
RO	**Luggage Rack** — SR	180	277

NISSAN PATHFINDER

Code	Description	Dealer	List
09254	XE 2WD 4-Dr (5-spd)	17043	19429
09214	XE 2WD 4-Dr (auto)	18113	20649
09654	XE 4WD 4-Dr (5-spd)	18508	21099
09614	XE 4WD 4-Dr (auto)	19709	22469
09754	SE 4WD 4-Dr (5-spd)	21938	25009
09714	SE 4WD 4-Dr (auto)	22903	26109
09814	LE 4WD 4-Dr (auto)	25438	28999
	Destination Charge:	375	375

Standard Equipment

PATHFINDER 2WD XE: 3.0L SOHC V6 engine, sequential multi-point electronic fuel injection, 5-speed manual overdrive transmission, power recirculating ball steering, power vented front disc/rear drum brakes, double-wishbone front suspension w/stabilizer bar, 5-link coil-spring rear suspension with stabilizer bar, rear wheel anti-lock braking system (ABS), flush-mounted halogen headlamps, tinted glass, dual outside mirrors w/passenger-side convex mirror, skid plates and tow hooks, chromed steel wheels, rear wiper/washer, reclining front bucket seats w/adjustable head restraints, split fold-down rear seats w/adjustable head restraints, reclining rear seatbacks, cloth seat trim, front and rear passenger-assist grips, front door map pockets, full carpeting, remote fuel-filler door release, tilt steering column, rear window defroster w/timer, side window defoggers, remote hood release, cargo area courtesy lamp, center console w/CD and cellular phone compartment, lockable glove box, rear cargo net, tachometer, trip odometer, digital quartz clock, coolant temperature gauge, high-output electronically-tuned AM/FM cassette stereo audio system with auto reverse/Dolby noise reduction/8-speakers, diversity antenna system, steel side-door guard beams, 3-point front seatbelt system, 3-point manual rear seatbelts in the outboard positions/center lap belt, center high mount stop lamp, child safety rear door locks, energy-absorbing bumpers, energy-absorbing steering column, front and rear outboard head restraints.

4WD XE-V6 (in addition to or instead of 2WD XE equipment): Automatic locking front hubs, integrated fender flare/mud flaps, rear heater ducts.

4WD SE-V6 (in addition to or instead of 4WD XE equip): Exterior spare tire mount w/cover, rear quarter window privacy glass, dual heated power remote-controlled mirrors w/pass side convex mirror, alloy whls, rear wind deflector, step rail, fog lamps, multi-adjustable driver's seat w/2-way head restraints/

seat cushion tilt/seatback recline/3-position lumbar·support & fore/aft adjustments, rear-seat fold-down armrests, power windows w/driver-side one-touch auto-down feature, power door locks, cruise control, remote rear window release, 2-speed variable intermittent windshield wipers, dual illuminated visor vanity mirrors, remote vehicle security system, map lamps, flip-up/removable glass sunroof.

4WD LE-V6 (in addition to or instead of 4WD SE equipment): 4-speed automatic overdrive transmission, power 4-wheel disc brakes, rear limited slip differential, exterior spare tire mount w/cover deleted, skid plates and tow hooks deleted, integrated fender flare/mud flaps deleted, six-spoke design alloy wheels, luggage rack, rear wind deflector deleted, running board/molded splash guards, step rail deleted, reclining front bucket seats w/adjustable head restraints deleted, leather seating surfaces w/heated front seats, cloth seat trim deleted, semi-automatic air conditioning with non-CFC refrigerant, compact disc player by Nissan, SE-V6 Leather Trim Package includes: leather seating surfaces, leather-wrapped steering wheel, parking brake handle, heated front seats w/individual controls.

Accessories

CODE	DESCRIPTION	DEALER	LIST
A01	**Air Conditioning** — XE, SE	843	995
	std on LE		
G01	**XE Convenience Pkg** — XE	1313	1550
	incls cruise control, power windows, power door locks, power liftgate release, intermittent windshield wipers, heated power mirrors, map lights, security system [reqs air conditioning]		
V01	**XE Sport Pkg** — XE	728	860
	incls limited slip differential (4WD), fender flares, cargo net, outside spare tire carrier and cover, foglights [reqs convenience pkg]		
T06	**SE-V6 Off-Road Pkg** — SE	635	750
	incls 4-wheel disc brakes, adjustable shock absorbers, limited slip differential, black items (bumpers, grille, mirrors, luggage rack and windshield molding [reqs air conditioning])		
X03	**Leather Trim Pkg** — SE 4WD	1063	1255
	incls leather upholstery/steering wheel/brake handle/shift knob, heated seats [reqs air conditioning]		
E10	**Two-Tone Paint** — LE	254	300
C01	**California Emissions**	128	150

OLDSMOBILE BRAVADA

BRAVADA 6 CYL

		DEALER	LIST
V06TR	4-Dr Sport Utility	23525	25995
Destination Charge:		475	475

Standard Equipment

BRAVADA: Gold metallic bodyside accent stripe, all-weather air conditioner, full-time all-wheel drive with viscous clutch, front and rear armrests, all-passenger seating position assist handles, Freedom high-capacity heavy-duty battery, power front disc/rear drum anti-lock brakes, front bumpers with integrated air dam and rear body color, cut-pile wall-to-wall carpeting with carpeted lower door panels, overhead console with digital compass/outside temperature readout/dual reading lamps; floor console with cupholders and dual auxiliary electrical outlets and power seat controls, rear convenience net, resume and acceleration feature cruise control, side window defoggers, electric rear window defogger, door locks with remote lock control package (includes two key-chain transmitters), 4.3 liter Vortec V6 engine with central port fuel injection, auxiliary front and rear carpeted floor mats, protective rear cargo mat, halogen headlamps, interior operated hood release, analog instrument panel gauge cluster includes: gauges for oil pressure/coolant temperature/voltmeter/fuel level/trip odometer/anti-lock brake monitor light; lamps include: interior dome/instrument panel convenience/under-hood/glove box/ashtray; front license plate bracket, power rear tailgate lock release, rooftop aero design luggage carrier with adjustable crossbar, inside day-night mirror with door-activated map lights, driver and passenger side electrically operated outside mirrors, moldings include: color-coordinated bodyside/rocker panel/wheel opening; locking rear differential posi-traction, Delco ETR AM stereo/FM stereo radio with seek-scan/auto-reverse cassette/music search/graphic equalizer/digital display clock/mast antenna; front reclining bucket seats with driver's side 6-way power adjustment, power lumbar adjustment for driver and passenger seats, folding rear bench seats with center armrest, power steering, leather-wrapped Tilt-Wheel steering wheel, independent front suspension system with torsion bars and stabilizer bar, rear semi-elliptic leaf spring suspension, high-pressure gas-assisted front and rear shock absorbers, P235/75R15 radial-ply all-season blackwall tires, full size spare tire, 4-speed automatic shift transmission, flo-thru ventilation w/console vent for rear seat passengers, auxiliary sunshade/extender visors, lighted vanity mirrors and convenience straps, cast aluminum 15" wheels (including spare), power side windows, Solar-Ray windshield/front door glass, deep-tint rear door/rear quarter/tailgate windows; pulse wiper system, rear-lift glass wiper and washer, foglamps.

Accessories

CODE	DESCRIPTION	DEALER	LIST
B94	Gold Pkg	52	60
K05	Heater, Engine Block	28	33
P16	Tire Carrier, Exterior Spare	137	159
QFN	Tires, P235/75R15 WOL All-Season	114	133
U1C	Radio, AM/FM Stereo w/Compact Disc	115	134
U52	Electronic Instrument Panel Cluster	168	195
WJ7	Custom Leather Trim	559	650
Z82	Towing Pkg, 5,000 Lb Capacity	219	255
NG1	New York Emissions	NC	NC
YF5	California Emissions	NC	NC

TOYOTA LAND CRUISER

		DEALER	LIST
6154	5-Dr 4WD Wagon (auto)	28614	34268
	Destination Charge: approximate	400	400

Standard Equipment

LAND CRUISER: Tilt steering column, heavy-duty battery, cruise control, rear heater, cloth upholstery, rear mud guards, front/rear stabilizer bars, front /rear carpeting, fender flares, tow harness, styled steel wheels, door map pockets, tachometer, trip odometer, variable intermittent wipers, rear window intermittent wipers, heavy-duty cooling system, locking center differential, tinted glass, heavy-duty transmission oil cooler, air cond, digital clock, door trim panels w/cloth inserts, reclining front bucket seats, rear fold-down bench seats, power steering, ignition key light, electric rear window defroster, diagnostic warning lights, power diversity antenna system, center console w/storage, soft urethane steering wheel, power front disc/rear drum brakes, remote fuel-filler door release, power windows w/driver side express down, P275/70R16 SBR BW tires, full-size spare tire, 4.5L 6 cylinder EFI 24-valve engine, power door locks, child-safety rear door locks, 4-speed ECT automatic overdrive transmission, dual color-keyed power mirrors, right illuminated visor vanity mirror, premium AM/FM ETR stereo radio w/cass, programmable equalizer, rear woofer and 9 speakers; transfer case/fuel tank skid plates.

TOYOTA

CODE	DESCRIPTION	DEALER	LIST

Accessories

TX	**Two-Tone Pkg**	208	260
AW	**Aluminum Wheels**	412	515
	incls five P275/70R16 tires, five aluminum wheels		
FE	**50-State Emissions**	NC	NC
SR	**Power Moonroof**	920	1150
AB	**Anti-Lock Brakes**	968	1180
	incls full floating axle, transfer case, power anti-lock 4-wheel disc brakes		
LA	**Leather Trim Pkg**	3224	4030
	incls leather-wrapped steering wheel, leather seating, dual power front seats, leather headrests, leather-wrapped transmission lever and transfer case knob, door panels w/leather inserts, leather-covered center console, third rear seat (reqs premium 3-in-1 Combo Radio)		
DL	**Differential Locks**	1568	1930
	incls transfer case, anti-lock 4-wheel disc brakes, lockable front and rear differentials, full-floating axle		
TH	**Third Rear Seat**	1116	1395
	incls rear 3-point seatbelts, split-fold-down rear third seat, rear assist grips, rear quarter sliding windows, privacy glass, cloth headrests, child-safety locking rear hatch		
DC	**Premium 3-In-1 Combo Radio**	600	800
	incls compact disc player, 9 speakers, premium AM/FM ETR stereo radio w/cassette, programmable equalization		

TOYOTA 4RUNNER

8642	SR5 V6 2WD 4-Dr (auto)	17769	21028
8657	SR5 4WD 4-Dr (5-spd)	16998	19998
8665	SR5 V6 4WD 4-Dr (5-spd)	18538	21938
8664	SR5 V6 4WD 4-Dr (auto)	19425	22988
	Destination Charge: approximate	400	400

TOYOTA

Standard Equipment

4RUNNER SR5 4-CYLINDER: Power steering, passenger assist grips, cloth upholstery, tinted glass, power rear window, 2.4L 4 cylinder EFI engine, digital clock, tachometer, front center console w/storage, front and rear mud guards, trip odometer, cut-pile carpeting (including cargo area), front and rear stabilizer bars, rear window wiper/washer, remote fuel-filler door release, dual rear storage compartments, dual black outside mirrors, power front disc/rear drum brakes, P225/75R15 mud & snow SBR BW tires, full-size spare tire, styled-steel wheels, reclining front bucket seats, split fold-down rear bench seat, child-safety rear door locks, skid plates (suspension, fuel tank, transfer case).

SR5 V6 (in addition to or instead of SR4 4-CYLINDER equip): Sport stripes, elec rear window defroster, transfer case skid plate deleted (2WD), AM/FM ETR stereo radio w/4 speakers, tilt steering column, 3.0L V6 EFI engine, variable intermittent front wipers, power front disc/rear anti-lock drum brakes.

Accessories

CODE	DESCRIPTION	DEALER	LIST
BR	**Bronze Tinted Glass** — V6	128	160
TW	**Tilt Steering Column** — 4-Cylinder	183	215
AC	**Air Conditioning**	764	955
VP	**Value Pkg 1** — 4-Cylinder models	1792	1991
	incls cruise control, Chrome Pkg, intermittent wipers w/timer, air conditioning, carpeted floor mats, leather-wrapped steering wheel, Power Pkg, deluxe AM/FM radio w/cassette & 4 speakers		
VP	**Value Pkg 1** — V6 models	1292	1436
	incls Chrome Pkg, cruise control, air conditioning, carpeted floor mats, intermittent wipers w/timer, Power Pkg		
VF	**Value Pkg 2** — V6 4WD models	2053	2281
	incls Value Pkg 1, chrome bumper (accommodating wider tire), alum whls		
VQ	**Value Pkg 3** — V6 4WD models	3227	3586
	incls Value Pkg 2, Leather Trim Pkg (reqs bronze tinted glass)		
CH	**Chrome Pkg**	196	245
	incls chrome windshield molding/grille/front & rear bumpers/outside door handles (4-Cyl models also include small chrome wheel opening moldings)		
SX	**Sports Pkg** — gray glass	360	450
	incls adjustable fore/aft spt headrests, cloth front sport seats, rear window gray privacy glass (req's Chrome Pkg or Value Pkg or aluminum wheels)		
SY	**Sports Pkg** — bronze glass - V6 models	232	290
	incls adjustable fore/aft sport headrests, cloth front spt seats, rear window bronze privacy glass (reqs Chrome Pkg, bronze tinted glass or Value Pkg)		
LA	**Leather Trim Pkg** — V6 4WD models	1344	1680
	incls leather-wrapped steering wheels, leather-trimmed sport seats, cruise control, rear window privacy glass, door trim panels w/leather inserts, 4-way adjustable headrests, intermittent wipers w/timer (reqs Power Pkg)		
CK	**All Weather Guard Pkg** — 4-Cylinder models	191	235
	V6 models	55	65
	incls rr window defroster (std V6), heavy-duty battery (V6 models), heavy-duty specifications for windshield wiper motor/starter motor/distributor cvr		
PO	**Power Pkg**	632	790
	incls power door locks, power windows w/driver side express down, dual chrome power mirrors (reqs cruise control and Chrome Pkg or aluminum wheels; or cruise control or Leather Trim Pkg)		
LK	**Anti-Lock Rear Brakes** — 4-cylinder	255	300
AB	**4-Wheel Anti-Lock Brakes** — V6	541	660
CA	**California Emissions**	130	153

CODE	DESCRIPTION	DEALER	LIST
PX	**Metallic Paint**	NC	NC
AW	**Aluminum Wheels** — V6 4WD	872	1090
	incls center wheel cap ornament, Chrome Pkg, large wheel opening arch moldings, five 31-10.5 R15 tires		
AY	**Aluminum Wheels** — w/P225 tires - V6	376	470
	incls center wheel cap ornament, P225/75R15 tires, small wheel opening moldings (reqs Value Pkg 1 or Chrome Pkg)		
CL	**Cruise Control**	300	375
	incls intermittent wipers w/timer, cruise control, headlights-on warning buzzer (V6 models), urethane-wrapped steering wheel (4-Cylinder models req tilt steering column, Power Pkg)		
EX	**Deluxe AM/FM ETR Radio w/Cassette** — 4-Cylinder	416	555
	incls 4 speakers		
EX	**Deluxe AM/FM ETR Radio w/Cassette** — V6	207	270
	incls power antenna, 4 speakers		
CE	**Premium AM/FM ETR Radio w/Cassette** — V6	506	675
	incls power antenna w/diversity reception, 6 speakers		
DC	**Premium 3-In-1 Combo Radio** — V6	1106	1475
	incls 6 speakers, AM/FM ETR stereo radio w/cassette and compact disc, power antenna w/diversity reception		
RH	**Rear Heater**	128	160
	incls large rear console box (req's All-Weather Guard Pkg)		
SR	**Power Moonroof** — V6	648	810

Dealer Incentives / Manufacturer Rebates

These are programs offered by the manufacturers to increase the sales of slow-selling models or to reduce excess inventories. While the manufacturer's rebates are passed directly on to the buyer, dealer incentives are passed on only to the dealer–who may or may not elect to pass the savings on to the customer. • The following incentives and rebates were in effect at time of publication. Please note, however, that these programs often change frequently. • For updated information regarding Dealer Incentives and Manufacturer's Rebates, call Nationwide Auto Brokers, Inc. at **313-559-6661**.

	DEALER INCENTIVE ($)	MFRS REBATE ($)		DEALER INCENTIVE ($)	MFRS REBATE ($)
CHEVROLET			**ISUZU**		
Astro		500	Pickup	400-1100	
Blazer S10 2-Dr		1000	Rodeo 4WD	750	
Chevy Van		500	Trooper	1000	
Lumina Van		750	**JEEP**		
S10 2WD PU (4 cyl)	500		Wrangler (4 cyl)		500
DODGE			**MITSUBISHI**		
Minivans		500	Expo/Expo LRV		500
Ram Van		1000	Pickup	800-1200	
Ram Wagon		1000	**NISSAN**		
FORD			Pathfinder	500	
Aerostar		750	Pickup	500-1000	
Bronco		1000	**OLDSMOBILE**		
Club Wagon		500	Bravada		1000
Econoline Van		500	Silhouette		1000
Ranger (2.3L)		300	**PLYMOUTH**		
GMC			Colt Vista		300
Jimmy		1000	Minivans		500
GMC Van		500	**PONTIAC**		
Safari		500	Trans Sport		750

READER QUESTIONNAIRE

To help us improve the information content of our books,
please complete this questionnaire and mail to:

Edmund Publications Corporation
300 N. Sepulveda Blvd., Suite 2050
El Segundo, Ca 90245

1. **Where did you purchase this Edmund's Book?**
   ❏ BOOKSTORE   ❏ NEWSSTAND   ❏ OTHER

2. **How many times have you purchased editions of Edmund's USED CAR PRICES books?**
   ❏ ONCE   ❏ TWICE   ❏ THREE TIMES   ❏ FOUR TIMES OR MORE

3. **What is your vehicle preference?**
   CHECK ONE: ❏ AMERICAN   ❏ IMPORT
   CHECK ONE OR MORE: ❏ CAR   ❏ VAN   ❏ TRUCK   ❏ SPORTS UTILITY

4. **What is your budget/price for buying a new vehicle?**
   ❏ UNDER $10,000   ❏ $10-15,000   ❏ $15-20,000   ❏ $20-30,000
   ❏ $30-40,000   ❏ $40,000 AND UP

5. **Which Edmund's NEW VEHICLE PRICE GUIDES have you purchased in the past?**
   ❏ AMERICAN CARS   ❏ IMPORTS   ❏ VAN, PICKUP, SPORTS UTILITY   ❏ ECONOMY

6. **Would you like to use a computerized version of Edmund's Price Guides?**
   ❏ NO   YES FOR: ❏ IBM PC   ❏ WINDOWS   ❏ MACINTOSH

ANY COMMENTS: _____

_____

_____

To be advised directly of special offers from Edmund's, please complete the following. Thank you.

NAME _____

ADDRESS _____

CITY, STATE, ZIP _____

TELEPHONE _____

S2801

Specifications and EPA Mileage Ratings

On the following pages, the list of ratings for 1993. Released by the Environmental Protection Agency in September, 1992. These ratings are estimates; whether you get better or worse mileage depends upon how you drive.

contents

VANS

Specifications and EPA Mileage Ratings		ASTRO VAN 2WD REG	ASTRO VAN 2WD EXTD	ASTRO VAN AWD REG	CHEVY VAN G10 110" WB	LUMINA VAN CARGO	LUMINA VAN PASS	SPORTVAN G10 110" WB	SPORTVAN G20 125" WB	SPORTVAN G30 125" WB	SPORTVAN G30 146" WB		TOWN & CNTRY FWD WGN
Length (in.)		176.8	186.8	176.8	180.0	191.5	191.5	180.1	204.0	204.1	225.0		192.8
Width (in.)		77.5	77.5	77.5	79.5	73.9	73.9	79.1	79.5	79.5	79.5		72.0
Height (in.)		76.2	76.2	76.2	79.0	65.7	65.7	80.0	79.5	81.9	82.3		66.7
Wheelbase (in.)	**CHEVROLET**	111.0	111.0	111.0	110.0	109.8	109.8	110.0	125.0	125.0	146.0	**CHRYSLER**	119.3
Curb Weight (lbs.)		4160	4241	4160	3900	3510	3344	4250	4300	4500	4650		3977
Gross Vehicle Wt. (lbs.)		5300/	5700/	5700/	4900/	5126/	5126/	5600/	6600/	7400/	8600/		5200/
- min/max		5700	5950	5950	6000	--	--	6000	6600	8600	9200		
Cargo Capacity (lbs.)		--/	--/	--/	1100/	1257/	500/	1050/	2100/	2590/	--/		150/
- min/max		1740	1914	1697	2200	--	800	1400	2627	4090	3457		450
Engine Type		V6	V6	V6	V6	V6	V6	V6	V6	V8	V8		V6
Displacement (liters/CID)		4.3/	4.3/	4.3/	4.3/	3.1/	3.1/	4.3/	4.3/	5.7/	4.3/		3.8/
		262	262	262	262	191	191	262	262	350	262		203.5
Horsepower		165	165	165	155	120	120	155	155	195	195		162
Torque		235	235	235	230	175	175	230	230	290	290		213
Steering Ratio		16/	16/	16/	17.2	17.6	17.6	17.2	17.2	17.2	17.2		18.3
		13:1	13:1	13:1									
Turning Circle (ft.)		39.5	39.5	40.5	42.7	43.1	43.1	41.3	46.0	48.5	54.0		43.0
Fuel Tank (gals.)		27.0	27.0	27.0	22.0	20.0	20.0	22.0	33.0	33.0	33.0		20.0
Transmission		4A	4A	4A	4A	3A	3A	4A	4A	4A	4A		4A
EPA City/Hwy (mpg) - manual		NA	NA	NA	NA	NA	NA	NA	NA	NA	NA		NA
EPA City/Hwy (mpg) - auto		16/21	15/20	15/20	16/21	19/27	19/27	15/19	15/19	13/17	13/17		17/22

Specifications and EPA Mileage Ratings	B150 VAN CARGO 110" WB	B250 VAN CARGO 127" WB	B350 VAN MAXI 127" WB	B150 WGN 110" WB	CARAVAN C/V CARGO	CARAVAN C/V EXTD CARGO	CARAVAN FWD PASS	GRND CARAVAN FWD PASS	AEROSTAR VAN	AEROSTAR WGN 119" WB	AEROSTAR WGN 119" WB
	DODGE								FORD		
Length (in.)	187.2	205.2	231.2	187.2	178.1	192.8	178.1	192.8	174.9	174.9	190.3
Width (in.)	79.8	79.8	80.0	79.8	72.0	72.0	72.0	72.0	71.7	71.7	71.7
Height (in.)	79.0	79.6	79.6	79.0	66.0	66.7	66.0	66.7	72.9	72.2	72.2
Wheelbase (in.)	109.6	127.6	127.6	109.6	112.3	119.3	112.3	119.3	118.9	118.9	118.9
Curb Weight (lbs.)	3785	3863	4368	4085	3135	3436	3306	3574	3296	3476	3580
Gross Vehicle Wt. (lbs.) - min/max	5000/ 5300	6010/ 6400	7500/ 9000	5000/ 6010	5200/ --	5200/ --	5200/ --	5200/ --	4920/ 5300	4900/ 5150	5000/ 5300
Cargo Capacity (lbs.) - min/max	1215/ 1530	2147/ 2502	3067/ 4407	1107/ 1876	1200/ 2000	2000/ --	1200/ 2000	2000/ --	1800/ 1950	--/ 139.3	--/ 167.7
Engine Type	V6	V6	V8	V6	I4	V6	I4	V6	V6	V6	V6
Displacement (liters/CID)	3.9/ 239	3.9/ 239	5.2/ 318	3.9/ 239	2.5/ 153	3.3/ 201.5	2.5/ 153	3.0/ 181.4	3.0/ 182	3.0/ 182	3.0/ 182
Horsepower	175	175	220	175	100	162	100	142	135	135	135
Torque	225	225	295	225	135	195	135	173	160	160	160
Steering Ratio	13-16	13-16	13-16	13-16	18.3	18.3	18.3	18.3	19.8-15.0:1	19.8-15.0:1	19.8-15.0:1
Turning Circle (ft.)	40.5	46.2	52.4	40.5	40.5	42.5	41.0	43.0	37.5	37.5	38.5
Fuel Tank (gals.)	22.0	22.0	22.0	22.0	20.0	20.0	20.0	20.0	21.0	21.0	21.0
Transmission	3A	3A	4A	3A	5M	4A	5M	3A	5M	5M	5M
EPA City/Hwy (mpg) - manual	NA	NA	NA	NA	20/30	NA	20/30	NA	17/24	17/24	17/24
EPA City/Hwy (mpg) - auto	15/17	15/17	13/17	14/16	20/26	18/23	20/26	19/24	17/23	17/23	17/23

Specifications and EPA Mileage Ratings	CLUB WGN 138" WB	ECONO VAN E150 138" WB	RALLY WGN G1500 110" WB	RALLY WGN G2500 125" WB	RALLY WGN G3500 125" WB	RALLY EXTD WGN G3500 146" WB	SAFARI VAN 2WD REG	SAFARI VAN 2WD EXTD	SAFARI VAN AWD REG	MPV 5-PASS 2WD WGN	MPV 7-PASS 2WD WGN
	GMC									MAZDA	
Length (in.)	211.8	211.8	180.1	204.0	204.1	225.0	176.8	186.8	176.8	175.0	175.8
Width (in.)	79.5	79.5	79.1	79.5	79.5	79.5	77.5	77.5	77.5	71.9	71.9
Height (in.)	80.9	80.7	80.0	79.5	81.9	82.3	76.2	76.2	76.2	68.1	68.1
Wheelbase (in.)	138.0	138.0	110.0	125.0	125.0	146.0	111.0	111.0	111.0	110.4	110.4
Curb Weight (lbs.)	4917	4470	4250	4300	4500	4650	4160	4241	3897	3595	3745
Gross Vehicle Wt. (lbs.) - min/max	6050/ 7000	6050/ 7000	5600/ 6000	6600/ 6600	7400/ 8600	8600/ 9200	5300/ 5700	5700/ 5950	5700/ 5950	NA	NA
Cargo Capacity (lbs.) - min/max	--/ 254.9	1310/ 2030	1050/ 1400	2100/ 2627	2590/ 4090	--/ 3457	--/ 1740	--/ 1914	--/ 1697	11/110 cu. ft	11/38 cu. ft
Engine Type	V6	I6	V6	V6	V8	V8	V6	V6	V6	L4	L4
Displacement (liters/CID)	4.9/ 300	4.9/ 300	4.3/ 262	4.3/ 262	5.7/ 350	5.7/ 262	4.3/ 262	4.3/ 262	4.3/ 262	2.6/ 159	2.6/ 159
Horsepower	145	145	155	155	195	195	165	165	165	121	121
Torque	265	265	230	230	290	290	235	235	235	149	149
Steering Ratio	17.0:1	17.0:1	17.2:1	17.2:1	17.2:1	17.2:1	16/ 13:1	16/ 13:1	16/ 13:1	22.1	22.1
Turning Circle (ft.)	50.0	50.0	41.3	46.0	48.5	54.0	39.5	39.5	40.5	36.1	36.1
Fuel Tank (gals.)	22.0	22.0	22.0	33.0	33.0	33.0	27.0	27.0	27.0	19.6	19.6
Transmission	4A	3A	4A	4A	4A	4A	4A	4A	4A	4A	4A
EPA City/Hwy (mpg) - manual	NA	NA	NA	NA	NA	NA	NA	NA	NA	NA	NA
EPA City/Hwy (mpg) - auto	14/18	14/17	15/19	15/19	13/17	13/17	16/21	15/20	15/20	18/24	18/24

Specifications and EPA Mileage Ratings	MPV 7-PASS 4WD V6 WGN	MERCURY	VILLAGER FWB PASS	MITSUBISHI	EXPO BASE WGN	EXPO LRV WGN	EXPO AWD WGN	NISSAN	QUEST XE VAN	OLDSMOBILE	SILHOUETTE FWD PASS	PLYMOUTH	COLT VISTA FWD WGN
Length (in.)	175.8		189.9		177.0	168.5	177.4		189.9		191.5		168.5
Width (in.)	72.3		73.7		66.7	66.7	66.7		73.7		73.9		66.7
Height (in.)	70.8		67.6		62.6	62.1	62.6		65.6		65.7		62.1
Wheelbase (in.)	110.4		112.2		107.1	99.2	107.1		112.2		109.8		99.2
Curb Weight (lbs.)	4040		3985		3020	2745	3219		3783		3720		2734
Gross Vehicle Wt. (lbs.)	NA		5200/		NA	NA	NA		NA		5126/		NA
- min/max			--								--		--
Cargo Capacity (lbs.)	11/38		1190		38/75	30/68	38/75		14/115		150/		35/79
- min/max	cu. ft		1290		cu. ft	cu. ft	cu. ft		cu. ft		300		cu. ft
Engine Type	V6		I4		L4	L4	L4		V6		V6		L4
Displacement (liters/CID)	3.0/		3.0/		2.4/	1.8/	2.4/		3.0/		3.8/		1.8/
	180		182		144	112	144		180.7		231		111.9
Horsepower	155		151		136	113	136		151		170		113
Torque	169		174		145	116	145		174		225		116
Steering Ratio	21.4		17.5		17.8	17.8	17.8		17.5		17.6		17.8
Turning Circle (ft.)	39.6		41.5		36.8	33.5	36.8		39.9		43.1		33.5
Fuel Tank (gals.)	19.8		20.0		15.8	14.5	15.8		20.0		20.0		14.5
Transmission	4A		4A		5M	5M	5M		4A		4A		5M
EPA City/Hwy (mpg) - manual	NA		NA		22/27	24/29	20/24		NA		NA		21/28
EPA City/Hwy (mpg) - auto	15/19		17/23		20/26	NA	19/23		17/23		17/25		20/26

Specifications and EPA Mileage Ratings	COLT VISTA SE FWD WGN	COLT VISTA AWD WGN	VOYAGER FWD PASS	GRND VOYAGER FWD PASS	PONTIAC	TRANS SPORT SE VAN	TOYOTA	PREVIA DX VAN	PREVIA LE VAN	PREVIA DX AWD VAN	PREVIA LE AWD VAN
Length (in.)	168.5	168.5	178.1	192.8		191.5		187.0	187.0	187.0	187.0
Width (in.)	66.7	66.7	72.0	72.0		73.9		70.8	70.8	70.8	70.8
Height (in.)	62.1	62.6	66.0	66.7		65.7		68.7	68.7	69.1	69.1
Wheelbase (in.)	99.2	99.2	112.3	119.3		109.8		112.8	112.8	112.8	112.8
Curb Weight (lbs.)	2734	3064	3306	3574		3600		3610	3730	3830	3950
Gross Vehicle Wt. (lbs.)	NA	NA	5200/	5200/		5126/		NA	NA	NA	NA
- min/max	--	--				--					
Cargo Capacity (lbs.)	35/79	35/79	1200/	2000/		300/		33/158	33/158	33/158	33/158
- min/max	cu. ft	cu. ft	2000	--		800		cu. ft	cu. ft	cu. ft	cu. ft
Engine Type	L4	L4	I4	V6		V6		L4	L4	L4	L4
Displacement (liters/CID)	2.4/	2.4/	2.5/	3.0/		3.1/		2.4/	2.4/	2.4/	2.4/
	143	143	153	181.4		191		148.8	148.8	148.8	148.8
Horsepower	136	136	100	142		120		138	138	138	138
Torque	145	145	135	173		175		154	154	154	154
Steering Ratio	17.8	17.8	18.3	18.3		17.6		18.6	18.6	18.6	18.6
Turning Circle (ft.)	33.5	33.5	41.0	43.0		43.1		37.4	37.4	37.4	37.4
Fuel Tank (gals.)	14.5	14.5	20.0	20.0		20.0		19.9	19.9	19.9	19.9
Transmission	5M	5M	5M	3A		3A		4A	4A	4A	4A
EPA City/Hwy (mpg) - manual	19/24	19/24	20/30	NA		NA		NA	NA	NA	NA
EPA City/Hwy (mpg) - auto	19/23	19/23	20/26	19/24		18/23		17/22	17/22	17/21	17/21

PICKUPS

CHEVROLET

Specifications and EPA Mileage Ratings	C1500 117" WB 2WD FLEETSIDE	C1500 131" WB 2WD FLEETSIDE	C1500 142" WB 2WD FLEETSIDE	C2500 155" WB 2WD FLEETSIDE	C3500 131" WB 2WD FLEETSIDE	C3500 155" WB 2WD EXTD CAB	C3500 168" WB 2WD CREW CAB	K1500 117" WB 4WD FLEETSIDE	S10 108" WB 2WD SB REG CAB	S10 118" WB 2WD LB REG CAB	S10 108" WB 4WD SB REG CAB	S10 118" WB 4WD LB REG CAB
Length (in.)	193.9	212.6	218.0	237.0	212.6	237.0	249.6	194.0	188.8	204.7	188.8	204.7
Width (in.)	76.8	76.8	77.1	76.8	76.8	76.8	76.8	77.1	67.9	67.9	67.9	67.9
Height (in.)	70.4	73.0	70.6	75.8	75.5	75.8	68.3	73.8	63.0	63.7	64.5	64.6
Wheelbase (in.)	117.5	131.5	141.5	155.5	131.5	155.5	168.5	117.5	108.3	117.9	108.3	117.9
Curb Weight (lbs.)	3717	4021	4032	4261	4261	4874	5176	4138	2822	2874	3356	2874
Gross Vehicle Wt. (lbs.)	5600/	7200/	5600/	7200/	9000/	9000/	9000/	6100/	4200/	4200/	4200/	4200/
- min/max	6200	8600	6200	8600	10000	10000	10000	6800	5150	5150	5150	5150
Cargo Capacity (lbs.)	1809/	2563/	1809/	2563/	3910/	3910/	3566/	1809/	1213/	1160/	1213/	1160/
- min/max	2298	3177	2298	3177	5098	5098	4794	2298	1567	1428	1395	1350
Engine Type	V6	V6	V6	V8	V8	V8	V8	V6	I4	I4	I4	I4
Displacement (liters/CID)	4.3/	4.3/	4.3/	5.7/	5.7/	5.7/	5.7/	4.3/	2.2/	2.2/	2.2/	2.2/
	262	262	262	350	350	350	350	262	133	133	133	133
Horsepower	165	165	165	210	210	210	210	165	118	118	118	118
Torque	235	235	235	300	300	300	300	235	130	130	130	130
Steering Ratio	13:1	13.1	13.1	13.1	13.1	13.1	13.1	13:1	17.5:1	17.5:1	17.5:1	17.5:1
Turning Circle (ft.)	41.3	44.6	49.0	52.9	45.7	52.9	60.9	40.3	36.9	40.1	36.9	40.1
Fuel Tank (gals.)	25.0	25.0	25.0	34.0	34.0	34.0	34.0	25.0	20.0	20.0	20.0	20.0
Transmission	5M	5M	5M	5M	5M	5M	5M	5M	5M	5M	5M	5M
EPA City/Hwy (mpg) - manual	17/22	15/21	15/21	13/18	12/15	11/14	10/13	15/19	23/27	23/27	23/27	23/27
EPA City/Hwy (mpg) - auto	17/21	16/21	15/20	14/19	11/14	11/14	10/11	15/18	20/26	20/26	20/26	20/26

PICKUPS

DODGE

Specifications and EPA Mileage Ratings	DAKOTA 112" WB 2WD	DAKOTA 112" WB 4WD	DAKOTA 124" WB 2WD	DAKOTA 131" WB 2WD CLUB CB	DAKOTA 131" WB 4WD CLUB CB	RAM 1500 119" WB 2WD	RAM 1500 119" WB 4WD	RAM 1500 135" WB 2WD	RAM 2500 135" WB 2WD	RAM 2500 135" WB 4WD	RAM 3500 135" WB 2WD
Length (in.)	195.3	195.3	207.3	214.2	214.2	204.1	204.1	224.3	224.3	224.3	224.3
Width (in.)	69.3	69.3	69.3	69.3	69.3	78.4	78.4	78.4	78.4	78.4	93.5
Height (in.)	64.2	66.4	64.2	64.2	66.4	72.0	75.9	72.4	72.4	75.9	73.4
Wheelbase (in.)	111.9	111.9	123.9	130.9	130.9	118.7	118.7	134.7	134.7	134.7	134.7
Curb Weight (lbs.)	2991	3634	3080	3508	3877	3958	4517	4121	4656	4949	5212
Gross Vehicle Wt. (lbs.)	4250/	5150/	4250/	4250/	5350/	6010/	6400/	6010/	7500/	7500/	10500/
- min/max	6200	6000	6200	6200	5900	6400	--	6400	8800	8800	--
Cargo Capacity (lbs.)	1250/	1450/	1250/	1450/	1450/	2052/	1787/	1889/	2844/	2509/	4900/
- min/max	2600	2000	2600	2000	2365	1883	2202	4104	3133	5288	5288
Engine Type	I4	V6	I4	V6	V6	V6	V6	V8	V6	V8	V8
Displacement (liters/CID)	2.5/	3.9/	2.5/	3.9/	3.9/	3.9/	3.9/	5.2/	3.9/	5.2/	5.9/
	153	239	153	239	239	239	239	318	239	318	360
Horsepower	99	175	99	175	175	175	175	220	175	220	230
Torque	132	225	132	225	225	225	225	300	225	300	330
Steering Ratio	16.0	14.0	16.0	16.0	14.0	16-13	16-13	16-13	16-13	16-13	17.5
Turning Circle (ft.)	39.8	38.5	43.5	46.6	44.4	40.6	40.6	45.2	45.4	45.4	45.4
Fuel Tank (gals.)	15.0	15.0	15.0	15.0	15.0	26.0	26.0	35.0	35.0	35.0	35.0
Transmission	5M	5M	5M	5M	5M	5M	5M	5M	5M	5M	5M
EPA City/Hwy (mpg) - manual	22/27	15/19	22/27	16/22	15/19	15/19	14/18	15/19	13/17	14/18	NR
EPA City/Hwy (mpg) - auto	NA	14/18	NA	14/18	14/18	15/17	13/17	15/17	13/17	13/17	NR

Specifications and EPA Mileage Ratings		F150 117" WB 2WD FLARESIDE	F150 117" WB 2WD STYLESIDE	F150 117" WB 4WD STYLESIDE	F150 133" WB 2WD STYLESIDE	F150 133" WB 4WD STYLESIDE	F150 139" WB 2WD SC STYLESIDE	F250 155" WB 2WD SC STYLESIDE	F350 168" WB 2WD CREW CAB	RANGER 108" WB 2WD SB	RANGER 108" WB 4WD SB	RANGER 114" WB 2WD LB	RANGER 125" WB 2WD SC
Length (in.)		197.1	197.1	197.1	213.3	213.3	219.1	235.3	248.7	184.0	184.0	196.0	198.2
Width (in.)		80.0	79.0	79.0	79.0	79.0	79.0	79.0	79.0	69.4	69.4	69.4	69.4
Height (in.)		71.0	71.0	74.0	70.8	74.0	70.8	74.0	71.0	64.0	67.4	64.0	64.1
Wheelbase (in.)		116.8	116.8	116.8	133.0	133.0	138.8	155.0	168.4	107.9	107.9	113.9	125.1
Curb Weight (lbs.)		3875	3886	4050	3982	4250	4186	4316	5200	2920	3260	2955	3208
Gross Vehicle Wt. (lbs.) - min/max	FORD	5000/	5250/	6100/	5450/	6250/	6050/	8800/	9200/	4140/	4580/	4260/	4460/
		6100	6100	--	6250	--	--	--	10000	4660	4860	4700	4860
Cargo Capacity (lbs.) - min/max		1040/	1350/	2070/	1470/	1980/	1780/	4035/	3985/	1050/	1250/	1250/	1240/
		2110	2170	--	2265	--	--	--	4585	1550	1550	1650	1550
Engine Type		I6	I6	I6	I6	I6	I6	V8	V8	I4	I4	I4	I4
Displacement (liters/CID)		4.9/	4.9/	4.9/	4.9/	4.9/	4.9/	5.8/	5.8/	2.3/	2.3/	2.3/	2.3/
		300	300	300	300	300	300	351	351	140	140	140	140
Horsepower		145	145	145	145	145	145	200	200	100	100	100	100
Torque		265	265	265	265	265	265	310	310	133	133	133	133
Steering Ratio		17.0	17.0	17.0	17.0	17.0	17.0	17.0	17.0	17.0	17.0	17.0	17.0
Turning Circle (ft.)		44.5	44.5	44.5	49.0	49.0	52.0	54.0	59.0	37.3	37.3	38.3	41.5
Fuel Tank (gals.)		34.7	34.7	34.7	37.2	37.2	34.7	37.2	37.2	16.3	16.3	20.0	20.0
Transmission		5M	5M	5M	5M	5M	5M	5M	5M	5M	5M	5M	5M
EPA City/Hwy (mpg) - manual		15/20	15/20	15/18	15/20	15/18	15/20	NR	NR	23/28	22/26	23/28	23/28
EPA City/Hwy (mpg) - auto		15/20	15/20	14/18	15/20	14/18	15/20	NR	NR	21/24	20/23	21/24	21/24

Specifications and EPA Mileage Ratings		SIERRA 1500 117" WB 2WD	SIERRA 1500 142" WB 2WD	SIERRA 2500 131" WB 2WD	SIERRA 2500 155" WB 2WD	SIERRA 3500 155" WB EXTD 2WD	SIERRA 3500 168" WB CREW CAB 2WD	SONOMA 108" WB 2WD RG CB	SONOMA 108" WB 4WD RG CB	SONOMA 118" WB 2WD LB RG	SONOMA 118" WB 4WD LB RG CB	PICKUP 2WD SWB
Length (in.)		193.9	218.0	212.6	237.0	237.0	249.6	188.8	188.8	204.7	204.7	177.3
Width (in.)		76.8	77.1	76.8	76.8	76.8	76.8	67.9	67.9	67.9	67.9	66.6
Height (in.)		70.4	70.6	73.0	75.8	75.8	68.3	63.0	64.5	63.7	64.6	64.2
Wheelbase (in.)		117.5	141.5	131.5	155.5	155.5	168.5	108.3	108.3	117.9	117.9	105.6
Curb Weight (lbs.)		3717	4032	4021	4261	4874	5176	2822	3356	2874	2874	2830
Gross Vehicle Wt. (lbs.) - min/max	GMC	5600/	5600/	7200/	7200/	9200/	9000/	4200/	4200/	4200/	4200/	4300/
		6200	6200	8600	8600	10000	10000	5150	5150	5150	5150	
Cargo Capacity (lbs.) - min/max		1809/	1809/	2563/	2563/	3910/	3566/	1213/	1213/	1160/	1160/	NA
		2298	2298	3177	3177	5098	4794	1567	1395	1428	1350	
Engine Type		V6	V6	V6	V8	V8	V8	I4	I4	I4	I4	L4
Displacement (liters/CID)		4.3/	4.3/	4.3/	5.7/	5.7/	5.7/	2.2/	2.2/	2.2/	2.2/	2.3/
	ISUZU	262	262	262	350	350	350	133	133	133	133	137.5
Horsepower		165	165	165	210	210	210	118	118	118	118	96
Torque		235	235	235	300	300	300	130	130	130	130	123
Steering Ratio		13.1	13.1	13.1	13.1	13.1	13.1	17.5:1	17.5:1	17.5:1	17.5:1	23.2/
												26.6
Turning Circle (ft.)		41.3	49.0	44.6	52.9	52.9	60.9	36.9	36.9	40.1	40.1	35.4
Fuel Tank (gals.)		25.0	25.0	34.0	34.0	34.0	34.0	20.0	20.0	20.0	20.0	14.0
Transmission		5M	5M	5M	5M	5M	5M	5M	5M	5M	5M	5M
EPA City/Hwy (mpg) - manual		17/22	15/21	15/21	13/17	NR	NR	23/27	23/27	23/27	23/27	21/25
EPA City/Hwy (mpg) - auto		17/21	17/21	16/21	13/17	NR	NR	20/26	20/26	20/26	20/26	NA

Specifications and EPA Mileage Ratings	PICKUP 2WD LWB	PICKUP 2WD SPACECAB	PICKUP 4WD SWB	PICKUP 4WD SWB V6	MAZDA	B2300 2WD PU BASE SB	B2300 2WD PU BASE CAB PLUS	B3000 2WD PU SE LB	B3000 2WD PU SE CAB PLUS	B4000 2WD PU SE LB	B4000 2WD PU LE CAB PLUS	B4000 4WD PU SE SB	B4000 4WD PU SE CAB PLUS
Length (in.)	193.8	193.8	177.3	177.3		184.5	202.7	197.5	202.7	197.5	202.7	184.5	202.7
Width (in.)	66.6	66.6	66.6	66.6		69.4	69.4	69.4	69.4	69.4	69.4	69.4	69.4
Height (in.)	64.2	64.2	68.5	68.5		64.0	64.0	64.0	64.0	69.4	69.4	67.5	67.5
Wheelbase (in.)	119.2	119.2	105.6	105.6		107.9	125.0	113.9	125.0	113.9	125.0	113.9	125.0
Curb Weight (lbs.)	2940	3110	3355	3475		2918	3208	2955	3275	3031	3418	3258	3516
Gross Vehicle Wt. (lbs.) - min/max	4300/	4300/	4700/	4700/		4660/	4820/	4700/	4820/	4700/	4820/	4840/	5040 --
Cargo Capacity (lbs.) - min/max	NA	NA	NA	NA		1250/	1240/	1650/	1240/	1650/	1240/	1550/	1500/ --
Engine Type	L4	L4	L4	V6		L4	L4	V6	V6	V6	V6	V6	V6
Displacement (liters/CID)	2.3/ 137.5	2.6/ 156.2	2.6/ 156.2	3.1/ 191		2.3/ 140	2.3/ 140	3.0/ 182	3.0/ 182	4.0/ 245	4.0/ 245	4.0/ 245	4.0/ 245
Horsepower	96	120	120	120		98	98	140	140	160	160	160	160
Torque	123	150	150	165		130	130	160	160	225	220	225	225
Steering Ratio	23.2/ 26.6	17.2	18.8	18.8		27.2	17.0	17.0	17.0	17.0	17.0	17.0	17.0
Turning Circle (ft.)	39.4	39.4	36.1	36.1		36.5	41.6	38.3	41.6	38.3	41.6	37.3	42.4
Fuel Tank (gals.)	19.8	19.8	14.0	14.0		16.3	19.6	19.6	19.6	19.6	19.6	16.3	19.6
Transmission	5M	5M	5M	5M		5M	5M	5M	5M	5M	5M	5M	5M
EPA City/Hwy (mpg) - manual	21/25	21/25	17/20	15/18		22/26	22/26	22/26	19/24	18/24	NA	18/22	18/22
EPA City/Hwy (mpg) - auto	NA	NA	NA	NA		NA	NA	NA	19/24	NA	17/23	NA	NA

Specifications and EPA Mileage Ratings	B4000 4WD PU LE CAB PLUS	MITSUBISHI	MIGHTY MAX 2WD TRUCK	MIGHTY MAX 4WD TRUCK	MIGHTY MAX MACRO CAB	NISSAN	2WD TRUCK STD LB	2WD TRUCK SE KING CAB	2WD TRUCK STD REG CAB	2WD TRUCK XE REG CAB	2WD TRUCK XE KING CAB	4WD TRUCK XE REG CAB	4WD TRUCK XE KING CAB
Length (in.)	202.7		177.2	177.2	188.2		190.0	195.5	174.6	180.1	190.0	180.1	195.5
Width (in.)	69.4		65.2	65.9	65.2		65.0	65.0	65.0	65.0	65.0	66.5	66.5
Height (in.)	67.5		58.3	64.4	59.6		62.0	62.0	62.0	62.0	62.0	66.7	67.1
Wheelbase (in.)	125.0		105.1	105.1	116.1		116.1	116.1	104.3	104.3	116.1	104.3	116.1
Curb Weight (lbs.)	3516		2600	3205	2780		3115	3235	2970	2970	2885	3390	3765
Gross Vehicle Wt. (lbs.) - min/max	5040		4165	4890	4325		NA	NA	NA	NA	NA	NA	NA
Cargo Capacity (lbs.) - min/max	1550/		1585/	3190/	1560/		NA 2000	NA 1400	NA 1400	NA 1400	NA 1400	NA 1400	NA 1400
Engine Type	V6		L4	V6	L4		V6	V6	L4	L4	L4	L4	V6
Displacement (liters/CID)	4.0/ 245		2.4/ 143.5	3.0/ 181	2.4/ 143.5		3.0/ 180.7	3.0/ 180.7	2.4/ 145.8	2.4/ 145.8	2.4/ 145.8	2.4/ 145.8	3.0/ 180.7
Horsepower	160		116	151	116		153	153	134	134	134	134	153
Torque	220		136	174	136		180	180	154	154	154	154	180
Steering Ratio	17.0		17.2/ 21.2	17.8	17.2/ 21.2		NA	NA	NA	NA	NA	NA	NA
Turning Circle (ft.)	42.4		35.4	40.0	38.7		36.7	36.7	33.5	33.5	36.7	33.5	36.7
Fuel Tank (gals.)	19.6		13.7	15.7	13.7		21.1	15.9	15.9	15.9	15.9	15.9	21.1
Transmission	5M		5M	5M	5M		5M	5M	5M	5M	5M	5M	5M
EPA City/Hwy (mpg) - manual	NA		21/25	17/22	21/25		19/23	19/23	23/27	23/27	23/27	18/22	15/19
EPA City/Hwy (mpg) - auto	16/21		19/23	NA	19/23		NA	18/24	NA	21/26	21/26	NA	16/19

PICKUPS

Specifications and EPA Mileage Ratings	4WD TRUCK SE KING CAB		2WD TRUCK STD REG CAB	2WD TRUCK DX XTRACAB	2WD TRUCK V6 SR5 XTRACAB	4WD TRUCK DX REG CAB	4WD TRUCK DX XTRACAB	4WD TRUCK V6 SR5 XTRACAB	T100 TRUCK DX 2WD V6	T100 TRUCK SR5 2WD V6	T100 TRUCK DX 4WD V6	T100 TRUCK SR5 4WD V6	1-TON TRUCK DX 2WD V6
Length (in.)	195.5		174.4	193.1	193.1	174.6	193.1	193.1	209.1	209.1	209.1	209.1	209.1
Width (in.)	66.5		66.5	66.5	66.5	66.5	66.5	66.5	75.2	75.2	75.2	75.2	75.2
Height (in.)	67.1		60.8	61.0	61.0	60.8	61.0	67.3	66.7	66.7	70.1	70.1	66.7
Wheelbase (in.)	116.1		103.0	121.9	121.9	103.0	121.9	121.9	121.8	121.8	121.8	121.8	121.8
Curb Weight (lbs.)	3855		2690	2970	3120	3585	3540	3815	3400	3450	3875	3910	3490
Gross Vehicle Wt. (lbs.)	NA	TOYOTA	4400/	4550/	4600/	5400/	5400/	5400/	5000/	5000/	5500/	5500/	6000/
- min/max	/		--	--	--	--	--	--	--	--	--	--	--
Cargo Capacity (lbs.)	NA		1760/	1675/	1490/	2015/	1820/	1545/	1650/	1650/	1655/	1655/	2570/
- min/max	1400		--	--	--	--	--	--	--	--	--	--	--
Engine Type	V6		L4	L4	V6	L4	L4	V6	V6	V6	V6	V6	V6
Displacement (liters/CID)	3.0/		2.4/	2.4/	3.0/	2.4/	2.4/	3.0/	3.0/	3.0/	3.0/	3.0/	3.0/
	180.7		144.4	144.4	180.6	144.4	144.4	180.6	180.6	180.6	180.6	180.6	180.6
Horsepower	153		116	116	150	116	116	150	150	150	150	150	150
Torque	180		140	140	180	140	140	180	180	180	180	180	180
Steering Ratio	NA		22.9/	22.9/	22.9/	26.2/	26.2/	26.2/	20.3	20.3	19.0	19.0	20.3
			19.5	19.5	19.5	29.9	29.9	29.9					
Turning Circle (ft.)	36.7		35.4	41.3	41.3	37.4	43.3	43.3	38.7	38.7	43.2	43.2	38.7
Fuel Tank (gals.)	21.1		17.2	19.3	19.3	17.2	19.3	19.3	24.3	24.3	24.3	24.3	24.3
Transmission	5M		5M	5M	5M	5M	5M	5M	5M	5M	5M	5M	5M
EPA City/Hwy (mpg) - manual	15/19		23/28	23/28	16/21	19/22	19/22	15/18	16/21	16/21	15/18	15/18	16/21
EPA City/Hwy (mpg) - auto	16/19		NA	22/25	18/23	18/19	NA	13/17	16/20	16/20	17/17	17/17	16/20

SPORT UTILITIES

Specifications and EPA Mileage Ratings	BLAZER FULL SIZE		BLAZER S10 2DR 2WD	BLAZER S10 4DR 2WD	BLAZER S10 2DR 4WD	BLAZER S10 4DR 4WD	SUBURBAN C1500 2WD	SUBURBAN K1500 4WD	SUBURBAN C2500 2WD		BRONCO 4WD WGN	EXPLORER 2DR 2WD	EXPLORER 4WD 2WD
Length (in.)	188.0		170.3	176.8	170.3	176.8	219.5	219.5	219.5		183.6	174.4	184.3
Width (in.)	77.1		65.4	65.4	65.4	65.4	76.7	76.7	76.7		79.1	70.2	70.2
Height (in.)	72.4		64.1	64.1	64.1	64.3	70.2	72.1	71.0		74.4	67.5	67.3
Wheelbase (in.)	111.5		100.5	107.0	100.5	107.0	131.5	131.5	131.5		104.7	102.1	111.9
Curb Weight (lbs.)	4710	CHEVROLET	3221	3397	3536	3776	4657	5114	5002	FORD	4570	3646	3863
Gross Vehicle Wt. (lbs.)	6250/		4350/	4850/	4700/	5100/	7200/	8600/	7200/		6050/	4580/	4780/
- min/max	--		--	--	--	--	--	--	--		6300	4780	5180
Cargo Capacity (lbs.)	53/99		28/67	35/74	28/67	35/74	51/149	51/149	51/149		50/101	33/69	43/82
- min/max	cu. ft.		cu. ft.	cu. ft.	cu. ft.	cu. ft.	cu. ft.	cu. ft.	cu. ft.		cu. ft.	cu. ft.	cu. ft.
Engine Type	V8		V6	V6	V6	V6	V8	V8	V8		V8	V6	V6
Displacement (liters/CID)	5.7/		4.3/	4.3/	4.3/	4.3/	5.7/	5.7/	5.7/		5.0/	4.0/	4.0/
	350		262	262	262	262	350	350	350		302	245	245
Horsepower	210		165	165	165	165	210	210	210		185	160	160
Torque	300		235	235	235	235	300	300	300		270	220	220
Steering Ratio	13/		17.5	17.5	17.5	17.5	13/	13/	13/		17.0	17.0	17.0
	16						16	16	16				
Turning Circle (ft.)	41.5		34.6	35.4	35.4	35.4	45.8	45.8	45.8		36.6	34.8	35.6
Fuel Tank (gals.)	30		20	20	20	20	42	42	42		32	19	19
Transmission	5M		5M	5M	5M	5M	4A	4A	4A		5M	5M	5M
EPA City/Hwy (mpg) - manual	13/17		16/21	16/21	15/20	15/20	NA	NA	NA		13/17	18/23	18/23
EPA City/Hwy (mpg) - auto	13/16		16/21	16/21	15/20	15/20	13/17	12/16	13/17		14/18	16/22	16/22

Specifications and EPA Mileage Ratings	EXPLORER 2DR 4WD	EXPLORER 4DR 4WD	GEO	TRACKER 2WD CVT	TRACKER 4WD HT	GMC	JIMMY 2DR 2WD	JIMMY 4DR 2WD	JIMMY 2DR 4WD	JIMMY 4DR 4WD	SUBURBAN C1500 2WD	SUBURBAN K1500 4WD	SUBURBAN C2500 2WD
Length (in.)	174.4	184.3		142.5	142.5		170.3	176.8	170.3	176.8	219.5	219.5	219.5
Width (in.)	70.2	70.2		64.2	64.2		65.4	65.4	65.4	65.4	76.7	76.7	76.7
Height (in.)	67.5	67.3		65.6	65.6		64.1	64.1	64.3	64.3	70.2	72.1	71.9
Wheelbase (in.)	102.1	111.9		86.6	86.6		100.5	107.0	100.5	107.0	131.5	131.5	131.5
Curb Weight (lbs.)	3844	4053	GEO	2189	2387	GMC	3221	3397	3536	3776	4657	5114	5002
Gross Vehicle Wt. (lbs.)	4800/	4800/		3300/	3300/		4350/	4850/	4700/	5100/	7200/	8600/	7200/
- min/max	5250	5360		--	--								
Cargo Capacity (lbs.)	33/69	43/82		9/32	9/32		28/67	35/74	28/67	35/74	51/149	51/149	51/149
- min/max	cu. ft.	cu. ft.		cu. ft.	cu. ft.		cu. ft.	cu. ft.	cu. ft.	cu. ft.	cu. ft.	cu. ft.	cu. ft.
Engine Type	V6	V6		I4	I4		V6	V6	V6	V6	V8	V8	V8
Displacement (liters/CID)	4.0/	4.0/		1.6/	1.6/		4.3/	4.3/	4.3/	4.3/	5.7/	5.7/	5.7/
	245	245		97	97		262	262	262	262	350	350	350
Horsepower	160	160		80	80		165	165	165	165	210	210	210
Torque	220	220		94	94		235	235	235	235	300	300	300
Steering Ratio	17.0	17.0		18-21	18-21		17.5	17.5	17.5	17.5	13/	13/	13/
											16	16	16
Turning Circle (ft.)	37.8	38.5		32.2	32.2		34.6	35.4	35.4	35.4	45.8	45.8	45.8
Fuel Tank (gals.)	19	19		11	11		20	20	20	20	42	42	42
Transmission	5M	5M		5M	5M		5M	5M	5M	5M	4A	4A	4A
EPA City/Hwy (mpg) - manual	17/22	17/22		25/27	25/27		16/21	16/21	15/20	15/20	NA	NA	NA
EPA City/Hwy (mpg) - auto	15/20	15/20		23/24	23/24		16/21	16/21	15/20	15/20	13/17	12/16	13/17

SPORT UTILITIES

Specifications and EPA Mileage Ratings	YUKON FULL SIZE	ISUZU	AMIGO 2WD	AMIGO 4WD	RODEO 2WD	RODEO 2WD V6	RODEO 4WD V6	TROOPER 2DR SWB	TROOPER 4DR LWB	JEEP	CHEROKEE 2DR 2WD WGN	CHEROKEE 4DR 2WD WGN	CHEROKEE 4DR 4WD WGN
Length (in.)	188.0		168.1	168.1	183.9	183.9	183.9	166.5	183.5		168.8	168.8	168.8
Width (in.)	77.1		70.1	70.1	66.5	66.5	66.5	68.7	68.7		67.7	67.7	67.7
Height (in.)	72.4		69.9	69.9	65.4	65.4	65.4	72.8	72.8		63.8	63.8	63.8
Wheelbase (in.)	111.5		91.7	91.7	183.9	183.9	183.9	91.7	108.7		101.4	101.4	101.4
Curb Weight (lbs.)	4710	ISUZU	3390	3615	3345	3775	3995	4060	4210	JEEP	2876	2928	3090
Gross Vehicle Wt. (lbs.)	6250/		4100/	4500/	4550/	4650/	4900/	5350/	5500/		4500/	4500/	4500/
- min/max	--		--	--	--	--	--	--	--		4650	4650	4650
Cargo Capacity (lbs.)	53/99		NA	NA	1005/	895/	905/	31/68	47/90		36/72	36/72	36/72
- min/max	cu. ft.				--	--	--	cu. ft.	cu. ft.		cu. ft.	cu. ft.	cu. ft.
Engine Type	V8		L4	L4	L4	V6	V6	V6	V6		I4	I4	I4
Displacement (liters/CID)	5.7/		2.6/	2.6/	2.6/	3.2/	3.2/	3.2/	3.2/		2.5/	2.5/	2.5/
	350		156.2	156.2	156.2	193.2	193.2	193.2	193.2		151	151	151
Horsepower	210		120	120	120	175	175	175	175		130	130	130
Torque	300		150	150	150	188	188	188	188		149	149	149
Steering Ratio	13/		18.7	18.7	20.5/	20.5/	20.5/	19.4	19.4		14.0	14.0	14.0
	16				23.5	23.5	23.5						
Turning Circle (ft.)	41.5		33.5	33.5	37.7	37.7	37.7	32.8	38.1		35.9	35.9	35.9
Fuel Tank (gals.)	30		21.9	21.9	21.9	21.9	21.9	22.5	22.5		20	20	20
Transmission	5M		5M	5M	5M	5M	5M	5M	5M		5M	5M	5M
EPA City/Hwy (mpg) - manual	13/17		16/20	16/20	16/20	16/19	16/19	16/18	16/18		20/23	20/23	20/23
EPA City/Hwy (mpg) - auto	13/16		NA	NA	NA	16/19	16/18	15/18	15/18		NA	NA	NA

SPORT UTILITIES

Specifications and EPA Mileage Ratings	GRND CHEROKEE 4DR 2WD WGN	GRND CHEROKEE 4DR 4WD WGN	WRANGLER S/SE 4WD	WRANGLER SAH/REN 4WD	LAND ROVER			MAZDA		MITSUBISHI
					RANGE ROVER COUNTY	RANGE ROVER COUNTY LWB	DEFENDER 90	NAVAJO DX 2WD	NAVAJO DX 4WD	MONTERO LS 4WD 4DR
Length (in.)	179.0	179.0	151.9	151.9	175.0	183.0	160.5	175.3	175.3	185.2
Width (in.)	70.9	70.9	66.0	66.0	71.4	71.4	70.5	70.2	70.2	66.7
Height (in.)	64.8	64.8	69.5	69.5	70.8	70.8	70.8	68.1	68.1	73.4
Wheelbase (in.)	105.9	105.9	93.4	93.4	100.0	108.0	92.9	102.1	102.1	107.3
Curb Weight (lbs.)	3530	3674	2943	3085	4401	4574	3560	3785	3980	4190
Gross Vehicle Wt. (lbs.)	5300/	5300/	4700/	4700/	6019/	6019/	6003/	NA	NA	NA
- min/max	--	--	--	--	--	--	--	--	--	--
Cargo Capacity (lbs.)	40/81	40/81	5/53	5/53	71/83	76/--	NA	33/70	33/70	9/73
- min/max	cu. ft.	cu. ft.	cu. ft.	cu. ft.	cu. ft.	cu. ft.		cu. ft.	cu. ft.	cu. ft.
Engine Type	I6	I6	I4	I6	V8	V8	V8	V6	V6	V6
Displacement (liters/CID)	4.0/	4.0/	2.5/	4.0/	3.9/	4.2/	3.9/	4.0/	4.0/	3.0/
	242	242	151	151	241	261.2	241	245	245	181
Horsepower	190	190	123	180	182	200	182	160	160	151
Torque	225	225	139	220	232	251	232	220	220	174
Steering Ratio	15.4	15.4	24.0	24.0	19.3	19.3	19.3	17.0	17.0	16.4
										18.0
Turning Circle (ft.)	36.6	36.6	32.9	32.9	39.4	44.8	40.0	35.6	35.6	38.7
Fuel Tank (gals.)	23	23	15	20	23.4	23.4	15.6	19.3	19.3	24.3
Transmission	5M	5M	5M	5M	4A	4A	5M	5M	5M	5M
EPA City/Hwy (mpg) - manual	--	16/21	18/20	16/20	NA	NA	13/16	18/23	17/22	15/18
EPA City/Hwy (mpg) - auto	NA	15/20	NA	15/16	12/15	13/16	NA	NA	NA	15/18

SPORT UTILITIES

Specifications and EPA Mileage Ratings	MONTERO SR 4WD 4DR	NISSAN		OLDSMOBILE	TOYOTA				
		PATHFINDER 2WD	PATHFINDER 4WD	BRAVADA 4DR 4WD	LAND CRUISER 4DR WGN	4RUNNER SR5 V6 4DR 2WD	4RUNNER SR5 4DR 4WD	4RUNNER SR5 V6 4DR 4WD	
Length (in.)	186.6	171.9	171.9	178.9	188.2	176.6	176.6	176.6	
Width (in.)	70.3	66.5	66.5	65.2	76.0	66.5	66.5	66.5	
Height (in.)	75.2	65.7	65.7	65.5	73.2	66.1	66.1	66.1	
Wheelbase (in.)	107.3	104.3	104.3	107.0	112.2	103.3	103.3	103.3	
Curb Weight (lbs.)	4440	NA	3885	4010	4762	4105	3825	4105	
Gross Vehicle Wt. (lbs.)	NA	NA	NA	5100/	6525/	5400/	5400/	5400/	
- min/max	--	--	--	--	--	--	--	--	
Cargo Capacity (lbs.)	9/73	31/80	31/80	35/74	75/91	44/78	44/78	44/78	
- min/max	cu. ft.	cu. ft.	cu. ft.	cu. ft.	cu. ft.	cu. ft.	cu. ft.	cu. ft.	
Engine Type	V6	V6	V6	V6	L6	V6	L4	V6	
Displacement (liters/CID)	3.5/	3.0/	3.0/	4.3/	4.5/	3.0/	2.4/	3.0/	
	213.3	180.7	180.7	262	273.3	180.6	144.4	180.6	
Horsepower	215	153	153	200	212	150	116	150	
Torque	228	180	180	260	275	NA	140	NA	
Steering Ratio	16.4/	NA	NA	17.5	18.6	26.2/	26.2/	26.2/	
	18.0					29.9	29.9	29.9	
Turning Circle (ft.)	38.7	35.4	35.4	39.1	40.4	37.4	37.4	37.4	
Fuel Tank (gals.)	24.3	20.4	20.4	20	25.1	17.2	17.2	17.2	
Transmission	5M	5M	5M	4A	4A	4A	5M	5M	
EPA City/Hwy (mpg) - manual	NA	15/18	15/18	NA	NA	NA	19/22	15/18	
EPA City/Hwy (mpg) - auto	14/17	15/19	15/18	16/21	12/15	17/21	NA	14/16	

We SELL...You SAVE

 SAVE MONEY

 SAVE TIME

 SAVE FRUSTRATION

YOU ARE OUR #1 PRIORITY.

- You will not pay more than $50-$125 over dealer invoice.

- Your purchase will be made from the comfort of your home.

- Your vehicle is available immediately due to our huge inventory.

- You may finance through GMAC, Ford or Chrysler credit.

- You may lease your vehicle.

- Your vehicle has a full factory warranty.

- You may choose your options and know exactly what each one costs.

- You can use your itemized option quote as a reference or as a bargaining tool for the future.

- Your vehicle will be shipped to the destination of your choice:
  1. Your designated local dealership as a pick-up point.
  2. You may pick up at our headquarters in Southfield, MI.
  3. Your home via ICC−bonded driveaway service.

- We have over 25 years of experience to put to work for you.

Please Note: Some specialty imports and limited production models and vehicles may not be available for delivery to your area through our pricing service. A message on your printout will advise you of this eventuality. You will still be able to use the printout in negotiating the best deal with the dealer of your choice. New car pricing and purchasing services are not available where prohibited by law. Some limited vehicles are slightly higher.

MAIL • FAX • PHONE

NATIONWIDE
AUTO BROKERS, INC.
17517 West Ten Mile Road • Southfield, MI 48075
810-559-6661 • FAX 810-559-4782

FOR YOUR ITEMIZED QUOTE, NATIONWIDE BREAKS DOWN THE PRICE OF A CAR – OPTION BY OPTION – LETTING YOU SEE JUST HOW AN[ ] WHAT YOU ARE PAYING FOR. EACH QUOTE IS ONLY $11.95.

Name _____

Address _____

_____

City _____

State _____

Zip _____

Phone _____

Fax _____

☐ MC/Visa/Discover ☐ Check ☐ Money Order
Card No. _____

Exp. Date _____

MAKE	MODEL/ DESCRIP.	BODY TYPE (Check all that apply)	PRICE EACH
		☐ 2 door ☐ 4 door ☐ station wagon ☐ diesel ☐ turbo ☐ automatic ☐ manual ☐ hatchback ☐ notchback ☐ front wheel drive ☐ all wheel drive	$11.95
		☐ 2 door ☐ 4 door ☐ station wagon ☐ diesel ☐ turbo ☐ automatic ☐ manual ☐ hatchback ☐ notchback ☐ front wheel drive ☐ all wheel drive	$11.95
		☐ 2 wheel drive ☐ 4 wheel drive ☐ diesel ☐ turbo ☐ 1/2 ton ☐ 3/4 ton ☐ 1 ton	$11.95

FAX PRICE: $6.95 for first two quotes of $11.95 each, $2.50 each additional fax. NOTE: Attach sheet with additional body type specs only if necessary (do not list options)

Total _____

Signature _____

NATIONWIDE
AUTO BROKERS, INC.
17517 W. 10 MILE RD. • SOUTHFIELD, MI 48075

1-800-521-7257
Mastercard/Visa/Discover customers only.
Michigan residents call 313-559-6661
Mon. thru Fri. 8:30 a.m. - 8 p.m.
Sat. 9 a.m. - 1 p.m. Eastern.

Edmund's CLASSIFIED ADS

Put the power
of the Nation's
**Original
Consumer Price
Authority**
to work for you!

Advertise in
Edmund's
series of automotive
reference books.

Call today
and reserve your ad!
407-767-0557

To Place a Classified Ad

Standard Rate:
  $5.00 per word.
  20 word minimum.
Bold Face Type:
  add $1.00 per word.
Borders:
  $25.00 per column inch.
Classified Display:
  $125 per column inch

Counting Words: Two initials, abbreviations, numerals and symbols are counted as one word. Telephone number including area code and zip codes are one word. (Zip code must appear in every ad with an address). Multiple name cities are counted as one word. Normal punctuation is no charge.

Payment must be received with copy. Check, Money Order, MasterCard or Visa accepted.

Payment:

❏ Check or Money Order

❏ Visa

❏ MasterCard

❏ P.O. No._____

_____
Credit Card #   Expires

_____
Cardholder Name:

_____
Signature

Call 407-767-0557 or fax 407-767-6583 or mail to: P.O. Box 1139, Longwood, FL 32752

Edmund's **SINGLE COPIES / ORDER FORM**

Please send me:

❏ **USED CAR PRICES** *(includes S&H)* ....$ 8.25

❏ **NEW CAR PRICES** *(includes S&H)*................................$ 8.25

❏ **VAN, PICKUP, SPORT UTILITY BUYER'S GUIDE** *(includes S&H)*....$ 8.25

❏ **IMPORT CAR PRICES** *((includes S&H)* ....$ 8.25

❏ **ECONOMY CAR BUYING GUIDE** *(includes S&H)* ....$ 8.25

Name _____

Address _____

City, State, Zip _____

Phone _____

IS2801

PAYMENT: ❏ MASTERCARD ❏ VISA ❏ CHECK or MONEY ORDER $_____

Make check or money order payable to:

Edmund Publications Corporation, *P.O. Box 338, Shrub Oak, NY 10588*

*For more information or to order by phone, call **(914) 962-6297***

Credit Card # _____ Exp. Date: _____

CardHolder Name _____ Signature _____

Prices above are for shipping within the U.S. and Canada only. Other countries please add $5.00 to the cover price per book (via air mail) and $2.00 to the cover price per book (surface mail). Please pay through an American Bank or with American currency. Rates subject to change without notice.

Edmund's SUBSCRIPTIONS / ORDER FORM

Please send me a one-year subscription for:

❑ **USED CAR PRICES** *(includes bulk rate shipping/handling)* ....$ **29.75**
CANADA $37.25/FOREIGN COUNTRIES $53.75 *(includes air mail shipping/handling)*
now 6 issues instead of 4

❑ **NEW CAR PRICES** *(includes bulk rate shipping/handling)* ....$ **15.00**
CANADA $18.75/FOREIGN COUNTRIES $27.00 *(includes air mail shipping/handling)*
3 issues per year

❑ **VAN, PICKUP, SPORTS UTILITY** *(includes bulk rate shipping/handling)* ....$ **15.00**
CANADA $18.75/FOREIGN COUNTRIES $27.00 *(includes air mail shipping/handling)*
3 issues per year

❑ **IMPORT CAR PRICES** *(includes bulk rate shipping/handling)* ....$ **15.00**
CANADA $18.75/FOREIGN COUNTRIES $27.00 *(includes air mail shipping/handling)*
3 issues per year

❑ **NEW VEHICLE PRICES** *(includes bulk rate shipping/handling)* ....$ **55.00**
CANADA $68.75/FOREIGN COUNTRIES $99.00 *(includes air mail shipping/handling)*
- includes the complete automotive market of new vehicles - 11books:

- 3 NEW CAR PRICES (Domestic)
- 3 IMPORT CAR PRICES
- 3 VAN, PICKUP, SPORT UTILITY
- 2 ECONOMY CAR BUYING GUIDE

❑ **NEW & USED CAR PRICES** *(includes bulk rate shipping/handling)* ....$ **59.75**
CANADA $74.75/FOREIGN COUNTRIES $107.75 *(includes air mail shipping/handling)*
12 books:

- 6 USED CAR PRICES
- 3 NEW CAR PRICES (Domestic)
- 3 IMPORT CAR PRICES

❑ **PREMIUM SUBSCRIPTION** *(includes bulk rate shipping/handling)* ....$ **84.75**
CANADA $106.00/FOREIGN COUNTRIES $152.75 *(includes air mail shipping/handling)*
- includes all of the above - 17 books:

- 6 USED CAR PRICES
- 3 NEW CAR PRICES (Domestic)
- 3 IMPORT CAR PRICES
- 3 VAN, PICKUP, SPORT UTILITY
- 2 ECONOMY CAR BUYING GUIDE

Name _____

Address _____ Phone _____

City, State, Zip _____

PAYMENT: ❑ MASTERCARD ❑ VISA ❑ CHECK or MONEY ORDER —AMOUNT $_____
Make check or money order payable to: ***Edmund Publications Corporation,***
P. O. Box 338, Shrub Oak, NY 10588   *Rates subject to change without notice.*
*For more information or to order by phone, call **(914) 962-6297***

Credit Card # _____ Exp. Date: _____
Cardholder Name: _____ Signature: _____

IS2801

Edmund's

SCHEDULED RELEASE DATES FOR 1994/95*

VOL. 28/29		RELEASE DATE	COVER DATE
I2801	IMPORT CAR PRICES	MAR 94	JUL 94
U2802	USED CAR PRICES	MAR 94	MAY 94
N2802	NEW CAR PRICES [Domestic]	MAY 94	NOV 94
S2802	VAN, PICKUP, SPORT UTILITY BUYER'S GUIDE	MAY 94	NOV 94
U2803	USED CAR PRICES	MAY 94	JUL 94
I2802	IMPORT CAR PRICES	JUN 94	DEC 94
E2802	ECONOMY CAR BUYER'S GUIDE	JUN 94	OCT 94
U2804	USED CAR PRICES	JUL 94	SEP 94
U2805	USED CAR PRICES	SEP 94	NOV 94
N2803	NEW CAR PRICES [Domestic]	NOV 94	FEB 95
S2803	VAN, PICKUP, SPORT UTILITY BUYER'S GUIDE	NOV 94	FEB 95
U2806	USED CAR PRICES	NOV 94	JAN 95
I2803	IMPORT CAR PRICES	DEC 94	APR 95
U2901	USED CAR PRICES	JAN 95	MAR 95
N2901	NEW CAR PRICES [Domestic]	FEB 95	JUN 95
S2901	VAN, PICKUP, SPORT UTILITY BUYER'S GUIDE	FEB 95	JUN 95
E2901	ECONOMY CAR BUYER'S GUIDE	FEB 95	JUN 95

*Subject to Change